Avijit Ghosh was born in Agartala and grew up loafing in the small towns of Bihar and Jharkhand—Dumka, Giridih and Arrah. He spent most of his college hours in cinema halls but managed to graduate in history from St Xavier's College, Ranchi. He devoted his JNU days to sitting outside the library canteen sipping tea while listening to his more gifted friends discuss Gramsci and Castro. A journalist for the past thirty years, he has worked for Press Trust of India (PTI), *The Pioneer*, *The Telegraph* and now *The Times of India*.

Avijit is the author of two novels, *Bandicoots in the Moonlight* (2008) and *Up Campus Down Campus* (2016); and two books on cinema, *Cinema Bhojpuri* (2010) and *40 Retakes: Bollywood Classics You May Have Missed* (2013). He has also written a monograph on film director Phani Majumdar for National Film Archive of India (NFAI).

He lives in Delhi with his wife and two children. He tweets from the handle @cinemawaleghosh and awaits your feedback at avijitghosh65@gmail.com.

WHEN ARDH SATYA MET HIMMATWALA

The Many Lives of 1980s' Bombay Cinema

Avijit Ghosh

SPEAKING TIGER BOOKS LLP
125A, Ground Floor, Shahpur Jat, near Asiad Village,
New Delhi 110049

First published by Speaking Tiger Books 2023

ISBN: 978-93-5447-460-6
eISBN: 978-93-5447-451-4

To Baba, Ma and Jamaibabu,
I miss you

CONTENTS

PREFACE

I went to college in the 1980s. The two things that drew the attention of my friends and me were girls and cinema. The girls, unfortunately, showed little interest in us. Options reduced, we gravitated towards cinema.

Memories of youth are usually hardwired in our brains. In my mind's eye, I can vividly recall the movies I saw those days, with whom and where. I can still see myself waiting for the ticket counter to open, all of us taking turns to stand in the queue during summertime. I can taste the potato chips and hear the canteen boys shout *'Thanda!'* while brushing the bottle openers against Gold Spot and Campa Cola bottles during the interval.

We weren't choosy about what we saw. From 'ladies picture' *Thodisi Bewafaii* to front bencher-friendly *Paanch Qaidi*; from Big B's fun-filled *Satte Pe Satta* to Ramsay horrors such as *Guest House*, we saw everything that came our way. This is why when book editor Shantanu Ray Chaudhuri asked me five years ago if I was interested in writing a book on Hindi cinema of the 1980s, an underwritten and under-explained period, I accepted with delight. Thank you, Shantanu. Without you, the book wouldn't have been conceived.

In popular imagination, the Eighties is a black mark, typified by mindless movies and perishable music. But perhaps Charles Dickens' first line from *A Tale of Two Cities*—'it was the best of times, it was the worst of times'—describes the period more aptly. The book strives to capture and explain the contradictions that typified the decade.

Let me explain briefly what this book is about. The first reel—as we have fondly decided to name the chapters—locates the socio-political and technological ecosystem in which the Hindi film industry functioned in the 1980s. The second reel details the extent and impact of film piracy which became rampant over the decade. The third is about the censors and their running battle with filmmakers. The great 1986 film industry strike, a forgotten but significant moment in the history of the Hindi film industry, is mapped in the fourth. The fifth and sixth reels talk about the state and fate of alternative cinema during this period.

In recent months, there has been some noise about southern films scoring over the North. The book explores the strong North and South interactions in the 1980s. Portions are also devoted to those who defined the decade—producers, directors, actors, writers—and those who slowly faded away. The book looks at the phenomenon of star sons, a dominant trend of the period, and delves into smaller genres such as devotionals and sex films.

The Eighties is largely considered to be a 'rough' period for 'good' music, both subjective terms. The book strives to show that the decade was also informed by its share of refined poetry and reflective compositions. The last reel describes the strong bonds between literature of every region and Hindi films.

I have spoken with a wide range of directors, producers, writers, actors, songwriters and distributors to get a better understanding of the subject. Many interviews were conducted on phone, partly due to COVID-19 restrictions. Along with English newspapers, trade magazines and Parliament replies, I have also referred to Hindi magazines such as *Madhuri, Dharamyug* and *Sarika.*

Several films were certified years after being released. Some films were released in different territories in different years. Reference sources such as IMDb, and even *Encylopaedia of Indian Cinema,* go by the certification date. At places where the difference is stark, I have gone by *Trade Guide* and *Film Information*, which listed all the films released annually. Interestingly, some films received national awards before they were released. The awards were advertised prominently to attract the gentry.

I express my thankfulness to the staff at the Pune-based National Film Archive of India, who were extremely helpful. I record my appreciation for director Prakash Magdum, librarian Veena Kshirsagar and assistant librarian Niraj Bhandwale. None of them work at the NFAI anymore.

The book took longer to finish than I expected: five years. The mission received a setback when the publishers I had signed up with lost interest after Shantanu left them. I had to look for a new publisher. Thankfully, Ravi Singh and Renuka Chatterjee of Speaking Tiger stepped in.

My utmost gratitude to Ravi and Renuka for supporting the book in the hardest of times. I must also record my fullest appreciation for Vandana Agarwal, friend and former colleague, for painstakingly editing and improving the book and I'm thankful to Dyuti Roy for her eagle-eyed editing. The errors are mine alone.

I also take the opportunity to thank a bunch of friends, colleagues and well-wishers who, directly or indirectly, helped me in my efforts: Devesh Kapur, Chandra Bhan Prasad, D. Shyam Babu, Pravin Kumar, Atul Thakur, Subodh Ghildiyal, Sanjiv Sankaran, Sunil Warrier, Suneel Sinha, Sunil Nair, Nirmal Sharma, Chanchal Mazumdar, Narayani Ganesh, Deepika Sahu, Anuradha Raman, Malini Sen, Renu Pachauri, Yeshi Seli, Sanjay Verma, Saeed Saud Akhtar, Neeraj Singh, M. Shankar, Mahesh Krishnamurthy, Sanjeev Kumar, Arjun Kumar, Rinki Roy Bhattacharya, Sushil Aaron, Susmita Dasgupta, Rakesh Batabyal, Badri Narayan, Bhaichand Patel, Ronojoy Sen, Rasheed Kidwai, Namrata Joshi, Gautam Chintamani, Shyam Shroff, Iqbal Rizvi, Sarbani Roy, Palash Roy and Sourav Roy. My sincere apologies to those I forgot. It's due to my advancing age, not for lack of respect.

Lastly, I am indebted to my wife Rachana Sharma, a fellow traveller in all my creative endeavours. I am also beholden to my son Abhishek for allowing me a decent share of the Wi-Fi and my daughter Diya for sharing her tea with me.

TRAILER

The Eighties was a time of disruption and change in Hindi cinema.

It was a time when the arrival of VCR and the menace of film and music piracy shook cinema out of its comfort zone. It was a time when expansion of television and the growth of ODI cricket changed the film business forever.

It was a time when these uncertainties created openings for brasher and brawnier players with bad and black money. It was a time when theatres entered a period of crisis, creating conditions for the birth and growth of the multiplex culture in coming years.

It was a time when the middle class deserted the theatres, forcing changes in the script and the method of celluloid storytelling. The entertainment 'needs' of the youth and the underclass, as understood by the industry, were catered to. They were, after all, the only ones who were still cinema regulars.

The Eighties was also a time of paradoxes.

It was a time when hundreds of shallow conveyor-belt movies swarmed the theatres. It was also a time when serious cinema won fulsome acclaim at premium foreign festivals and when umpteen films on Indian and world literature were made.

It was a time when stars played gods, distributing time in four-hour shifts. It was a time when markets shrunk and flops reached an unprecedented high.

It was a time when songs devolved into ditties and dominated the charts. It was a time of sensitive poetry and meditative music.

It was a time when many kneeled before the government. It was a time when many refused to kowtow before the government.

The Eighties was the precursor, almost an opening act to the satellite revolution that struck India in the Nineties.

The Eighties acted as a hyphen between the past and the future. It was also a decade that tasted the future.

REEL 1

EXPLAINING THE EIGHTIES

*When a film begins to bore, the front-stallers start catcalling,
the rear-stallers trickle out to the galleries and only
the critics are obliged to sit out.**

Early 1970s! India was in the middle of a collective orgasm
called Rajesh Khanna. Men aped him. Women of all ages
adored him. Some smeared his car with lipstick, wrote letters in
blood and married his photograph. But like a tropical fever, the
fervour vanished in a few years. The romantic star, whose name
was synonymous with fan hysteria and box-office gold, was
felled by a cache of duds even before the decade had touched
the midway mark.

Politics turned out the same way. In the early '70s, Prime
Minister Indira Gandhi was riding a tsunami of popularity
following the nationalisation of fourteen private banks (1969)
and the abolition of privy purses (1971). A decisive victory
over Pakistan in the 1971 war added to her growing cabinet
of accomplishments and furthered her image of a strong leader,
'the only female in the cabinet'.

But rising prices, growing inflation and spiralling
unemployment, among other things, soon created a climate

---

*'Film Review: Nasihat', *The Statesman*, Delhi, 27 July 1986

of political disenchantment against the Congress government. The unrest gave rise to the students' movement (1974), first in Gujarat and later in Bihar. Jayaprakash Narayan, a luminary of the freedom struggle, marshalled them.

It's almost a cliché now, but it must be repeated that this larger ecosystem of discontent and disenchantment contributed to the emergence of a new celluloid hero, Amitabh Bachchan, whose bottled rage matched the moment's mood, especially among the young and the restless. Khanna's smile could bring out the sun. Bachchan preferred grunts to grins. Khanna flourished singing some of the finest numbers that Kishore Kumar ever crooned. In *Zanjeer* (1973) and *Deewaar* (1975), the two films that gave us Salim-Javed's famous Angry Young Man persona, Bachchan did not lip-sync a single number. Fists, not songs, became Hindi cinema's red-hot currency.

Mrs Gandhi, too, went into action mode. Growing insecurity caused by an adverse Allahabad High Court judgment made her proclaim a state of emergency on 25 June 1975. Democracy went on forced leave for the next twenty-one months. Opposition leaders were dumped into jail. One of them, Atal Bihari Vajpayee, penned humour poetry during his incarceration. Civil liberties were snatched away; thousands were forcibly sterilised. For a change, though, trains ran on time. And the clerks, cribbing furiously, sat at their desks to work.

Movies were censored. All prints of *Kissa Kursi Ka*, a scathing indictment of ugly power politics, were burnt allegedly at the behest of top Congress leaders. Newspapers were censored too. Gulzar's *Aandhi*, whose protagonist woman politician resembled the PM, was banned briefly. In normal times, the news might have made huge headlines. *The Times of India* published a bikini-sized paragraph.

There was a diktat against showing excessive sex and violence. Of course there were exceptions, most notably *Sholay* (1975). Drinking on screen was disallowed. The mainstream Bombay film industry often found ways to laud the government. In Narendra Bedi's *Mahachor* (1976), the hero (Rajesh Khanna) enlightened the viewer on how the government's policies will make the country a 'sone ki chidiya' again.

Toadying was the norm. Those who dared to differ were dealt with sternly. In his autobiography, *Romancing with Life*, Dev Anand recalled an occasion during the Emergency when fellow actor Dilip Kumar and he were invited to New Delhi to attend a Youth Congress rally led by Sanjay Gandhi. They obliged. But when they were asked to go to the television centre in the evening and endorse the 'dynamism' of Gandhi junior, both were wary.

Dev Anand wrote, 'While Dilip also hesitated to go to the TV centre to participate in any propaganda in favour of the Emergency, I vehemently and vociferously opposed the suggestion, with the result that not only were all my pictures banned from being screened on television, but also any mention of or reference to my name on an official media was forbidden, along with Kishore Kumar's, who had also refused to go and sing in one of their programmes.'[1]

The unofficial ban on the singer began on 4 May 1976 and was lifted a month and a half later, on 18 June, after he promised to hold a Kishore Kumar Nite in Delhi. The proceeds of the show held on 23 January 1977 amounted to Rs 16 lakh and went to the Delhi Flying Club, wrote film scholar Aruna Vasudev in her book, *Liberty and Licence in the Indian Cinema*. Sanjay Gandhi was the club's 'patron saint'.

Extraordinary things were also happening on celluloid. *Sholay*, panned by most critics, became a monster hit. The film's dialogues, penned by Salim-Javed, were peddled as a long-playing record by Polydor and blared non-stop across cities, towns and kasbahs. The movie also started the trend of multi-starrers in Bombay cinema, which found its extreme form in Rajkumar Kohli's *Nagin* (1976), a shape-shifting snake's quest for revenge. It was tough to match *Nagin's* record of seven heroes and five heroines. But many producers thereafter managed to incorporate at least two heroes and an equal number of heroines in their films.

In 1977, multi-starrers hit the stratosphere when Manmohan Desai released three lost-and-found movies: *Dharam-Veer, Chacha Bhatija* and *Amar Akbar Anthony*. *Parvarish* had a similar theme but with a minor variation. Three of them—*AAA, Dharam-Veer,* and *Parvarish*—were among the year's four biggest hits; Nasir Hussain's *Hum Kisise Kum Naheen* being the fourth. *Trade Guide* ranked them in the AII (superhit) category. Even *Chacha Bhatija* was a runaway winner. In the history of Hindi cinema, no director had ever delivered four megahits in the same year.

Politically, too, 1977 was a watershed year. The Emergency ended on 21 March. From the mainstream film industry, Dev Anand came out openly and boldly for the Opposition. The evergreen star addressed a Bombay rally for lawyer-politician Ram Jethmalani and was proclaimed a real hero. Later he also founded the still-born National Party of India.

The Janata Party, a conglomerate of disparate ideologies and dominant individuals with vaulting ambitions, stormed to power in the 1977 general election. In January 1978, the Morarji Desai government demonetised 1,000, 5,000 and 10,000-rupee notes to control black money, but without much success—a lesson hardly learnt, as subsequent events show.

Tinsel town was believed to be among the biggest playing fields for black money. But when news of the demonetisation wafted over Akashvani and Doordarshan, the film industry was quietly smirking. Journalist Ashok Row Kavi wrote, 'There was no panic, no breast-beating. There was calm everywhere. It did not mean there was no black money lying around in film land. It was there but had already been converted into substantial capital holdings. Bombay's film-folk have known how to grease the parallel economy long before freedom dawned over the sub-continent.'[2]

But the crisis all set to strike the film industry with the force of a George Foreman punch was simmering far away. A stark dip in the Bombay film market abroad was noticed by trend-watchers and trade magazines. 'Business of films overseas [particularly the UK] was slack. Some countries either stopped the import of Indian films or increased the duty manifold,' trade magazine *Film Information* reported, summing up 1979.[3] Back home, Bombay cinema remained blissfully unaware of the gathering storm.

It was in this backdrop that the 1980s arrived.

The Eighties was essentially a decade of contradictions in Hindi films.

It was the time of *Ardh Satya* and *Himmatwala*. Of K. Raghavendra Rao and Govind Nihalani. Of *Paap Ko Jalaa Kar Raakh Kar Doonga* and *Satah Se Uthata Aadmi*. Of Velankar and Mogambo. Of Indeevar and Vasant Dev. Of Bappi Lahiri and Vanraj Bhatia. Of Kundan Shah and Kader Khan.

This was a time when films flopped with alacrity yet production figures soared with abandon. At the core of this paradox stood an inexorable fact—the Hindi film industry was in furious flux. The rules of the game in every key sector—financing, production, distribution—were being battered beyond recognition due to the onset of new disruptive technology. Much of the Eighties was a sort of unnerving and awkward interplay between the forces that held the Hindi film industry together and the energies that took them apart.

And this was reflected in the movies. The average commercial producer and financier were generally allergic to experimentation. But uncertainty and insecurity pushed them further into the arms of the familiar. Scripts avoided surprise, stereotyping received support.

Action, emotion, drama, fights, titillation, songs, comedy—everything was sloshed together in the hope of creating an appetising goulash for the audience. As actor Rakesh Bedi recounted, 'Producers used to say, *"Kamal ka subject hai"*:

six songs, four fights, one chase….The story was divided into scenes for choreographers and fight masters.'[4] This was cinema of ingredients at its puerile purest.

Speaking to *Film Information* in 1987, writer Salim Khan (of Salim-Javed fame) categorised Hindi film writers into two types. There were the literary writers, who were 'knowledgeable, learned and observant' but who neither understood the film medium nor wanted to understand it. The second breed, Khan said, could write only 'after seeing Indian hits and foreign films'. He sarcastically elaborated, 'These writers must understand that if they can see these films on video [and copy scenes from them], the audience too must have seen such films on video. I don't say that one cannot draw inspiration from earlier films. But for heaven's sake, don't draw the total scenes from previous hits.'

—————————— SHORT TAKE ——————————

Cinema mags (and rags) flourish

The Eighties bustled with film magazines which provided good, bad and indifferent employment to hundreds of journalists. A record number of magazines—*Filmfare, Stardust, Star & Style, Showtime, Movie, Picturpost, Screen, Madhuri, Filmi Duniya, Mayapuri, Filmi Kaliyan, Shama* and dozens of others—were published in various languages and thrived on their readership's insatiable appetite for gossip about the private lives of stars. Magazines like *Madhuri*, which had a literary flavour, were rare.

When the 1980s arrived, cinema was India's primary mass entertainment. Plays, circus, fairs, exhibitions and others offered feeble competition to the magic of moving images in a dark auditorium. And it didn't matter that you could sniff most of the toilets from a distance and the seats often served as blood donation counters for bedbugs.

According to film historian B.V. Dharap, 420 cinemas existed in India in 1931. With the arrival of the talkies (*Alam Ara*) the same year, the number vaulted to 1,265 in 1939. By 1950, the nation had around 4,000 theatres.[5]

By 1980, as per *Encyclopaedia of Indian Cinema*, the country had 6,368 permanent cinemas and 4,024 temporary 'touring' theatres—a total of 10,392. The 'travelling' theatres were generally makeshift structures such as tents where movies were shown regularly, especially in the kasbahs and villages, during fairs. Apart from single-screen permanent halls, there were a handful of military cinemas too. By 31 March 1987, a working group on National Film Policy noted, the number of cinemas had grown to 12,732.[6]

In 1981, as per the census, India's population stood at 68.52 crore. That's a pitiable ratio of roughly 54,000 viewers per cinema.

The ratio is far worse if you keep in mind that the four southern states—Tamil Nadu (2,135), Andhra Pradesh (2,131), Kerala (1,282) and Karnataka (1,226)—accounted for 6,774 cinemas or 53 per cent of the total cinemas in India.[7] In these states, Bombay cinema had limited reach, which means that the target audience for Hindi films was smaller than what a cursory look at the numbers suggests.

The skewed demand and supply should have made the theatres hot property. Yet as early as 1982, N.F. Damania, president, Theatres Owners Association, said that running cinemas had ceased to be lucrative.[8]

Damania also narrated an anecdote to illustrate the point: A women's delegation met a group of cinema hall owners to put forward a list of grievances. The exhibitors were trying to explain their position when one of the delegation members got agitated. She said, 'I know Indira Gandhi. I will get your theatre demolished.' To this, a theatre owner quipped, 'If you can do that, I will give Rs 2 lakh to your organisation.'[9] In Bombay, theatres such as Rex, Majestic, Broadway and Neptune had already been razed and recast as shopping centres.

Clearly, even before the video storm hit India, some theatre owners were already thinking of their cinemas as real estate. A slow, subterranean crisis was brewing in the theatre business in this pre-multiplex era.

In the 1980s, air-conditioned theatres were exceptions, not the rule. Most cinemas were either air-cooled or had fans. Not every fan moved. The light and sound quality was uneven. Electricity cuts were common.

What made a theatre special in that era? In 1982, K.C. Khanna, manager of Indore's Prem Sukh cinema, told *Madhuri* magazine that his theatre's USP was underground parking, which no other cinema hall in the city provided. Efforts were made to make women cine-goers feel more comfortable. Chhavinath Shukla, manager of Prakash Talkies in Ujjain said the theatre offered a separate enclosure for women in the first class. 'They are given tickets from a separate counter and have a separate entrance too,' he said.[10]

This was the era of mega theatres. Satyam in Madras had 1,255 seats. Prem Sukh in Indore offered 1,077 seats.[11] Delhi's Liberty cinema, founded in 1956, had 959 seats.

Scalping of tickets was a regular business. Commonly known as black marketeers or blackiyas, these crooks ran a mini ticket-selling scam, often in collusion with cops and, in many cases, with theatre staff. The theatre employees, seldom well paid, were caught between a rock and a hard place. Some of them cooperated with the goons partly to make some extra money and partly out of fear.

In many cases, theatre staff were paid below the minimum wage. A gatekeeper told *Madhuri* in 1982 that he received a mere Rs 90 per month and an additional Rs 30 for overtime. The owner made him sign on vouchers for more than what was paid, he said.[12] As per a 2006 *Economic and Political*

Weekly study, even a daily wager in agriculture earned between Rs 10-20 every day in 1980s Bihar.

Yet jobs in cinemas were sought after. Shahzad Ahmad, a projectionist in Saharanpur's Kalpana cinema for more than forty years, recalled that the job gave him a certain clout. 'At government offices, I was treated with respect and got preferential treatment,' he said.[13] People curried favour hoping to get tickets on crowded weekends.

SHORT TAKE

Scalping tickets in small towns

In the towns I grew up in—Arrah (Bihar) and Ranchi (then south Bihar, now Jharkhand)—selling tickets in black was common practice. In some theatres, ticket counters would open for barely fifteen minutes before the housefull board was put up. In Ranchi, the only cinema which functioned honestly and smoothly was Sainik Theatre (earlier known as Garrison), which was run by the Army.

In November 1980, *Screen* published a story on the modus operandi of selling tickets at inflated prices outside a Bombay theatre. The black marketeers would get about twenty urchins to stand in a queue for a tip of Rs 2 each. Each boy would buy four tickets for him to sell at a higher price. One theatre owner and two scalpers told the reporter that the Amitabh Bachchan phenomenon had given 'an unprecedented fillip' to professional scalping.[14]

In the Eighties, television and cricket emerged as strong rivals to popular cinema. Television had arrived in India in 1959. But until as late as the early Eighties, only a select minority in urban India had tasted its pleasures. Entertainment options were limited on the state-run Doordarshan. Barring the Sunday movie and a few film-based programmes like *Chitrahaar*, the staple was pro-government programming. For the average middle-class household still struggling to buy a fridge or a scooter, the TV didn't even figure as an object of desire. This changed dramatically as the Eighties progressed.

For television, 1982 was a milestone year. National programming became possible following a steady satellite link between New Delhi and other transmitters. Colour transmission began the same year on Independence Day. Affluent urban India enjoyed the 1982 Asian Games in colour. A massive expansion followed. In a written reply, Union I&B minister Ajit Kumar Panja told Lok Sabha on 20 April 1987 that India had 197 working TV transmitters—forty-six high-power and 151 low-power ones.

The landscape of cities and towns changed dramatically. Unaesthetic antennas came up on every other rooftop. People shifting the direction of antennas for better reception was a common sight in middle-class colonies. Quoting official statistics, business journalist Vanita Kohli wrote in her book, *The Indian Media Business*, that the number of TV homes vaulted from 1.1 million in 1979 to 22.5 million in 1989. The increasing number of TV sets also meant more middle-class families could watch live sports on the small screen. Interestingly, as per NRS data in the book, cinemagoers plummeted from 12.2 million in 1986 to 5 million in 1992.

One-Day cricket was a key agent in India's altering idea of home entertainment. In 1983, India's World Cup triumph whetted the national appetite for the fifty-over game. Purists scoffed at ODI cricket as they now sneer at T20. But Board of Control for Cricket in India (BCCI) was quick to spot the golden goose. International engagements of the shortened variety swelled.

Between 1974 and 1983, India had played just fifty-five ODIs, roughly 5.5 games every year. Between 1984 and 1989, the number rose to 113 ODIs, roughly nineteen games a year and a three-time jump from the pre-1983 era. It was a new obsession that had millions of young Indians hooked. Its fans wouldn't even dream of going to watch a movie when a game was on. On such days, noon and matinee shows would lose some of its core patrons to cricket. The seven-hour event, often telecast live on DD, played out like two back-to-back movies. In other words, in the Eighties, cricket and cinema, two of India's greatest passions, came into market-conflict with each other.

Distributors and theatre owners were big losers. The popularity of ODI cricket and live telecast scared the film industry. Two months before the 1987 Reliance World Cup (1 October-9 November), film trade magazines pointed out that each week was scheduled to have three games. 'This being the biggest opposition one can think of, no major film will be released during this period,' noted a trade magazine.[15]

Actor Rishi Kapoor used an imaginative analogy to explain the situation. 'This [Reliance Cup] is the biggest multi-starrer running now. It has eleven heroes [one team] and eleven villains [the rival team]. And two heroines too [umpires], if you please, who'll be dancing on the field! Who would be interested in seeing our one, two or three hero films in preference to this multi-multi-starrer?'[16]

Close on the heels came sponsored television serials. *Hum Log* (July 1984), Doordarshan's first soap, was a game-changing event. The serial's wild popularity, especially among north India's middle class, opened the doors for more shows: *Buniyaad, Khandaan, Yeh Jo Hai Zindagi* and others.

Following the lives of fictional families became a real-time preoccupation. As the number of sponsored shows grew, the idea of an evening well spent got redefined. Common middle-class behaviour such as dropping in unannounced at a friend's place became infrequent.

As TV started capturing more public time and mindspace, cinema cash collections started shrinking. Trade magazines kept worriedly writing about more and more sponsored serials being introduced on national TV which would 'prove to be a formidable opposition to the evening film shows'.[17]

Nothing illustrated the dazzling rise of the idiot box better than film magazine *Madhuri* putting TV stars on its 7 June 1985 cover, with the catchline, '*Ghar ghar ke chahete* (Darlings of every household).' TV stars of *Yeh Jo Hai Zindagi*, Satish Shah and Swaroop Sampat graced the cover, once reserved for top film actors.

The trend was clear. As producer Pranlal Mehta said a year later, 'We have two kinds of audiences: youth and ladies [for films]. The women-oriented subjects are good for the 12 and 3 p.m. shows. The 9 p.m. audience is now lost to television. The upper class does not go to the cinema halls because they are in such a bad state and they have their televisions and videos. What is left is the youth; nobody can keep them indoors. They love the songs and dances. The audience for this kind of film is from age nine onwards.'[18]

In a January 1987 interview, distributor R.R. Khajanchi of Khajanchi Film Exchange in Amravati reaffirmed that evening television was hurting collections. 'Previously on Sundays, every film used to be housefull. But now due to so many programmes, serials and feature films, business has come down to 60 per cent.'[19]

With cable TV, the situation worsened. Distributor Trilok Singh of United Charuchitra, Jaipur said, 'Earlier video parlours and TV were affecting business and now disc TV has made serious inroads at many places...Weaker pictures have no chance.'[20]

Ramayan (1987-88) and *Mahabharat* (1988-90) further underlined how television could influence an entire nation's social calendar.

The politics of violence further shrivelled the cinema pie. Film business in Punjab was shocked into submission by extremism in the 1980s. In several towns, show timings were altered. Restrictions on movement of scooters and motorcycles at police checkposts also added to cinegoers' inconvenience.

In Batala, the main town of terror-hit Gurdaspur district, going to the movies became a dangerous pastime. 'During 1983-84, militants twice tried to set fire to Krishna Talkies. A desi bomb was also hurled once. People were too scared to visit theatres,' recalled the theatre's former co-owner Krishna Swarup.[21]

The bomb blasts changed the town's behaviour. Journalist Rakesh Rekhi, who grew up in Batala, said, 'After the attacks, the night show [9 to 12] was discontinued. Families stopped visiting the cinema halls. Only the young and the reckless kept visiting the theatres which started screening soft-sex movies with adult clips surreptitiously inserted.'[22]

There were other setbacks in store for the strife-torn northern state. Punjabi filmstar Virendra (*Yaari Jatt Di, Sarpanch*) was shot dead by suspected terrorists during the shooting of *Jatt Tey Zameen* on 6 December 1988. The actor, who also directed the Hindi film, *Khel Muqaddar Ka* (1981), was a cousin of Dharmendra.

Picture-postcard Kashmir was the preferred location for love stories ever since Bombay cinema discovered colour and snow in the 1960s. In September 1986, Mohiuddin Shah, director of tourism, J&K government, flew down to Bombay to find out the reasons behind a drastic reduction of film shoots in Kashmir. He promised to look into the problems faced by film units.[23]

How the scenario altered within three years! In 1989, the rise of violent separatism changed everything. The Valley was convulsed by cries of '*azaadi*'. A cinema hall in Srinagar was one of the two targets of bomb explosions on 8 May.[24] In the months that followed, cinema halls became an ideological casualty. Militants enforcing a conservative version of Islam ordered their closure. Gradually all theatres—Palladium, Broadway, Neelam, Regal, Naz, Shah, Khayam, Khyber, Shiraj and Firdaus—shut down in Srinagar.

Kashmir was part of the Punjab distributors' territory—and it ceased to be a collection point. From all accounts, though, illegal video cassettes continued to be popular.

—————————— SHORT TAKE ——————————

Lost passion

Visiting Srinagar as a reporter in 2013, I spoke with a few Kashmiris on the Hindi films scene in the 1980s. Mohd Yousuf Mir, who ran a small transport business, recalled renting a VCR for Rs 250 for a night to watch three Hindi movies at one go. '*Par woh junoon khatam ho gaya* (That passion is gone),' he said.[25]

Politics adversely affected films in other parts of India too. The Assam student movement (1979-85) hurt film business in the eastern state.

The screening of Amitabh Bachchan's *Mard* (1985) was stopped midway during the first show at Surya cinema in North Lakhimpur in north-east Assam. Bachchan was a Congress MP and had addressed several rallies in the polls. The call for discontinuing the film came from the rival Asom Gana Sangram Parishad. Advance booking amounts were refunded. Scared of repercussions, the owner of Aditya cinema decided not to screen the movie at all.[26]

In 1986, Hindi films screenings in Tamil Nadu were forcibly stopped by students and members of the DMK. A resolution was arrived at later. A year later, anti-Hindi agitators stopped Hindi film shows in Pondicherry, Madurai and Trichy.[27]

Hindi cinema also faced a boycott in parts of West Bengal, from the Gorkhaland National Liberation Front (GNLF), then spearheading an agitation for a separate hill state. The boycott was in reaction to an advertisement published in Calcutta newspapers, which had described the GNLF agitation as 'anti-national'. The ad carried an appeal signed by more than 100 film personalities associated with the Bengal and Bombay film industries. There were six cinemas in the affected area (Darjeeling, Kalimpong and Kurseong) which mostly exhibited Hindi films.[28]

To sum up, the Bombay film market shrank throughout the 1980s. And that was bad news for all stakeholders.

Clearly, the film industry was getting pushed into a tight corner. Yet curiously, the 1980s marked a record high in the number of Hindi films made over a decade. Year 1985 saw the production of an eye-popping 185 films which overtook the previous record of 183 films in 1947.

In the 1980-89 period, 1,594 Hindi films were censored, roughly 160 every year. This was a dramatic leap from the previous decade (1970-79) when 1,105 Hindi films were censored, about 110 per annum. The previous decadal record was 1,164 from 1940-49.

Interestingly, despite the growing number of flops, more films were produced in the second half of the 1980s than the first. In 1985-89, 852 films were censored, compared to 742 in 1980-84.

In the latter half of the 1980s, film production surged as if on steroids. Multi-starrers were launched with alacrity and dumped midway with abandon. *Film Information* noted that between 1 January 1987 and 22 May 1987, as many as 196 new Hindi films were announced or launched. To detail the development, in a period of 142 days, forty-eight films went on the floors, eighty were launched with song recordings or mahurats, and sixty-eight films were announced with cast and credits.[29]

Screen magazine described 1987 as the year of 'stars, lavish mahurats and gala parties' but also spotted a crucial contradiction at work. At the beginning of the Eighties, the cost of a multi-starrer was about Rs 1 crore. Now the expense had doubled without any corresponding increase in the number of cinema houses or territories.

Mainstream news magazines too noted the trend. In 1988, *India Today* highlighted the manic but mindless production activity that had gripped Bombay's moviedom. Uday Row Kavi, editor of film trade weekly *Box Office*, told the magazine that 'an astonishing 783 new productions were announced in 1987. In just one month, August, there were eighty-seven mahurats, virtually three a day.'[30] An estimated 400 films were being lensed, their average cost calculated at Rs 75 lakh per film. Total potential investment was assessed at Rs 300 crore. The magazine further guesstimated that only a third of them were likely to be completed; the rest were to be abandoned at a certain stage before completion.[31]

This was happening at a time when the number of cinema goers was plummeting. From 12.2 million in 1986, it dropped to 5 million in 1992, as data from National Readership Survey later showed.[32] Trade magazines of the time list an astounding number of unfinished films. There was also a long inventory of complete but unsold films. With supply vastly exceeding demand, releasing a film in theatres was as difficult as making it. The vital question, therefore, was: who would want to invest in movies at a time when the chances of a film's success were hardly any better than India defeating the West Indies in Test cricket?

The arrival of new black money propelled this skewed game of demand and supply. Gresham's law says bad money drives out good money. In Bombay cinema, old money was gradually eased out by new money, part of which was 'bad' too. Gradually, a new financial regime of fresh financiers and inexperienced producers was created.

The new men with money were 'super-rich diamond merchants, expatriate Indians from Dubai, real-estate and bullion speculators, and most ironically, video pirates who made tidy fortunes hijacking Hindi films in the past.'[33]

You can append underworld money to that list. Money earned by dubious means had entered Bombay cinema long ago. In his autobiography, *Khullam Khulla,* Rishi Kapoor revealed that Rattan Khatri, then the 'matka king' of Bombay, had produced one of his movies, *Rangilla Ratan* (1976).[34] Matka was an illegal but hugely popular form of public gambling in those days, especially in Bombay.

Film scholars have taken note of the invasion of dirty money. Global security think tank RAND wrote in a study that don Dawood Ibrahim's 'D-Company moved into the entertainment industry in the late 1980s to cultivate a more acceptable social image, to expand its rackets, and to find new vehicles for laundering money...They began at the production level, focusing their control on the financing and production of new films.'[35]

To find out the main sectors where black-income activities were carried out, noted economist Shankar N. Acharya and his associates prepared a questionnaire and distributed it to all commissioners of income tax. The senior officials were asked to rank twenty sectors in any of the four categories— most important, very significant, significant and minor—in the decreasing category of black money being parked in those sectors. The findings, incorporated in a book, *Aspects of the Black Economy in India* (1985), are revealing.

As per the survey, only real estate (83 per cent) and large-scale manufacturing (78 per cent) were bigger storehouses of unpaid tax money. The film industry (producers, directors, stars, theatre owners, etc.) finished third on the podium—67 per cent officials felt that it belonged to the most important category and 23 per cent assessed that it was in the very significant category as a sector where black-income activities abounded.[36]

Stars, crew and technicians were all paid partly in black. Yet filmstars continued to be callous in clearing their income-tax dues. Union minister of state for finance B.K. Gadhvi told Lok Sabha that seventy-two stars had income-tax arrears exceeding Rs 1 lakh as on 31 March 1987. Jaya Prada headed the list with Rs 65.12 lakh, followed by Rajesh Khanna with Rs 63.83 lakh.[37] The trend continues.

On the surface, it was business as usual. But no amount of gloss could paper over the grim reality of a shrinking market. Intra-industry debates at the time reveal a sharp friction among all parties concerned: producers, distributors, exhibitors and actors. Going through these debates published by trade magazines is like reading the story of the blind men and the elephant. Every side, barring the actors, claimed that the system was loaded against them. High production costs, too many films, too few theatres, and too little profits—that was the scenario.

To control the chaos, a new system came into place. Most distributors stopped buying a film outright as was the earlier practice. The producer was now expected to become his partner to minimise his risk. Veteran producer-distributor N.N. Sippy explained that since the supply of films was greater than demand, a distributor could afford to be choosy in a competitive market. He said, 'Producers, therefore, are helpless. They have to accept the terms of the distributors and become partners with them. It's all a case of over-production....'[38]

Sippy further elaborated, 'And why has risk increased so much? It is because of the steep rise in cost of production. As producers, we are not able to control costs. And how can we? Artistes and technicians are charging exorbitant rates. The amount of wastage resulting from the practice of artistes to give just a few hours for shooting for a film in a day is unbelievable. This adds to the cost of production.'[39]

The happiest people in this maddening scenario were the top stars. There were only a handful of actors whose name could draw a respectable queue outside the advance booking counter. Producers buzzed around them like flies in a sweet shop. Mithun Chakraborty acted in at least 110 Hindi films between 1980 and 1989. Film business reports show that less than a fifth of his movies made profits. Yet in February 1987, answering a fan's question in Hindi film magazine *Madhuri*, Mithun said that his dates were booked for the next two-and-a-half years!

Stars rationed shooting dates like kerosene in public distribution outlets. Middling producers were invariably hard-pressed for time. Being late for shooting was a status symbol. Producer-director Deepak Bahry (*Agent Vinod, Taraana*) remembers, 'If you were to start shooting at 9.30 a.m., a star would turn up at 3 p.m. and say he wants to leave by 5 p.m. Now what could a director do in two hours? You had to be sharp and inventive to finish your work in such a short time. The problem was so rampant that we had ceased to see it as a problem. That was the normal way you worked. Sometimes you used a duplicate for longer shots and blended it with the star's close-ups.[40]

In an interview to *Movie* magazine before the release of *Qayamat Se Qayamat Tak* (1988), Aamir Khan revealed why he opted not to become a producer. 'My dad [Tahir Hussain],' said the young Khan, 'being a producer paid the directors and artistes; yet, had to regularly chase them, as they would play musical chairs with him before completing his films. Seeing these unfavourable conditions, I vowed that I would never become a producer or have anything to do with films.' Aamir did become a producer much later, but on his own terms.

Fudging box-office figures was part of a game played by stars, producers and theatre owners in tandem. Moderately successful films running in half-empty theatres were upgraded to silver jubilee status with the help of filmstars and producers. In a 1982 interview, N.F. Damania, president, Theatre Owners' Association, revealed, '*Yaarana's* ticket sales are Rs 20,000 and the theatre rental is Rs 32,000. But it is running. *Ek Hi Bhool* has been making losses after tenth week but will be taken off only after it celebrates silver jubilee. *Satte Pe Satta's* ticket sales are the same as its rentals but the film isn't changed. If flop films continue to be shown after making losses, how will other films run?'[41]

He further expounded on the economics of rigging. 'The filmstar and the producer join hands to make up for the losses. The success or failure of a film has repercussions on their forthcoming films. It affects their fees...Since we do business with them, we agree to their request. Otherwise they won't give us their next film.'[42]

Hits or flops, even B-list stars had producers chasing them. Feeble efforts were made to rein them in towards the end of the decade. In a meeting of producers and filmstars, it was unanimously decided that from 15 March 1989, all stars will work for two shifts only and that each shift will not be less than six working hours. The first shift will begin from 8 a.m. and second from 3 p.m.[43] It didn't work.

Looking back, director Sudhir Mishra (*Yeh Woh Manzil To Nahin*, 1987) felt that the 1980s was 'a bad place' to be. He summed up, 'Single screens were deteriorating. Multiplexes had not yet arrived. The middle class had stopped going to cinema halls. The nature of money coming into cinema was gradually changing. The stars had taken over. And the cost of filmmaking could no longer be justified by its revenues.'[44]

And yet, in a parallel world, the finest of Hindi cinema also came to life in this era—'It was the best of times, it was the worst of times.'

Stars and Stardust in Lok Sabha

Before the 1980s, filmstars were a rare presence in the Lower House. Telugu actor Kongara Jaggaiah (Congress) was probably the first actor to win a Lok Sabha seat in 1967. But in 1984, everything changed as the Bombay film industry firmly planted its feet in Parliament.

Rajiv Gandhi's Congress swept the Lok Sabha polls, riding a sympathy wave generated by his mother Indira Gandhi's assassination. Three stars and one lyricist were elected to the Lower House. All of them contested on a Congress ticket. Incidentally, three exhibitors were also elected in 1984. They also represented the Congress.

In Allahabad, Amitabh Bachchan defeated the seemingly unbeatable heavyweight politico Hemvati Nandan Bahuguna of the Lok Dal by a handsome 1.87 lakh votes. In North-West Bombay, Sunil Dutt polled more than double the votes from his nearest rival, BJP's redoubtable lawyer Ram Jethmalani. Margin: a healthy 1.54 lakh. Vyjayanthimala overcame the unbeaten Era Sezhiyan in Madras South by 48,000-plus votes in a tough contest. The fourth industry person was poet Balkavi Bairagi, who wrote songs in films like *Reshma aur Shera* and *Ankahee*. He won from Mandsaur—his third LS poll triumph—by over 59,000 votes.

Film business weekly broadsheet *Screen* went euphoric. The front page had the caption: 'Look! The New Leaders.' 'Something so spectacular, something so exciting, has rarely happened in the history of the world of Hindi films,' it gushed.

गुलछड़ियां (अभिनंदन)

— कपिल कुमार

जेठमलानी के लिए भारी पड़े सुनील,
काम न आई एक भी उनकी लिखी अपील ।
उनकी लिखी अपील हो गई हिरविल मेवा,
इतना बड़ा वकील करे अब लाला चेगा ।
कहे 'कपिल' समझाय, अदालत की चतुराई,
मतदाता ने बहुमत से नापास कराई ।

जीत लिया अमिताभ ने मतपेटी का युद्ध,
पुत्र इलाहाबाद का निकला सोना शुद्ध ।
निकला सोना शुद्ध, बिलावट वाला हारा,
देवता नंदन को उत्तर मिला करारा ।
कहे 'कपिल' समझाय, हाथ का साथ निभाया,
नेता बन कर, अभिनेता संसद में आया ।

वैजयंती माला फिरी नगर-गली-घर-गांव,
पूंछ बोले पर से, देखी धूप न छांव ।
देखी धूप न छांव, धूल सड़कों की छानी,
किसी औरत ने लिख डाली नई कहानी ।
कहे 'कपिल' समझाय, लगाया पावन नारा,
पूरब-पश्चिम-उत्तर-दक्षिण सभी हमारा ।

Lyricist Kapil Kumar penned a paean after the triumph of Amitabh Bachchan, Sunil Dutt and Vyjayanthimala in Lok Sabha polls. (Photo Credit: *Film Information*)

Cine exhibitors and distributors Nihal Singh (Agra) and Manphool Singh (Bikaner) also won on Congress tickets.[45] Unlike Nihal Singh, though, Manphool described himself as 'an agriculturist' in his Lok Sabha bio. Shantaram Potdukhe of Congress, who was elected from Chandrapur constituency for a third time, owned a cinema hall, Abhay Talkies.

REEL 2

THE GREAT PIRACY BAZAAR

*The sanctity of the cinema hall is going away. Cinema is like an aging whore who is losing her seductive power, but hoping her youth will return. But it's too bad there's a new bitch in town: video and TV—Mahesh Bhatt, 1988**

In the 1980s, a little gizmo became the unlikely villain that would torment the mighty Bombay film industry for years. The device was roughly the size of a ludo board, a few inches thick and light enough to be lifted by a kid. Slick for its time, it was called the video cassette recorder or VCR. In India, many simply called it 'video'.

If the VCR set was the hardware, magnetic tapes were the software. A feature film, about 160 minutes long, could be recorded on a single tape. The VCR and the magnetic tape, hooked to a television set, became the VHS (video home system). Together they revolutionised drawing-room entertainment and transformed movie watching forever.

The video cassettes were supplied by your friendly, neighbourhood video librarywala, the ubiquitous retail stores of the pirates. Till now, the audience went to the cinema. Now the cinema of your choice was delivered at home—often

---

**India Today*, 31 May 1988

on a two-wheeler. The VHS was to the 1980s what OTT or streaming services are to the 2020s.

Most novel technologies with scaling-up potential unsettle the existing financial order. The VHS was no exception, especially after bootleggers took charge. The film industry got financially bruised and emotionally battered.

The VHS ended up creating one of the biggest technical disruptions in the history of films. Mobility and accessibility were its main strengths. The appliance could be set up at home or in a vehicle. Inter-city buses would describe themselves as 'video coach', often flaunting their misspelt versions: VDO, or just BDO. Travellers would inquire in advance about which films would be shown; these were the best part of the journey.

Piracy was as rampant and troublesome as toothaches. Veteran film publicist and columnist Vasant Sathe wrote in *Screen*, 'It is no longer a secret that air-conditioned luxury buses going from Bombay to Goa or Bangalore or going from Delhi to Chandigarh are regularly showing Indian films on videos.'[1]

Cable TV further expanded the reach and revenue of the free-booting industry. Residential apartments got connected and hooked. Hotels took to cable TV like kids to candy. As Sathe noted, 'Several hotels situated on hill stations like Mussoorie, Nainital, Matheran, Mahabaleshwar are showing every night for their guests feature films...Like radio and TV, video is becoming a regular feature of every room in five-star hotels.'[2]

Producer-director Atma Ram (*Shikar, Yeh Gulistan Hamara*) summed up the problem in Filmotsav 1984. He said, 'The video operators paid no sales tax, no income tax, no excise levy, no custom duty and no royalty to producers. A lot of black money went into the business.'[3]

It is 'nothing short of a mafia,' he exclaimed in desperation.[4]

It was merely demand and supply at work. The Bombay film industry's sluggish modus operandi worked perfectly for the piracy industry. In the 1980s, a yawning gap existed between a film's date of release and its eventual exhibition in small-town India. Like an overworked daily wager, the prints would arrive broken and tired after hundreds of screenings. Routinely patched up, they would be jumpy at places, resulting in skipping of frames. The projectionists often suffered the most colourful of abuses in such situations. Illegal video cassettes would arrive long before the film prints and mop up the market. In time, as the bootleggers got more organised and daring, video cassettes would be available in mega cities even before the release of a film.

Not surprising then, it was easy to be seduced by the home video even though it was ethically and legally wrong. 'New films became like trailers on VHS. Only the best was watched at theatres,' recalled Delhi-based film distributor Sanjay Mehta.[5] The rest were rejected after the video 'screen test'.

Director K. Ravi Shankar (*Sindoor, Dariya-dil*) remembered how he panicked after discovering that top-quality cassettes of *Ghar Ek Mandir* (1984), a film produced by his father A. Krishnamoorthy, were freely available at Delhi's underground Palika Bazaar, a pirates' paradise. 'It was the first day of the film's release. The situation was beyond our control. But we never lost hope. We thought, if the audience likes the movie on VHS, they will come back to watch it on the big screen. And they did,' he said.[6] The high-voltage family drama came out a winner.

Film director B. Subhash recounted a similar anecdote about *Tarzan* (1985), primarily remembered for its desi Jane, Kimi Katkar. 'Those days we used to give the film's print seven days in advance to the overseas distributor. The pirated version was out on the day of the film's release. The video librarywala came to my home and asked my wife, "*Aapko Tarzan chahiye* (Do you want *Tarzan's* cassette)". She wondered, "*Kaun si Tarzan?*" He said, "*Aap ki Tarzan*".'

An agitated Subhash called up the overseas distributor and screamed, 'What have you done? You have destroyed the film.' But his blood pressure stabilised after his Bombay distributor called. 'He congratulated me and said, "There's a long queue for advance booking." I asked the manager of Shalimar theatre, "Really? How?" The manager said, *"Film ka video report achha hai* (The film's video reports are good)".'[7]

───────────────── SHORT TAKE ─────────────────

Video film magazines

A byproduct of this development was the emergence of video film magazines. Like a regular film magazine, they showed interviews with stars, trailers of forthcoming films, even spot reports of film shooting. Among them, *Lehren* was the most popular. Excerpts from *Lehren*, *Movie Video* and *Ekanth* are now available on YouTube.

Bombay cinema's foreign market was the first to be bloodied by video piracy. *Screen* magazine wrote in 1980 that fifty of the 129 cinemas-showing Indian films in the United Kingdom had shut shop by 1979. Film exporter Rajendra Singh said that economic depression in the UK and the consequent fall in the purchasing power of people of Asian origin was the larger reason behind the collapse of the UK market.[8]

It wasn't the only reason though. Singh further pointed out that movie ticket prices had jumped from 85 pence to 1.85 pounds in the lower class and from 1.50 pounds to 2 pounds in the upper class. 'As illegal videos could be hired for as little as 2 pounds for forty-eight hours, this had prompted people to stay indoors and watch films in the comfort and privacy of their homes.'[9]

In 1980, Hollywood and Broadway director Krishna Shah

(*Rivals* and *River Niger*) secretly filmed his encounter with a London shopkeeper selling pirated video cassettes of his film, *Cinema Cinema*. Shah, who had earlier delivered the much talked-about Hindi flop, *Shalimar*, asked for a cassette and was told that it would cost him 32 pounds. The shopkeeper also told him that he had already sold 500 cassettes of the film![10]

A year later, Bombay's film business weekly *Trade Guide* briefly noted, 'With the UK market fully going video, the overseas market [has] fully crumbled.'[11]

The report also said that many theatres had shut down in Thailand and Malaysia. At this stage, the entire video market was illegal. By May 1984, only two Indian theatres were left in the UK.[12]

Amit Khanna, then vice-president of the Film Producers' Guild, said, 'An Indian blockbuster used to fetch 1,00,000 pounds in the UK alone; now the overseas distributor is lucky if he can sell the rights for the UK at 5,000 pounds.'[13]

Official statistics support this view. Information and Broadcasting Minister Ajit Kumar Panja told Lok Sabha in 1987, 'There has been a decline in the export of feature films canalised [*sic*] through NFDC. Earnings from export of feature films [including video rights of feature films] have come down from Rs 15.07 crore in 1980-81 to Rs 7.18 crore in 1986-87.'[14]

In a written reply, Panja furnished further evidence of falling film exports—1984-85: 525; 1986-87: 413. 'The export of Indian films has shown a decreasing trend. This is mainly due to video piracy,' he said.[15]

Video piracy was a chaotic market, hydra-headed in nature, making it difficult to curb and almost impossible to eradicate. The entire process was choreographed in three steps. First, the film's print was transferred into a master magnetic tape. The master tape's contents were reproduced on duplicating machines and packaged. Second, the tapes were taken to the supply hubs from where they were bought by video library owners across the country. Third, the tapes were rented out from these libraries in cities, towns, kasbahs and villages. The illegal business functioned with test-tube precision.

A 2009 research paper, *Film Piracy, Organized Crime, and Terrorism*, referred to the role of mafia boss Dawood Ibrahim in the business. The paper noted, 'In his early years, [Dawood] Ibrahim operated his gang, D-Company, by standard crime-syndicate practices: extortion, smuggling, and contract killings. During the 1980s, Ibrahim and his cohorts were able to vertically

Cricketer Sandeep Patil played the male lead in the flop, *Kabhie Ajnabi The* (1985)

integrate D-Company throughout the Indian film and pirate industry, forging a clear pirate monopoly over competitors and launching a racket that controlled the master copies of pirated Bollywood and Hollywood films.'[16] Cassettes duplicated from a master tape were of superior quality.

The copycats were so well organised that veteran film director Yash Chopra once admitted that pirated prints of the latest Friday release were out the same weekend itself.[17]

At the retail level, piracy became a kitchen industry. A Bombay library owner revealed that 'a number of rich Malabar Hill housewives had got into the duplicating business.'[18]

Small-time traders and businessmen out to make a fast buck also copied films inside theatres. These cassettes made for unsatisfactory viewing. But they could still be in demand, if the blurry scenes belonged to a recent box-office smash hit or a half-forgotten gem. In the kasbahs, where viewers waited for months for the film to arrive at the local theatre, even camera prints had a market. It was common practice among middle-class families to rent a VCR for Rs 50 for an all-night binge on weekends. Group viewings were common even in college hostels, a late-night *vilayati* porn flick being the centerpiece.

In Bombay, video libraries had started mushrooming by 1981. By 1984, there were about 500 libraries, mainly in well-heeled areas and the suburbs. Industry bigwig Amit Khanna estimated in 1984 that there were about 5,000 video libraries, 2,000 video coaches and 20,000 video bars and parlours in the country. The total turnover was assessed at Rs 100 crore.[19] Khanna, a producer-lyricist, also chaired the Copyright Protection Committee of the All India Film Producers' Council.

The illegal industry grew multifold in the next five years. By May 1988, *India Today* guesstimated that there were 15 lakh video cassette recorders (VCRs) in the country. It further assessed, 'One lakh video libraries, one lakh video parlours and theatres, and thousands of hotel and private cable TV connections now provide a ready market for three lakh video cassettes every month. The annual turnover of the video market in India is now estimated at Rs 1,000 crore, about the same as the gross collections in the nation's 12,732 cinema theatres.'[20]

Even Dharavi, Asia's largest slum colony, was home to thirty-six video joints.[21]

Bombay's Lamington Road and Manish Market were the go-to places for retail video cassette buyers. Behind the façade of legitimate small-time businesses such as electronic goods stores, smuggled cassettes were peddled. The buyers came from everywhere—Delhi, Ahmedabad, Bangalore, Madras and small towns nearby—placing orders ranging from fifty to 500 cassettes.[22]

The rise of the video business meant a fall in lending rates. Piracy flourished because watching a film's video at home gradually became much cheaper and more convenient than going to the movies.

The Times of India took note of the change in 1984: 'Video libraries in Bombay began initially lending out cassettes at Rs 150 a day, by the end of last year [December 1983] in parts of the city they were available for Rs 8. In early 1982, hiring charges for a VCR and TV were Rs 300 for twenty-four hours, today [January 1984] it is Rs 150.'[23]

The video boom forced trade magazines to devote an entire section to the phenomenon. Every week *Film Information* diligently compiled video-related reports published in newspapers across state capitals and other towns.

A report from Khamgaon, a small town in Maharashtra, said films such as *Kalaakaar, Karate, Do Gulab, Fifty Fifty, Shaan* and *Gehri Chaal* were being shown at six video parlours. Interestingly, due to intense competition, the admission fee had dropped to 50 paise from Rs 5. One video joint was even charging 25 paise. In Maharashtra, videos had made inroads in most small towns, kasbahs and villages: Jalgaon, Buldhana, Malkapur, Shegaon, Nandura, Amrapur, Matargaon, Kamleshwar, Mangrool and Navaghare.[24]

It was the same story in Rajasthan. At the hugely popular camel fair at Pushkar, new Hindi films ran to packed shows at four video centres. 'I imagined these screenings would be badly organised, the print lousy,' said a photographer from Bombay. 'But I was wrong. The print was superb, they'd put up two speakers, and outside a man with a megaphone was chanting the names of the films.'[25]

Video joints had sprouted even in the boondocks of Madhya Pradesh. About thirty such hangouts were spotted in Chirimiri coalfields located in the mineral-rich Surguja district, now in Chhattisgarh.[26]

The illegal video parlours operated with impunity. At Bhavnagar in Gujarat, some would even advertise in local dailies, giving the names of the films being shown: *Zanjeer, Bekaraar, Main Awara Hoon* and *Pukar*. The video operators of Bhavnagar district also formed their own association.[27]

The cassettes were riotously popular abroad as well. In Bangladesh, small video theatres sprouted in cities and towns. Films such as *Disco Dancer, Qurbani, Kabhi Kabhie, Silsila, Love Story* and *Shaan* were available for an admission price of 10 taka only. 'Nightly rentals of VCRs with four or five videos of Hindi films also became very popular. Amitabh Bachchan, Mithun, Zeenat Aman and Hema Malini quickly became familiar names and popular icons among the middle and lower middle-class viewers here quickly amid the "culture war" between India and Bangladesh,' wrote Zakir Hossain Raju in the essay, 'Bollywood in Bangladesh: Transcultural Consumption in Globalizing South Asia'.[28]

—————————— SHORT TAKE ——————————

Aisa bhi hota hai

Actor-director Sanjay Khan once disclosed that a dealer of video cassettes in Dubai presented him with a pirated copy of *Abdullah*, a film directed and produced by him! 'It was a gift and so I accepted it with a smile,' he said. Even though the film's video rights to the Gulf hadn't been sold yet![29]

In the pre-VCR era, producers and distributors enjoyed a comfort level with each other. With a shrinking revenue pie, those bonds of trust were broken. Allegations and counter-allegations mounted. A Mysore distributor, suspected of lending the prints of *Karamdaata* (1986) to pirates, was beaten up by the producers.[30]

Distributor S.K. Surana of Pushpa Pictures in Bhusawal, Maharashtra said that even exhibitors from B and C class stations (small towns and kasbahs), who had once paid attractive rates, had stopped doing so after the introduction of big-sized videos.[31] Narain Dass Mukhija of Shri Navchitra Distributors, Jaipur estimated that illegal screenings had taken away at least 25 per cent of the business.[32]

Many theatres shut down in India, as they did abroad. Only those with a strong management and healthy financial back-up could weather the storm. Many cinema halls died a slow death. But it would be erroneous to say that video piracy was the only cause of their demise. Several other factors—high maintenance expenses, prohibitive taxes, slack management—were also at work. It would be more appropriate to proffer that piracy was a critical nail in the coffin.

A 1984 news report from Ahmedabad, a city of ailing textile mills then, said 'the film exhibition industry in the city, reeling under the impact of video piracy and the television boom, has forced a section of theatre owners to sell their theatres for other purposes.'[33] Two theatres, Model—one of the oldest in the city—and Dipali on the fashionable Ashram Road, had been sold and were slated to be replaced by multi-storeyed office complexes.[34]

In 1986, Ajanta and Ellora, two prominent Ahmedabad cinemas called it curtains. The closure notice said: 'The notice put up by the management outside their premises declares that the cinemas have been closed in view of the houses' inability to survive in the face of competition from video and TV and failure in getting enhanced rental from distributors.'[35]

In Jabalpur, Vaibhav cinema closed on 15 June 1989. Earlier, Mahaveer, Savitri, Sheila, Subhash and Navneet had also shut down in the same city.[36] It was the same story across the country.

Efforts to counter piracy were as sincere as a politician's promise. Occasionally, the police would swoop on hotels, libraries and homes, and confiscate cassettes and VCRs. But the menace remained rampant.

In a major operation in the UK in 1984, cops and other enforcement officials seized more than 10,000 Asian cassettes and hundreds of VCRs in raids on video dealers and private houses in West London. 'The raids...were concentrated in Southall, Wembley and Wealdstone, and more than 100 VCRs were found in one premises,' UK's *Video Week* magazine reported.[37]

Indian Videogram Association vice-chairman Rajesh Mehra felt that this was only the tip of the iceberg. 'There is still a long way to go. We estimate these raids accounted for about 20 per cent of the Asian piracy operators in the UK,' he said.[38]

Back home, the pirates were engaged in a see-saw battle with the law. While several video parlours were raided and shut down, at least in one case a court ruled in their favour.

Two reports highlight this contradictory approach. After raids on video libraries and cafes on 23-24 December 1983 in Jodhpur, 'almost all the dozen video joints in the city downed their shutters'.[39] It was a different story in Calcutta. Many video libraries, forced to shut shop after police raids and seizures of cassettes, reopened after a court intervention which restrained police from raiding the parlours and seizing cassettes.[40]

The Indian Motion Pictures Producers' Association (IMPPA) formed an anti-video piracy sub-committee with B.K. Adarsh as its convener and offered an incentive-based scheme for workers who participated in the raids. In one week, forty-two raids were conducted.[41]

Arrests were rare. Those detained were invariably low-level operators. In 1987, IMPPA carried out its biggest-ever raid, seizing 100 VCRs, three TVs, two U-Matic machines, two U-Matic tapes and 346 uncensored video cassettes. For the first time a bail amount as high as Rs 10,000 was fixed for the accused by the court.[42] U-Matic machines were used for recording on video cassettes those days.

But such raids were too infrequent and the punishments too light to act as a deterrent. Piracy awareness among law enforcers was ridiculously low. Khanna recalled going to police stations to complain about films being illegally shown in video parlours. 'The cop would ask, "What has the thief taken away?" We would say, "He is showing films illegally." He would then say, "What can I do?" They thought since there is no physical theft, there is no crime,' he said.[43]

The video dramatically changed movie content and, consequently, the nature and demographics of the audience. With the arrival of the video cassette or the VHS player, middle-class families slowly retreated from theatres, many of which were uninviting.

The movie halls primarily became the abode of the

underclass and the young middle-class male, especially in small towns. Scripts were written and tweaked keeping the front-stall and rear-stall ticket holders in mind because they became the primary audience and remained relatively loyal to the theatres. Balconies, too, were often filled by this class of audience, which was passionate enough to overspend on a ticket if it meant watching a favourite actor in the first week.

Young directors were forced to alter the kind of films they were making. Director Anil Sharma said *Bandhan Kuchchey Dhaagon Ka* (1983) was appreciated by those who saw it. 'But it was seen more on the pirated video circuit than in theatres. People were saying, video has come and *film line band ho jayegi* (the film industry will shut down). I felt my career was over at the age of twenty-four,' Sharma recalled.[44] His observations illustrate what many young directors went through.

The technological changes in the Eighties emerged out of a compulsion to outdo the bootleggers. For some time, 3D seemed to be the answer. The technology was impossible to duplicate on VCR. The fad surfaced after *Chhota Chetan* (1984), the dubbed version of Malayalam film, *My Dear Kuttichathan*, became the year's largest grosser.

Apart from *Shiva Ka Insaaf* (1985), directed by producer Romu N. Sippy's brother Raj N. Sippy, a few other filmmakers tried their luck with the eyeball-grabbing technology. Cinematographer-director V.S.R. Swamy's *Maha Shaktimaan* (1985) was a superhero film. The Ramsay brothers unleashed *Saamri* in 3D, a modest success the same year. As the novelty wore off, the technology was abandoned.

Some filmmakers felt that visual gloss—spectacular pageantry, eye-popping action scenes—could seduce the audience back to the big screen. Opting for 70mm or cinemascope films was another way to counter the copycats. 'The frames of movies made in these formats got chopped from the side, top and bottom on VCR,' cinematographer S.M. Anwar said.[45] But opting for the 70mm format was costly and only a few A-list producers could afford the investment.

In a sense, the VCR readied India for the satellite TV revolution of 1991. Before that, Hollywood films were mostly accessible only in metropolitan cities and A-class towns. With VCR, these limitations were bypassed. Many English movies were available at video stores across the country. Suddenly, the choice was endless.

Dennis Pereira, India representative of the Motion Picture Export Association of America, discovered that mini video parlours in small-town Amravati were playing Hollywood flicks such as *Tarzan The Ape Man*, *The Towering Inferno*, *Man with the Golden Gun* and *Visiting Hours*. The last one was yet to be released in India.[46]

Porn films also became readily available. Before the VCR, porn in India was largely limited to reading cheap pulp fiction. Often wrapped in yellow cellophane paper or stapled to avoid those looking for a free peekaboo, vernacular porn fiction was sold on the pavement under the popular premium brand, Mastram. Imported adult magazines such as *Playboy* or *Screw* also provided succour to the desirous but denied among the English-speaking upper class. Now porn cassettes were devoured by the eager and the starving. Censorship became irrelevant— and not for the last time.

In the early 1980s, newspaper reports about the government working on a law to check video piracy were routine. Nothing concrete happened. In Filmotsav 1984, the government announced the need for proactive intervention. I&B minister H.K.L. Bhagat assured the film industry that the government was concerned by the video piracy threat and was actively considering various ways to control the menace. He also said that the government was working on a comprehensive amendment to the Copyright Act, the Censorship Rules and the Cinematograph Act, if necessary.[47]

However, there was little attempt to walk the talk. As late as 1990, the government was still talking about forming an expert group to 'study the necessary amendments to the Copyright Act, Cinematograph Act and the Indian Wireless Act to handle the problems posed by video piracy and cable television more effectively'.[48]

Possibly, the government wasn't keen to intervene proactively. Video piracy was also an employment generator. It wounded the organised, tax-paying film industry but created a parallel self-employment industry. Video library owners were also employers. The chain of cassette production and distribution engaged thousands. Probably, weighing the pros and cons, the state opted for a go-slow policy.

In the end, the industry was left to fight its own battles. In 1987, the legit home video came to life with 'simultaneous home video release'. Star Video, a video house formed by a group of producers, released its first cassette, *Imaandaar*. The effort to legitimise the market got a further boost when a major industrial house, Garware, entered video production. The Garwares had the infrastructure to manufacture video cassettes and set up a recording unit too.[49]

But there were sharp differences over the division of spoils between producers and home video distributors. The Film Federation of India and All India Film Distributors' Council tried to sort out differences over the marketing of home-viewing video rights. It was felt that revenue from videos should be shared 50:50 between producers and all-India distributors.[50]

But the strategy failed to seriously dent piracy because the legit market failed to take off.

Video Film Industry: Short and Sweet

In the mid-1980s, video features made an unobtrusive entry into the chaotic film market. These video features were not shown on Doordarshan or in movie theatres. They were retailed directly to the home video audience. Like feature-film cassettes, you could rent them from the neighbourhood store.

These films were mostly produced by Nari Hira, owner of *Stardust* and a cache of other film magazines. He is also credited with the stories of some films. Actors like Aditya Pancholi, Kanwaljit Singh and Neeta Puri, all newcomers then, were regulars in these ventures, made under the banner of Hiba Films. Some of them were 'bold' in content like the cult hit *Shingora*, now available on YouTube. The film, starring Persis Khambatta, Marc Zuber and Pancholi became a rousing favourite for its steamy scenes. Om Puri (*Shahadat*), Supriya Pathak (*Naqli Chehra*), Zarina Wahab (*Kalank Ka Tika*) and others also made the odd appearance. So did a very young Urmila Matondkar (*Naqli Chehra, Scandal*).

These films were a departure from the regular Hindi feature. Pavan Kaul, who directed a bunch of films including *Naqli Chehra* and *Kalank Ka Tika*, recalled, 'You couldn't see a film like *Shingora* on the Indian screen then, the kind of character Persis Khambata played, a woman who sleeps with both father and son. That was very bold for its times. In *Kalank Ka Tika*, Kanwaljit Singh played a man who lures innocent village girls on the pretext of marriage and sells them to brothels in Bombay.'[51]

Anil Tejani (*Shingora*) was another prolific director of these video features.

It was a carefully controlled operation. Kaul explained, 'Most new actors such as Aditya Pancholi, Neeta Puri and Jeet Upendra received monthly wages. Like the old Hollywood studio model, the whole team—directors, writers—were put on contract and earned regular salaries. Everyone was modestly paid. We received a small bonus when a video did well. Our provident fund money was deducted. The production house even had its own anti-piracy cell. Their musclemen went around video libraries checking if there were any pirated copies.'[52]

The films were shot over thirty to thirty-five days, mostly at Nira Hira's two bungalows on Madh Island, Bombay, which functioned like studios. They were shot with the early models of Sony low-band, pre-CCD, tube cameras. The film's overall budget amounted to roughly Rs 3-4 lakh.

These films, routinely advertised in film magazines, had a decent run for a couple of years starting 1985. But cable piracy forced the market to fold up by 1988.

Music piracy was an adjunct to film piracy. HMV and Music India (earlier Polydor) were the big daddies of the music business. The bootleggers—some of whom have gone legit since—invaded the market. They not only grabbed a huge slice of the small money pie but also expanded the marketplace. Until then, music LPs or cassettes were sold in select shops located only in cities and towns. By its own admission, HMV had 1,500 authorised dealers, 8,000 titles and covered sixty-four countries. Piracy made the music available in lakhs of small stores all over India. The pirates aided the massification of music.

If the software was omnipresent, could the hardware be far behind? Earlier people couldn't buy personal music systems because they were too expensive. Now tape recorders and cassette decks, many of them smuggled from Nepal, flooded the market and entered lakhs of homes.

Buying pirated music cassettes became as common as shopping for veggies. A legit cassette—of HMV or Music India—would cost Rs 35 or more. A pirate would pack songs of three films in a single tape and sell it for Rs 20-25. Sometimes the audio quality of the pirated versions was better than the original. The music companies would release ads warning customers that pirated cassettes could damage their equipment. Few seemed to care.

Film journalist Anupama Chopra wrote that in the mid-80s, the Hindi music market was a little less than Rs 100 crore. 'A Rs 1 lakh royalty payment from a music company was an occasion for a producer to throw a party. Venus bought its first film, *Jaan Ki Baazi*, for Rs 50,000 in 1985...And then fruit juice man-turned-music moghul Gulshan Kumar [of T-Series] walked in. He lowered the price of tapes to less than Rs 25 and hiked audio payments to several lakhs.'[53]

There was a method to the T-Series tactics. Media scholars Lawrence Liang and Ravi Sundaram wrote in a 2011 research study that 'T-Series was a profoundly disruptive force in the Indian music market, in large part because it was a tremendously successful pirate. The company built its catalogue through a variety of quasi-legal and illegal practices, notably by abusing a provision in the fair-use clause of the Indian Copyright Act, which allowed for version recording. On this basis, T-Series released thousands of cover versions of classic film songs. It also engaged in more straightforward copyright infringement in the form of pirate releases of popular hits, and it often illegally obtained film scores before the release of the film to ensure that its recordings were the first to hit the market.'[54]

Producer-director Vinod Pande recounted an anecdote to emphasise how big and blatant music piracy was. 'Mr B.R. Chopra once told me that a well-known pirate confessed cheekily to him that he had made a profit of Rs 80 lakh from *Nikaah's* music.'[55] Chopra had produced and directed *Nikaah*. Despite the piracy, HMV put out an ad in *Screen* magazine in 1982, celebrating the platinum disc of *Nikaah*.

Hasan Kamal, who wrote *Nikaah's* lyrics, said the film's offbeat music had disappointed HMV music executives, who seemed to have little understanding of what the public wanted. 'They felt that this wasn't music of the time. Only 5,000 cassettes were released as a test case. By the time, the HMV people realised that the songs had become popular and came out with fresh stock, the pirated cassettes were already out,' he said.[56] In other words, the pirates had a better sense of the market.

Liang also wrote about the positive impact of T-Series, how the company changed the rules of distribution in ways that permanently transformed the music industry. He said, 'It [T-Series] also expanded the music-consuming public by focusing on genres and languages that had been ignored by the dominant Indian record labels and distributors, notably HMV. HMV had viewed recording in languages other than Hindi as unprofitable due to the small scale of the respective markets. T-Series proved that it was possible to expand these markets with stronger distribution and lower price points.'[57]

The established players tried their best to counter the pirates by reworking their pricing policy. HMV priced *Ram Lakhan's* music cassettes (1989) at Rs 16 a piece, less than half the selling price of an HMV cassette in early 1980s.[58]

Similarly, when HMV found that it could not meet the demand for one of its biggest hits, *Maine Pyar Kiya* (1989), it reportedly entered into an agreement with pirate cassette producers to raise their price on the album from Rs 11 to Rs 13 and pay HMV half a rupee for every unit sold. HMV, in return, promised not to sue them or raid their businesses. Other producers also colluded with pirates to minimise their costs, taxes and royalty payments to artistes.[59] These short-term strategies helped only marginally. The pirates were always miles ahead in the game.

At least one production house invested hugely in improving the quality of recording to counter film and music piracy: the Barjatyas. This delayed the release of debutant director Sooraj Barjatya's *Maine Pyar Kiya* by several months because the recordist had 'to incorporate the various effects of music and dialogue'.[60] Sooraj's father, producer Rajkumar Barjatya once explained the rationale behind doing so, citing the US example: 'Their enemy too was video, television. They evolved in a healthy way to compete with this menace—the 70mm, six-track stereophonic system and Cinemascope with 4-track system. It sent audiences scurrying back to the cinema houses and the box-office collection improved once again.'[61]

Music director Raamlaxman said he worked continuously for two-and-a-half years to compose the music for *Maine Pyar Kiya*. 'And I spent around three months trying to perfect the background music,' he added.[62]

In all, the Rajshris spent Rs 30 lakh on the music, more than the cost of some of their movies. The idea was to give the audience something special that becomes a talking point and lures many more to the theatre. The effects did enhance the audience experience and likely played an important part in the film's box-office triumph.

The 1980s exposed the negotiable morality of the middle class. Film piracy was criminal theft; so was music piracy. Yet few saw anything wrong with it.

Visiting the cinema required careful planning and preparation for families. Transport, parking and refreshment costs added to the expenditure. With piracy, watching a film became easier and came at a much-reduced price, even though the experience was not quite the same.

Watching movies at home had another fallout. Till then, cinema viewing was a patriarchal project where the male family head controlled what the women of the family would watch. This was true for majority of Indian homes. That changed. Now women could order their own video cassettes and watch films of their choice during afternoons. And young male adults, college students and others could watch the 'forbidden' stuff.

With the arrival of the Walkman, even listening to music got personalised. The 1980s marked the beginning of the individualisation of entertainment.

REEL 3

CUT, CUT, CUT! THE ART OF GETTING AROUND SCISSORHANDS

*I'm the last person to be talking about the Censor Board.
I've spent my whole career dancing between a pair of
scissors—Helen, 1980**

The relationship between the Bombay film industry and Central Board of Film Censors (CBFC), commonly described as the censor board, was always awkward at best, antagonistic at worst. The government body, which functions under the union information and broadcasting ministry, got itself a friendlier name in 1983: Central Board of Film Certification (CBFC). But the new name hardly brought any noticeable change in its attitude or behaviour. Even today the body continues to be referred to and identified by its old shortened moniker, the censors.**

In post-Independence India, the tussle between the Bombay mainstream filmmakers and the censors was primarily rooted in a difference of views about the social objective of movies. The

---

*Quoted in *India Today*, 15 October 1980

**For a more detailed analysis of film censorship in India, read, Aruna Vasudev's *Liberty and Licence in the Indian Cinema* and Monika Mehta's *Censor and Sexuality in Bombay Cinema*

CBFC, an implicit representative of the government's position on thorny cultural and political issues, saw itself as a moral custodian of society. Its central point was that movies had a larger purpose and the industry's focus on entertainment had negative side-effects. Most producers, on the other hand, operated on the underlying principle that films were a commercial enterprise and their job was to provide recreation and make money.

It was always a game of hide and peek between the censor board and the industry. Scenes and sequences related to sex, violence and politics were three constant areas of conflict. Filmmakers tried to find innovative ways to work past the restrictions. Movies that did not meet the guidelines were suitably spruced, even banned. It is another matter that the bans were often overturned in courts.

Several committees and panels on censorship were set up over the years. In 1969, the Enquiry Committee on Film Censorship, under the chairmanship of former Chief Justice of the Punjab High Court, G.D. Khosla, submitted its report. The committee recommended, among other things, lesser governmental influence and more aesthetic freedom. The report also spoke up in favour of celluloid kissing, which created a furore. The Khosla Committee recommendations found their way to the Cinematograph Act of 1974. But the Act got nullified later. Back to square one.

The battle between censors and Bombay cinema raged through the 1980s. One of the reasons the censor board didn't command respect was because it often did not follow its own rule book. Guidelines would be winked at to favour heavyweight producers who had a hotline to New Delhi's people in power.

Actor-producer-director Sanjay Khan was one of them. When his film *Abdullah* (1980) landed in major censor trouble, Khan revealed that he was asked by then censor board chairman M.L. Khandpur to see him. 'I will pass your film with a few cuts,' the chairman told him. 'But I was within my rights to appeal to a higher authority. Then the man says to me: "*Aap ko Delhi jaane ka bahut shaukh hai* (You are fond of going to Delhi)." To which I replied: "*Aap hi ne paida kiya hai* (You have created it)".'[1]

Khan's film had the kind of body-and-bosom show that the censor loved to snip. The song, 'Bheega badan jalne laga', is as voyeuristic as it gets: Zeenat Aman and her friends dance and bathe under an artificial waterfall, unaware that a bunch of dacoits are ogling at them. Aman, never a shy lily in her career, said in an interview later: 'If there's anything I regret it's the bathing scene in *Abdullah* which I thought was in bad taste.'[2] She was in a relationship with Sanjay Khan then.

But the movie not only managed to get a U-certificate but also a tax waiver in Delhi. *India Today* reported that the film's premier was attended by I&B minister Vasant Sathe and influential Congress politicians Yashpal Kapoor and Jagdish Tytler.[3]

The magazine also wrote that Khan had presented a show before Indira Gandhi at the Son of India exhibition in Trade Fair Authority of India (Pragati Maidan), Delhi.[4] Sanjay Gandhi, who had died in a plane crash on 23 June 1980, was the subject of the show.

The filmmaker wasn't the only one. His brother Feroz Khan's *Qurbani* (1980) began with a 98-second-long panegyric to Mrs Gandhi and Sanjay. The visual tribute, with a voice-over by the producer-director himself, was interspersed with black-and-white images of the Gandhi scion. Gandhi junior's dreadful role in the Emergency had already been exposed in the post-Emergency years (1977-80). The tribute went like this:

Shri Sanjay Gandhi, the Prince sleeps in peace. Thirty-three years old and too young to die. Beloved mother, the honorable Prime Minister, the Iron Lady of our nation, humanity bows before you in this hour of grief. But unfortunately life is a bubble and every day is a bonus. We can only pray to God that he grants us this bonus in you as long as providence and mortality permits to guide the destiny of our nation which is synonymous with you being with us.

The nation and I salute the Sleeping Prince. His talented family members, friends and critics. Inshallah, may his soul rest in peace. I dedicate my loyalty to the living memory of the prince whom I never met but whom I salute and hope to meet in Judgement before the Almighty.

Respected mother of our great nation, with your kind permission I wish to dedicate the proceeds of the premieres of Bangalore and Delhi to the memory of the Sleeping Prince. Inshallah, may his soul rest in peace.

Such a healthy dose of obsequiousness to the benefit of *Qurbani*, a guns-and-bikini thriller. 'The controversial tax exemption to the film by the then Maharashtra Chief Minister A.R. Antulay, who had also extended the same facilities to Feroz Khan's younger brother Sanjay Khan's *Abdullah*, was widely discussed in the media.'[5]

Shatrughan Sinha also felt that tax exemptions were politicised. Speaking to *Film Information* in December 1984, the actor-producer said, 'While *Kalka* was granted tax exemption status by many state governments solely on the film's merits, in Madhya Pradesh I was asked if I had any political influence. I said I don't want to use my political influence as I was sure that my film has merits enough to qualify it for tax exemption. What is the use of seeking tax exemption for your good films if the only qualification for tax exemption is your political influence?' *Kalka* (1983) was a coalminer drama produced by Sinha.

Producers openly promoted the ruling party. When producer Pranlal Mehta advertised his 1985 film *Balwaan*, the blurb was 'Congress I emerges Balwaan'. The opening credits of Pramod Chakraborty's *Shatru* (1986) made the following flattering proclamation: 'Inspired by the Prime Minister Rajiv Gandhi's crusade against red-tapism, favouritism and corruption, the greatest enemy of country's progress, and dedicated to honest policemen who laid their lives for this crusade.'

Political flattery was common in the 1980s.

Deference to the ruling leadership was displayed in various ways. *Jawani Ki Kahani* (1986), a surprise hit with a couple of 'hot' scenes, took care to show footage of Nehru, Indira Gandhi and Rajiv Gandhi, during a song built around a family planning slogan: *Ek ke baad abhi nahi, do ke baad kabhi nahi.* B. Subhash's action thriller *Commando* (1988) started with the line, 'Excepting [*sic*] our beloved prime minister late Shrimati Indira Gandhi, all characters in the film are fictitious.' Early in the film, a woman playing the role of Indira Gandhi delivers a speech, which is pretty close to a real speech made by the Prime Minister shortly before her assassination by her bodyguards in 1984. When *Commando* was released in 1988, her son Rajiv Gandhi was the Prime Minister.

Raj Kapoor's *Ram Teri Ganga Maili* (1985) made a USP of heroine Mandakini showering under a waterfall. The nipple-baring scene was far more revealing than generally permitted. In an age when most films landed in trouble for excessive skin show or extreme violence, Kapoor's film waltzed past the censors. Undeniably, Kapoor's *Satyam Shivam Sundaram* (1977) would have received more cuts if helmed by a lesser luminary. This was not a one-off case. The system was rigged to favour the big cats.

Not everyone was a Khan or Kapoor. It was a different story for low-budget producer-director Vinod Talwar's *Raat Ke Andhere Mein* (1987), a C-grade horror-suspense flick, where a masked monster rapes and kills women. The film was complete, Talwar says, in eight months but got stuck with the censors for another nine months. 'They chopped off so many scenes. *Film ko trailer bana diya* (The film became a trailer). I wanted to reshoot it for three to four days. But because of the controversy, the film got publicity and the distributor wanted to release it. He said, "*Aise hi de do.* (Give it to us as it is)".' Due to the savage cuts, the film incoherently lurches from one reel to the next, but strangely that did not adversely affect its box-office fate. 'It cost about Rs 15 lakhs. But I made a profit,' claimed Talwar.[6] *Trade Guide*, however, lists it in the flop section.

Between 1979 and 1983, producers of at least eleven films—ten Hindi and one Urdu—sought justice in the courts, challenging either a ban or what they felt was harsh certification by the censors. The films were: *Jaadu Tona, Jaani Dushman, Lok Parlok, Private Life, Chor Police, Abdullah, Meri Aawaz Suno, Andhaa Kaanoon, Jaanwar, Prem Rog* (all Hindi) and *Nikaah* (Urdu).[7]

The reasons were: too much violence (*Chor Police, Meri Aawaz Suno, Andhaa Kaanoon*), too many sex scenes (*Private Life*), promoting superstition (*Jaadu Tona, Jaani Dushman*), or allegedly offending religious sensibilities (*Lok Parlok, Nikaah*).

SHORT TAKE

What's in a name?

Manoj Kumar's *Kalyug ki Ramayan* was changed to *Kalyug Aur Ramayan* to avoid hurting religious sensibilities. Films such as *Durgaa Maa* and *Jeeva* emerged bruised but triumphant in their struggles with the censors. Dada Kondke's *Aage Ki Soch* also faced major problems with the censors before reaching the theatres.

Sometimes the objections to cuts turned ugly. A regional film censor panel member in Madras was warned that his legs would be chopped off if he continued to make 'adverse' recommendations.[8]

Some efforts were made to fight misogyny. R.J. Beley, regional officer, CBFC, communicated to the Indian Motion Picture Producers' Association to advise its members (producers) not to make use of words like *saali*, *haraamzadi* and *kutiya ki aulad* as they are derogatory to women and resented by womenfolk. The censor board also advised filmmakers not to show women in a bad light, following a memorandum submitted to the Prime Minister by the Committee on the Portrayal of Women in the Media.[9] If implemented with any degree of seriousness, that would have ended up in snipping off thousands of feet of film every year.

At times, the All India Film Producers Council (AIFPC) protested. In 1986, AIFPC decided to boycott the censor board. Reason: Delay in getting clearance and films often being sent to the revising committee. But the threat didn't last too long.[10]

In 1986, the Indecent Representation of Women (Prohibition) Act was also passed in Parliament. The Act said, 'No person shall produce or cause to be produced, sell, let to hire, distribute, circulate or send by post any book, pamphlet, paper, slide, film, writing, drawing, painting, photograph, representation or figure which contains indecent representation of women in any form.' But it hardly made any difference on the ground.

The case of producer-director Rajkumar Kohli's *Insaniyat Ke Dushman* (1987) encapsulates the tussle between censors and the Bombay film industry. Kohli began his career producing small-budget action movies in the 1960s but struck gold directing mega multi-starrers such as *Nagin* and *Jaani Dushman* in the 1970s.

His *Jaani Dushman*, briefly banned for encouraging irrationality, was cleared by Bombay High Court. In the film industry Kohli was well known, but as his travails with *Insaniyat ke Dushman* indicate he did not have a hotline to the men who mattered.

Kohli submitted the film's print to CBFC for certification on 20 June 1986. The examining committee watched the film and refused to certify it. In a 4 July letter, the committee said, 'The film is full of violence and it contains scenes of gruesome murder and rape. A senior respectable lawyer is seen bribing a woman to give false evidence in the court. A police officer is shown as shooting and killing for personal revenge. Thus, both the police and law are shown in an unprofessional manner. The medical profession is also shown as behaving in a negligent and irresponsible manner. Hence judging the film in its entirety, from the point of view of its overall impact, it has been decided by the censor board to refuse a certificate to the film under guidelines 2 (i), (ii), (iii), (iv) and 3 (i).'[11]

The examining committee was factually correct. But several films with similar scenes had been passed earlier. A harried

Kohli put forward an application to the revising committee on 6 July. The committee saw the film three weeks later, on 28 July and, like its predecessor, refused a certificate. In a letter on 6 August the committee said, 'The film is full of morbidity, violence, vulgarity, obscenity and depravity...'

A revised version was submitted in early September and viewed by the examining committee, which again refused to issue a certificate. The committee also raised fresh objections in a letter written on 6 October. After the second refusal, Kohli went to the Appellate Tribunal in November. As per the director, the tribunal was willing to grant an 'A' certificate, but only after making forty cuts. Kohli refused. At this stage, he discovered that a recently released film, *Insaaf Ki Awaaz*, had several similar scenes. The producer-director pointed out the anomaly. At his request, the tribunal saw *Insaaf Ki Awaaz*! The cuts came down to fourteen which Kohli accepted.[12]

For the record, one of the scenes cleared by censors had a villain hanging a five-year-old girl child in front her parents. Even by Kohli's modest standards, there was no art or craft in the movie's filming. In all, the film's release was delayed by five months and it cost the producer an additional Rs 10 lakh in interest. It was a middling success at the box office.

There were several similar cases. Amarlal Savlani's *Saat Bijliyaan* hung in limbo for over a year. The film was finally cleared by the Appellate Tribunal. The CBFC had refused to certify the film insisting that 'on the pretext of portraying the theme of good versus evil, the film depicted visuals of vulgar movement of girls, two songs were full of vulgar scenes and some of the lines had double meanings. And, also that violence had been glorified; and institutions of law degraded.'[13]

Director Govind Nihalani's *Tamas*, the serialised tele-film on communal violence during Partition, caused an outcry and got embroiled in a raging controversy. The film had to be cleared by a court.

Not everybody was unhappy with the censors. In her autobiography, *Freedom: My Story*, film director Arunaraje Patil writes about her positive experience during the certification of *Rihaee*. The film sensitively explored a married woman's conjugal rights when her husband goes to the city for livelihood. Patil was expecting the film to be mauled and mangled when she received a call from CBFC.

She wrote, 'The officer was a lady but that didn't mean anything because I had dealt with righteous, holier-than-thou ladies who were highly moralistic. As I sat down ready for battle, the officer looked at me and said, "Congratulations, I loved your film. It is so rare that we get to see a film like this..." She said that they didn't want to cut anything—not even a frame but would I take an "A" certificate, which meant adult viewing only. Relief washed over me that there were to be no cuts but an "A" would restrict the business, I had been told. I asked her if we could make it "UA" but she said the content would be too controversial and it would be safer for me to go with the "A" certificate.'[14] According to an estimate, a producer or financer lost 30 per cent of business if the film got an 'A' certificate as opposed to a 'U'.

Producer Manmohan Shetty was also pleasantly surprised when *Ardh Satya* was cleared without delay. 'We were expecting *Ardh Satya* to have censor problems because it dealt with police and politicians. But it was passed with an adult certificate in one screening,' he said.[15]

The experiences of the makers of *Rihaee* and *Ardh Satya* show that the censors weren't always prudish. The body could be liberal when it felt that there was an artistic reason for a sexually explicit scene or the use of foul language. On the other hand, the censors were stricter when they felt that scenes of sex or violence were purely for commercial exploitation.

Doordarshan too, it seemed, had its own 'special code' of what was meant to be shown and what was to be omitted. There were no direct instructions but some unwritten dos and don'ts had been established over the years. Cabarets, mujras, rapes and abusive words were taboo. Songs on *Chitrahaar* were also edited. A DD official once said, 'We don't allow repeated shots of two flowers touching, or far too frequent shots of a hill, the moon, or a stream which are used far too suggestively by our filmmakers.'[16]

In March 1986, DD cancelled the telecast of the award-winning *New Delhi Times* a day before it was to go on air. Director Ramesh Sharma's film explored the nexus between politicians and criminals.[17]

K. Vishwanath's *Jaag Utha Insan* was dropped from the menu when it was discovered that the caste conflict between Harijans and Brahmins was part of the storyline. Substantial footage was scissored from *Ek Chadar Maili Si* because of 'vulgar language'. A scene in *Alibaba aur 40 Chor* showing pigs being roasted was sliced off.[18]

The Hindi film song became an arena of skirmish as well. This was a time when pelvic thrusting, bosom heaving, lewd lyrics and double entendre were widespread. Titillation was the name of the game.

Film Information pointed out that objections were raised about the picturisation of two songs from *Hukumat* and one song each from *Goraa* and *Kaun Kitnay Paani Mein*. Some were cleared only after cuts.[19]

Producer Vimal Kumar of *Dariya-dil* said, 'I had to practically reshoot a Kimi Katkar and Govinda song in the rain. The song went, *"Barse re sawan kaanpey mera mann, bheeg jaye na badan mera, apni chhatri me mujhko chheepa le re, paas apne tu mujhko bula le re"*.'[20]

'Again I had to completely reshoot the song, 'Mera naam hai Ragini', picturised on Aruna Irani and Ravi Baswani in *Ghar Sansar*. They found the picturisation objectionable,' he recalled.[21]

Producer-director K. Ravi Shankar said *Ghar Ek Mandir* (1984) was initially given an 'A' certificate. He recalled, 'The film was censored in Chennai. A new regional officer, who had come from Odisha, found something offensive in the comedy scenes of Asrani and Aruna Irani. He felt some dialogues had double meaning, ordered some cuts and said, it is fit for an 'A'. We were shattered. If a movie named *Ghar Ek Mandir* has an 'A' certificate, I don't think the audience would have come in. It was like killing the film. We went to the revising committee, presented our case. After a little struggle, we got a 'U' certificate with some cuts.'[22]

The cat-and-mouse affair continued because there was no long-term solution, only quick-fix jobs on a case-to-case basis. Even CBFC Chairman Bikram Singh wondered, 'We can't define vulgarity precisely. What is vulgarity? Is it a particular dialogue of double meaning? Or is it just innocent humour? These questions do not have a readymade set of answer. Here we've got to exercise our moral and cultural judgment.'[23]

Meri Aawaz Suno: Bans Mean Box Office

Bans raise audience curiosity and often work to the film's advantage. A good example was Jeetendra's *Meri Aawaz Suno*. A remake of the Kannada hit, *Antha (The End)*, the film was released with an 'A' certificate in December 1981. Far less violent than the original, it was banned a couple of weeks after release.

Two days before the imposition, Ghulam Nabi Azad, then Youth Congress (I) president, had demanded its banning in

Parliament. 'Azad's objection was that the film depicted a Union home minister, home secretary and inspector-general of police as heading "a gang of smugglers and anti-social elements" which, he concluded, was not only in "bad taste" but also defamatory. Azad further urged that exhibition of the film should be stopped at once and action taken against its producer.'[24]

The film's producer and distributor rushed to the courts to obtain stay orders. Top lawyers Soli Sorabjee and Siddhartha Shanker Ray were engaged. The media too lambasted the ban. The *Hindustan Times* wrote an editorial headlined, 'Ill-conceived Ban'. Even the Congress-backed *National Herald* urged the central government to change its decision.

A modest success till then, the movie became a monster hit after the ban was lifted. 'In Ulhasnagar, an industrial township near Bombay, twin cinemas called Anil and Ashok held seven shows a day for four days following news of the ban. The ban hysteria generated so much viewer excitement that even post-midnight shows at one o'clock and four o'clock in the morning ran to full houses.'[25]

REEL 4

THE GREAT STRIKE OF 1986

In the history of Bombay cinema, the strike of 1986 is a singular event. Who would have thought that the chaotic industry, divided into disparate camps and riddled with bloated egos, would come together to raise the banner of collective protest against the Maharashtra state government and behave, to use a Marxian term, like 'a class for itself'?

This wasn't the first time that filmwallahs had stepped out of the screen and demonstrated on the streets. Back in 1949, burdened by backbreaking taxation and a string of octroi duties, the industry had struck work. But the 1986 strike remains one of a kind for its extended duration and its method of struggle. The lockdown began on 10 October and ended on 10 November, lasting a staggering thirty-one days.

The roots of the protest can be traced back to the Janata Party rule (1975-77) when finance minister Charan Singh imposed an additional levy on film prints after the first twelve copies. After 1980, increased levies further raised print costs. Film journalist Anil Saari wrote in a detailed exposition of the crisis that in effect, this doubled the cost of each print for the distributor on whom the producer shifted the burden.[1]

The raised levies were not an isolated problem. Costs of all commodities and services associated with film production had vaulted. The entertainment tax of 177 per cent—yes, 177 per cent!—on cinema tickets in Maharashtra was said to be the highest in the world. There were demands to abolish a surcharge claimed for Bangladesh refugees who had come fifteen years earlier during the 1971 Indo-Pak war. Theatre rentals had also skyrocketed. Most importantly, the audience was shrinking due to rising ticket prices, not to forget the video boom. The entire ecosystem had become too challenging for the film business.

Saari wrote, 'Consequently, the film distribution network outside Bombay simply collapsed. The old distributors shut up shop, preferring to stick to films they had bought previously. Though films continued to be produced in Bombay, there was difficulty in releasing them through the old distribution system.'[2]

In this perfect storm of grievances, the immediate reason for the protest was the imposition of a 4 per cent sales tax on the leasing of films by distributors and the hiring of production equipment.

In his autobiography, *Unfinished Innings: Recollections and Reflections of a Civil Servant*, Maharashtra's finance secretary Madhav Godbole wrote that the levy of sales tax on the leasing of films turned out to be 'the proverbial last straw' for the industry.

He also pointed out that 'in Maharashtra, the Act for levy of such a tax received the governor's assent in August 1985 but its implementation was kept in abeyance for more than a year, and the Act was made applicable only from 9 October 1986.'[3]

In August 1986, the state government had appointed a high-level committee to scrutinise the industry's demands and make appropriate recommendations. The committee was headed by Godbole. Others in the panel were revenue secretary J.C. Kanga, education secretary M.R. Kolhatkar and cultural affairs secretary S.S. Menon. But before the report was readied, the industry struck work on 10 October.

The industry's list of demands was placed before Parliament in a written reply by I&B minister Ajit Kumar Panja. The reply, ironically, was provided on 10 November 1986, on the day the strike ended.

1. Withdrawal of new sales tax on the film industry and reduction of sales tax on raw films

2. Reduction of entertainment tax rates and abolition of surcharge on cinema tickets

3. Permission to exhibitors to recover tax-free service charge from cinegoers

4. Reduction in existing rates of electricity tariff which should be charged at concessional rate

5. Establishment of special courts and special police cell to try video piracy cases

दस अक्तूबर को फिल्मोद्योग ने अनिश्चितकालीन हड़ताल की घोषणा कर दी. महाराष्ट्र के तमाम सिनेमाघर बंद हो गये. फिल्म निर्माण की सारी गतिविधियां ठप्प कर दी गयीं...हड़ताल के बारहवें दिन फिल्मकारों, सितारों और कामगारों का अभूतपूर्व मोर्चा सड़कों पर निकल पड़ा....

(Photo Credit: *Madhuri*)

6. Tax holiday for new cinemas and subsidy for renovation of existing cinemas, as given in other states

7. Allotment of land to the film industry in Film City

8. Permission to existing and new cinemas for construction of commercial complexes to make cinemas economically viable or allow demolition of cinemas as in other states

9. Cash incentives and/or subsidy for all films produced in Maharashtra

Panja also said that the government had not made any assessment of the loss suffered by the film industry due to the strike.

On 21 October, the twelfth day of the strike, a cavalcade of about 150 cars and trucks gathered in the Shivaji Park area. Producers, directors, distributors, actors, singers, songwriters and technicians crammed into them. Many preferred to walk.

The march was a multi-starrer. Prominent participants included V. Shantaram, Sunil Dutt, Dev Anand, Rajesh Khanna, Rohini Hattangadi, Raj Babbar, Tina Munim, Anil Kapoor, Anil Dhawan, Suresh Oberoi, Govinda, Khushboo, Farah, Meenakshi Seshadri, Javed Akhtar, Shabana Azmi, Sanjay Khan, Akbar Khan, Yash Chopra, Mithun Chakraborty, Shashi Kapoor, and many more. Rajesh Khanna was the press convener of the action committee.

Wrestler-turned-actor Dara Singh said, rather sarcastically, 'In the past we hit the streets to collect funds for wars, floods and famine. *Lekin aaj sarkar ne humein sachmuch sadakon par khada kar diya* (But today the government has forced us on to the streets).'[4]

Around 9.30 a.m., the caravan rolled towards Dadar. The march was led by Congress MP and actor Sunil Dutt. Crowds gathered on both sides of the road to catch a glimpse of the stars. Some joined the march. At one point, the number of participants swelled to 40,000. Around 2 p.m., the procession reached Azad Maidan. Then the bandwagon moved towards Mantralaya but was stopped by the cops near Bombay University.[5]

Under Dutt's leadership, action committee president Ramraj Nahta, senior actor-director Chandrashekhar, producer N.N. Sippy and other industry bigwigs presented a memorandum to CM S.B. Chavan. The delegation included three MPs from the city and sixteen MLAs.

On returning, Dutt said that he had received an unfavourable response. He said, 'The Chief Minister says that you shouldn't indulge in morchas and that until the high-level committee submits its report, he cannot do anything.'[6]

In the days that followed, there were more marches, and at least two actors went on hunger strike: character actor Jankidas and comic actor Ravi Baswani. The latter, who played a stellar role in the comedy classic *Jaane Bhi Do Yaaro* (1983), fasted at New Delhi's Boat Club, the preferred location for protesters in those days.

Jankidas, then seventy-five, called off his three-day 'fast unto death' following an assurance from Shiv Sena chief Balasaheb Thackeray that a statewide bandh would be called in support of the film industry's demands.[7] Jankidas, who acted in over 300 films, was also a cyclist of repute.

Several stars freely expressed their dissent during the strike. Dharmendra said, 'I've seen the film industry being slapped and bullied by the political bosses. Still, it has the capacity to survive. I can't believe why they want to kill us. After all, we are no terrorists.'[8]

Shabana Azmi was more directly critical of the government. She said, 'I have always wanted to believe in my government but time and again I have been disappointed. Rajiv Gandhi has been my hero but I feel let down by his government.'[9]

Initially, production units were permitted to shoot films outside Maharashtra. Film laboratories also remained functional. But as the campaign generated steam, the industry came to a near standstill.

Director Rahul Rawail stopped shooting for *Dacait* when it was just ten days short of being completed. He said, 'I had to leave my set standing at Chandivali Studios. It doesn't matter, of course, because we have to leave our personal problems aside. The strike hasn't [just] affected me, it has affected everyone. And like all other producers and directors, I'll start where I left off once the strike is called off.'[10] That was the general mood in the industry.

Cinemas stopped screening films in Maharashtra. Foreign news agency UPI reported that 'work on about 200 films was halted paralysing about fifty-four million rupees in investments... About 1,50,000 people went out of work.'[11]

The movement struck a chord with the film fraternity countrywide. The South Indian film chamber of commerce expressed full support to the agitation. On 29 October, cinemas, laboratories, music recording studios and distribution offices were shut across India to express solidarity with the Bombay film industry.

On 7 November, the New Bombay Taximen's Union appealed to CM Chavan to bring an early end to the strike. A union press note said about 35 per cent of the city's taxis had been affected by the closure of cinema halls.[12]

To ease film workers' economic woes, about Rs 20 lakh was raised. Every card-carrying member of each association was given Rs 100 every week.[13]

Lyricist and industry honcho Amit Khanna, who was closely involved with the action committee, recalled that the strike was highlighted by national and foreign media. He remarked, 'The government got rattled.'[14]

The proposed tax affected distributors and producers who began to look for alternative channels of survival. 'Undoubtedly, most of the film industry's units would have shifted their head offices out of Bombay and Maharashtra so that they could escape paying a sales tax on the sale of the completed film's distribution rights,' wrote Saari, adding that the industry also toyed with the idea of making films in Hyderabad-Secunderabad, Gujarat, even West Bengal.[15]

In 1984, Lok Sabha had seven representatives associated with the film business, including Sunil Dutt and megastar Amitabh Bachchan. All had triumphed on a Congress ticket. It is possible that the presence of these MPs—Bachchan was a childhood friend of Rajiv—might have injected an added dose of confidence among the protesters about the outcome of the strike.

That's why the most talked-about absentee from the 21 October rally was Bachchan. Many guesses were made in newspapers and magazines over his non-attendance:

1. He was visiting his kids in Switzerland

2. He was on the hit list of Punjab extremists, hence avoiding public exposure

3. Quoting sources close to him, *Madhuri* magazine said he had to gone to the US due to a sudden reappearance of *myasthenia gravis*, a neuro-muscular disease that had afflicted him earlier

Reason No. 1 was close to the truth. Nearly a fortnight later, a UNI report said Bachchan was in Switzerland for medical treatment and had returned to India on 4 November.[16]

Shabana Azmi was sharply critical of Big B's absence. She asked, 'Where is Amitabh Bachchan? There can be no reason good enough to explain his absence. If this is diplomacy, it will misfire. I don't believe that he will offend Rajiv Gandhi if he joins us. Surely, even the Prime Minister expects Amitabh Bachchan to stand up for his industry. In fact, this was a chance for Amitabh to become a hero, never mind if he lost favour with the government. Nobody has the guts to question Amitabh's actions. I think a strong letter must be sent to him, demand must be made that he should come here.'[17]

However, actor Amjad Khan offered an alternative perspective in an article he wrote for *The Times of India*. '...Amitabh Bachchan's role or lack of role in the strike...has been blown out of proportion. People expect some kind of miracle from Amitabh. I do not. Amitabh cannot knock on the Prime Minister's door in the middle of the night, wake him up and say, "Look, I've got some good friends in Bombay, do something for them." We are aware that film workers are asking, "Why isn't he intervening? Why isn't he solving the problem?" That is because they are affected by what they read in the papers and by idle chatter. This is wrong. Amitabh is no superhero or a supergod.'[18]

After coming back from Switzerland, Bachchan promised to help sort out the issue. Reports quoting 'high-level aides' said that on 5 November, he was locked in a 'high-level meeting' with representatives of the film industry. But the same day, the megastar also angered many by not turning up for 'a meeting organised by the action committee at Gaiety Cinema, Bandra. More than 100 people waited in vain [for him] for nearly three hours.'[19]

A day later, Bachchan told reporters in New Delhi that he had met Prime Minister Rajiv Gandhi. The PM, he said, had put him in touch with the cabinet secretary. 'I will seek the Prime Minister's intervention if things do not work out,' he told reporters in Delhi.[20] As in the roles he often enacted, he wanted to play the lone ranger in real-life too.

The peace pipe was smoked on 10 November. An agreement was arrived at after six hours of intense negotiations which carried on past midnight. The meeting was attended by CM S.B. Chavan, Congress leader Sushil Kumar Shinde and industry representatives such as Ramraj Nahta, N.N. Sippy, Gunwant Desai and actor-turned-Congress politician Baldev Khosa.

Chavan thanked both Sunil Dutt and Bachchan for playing 'a leading role' in bringing about a settlement.[21] 'World's largest film industry strike ends,' reported global news agency UPI.

As per the deal, the cinema ticket surcharge was reduced from Rs 15 crore to Rs 5 crore per year. In other words, the government made an ex-gratia grant of Rs 10 crore, intended to reduce the surcharge on cinema tickets. It also suspended the levying of the new sales tax until the finance secretary submitted his report on 15 December.

It was unclear at the time whether the stir had ended or was suspended. One school of opinion felt it was 'an honourable settlement', another strongly believed it was 'a total sellout'. In the latter narrative, Bachchan and Dutt were villains of the piece.

At a crowded meeting in a Bombay suburban theatre, a day after the strike was called off, Bachchan was panned by several speakers. Some claimed he had betrayed the industry and demanded his effigies be burnt. The meeting also decided to return a cheque of Rs 2 lakh which the actor-politician had donated for film workers, the worst hit during the shutdown. A disappointed Dev Anand tersely said, 'The film industry must have its own independent leadership and not depend on star MPs.' Ramraj Nahta, who headed the All India Film Producers' Council, submitted his resignation to the action committee.[22]

In an editorial headlined 'Bitter-Sweet Eid', *The Indian Express* sarcastically wrote that the film industry strike had ended 'in a typical Hindi movie face-saving formula'. However, the editorial was sympathetic to film industry MPs.

'Though Mr Amitabh Bachchan and Mr Sunil Dutt played a decisive role in ending the stir, certain sections of the film industry are sore at the terms of settlement. They have dubbed the accord as a total sellout. This seems an overreaction in which personal egos of film personalities seem to be having a free play...In any case, nothing is lost. Further discussion will follow once the Godbole Committee submits its report.'[23]

In his autobiography, Godbole also praised the two MPs. He wrote that Bachchan and Dutt had actively interceded on behalf of the film industry. The bureaucrat said, 'Amitabh Bachchan who was close to Rajiv Gandhi had requested the Prime Minister to intervene. There were clearly two groups in the film industry: one which was conciliatory and reasonable, and another which was militant and headstrong and was opposed to any compromise.'[24]

Godbole also revealed that during the time the committee was working on the report, Bachchan was continuously in touch with PM Rajiv Gandhi. At that time Gopi Arora was the additional secretary in the PMO and B.G. Deshmukh, the cabinet secretary. '...when I met Gopi, he told me that Bachchan had been talking to the Prime Minister and PM would like the film industry's demands to be considered sympathetically, so as to give it maximum possible relief...'[25]

The report was submitted on 19 December. Relief for the film industry included reduction in entertainment duty and abolition of surcharge (worth Rs 16 crore), exemption of entertainment duty on award-winning and children's films (worth Rs 2 crore) and a proposed incentive scheme for construction of new cinema houses by way of refund of entertainment duty in the form of an interest-free loan (amounting to Rs 1.5 crore). The committee also recommended setting up an advisory committee and special police cells to check piracy.

The report was discussed by the government and the industry's action committee on 20 December. The action committee accepted the recommendations; it decided to end the industry's boycott of Doordarshan and withdrew the threat to ignore the International Film Festival scheduled to be held in Delhi in January 1987. The Maharashtra cabinet gave its seal of affirmation on 25 December 1986. Cinema halls had already opened by then. In any case, the common man was not entirely deprived of movies during the strike, courtesy video and TV.

Despite the agreement, a section of the film industry, particularly workers, continued to view Amitabh in a negative light. The Rs 2 lakh cheque gifted by the actor to the striking film industry workers was kept in abeyance till 1 January 1987 before being accepted.

BOMBAY CINEMAS

The new admission rates of some of the cinemas of Bombay were published in these columns last week. Some more are given below (with old rates prior to Oct. 10 in brackets, wherever available):-
Metro 8, 7, 3.80 (8, 6, 4); Liberty 7, 5.50 (8, 7); Regal 7, 5; Sterling 8, 6 (8, 6); Strand 8, 6 (8, 6); Akashwani 5, 3.80 (6, 4); Maratha Mandir 7, 6, 5 (8, 6.60, 5.50); Minerva 7, 6 (8, 7, 6); Apsara 7, 6 (8, 7, 6); Novelty 6.50, 5.50 (8, 7, 6); Shalimar 6, 5, 4.50 (7, 6, 5); Super 5, 3.80, 2.95 (5.50, 4.50, 3); Dreamland 6, 5 (8, 7, 6, 4.95); Gaiety-Galaxy-Gemini, Bandra 6.50 and 5.50 from Jan. 9 (7, 6); Ambar-Oscar, Andheri 7.50, 6.50, 5.50 (7.50, 6.50, 5.50); Kamran, Kurla 4.50; Kalpana, Kurla 4.50, 3.50; Anand, Thana 4.50, 3.80; Sharda, Dadar 5, 3.80; Shyam, Jogeshwari 5, 3.80, 2.95; Ram, Jogeshwari 3.80, 2.95; Mayur, Kandivli 3.80, 3.45; Sona, Kandivli 5.50, 4.50; Milap,

Admission rate in Bombay cinemas in 1987.
(Photo Credit: *Film Information*, 10 January 1987)

During the strike, filmstars had often spoken about organising a musical nite for the technicians and workers who had suffered financial losses. The outcome of that gracious idea was Hope 86. The function took place at Bombay's massive Brabourne Stadium, once the venue for cricket tests. A news report pegged collections from ticket sales and private donations at around Rs 75 lakh.[26]

The show started at 8.30 p.m. and ended at 4 a.m. Among those who performed were Lata Mangeshkar, Laxmikant-Pyarelal, Rekha, Vinod Khanna, Kalyanji-Anandji, Bappi Lahiri, Govinda, Neelam, Jeetendra, Jaya Prada, Kim, Meenakshi Seshadri, Sridevi, Johny Lever, Dharmendra, Anil Kapoor, Rajesh Khanna, and many more.

Despite the controversy surrounding his role in the strike, Big B emerged as the star of the show. His performance drew deafening applause from the audience who remained glued to their seats till deep into the night. 'His act was reserved for the finale which was only around 3 a.m. For over an hour, he danced, sang and recited some passages of dialogue from his films. After that practically all top stars joined him for a closing group song.'[27]

Hope 86 had a Calcutta edition too, where Mithun Chakraborty took the lead. Other key stars engaged with the project included Rajesh Khanna and Shatrughan Sinha. Mithun harnessed his closeness with CPM leader and sports minister Subhash Chakraborty to organise the show, which initially met resistance from Opposition politicians as well as Left leaders. Bengal CM Jyoti Basu finally green-signalled the event which was held successfully at Salt Lake Stadium in the last week of December.

The 1986 strike gave the industry a glimmer of hope at a time when video piracy was eating into revenues. Few labour movements end in 100 per cent success. The 31-day strike was a modest triumph for the Bombay film industry. The movement uplifted spirits and many became aware of being part of a larger community. The shutdown underlined the power of one. Summing up the year, *Screen* magazine wrote, '1986 then was the year of the great revolt, the great awakening, something that was the need of the hour.'[28]

The strike had far-reaching consequences. It gave everyone a first-hand taste of the power of organised protest. Film workers' unions were emboldened to carry out a strike for better wages in 1987. After a 36-day shutdown of film production activities due to differences between producers' and workers' bodies over daily-rated workers' wages and service conditions, an accord was signed on 5 August 1987.[29]

The agreement dealt with wage increment, shift timings, etc. For the first time, *Film Information* noted, terms of employment were clearly defined in black and white. Producer-director Shakti Samanta was the chairman of the joint negotiations committee.

To sum up, Bombay cinema in the Eighties had multiple personalities. Organised resistance, albeit briefly, was one of them.

REEL 5

NEW WAVE 2.0:
PROGRESS AND STAGNATION

In 1969, three movies emerged like nymphs out of a lake, defying existing classifications in Bombay cinema: Mrinal Sen's *Bhuvan Shome*, Basu Chatterjee's *Sara Akash* and Mani Kaul's *Uski Roti*. In these films, stock figures of the mainstream consommé—the villain, the comic, the mandatory six songs—went missing in action. But for those in search of a more thoughtful time at the theatres, these films, diverse from each other in style and themes, stood apart and above. This was the inauguration of New Wave 1.0.

Slowly over the next decade, a bouquet of terms—Parallel, Art, Arthouse, New Wave, Offbeat, Alternative, Meaningful, Experimental and (just) New—entered the lexicon to describe this fresh category of films. Some of these terms became subjects of furious debate. Traditionalists argued that there are only two kinds of cinema, good and bad, and these categories didn't make sense. But as such films increased in numbers, these terms came to be accepted in media, academia and the public.

Parallel cinema wasn't scripted on a blank slate; it was the product of a process that had started several decades ago. Film societies across India played a key role in readying moviegoers for this new form of cinema. The movement started with the formation of the Calcutta Film Society in October 1947, Satyajit Ray being one of its founder members. His early movies, notably *Pather Panchali* (1955), influenced both aspiring filmmakers and the audience. Over the next three decades, apart from metropolitan cities such as Delhi, Madras and Bombay, film societies sprang up in small towns like Patna, Agra, Faizabad, Roorkee, Lucknow, Bhopal and elsewhere.[1]

These associations showcased the masters: Sergei Eisenstein, Vittorio De Sica, Alfred Hitchcock, Satyajit Ray, Akira Kurosawa, Jean Luc Goddard, and many others. They introduced and familiarised the audience with an entirely different vocabulary of cinema. The shows, generally organised on Sunday mornings, attracted students, bureaucrats, teachers and other members of civil society. Through them, a larger audience for serious, cerebral cinema was created.

In 1980, the Film Enquiry Committee headed by Dr K. Shivarama Karanth calculated that India had 200 societies with around 75,000 members. The report further pointed out that about 300 societies had applied for affiliation with the Federation of Film Societies of India.[2]

Hindi cinema had a bunch of intermittent precursors to parallel cinema. Chetan Anand's *Neecha Nagar* (1946), Bimal Roy's *Do Bigha Zameen* (1953), Amar Kumar's *Garam Coat* (1955) and several other films showcased neo-realism, which was to become the movement's hallmark.

Right through the 1970s, filmmakers such as Shyam Benegal (*Ankur, Nishant, Manthan*), Satyajit Ray (*Shatranj Ke Khiladi*), Saeed Mirza (*Arvind Desai Ki Ajeeb Dastaan*), Muzaffar Ali (*Gaman*), Avtaar Kaul (*27 Down*), Prem Kapoor (*Badnam Basti*), Mrinal Sen (*Ek Adhuri Kahani*) and others furthered Hindi arthouse cinema. Mani Kaul (*Ashadh Ka Ek Din, Duvidha*) and Kumar Shahani (*Maya Darpan*) formed a sub-category within this group. Their cinema was low on accessibility but stunning in the way it expanded the medium's language and creative space.

The 1980s ushered in New Wave 2.0. The films that defined the era felt more raw and urgent, like a calling attention motion in Parliament. Tribal exploitation (*Aakrosh*), student unrest (*Holi*), religious obscurantism (*Debshishu*), darkly comic take on corruption (*Jaane Bhi Do Yaaro*), caste discrimination (*Damul*), phoniness of the educated upper class (*Party*), contemporary retelling of Mahabharata (*Kalyug*) and Aesop's Fables (*Katha*), reworking ancient folktales (*Parinati*), expoloring a poet's interior world (*Satah Se Uthata Aadmi*)—the 1980s saw milestone movies on these subjects and more. Most were evolved and engaging. Accolades and awards, both national as well as international, were the norm, not the exception.

Explaining his aggressive and subversive cinema, Govind Nihalani, who had directed *Aakrosh* and *Ardh Satya*, wrote in *Dharamyug* in 1985. 'Putting a sheet over garbage doesn't stop the stink. On the contrary, more bacteria are born and the chances of a widespread epidemic increase. It would be nice if one removes the sheet and lets people see the dirt. If we don't do it, it means we are deceiving ourselves.'[3]

Fellow director Prakash Jha (*Damul*, 1985) caught attention with his documentary on the Bihar Sharif communal riots of 1981, *Faces After the Storm* (1982). He told the same magazine that no effort was made by the film industry to create socially aware people in post-Independence India. He said, 'Whatever was served in the name of emotion were nudity, debauchery and nonsensical acts, which were miles away from reality. This wasn't entertainment, just opium, which our professional filmmakers showed and earned pots of money. What did they give in return: An impotent environment, where the common man doesn't even want to react?'[4] Both

Nihalani and Jha moved away to a more mainstream cinema in the 1990s.

The second wave of arthouse movies made bigger commercial breakthroughs in a way the first wave couldn't. Among the early success stories, both critically and commercially, was Sivakasi-born director Rabindra Dharmaraj's *Chakra* (1981), a pitiless yet sensitive sketch of life and love in a Bombay shanty town. A graduate in English literature from St Stephen's College, Dharmaraj had also covered the Vietnam War as a photojournalist. He had trained in filmmaking in the University of California, made documentaries (*Crisis on the Campus*) and assisted Shyam Benegal.

Made for a mere Rs 9.5 lakh, *Chakra* was an artistic triumph and, more surprisingly, made money. *Trade Guide* ranked the film among the ten biggest hits of the year. One of the reasons attributed to the film's commercial success was the voyeuristic posters of Smita Patil bathing in the open. 'It is difficult to quantify but the poster did provide a little impetus to the opening,' admitted co-producer Manmohan Shetty.[5] Dharmaraj died of a stomach ulcer shortly after completing the film. He was thirty-three. The film went on to earn the national award for best actress for Smita and won the Golden Leopard at Locarno.

There were other major New Wave 2.0 winners at the box office. *Trade Guide* listed *Aakrosh* (1980) among the profit earners of 1980. *Ardh Satya* (1983) drew queues of the kind generally associated with Big B movies of the time. *(More details in next reel.)* Ironically, Nihalani had Bachchan in mind for the title role, which fortunately did not materialise. Puri's Anant Velankar is the definitive cop of the decade. Velankar, a survivor of domineering parenting and a victim of departmental politics, is all unreleased rage. The sense of being wronged is vented by thrashing a petty thief and leads to a gut-wrenching climax. The film earned him the national award for best actor as well as top honours at Karlovy Vary. *Trade Guide* rated *Ardh Satya* among the five biggest hits of the year alongside mainstream masala flicks such as *Andhaa Kaanoon, Avtaar, Betaab* and *Coolie*.

Many, including the director himself, read the success as a sign of a maturing audience. Nihalani said, 'In a very short span of time, meaningful cinema has forced many people to debate on the fact that we are living through horrible times. After the release of *Aakrosh* and *Ardh Satya*, the thought process has gathered pace in newspapers, magazines and universities.'[6]

More lay in store. Mirza's *Albert Pinto Ko Gussa Kyon Aata Hai* (1981) became a talking point prompting hoardings and headlines. *Mid-Day* advertised a forthcoming column with the caption, 'Shobha Kilachand Ko Gussa Kyon Aata Hai'. The same week, *Screen's* editor B.K. Karanjia wrote a front-page editorial headlined, 'Filmi Logon Ko Gussa Kyon Aata Hai'. He said, 'Within a couple of weeks after its release at Bombay and Calcutta in mid-January, the title of Saeed Mirza's film... has entered the language, become an integral part of the slangy, colloquial cultural idiom that had hitherto been influenced only by the big-budget spectacles of the commercial industry, films like *Sholay, Bobby* and *Amar Akbar Anthony*.'[7]

More positive news was on its way. At a time when the commercial film market abroad was rapidly dwindling, arthouse films were finding an alternate revenue stream away from home. In 1983, National Film Development Corporation (NFDC) director Malati Tambay Vaidya spoke of a growing demand for offbeat Indian films for television in West Europe. *Chakra, Albert Pinto...* and *Duvidha* had been sold to German television. A Hungarian delegation had selected a bunch of films for television screenings. The NFDC director also said that Saeed Mirza's *Arvind Desai Ki Ajeeb Dastaan* (1978), which was yet to be released in India, had earned 1,00,000 marks (Rs 4 lakh) from West German television.[8] The stars indeed seemed to be aligning in favour of art cinema.

Several other movies—to be regarded as classics later—were made during the period. Top of the list was Kundan Shah's cerebral comedy *Jaane Bhi Do Yaaro* (1983), a delightful, dark yarn that showcased how corruption had seeped into every ligament of public life: politics, media and bureaucracy. The film was like a giant jigsaw puzzle where every missing piece maddeningly and miraculously fell in place. Director Sudhir Mishra, who co-wrote the film's story and screenplay, remembered fondly how 'everyone who had acted in the film thought that the film would be absolute nonsense. There has never been another film like *Jaane Bhi Do Yaaro*, before or after.'[9]

Parallel cinema also tried to explain the noises in the head. Filmmakers were also exploring existentialism and alienation as understood by French philosophers Jean Paul Satre and Albert Camus. Director-producer Ashok Ahuja experimented with the autobiographical genre in *Aadharshila* (1981), where an FTII graduate visits his alma mater and is gripped by a desire to make art movies.

Mani Kaul's experimental *Satah Se Uthata Aadmi* (1980) constructed the inner world of modernist Hindi poet Muktibodh through the camera. M.K. Raina, who acted in the film, recalled, 'Kaul saw cinema as an art, like painting or music. He wanted to create a new structure in cinema like music: aalap, dhrut and other changes in a raag.'[10]

The film was invited for the Cannes Un Certain Regard section. Raina recalled the ordeal they had to undergo to send the film there. 'Mani was in Bombay and he had no money. As Mani's friends, Sufi singer Madan Gopal Singh and I took cans of the film on our backs to Loknayak Bhavan near Khan Market where the Directorate of Film Festival of India was located those days.'[11]

In noted Marathi poet Dilip Chitre's debut directorial feature, *Godam* (1983), a desolate colonial-era godown stood as a metaphor for the bleakness of life. The setting underlined that the beast and the compassionate cohabit in the same human being. Chitre also composed the film's music. Nihalani was the lensman. *Godam* deserved a bigger audience.

Veteran filmmaker K.A. Abbas made *The Naxalites* (1980), an ideologically uncompromising but cinematically dissatisfying effort on the radical Reds. Calcutta-born director Biplab Roy Choudhury followed up his award-winning *Shodh* (1979) with *Spandan* (1982), based on the sale of aborted foetuses as a means of survival. Kumar Shahani 'realised his theory of epic cinema' in *Tarang* (1984). One of the most underrated but powerful representatives of arthouse radical cinema, Buddhadev Dasgupta's hard-hitting *Andhi Gali* (1984) cross-examined the linkage between the political and the personal in the backdrop of the Naxalite movement.

Sagar Sarhadi poignantly and profitably balanced meaningful cinema in *Bazaar* (1982). The film, set in Hyderabad, touched the right social chord at a time when young girls were married off to rich, aging men from the Gulf. Jabbar Patel's *Subah* (1982) was another forward-looking film on women's identity and freedom of choice.

While public interest seemed to dwindle in the second half of the Eighties, new cinema continued to produce mini gems. Vijaya Mehta's *Rao Saheb* (1985), a sad story of love and denial set in colonial India, deserved more attention. So did *Pestonjee* (1987), a bittersweet tale of friendship between two Parsis.

Pradeep Krishen's *Massey Sahib* (1986), the story of a 'native' who is simple yet crooked, didn't critique colonialism upfront, rather laid bare its hidden, hegemonic influence. The movie, produced by NFDC, won a cache of best actor awards for Raghubir Yadav, whose enlivening act was the movie's spine:

Silver Peacock at IFFI, Delhi, and the Fipresci critics' prize at Venice.

Producer-director M.S. Sathyu, whose place in the celluloid pantheon was assured by the Partition classic, *Garm Hawa* (1974), had to wait endlessly to release *Kahan Kahan Se Guzar Gaya* (1986). The film, which got a financial grant from the West Bengal government, starred Anil Kapoor and singer-actress Sharon Prabhakar. Kapoor played an affluent young man prone to existential angst. Using his life as a matrix of sorts, Sathyu's movie told the larger story of Calcutta in 1981 and its violent Left vs Congress politics. The movie journeyed through Kapoor's speckled life—his rebellion against his father, his intense intimacy with a pop singer, his bonding with a model, his friendship with a radical Left worker, his own initiation into politics via *Das Kapital*, his de-classing routine, his involvement in acts of violence and his ultimate realisation that he is not cut out for it.

Another film with a Calcutta background, Aparna Sen's bilingual venture *Paroma* (1985), with Rakhee in the title role, took a feminist view of an extramarital affair. The Hindi version was released in Bombay in 1987.

Mira Nair's *Salaam Bombay* (1989) was the first super success of offbeat cinema after *Ardh Satya*. Nair filmed Bombay using a fresh sensibility, warts and wonders included. A precursor to *Slumdog Millionaire*, the film felt like an updated version of parallel cinema. The unrealised love story of an urchin and an underage sex worker reaffirmed that the audience hadn't moved away from 'art' cinema but needed a newer style of storytelling. Among other trophies, *Salaam Bombay* also received the national award for best feature film and the Camera d'Or at Cannes. The film, partly financed by NFDC-Doordarshan, became a goldmine for distributors at home and abroad. Last heard, the most celebrated of the slum kids, Shafiq Syed, was an auto driver in Bangalore.

Muzaffar Ali's poetic examination of the plight of chikankari workers, *Anjuman* (1986), belongs to this list. So does director Chandrakant Joshi's *Sutradhar*, dedicated to the memory of Smita Patil who passed away before it was released in 1987. The movie is a commentary on the seductive nature of power and how it often corrupts those who once fought against it. Sudhir Mishra's debut feature, NFDC-financed *Yeh Woh Manzil To Nahin* (1987), was a rumination on the decisions we take and try to justify. He got the national award for best debut feature by a director. Mishra's *Main Zinda Hoon* (1988) investigated gender hypocrisy and cruelty.

Utpalendu Chakraborty's *Debshishu* (1987) was a relentless examination of poverty, belief and hopelessness. The story of how a child born with more than one head is converted into a god was uplifted by a finely grained performance by Smita Patil. Another NFDC production, *Mahananda* (1987), directed by Mohan Kaura, was a refined and realistic take on the devadasi system.

Writer Nabendu Ghosh made a late directorial debut with *Trishagni* (1988), which interrogated desire in the backdrop of Buddhism in ancient India. Prakash Jha's *Parinati* (1989) was a tragic morality tale of greed and obsession. The film hardly created a ripple even among critics.

Director Kamal Swaroop's post-modernist *Om-Dar-B-Dar* (1988) found theatrical release twenty-five years after its certification, in 2013 but had already acquired cult status among the cineastes. Watching the experimental film is like being part of an aimless, unattainable, self-engrossed dream in an irrational world.

Far more gripping was Saeed Mirza's *Salim Langde Pe Mat Ro* (1989), which took a gritty yet elegiac look at the life and times of a ghettoised urban Muslim youth sucked into a world of crime. Regarded as a classic now, the film had few viewers at the theatres when it was first released.

At the heart of meaningful cinema's growth was the much-maligned Indian state. Most of them were funded by the government even though quite a few were critical of the state. Funding through the Film Finance Corporation (later NFDC) allowed these filmmakers to avoid commercial compromises. Take any twenty random New Wave films of the 1980s, the most common name in the credits will be NFDC. In the 1960s and 1970s too, Film Finance Corporation had financed many movies. But records show that in the 1980s, NFDC expanded its role in several new areas, notably film production.

NFDC assistance happened primarily on three fronts:

(a) Funding and producing films

(b) Assisting infrastructure projects for small cinema halls

(c) Selling these films to foreign TV channels

That apart, NFDC managed film festivals during 1981-88 and published a quarterly journal, *Cinema in India*, from 1987 onwards.

Statistics underline the first point. Between 1984-85 and 1986-87, NFDC received fifty-five financial applications to produce Hindi films; fifteen were sanctioned.[12]

From 1980 to 1988, NFDC funded fifty-four movies. Initially the finance body lent a maximum 75 per cent loan for a movie project, with an upper limit of Rs 3.5 lakh. Later the amount was increased to Rs 4.5 lakh. The NFDC also turned producer, financing several projects.[13]

Returns show that parallel cinema wasn't exactly a losing proposition at the box office. Between 1980-81 and 1989-90, NFDC disbursed Rs 3.28 crore worth of loans to producers. The amount recovered, including both principal and interest, was Rs 3.05 crore. The principal amount outstanding was Rs 1.6 crore, primarily because NFDC inherited about Rs 90 lakh as outstanding amount from FFC, its previous avatar. NFDC also wrote off bad debts totalling Rs 10.17 lakh during this period.[14]

The NFDC created an avenue for many filmmakers who had an offbeat story to tell but were unable to raise the money. 'The

NFDC's loans to low-cost budget films without asking for any collateral security became a starting point for many filmmakers who neither had large budgets nor were recognised yet,' said Manmohan Shetty, who teamed up with Pradeep Uppoor to produce *Aakrosh, Chakra* and *Ardh Satya*.[15]

Even for established filmmakers, there were distinct advantages. Director Shyam Benegal said, 'FFC financed films. NFDC...took a step forward: it also produced films. The big advantage was that the filmmaker now didn't have to concentrate on its marketability, but could concentrate on its making.'[16]

Film magazine *Madhuri* reported that *Ardh Satya* was made for Rs 12 lakh, of which Rs 6 lakh was provided by NFDC.[17] However, producer Shetty said the film took Rs 16 lakh to complete.[18] The movie grossed Rs 50 lakh, of which Rs 30 lakh was earned in Bombay alone.

Most NFDC films were made for less than Rs 15 lakh. *Jaane Bhi Do Yaaro* cost Rs 7.54 lakh and got a return of Rs 29 lakh, according to the *Madhuri* report. Jai Arjun Singh's book on the film says NFDC invested Rs 6.84 lakh in the film.[19] The NFDC figures also show that *Jaane Bhi Do Yaaro* grossed over 300 per cent more than the cost. *Trade Guide*, however, put it in the 'broke even' category.

Some NFDC films that earned profits were: *Massey Saheb* (cost: Rs 10.40 lakh, return: Rs 14 lakh), *Mirch Masala* (cost: Rs 25 lakh, return: Rs 39 lakh), *Pestonjee* (cost: Rs 13 lakh, return: Rs 23 lakh).

Films where NFDC lost money were: *Godam* (Rs 8 lakh, return: Rs 5 lakh), *Tarang* (Rs 16.50 lakh, return: Rs 10 lakh). *Party* (cost: Rs 18 lakh, return: Rs 13 lakh).

Trishagni was made by writer-director Nabendu Ghosh for Rs 12 lakh, of which Rs 10 lakh came from an NFDC loan, his son, director Subhankar Ghosh (*Woh Chhokri*), said.[20]

Interestingly, while NFDC was relatively tightfisted in dealing with Indian filmmakers, Richard Attenborough's *Gandhi* received Rs 6.87 crore, a staggering sum by the organisation's standards. The project had the backing of Prime Minister Indira Gandhi. The money turned out to be well-spent though. The Oscar-winning film, largely distributed by Columbia Pictures, also harvested megabucks globally but by early 1984, NFDC had got back only Rs 7.78 crore. The amount took care of the loan but neither the full interest (19 per cent annually) nor a share of the profits. NFDC director Malati Tambay Vaidya had raised the question—Where's the profit gone?—at a board meeting, *India Today* reported in May 1984.

In this era, state governments also financed and produced films. The beneficiaries were generally ideologically aligned, well-connected directors. CPM-ruled West Bengal financed Benegal's *Arohan*. Uttar Pradesh's Ganna Beej Evam Vikas Nigam (Sugarcane Seed and Development Corporation) backed Muzaffar Ali's *Aagman*. Ali contested the 1998 Lok Sabha polls on a Samajwadi Party ticket. The film, which started Anupam Kher's career, was dedicated to workers and peasants.Sometimes such initiatives were taken to celebrate a son of the soil. Madhya Pradesh government was responsible for *Satah Se Uthata Aadmi*. The film was based on the works of poet Muktibodh, who was born in Sheopur, then part of Central Provinces, now Madhya Pradesh.

Doordarshan also got involved in film production. Satyajit Ray's telefilm *Sadgati* and Tapan Sinha's *Aadmi Aur Aurat* (1984) were produced by the state broadcaster. DD began its colour TV telecast with *Sadgati* and *Shatranj Ke Khiladi* on 25 April 1982. Calcutta Doordarshan produced Mrinal Sen's *Tasveer Apni Apni*.

The most influential and widely discussed DD film of the decade was Nihalani's limited series *Tamas*, which was based on Bhisham Sahni's gut-wrenching novel on Partition. Nonetheless, Nihalani later said that the dependence on TV affected art cinema negatively. 'The strength of this cinema comes from its unconventionality and boldness. This is not possible on TV since it's controlled by the government and big-money corporations. Their sole ambition is to use it to keep themselves in power,' he said.[21]

Making movies wasn't enough though. Offbeat cinema needed a larger ecosystem to thrive. It needed the infrastructure of small theatres in a city's cultural hub where it could be easily accessed by the art-loving, serious cinema crowd.

Film critic Anil Saari wrote, 'Producing a small film may be easy for a producer with a few lakhs of rupees to spare, but selling it is extremely difficult. Most small films lie in the cans for months, and even years, before they find a distributor to release them even at one centre in the country...Getting the right theatre is the key for marketing of new films.'[22]

To plug this lacuna, Film Finance Corporation initiated the process of building theatres in India in 1979. In 1983, NFDC director Malati Tambay Vaidya said the financing body had sanctioned thirty-seven loans; six of the borrowers had completed their theatres and started screening films.[23]

To a question in Parliament, I&B minister V.N. Gadgil said, 'To ensure that good artistic films have adequate exhibition outlets, Corporation [NFDC] provides loans for construction of low-cost theatres in different parts of the country. It also exhibits good-quality, artistic films in Akashwani theatre, Bombay procured by it and in the theatres, the construction of which is financed by it.'[24]

But there was a huge gap between promise and practice. Distributor and film producer N.N. Sippy pointed out that NFDC was building castles in the air in the name of *janta* (people's) cinema. He said, 'It is providing loans worth Rs 4-5 lakh. Who would tell them that for this amount, you can't even buy a theatre's furniture, forget a theatre.'[25] Film industry sources estimate that in the 1980s, building a cinema hall would have cost at least Rs 2-3 crore, depending on the city and the location.

N.F. Damania, president, Theatre Owners' Association, was cynical about the NFDC deal to build cinemas. 'The NFDC is putting out advertisements that say, *"Rin lo, cinemaghar banao* (Take a loan, build a theatre)." But nobody is coming forward because they only provide Rs 3-5 lakh as loan. How can you make a cinema hall with such meagre money?'[26]

The NFDC 2005-06 annual report shows that between 1980-81 and 1989-90, the NFDC disbursed loans totalling Rs 5.30 crore for construction of film theatres and received a combined (principal plus interest) total of Rs 4.87 crore.[27]

Overall, the government disbursed Rs 7.60 crore worth of loans to build movie theatres between 1980 and 2006 and recovered an overall Rs 11.51 crore (Rs 7.04 crore as principal and Rs 4.46 crore as interest). Clearly, the amount was negligible and made little difference to the situation on the ground.[28] The money would have helped repair cinemas, not build them.

The NFDC also adopted another modus operandi to intervene in the exhibition network. In 1980, Lotus cinema in Bombay was hired to screen alternative cinema. This was followed by control over two other theatres: Akashwani and Gemini. In Ahmedabad, NFDC took Advance Cinema on long lease. However such attempts were not enough to make any difference. As Muzaffar Ali said, 'NFDC made pictures but did not take them to the people.'[29]

Interestingly, Ali recalled that producer-director Basu Bhattacharya tried to find an alternative called Mukt (Marketing Union of Kinematographic Technicians), which was meant to facilitate distribution of such films. But nothing came of it.[30]

The parallel cinema movement never progressed beyond a point. Why? And who was to blame? M.K. Raina felt that the bureaucrats were at fault. He said, 'They had no vision. They did a job but had no plan or passion. The NFDC could have developed more theatres and helped build a parallel distribution network.'[31] But the truth is that the film body wasn't provided the financial muscle required to build theatres across the country.

The shortage of cinema halls to exhibit art films was a fundamental problem. Theatres such as Shakuntalam in New Delhi, Lotus or Akashwani in Bombay or Nandan in Calcutta were rare. Many movies languished in the cans. Even films with saleable stars such as Kumar Shahani's epic *Tarang* (Smita Patil, Amol Palekar, Girish Karnad, Om Puri) or Sagar Sarhadi's questioning of the justice system, *Tere Shaher Mein* (Kulbhushan Kharbanda), failed to get a theatrical release. '*Damul* couldn't be commercially released; it was shown only on television and in the festival circuit,' said producer Shetty.[32] Some films were only shown in film society screenings.

Piracy worsened matters. Copies of *Ardh Satya* were often seized in raids conducted on illegal video parlours. One can only speculate on the amount of revenue lost to piracy.

Shyam Benegal felt that the alternative cinema movement was only partially successful, and blamed 'self-involved filmmakers making self-involved films', which lacked connect with people.[33]

'They would say, you want to communicate, what kind of art is that? Self-expression is more important. This became a peculiar kind of debate, almost suicidal: making films no one wanted to see. It was a confusing time, without clarity. Films are also a product to entertain and engage. It should have that quality without which people will not pay money to see the film,' the filmmaker said.[34]

Director Saeed Mirza lamented that though his film *Salim Langde Pe Mat Ro* (1989) worked, the earnings never reached the filmmaker. 'What most of us realised was that we could never really compete with the great extravaganzas. In fact we didn't even want to. What we needed was a fair share of the distribution network and, we believed, our films would work financially. We felt there were enough serious viewers around the country to make that happen. The problem was that we could not reach them till much later,' he said.[35]

The expansion of television's footprint and audience unleashed a plethora of government-funded or sponsored programmes on Doordarshan. Serious filmmakers sensed an opportunity, leading to a mass migration to the small screen.

Benegal's epochal *Bharat Ek Khoj* translated Indian history into celluloid and *Katha Sagar* brought Indian literature to television. Ketan Mehta made everyone participate in the comic adventures of Mr Yogi on DD. Mirza's *Nukkad*—a wry look at working-class, street-corner life—became a cult serial; he also made *Manoranjan*. Amol Palekar directed the tender *Kacchi Dhoop* and *Naqab*. Apart from the successful *Chashme Buddoor* and *Katha*, Sai Paranjpye also made two TV serials, *Ados Pados* and *Chhote Bade*.

Director Sudhir Mishra felt the migration ended up damaging cinema in the long run. He said, 'With TV, you could get away with mediocre work. Many filmmakers went away from the cinematic way of telling their stories. A lot of parallel and middle cinema filmmakers went into DD. They might have been [doing] good work in terms of stories but it messed up their cinematic abilities, which were no longer required. From being filmmakers, they became content makers. For TV, you did not require the flair of a *Mirch Masala*. The whole idea of the big screen, the sound, the audio-visual way of storytelling disappeared in the 1980s.'[36]

The larger question is, what was art cinema supposed to achieve? Was it just meant to sensitise the urban audience towards India Ignored? Was it just intended to improve their 'taste' of cinema? Or was it meant to shake them out of a political stupor and propel them towards a more activist role in life?

Mishra said there was a belief that 'cinema was supposed to be more'. The word 'more' is open to interpretation here. But probably it signifies that cinema was meant to show the path to a better society. That didn't happen. He said, 'It wasn't our job to determine what happens. Our job wasn't to find the solution...Maybe some filmmakers ran out [of steam].'[37]

Several star directors of the art cinema movement were Left-inclined. Their belief system received a sharp jolt with the collapse of communism in the Soviet Union and East European states. These governments were overthrown by the very people whom they claimed to represent. Mishra said, 'When the Berlin Wall fell and the Soviet Union collapsed, disillusionment with the Left set in.'[38]

The fade-out of parallel cinema wasn't an event but a process. It didn't happen in a year or two. Even in the 1990s, meaningful cinema continued to survive, if not thrive: Sai Paranjpye's *Disha* (1990), Amol Palekar's *Thoda Sa Roomani Ho Jayen* (1990), Govind Nihalani's *Drishti* (1990) and *Rukmavati Ki Haveli* (1991), Shyam Benegal's *Suraj Ka Satwan Ghoda* (1992) and Sudhir Mishra's *Dharavi* (1992). But overall, offbeat cinema fell off the mind-map of the audience.

REEL 6

NEW WAVE 2.0:
MOVERS AND SHAKERS

A bunch of committed players—producers, directors and actors—created a new parallel cinema in the Eighties.

Govind Nihalani

Two visceral movies of the 1980s are hardwired into the memory of a generation of filmgoers: *Aakrosh* (1980) and *Ardh Satya* (1983). Both were directed by the Karachi-born cinematographer-director Govind Nihalani, who emerged as the poster boy of New Wave 2.0.

Based on a real-life occurrence in Bhiwandi, *Aakrosh* typified the new, direct and angrier political cinema. The film was about the coiled anguish of an Adivasi whose wife has been raped and murdered by a small town's prosperous and powerful cabal. His climactic cry after axing his own sister is among the most cathartic moments in Indian cinema.

With low lighting, sharp editing and an unsettling background score, the movie created a sense of foreboding all along. The first dialogue in this neo-realist thriller is spoken after 9.36 minutes. The film is like a mugger that grips you by the throat and never lets the grasp ease. You watch *Aakrosh* with a degree of anxiety.

The film reaped awards as if they were on discount: the

national award for best feature film and the prestigious Golden Peacock Award for best film at the International Film Festival of India (IFFI), Delhi. Even in small-town India, it found audience and appreciation.

Interestingly, a new technological development was key to the making of the movie. *Aakrosh* was among the first Hindi films to be shot in 16mm and enlarged to 35mm for the big screen. Producer Manmohan Shetty recalled, 'I started a facility at Adlab in Bombay which allowed filmmakers to shoot a film in 16mm, process the negatives and blowup the prints to 35mm. The technology saved about 30 per cent of the raw stock's cost. Nobody seemed to be convinced or interested in the idea, so I thought, let me produce the film and do it myself. We started with *Chakra* (1981). But *Aakrosh,* which used the same technology, was released a year earlier.'[1]

The technology gave a boost to small producers seeking to make low-cost, socially conscious movies. Among some other films, which used the technology was M.S. Sathyu's *Kahan Kahan Se Guzar Gaya.* In time, shooting films in 16mm became common, especially in regional cinema. The technology wasn't too conducive to long shots though. *Aakrosh* is packed with close-ups.

But it was *Ardh Satya,* released three years later, that rocked the box office and shook the Bombay film world. The film bared the corrupt politician-crooked cop nexus wide open, and prompted imitations galore. *Ardh Satya* became the magical crossover movie—a cash-counter biggie and an award collector—that parallel cinema bhakts had wet dreams about. Its lead actor Om Puri once confessed, 'We were sure of *Ardh Satya's* success. But we just did not imagine the degree of its success.'[2]

To its producers, *Ardh Satya* not only earned money but also brought prestige. 'Even now, over thirty-five years later, whenever people come to know that I am the producer of *Ardh Satya,* they react respectfully,' said Shetty.[3]

While *Aakrosh* and *Ardh Satya* got attention, Nihalani showcased his versatility as a director, crisscrossing from one theme to another. *Aakrosh* was followed by the vastly underrated *Vijeta* (1982), a rare instance then of a turbaned Sikh as the male lead. The movie mapped the angst and self-doubt of an Air Force cadet who nurses bitter feelings against his father. *Vijeta* did not glamorise or muscularise the soldier; it humanised them. A family torn by bitterness and the evolution of a slacker to a fighter pilot are two seemingly disparate subjects. But the director, who got the *Filmfare* award for best cinematographer, managed it adeptly, aided by the exceptional writing of Satyadev Dubey and Dilip Chitre. It is possible the film did not receive the same attention because it was too mellow and nuanced, and maybe also seen as statist, as it glorified the Indian Air Force.

Ardh Satya, whose title was taken from a poem and was written by Chitre, was followed by *Party* (1984), a voyeuristic yet critical view of the hypocrisies that consume the thinking literati. Verbose but ideologically intense, *Aaghat* (1985) tried to make sense of the changing trade union scene in Bombay from the Left's point of view. The film was followed by the dark and haunting tale of Partition, *Tamas* (1988) on DD, which remains one of his most distilled works.

Nihalani developed a reputation for meticulousness; sometimes to the point of overdoing it. M.K. Raina recalled how the director required twenty-two takes for an uncomplicated shot of Deepa Sahi walking into the hospital to meet her injured husband. 'In fact, Deepa felt so humiliated that she started weeping after the shot. Rajkumar Santoshi, who was assisting him in the film, was left with the thankless job of consoling her,' Raina said.[4]

In his biography, Om Puri referred to Govind as 'my Alkazi in Bollywood'. He said, 'Just like Ebrahim Alkazi was my mentor in theatre, Govind is my mentor in films. He is an actor's director. I have given my life's best performances with him...'[5]

'But he is a very greedy director and squeezes every last

drop from an actor. Just like those sugarcane juice machines. I jokingly tell him that he is always hungry and *bahut footage khata hai* (wastes a lot of footage). He literally consumes raw stock like a maniac. After editing a Govind Nihalani film, one can actually make another film with the discarded raw stock,' Puri said.[6]

Saeed Mirza

Bombay-born Saeed Mirza marked his presence with *Arvind Desai Ki Ajeeb Dastaan* (1978), a study in young bourgeois alienation in a capitalist world. Long film titles became Mirza's signature, much like Nasir Hussain in mainstream Bombay cinema in the 1950s and '60s.

Mirza's *Albert Pinto Ko Gussa Kyon Aata Hai* (1981) was a subtle examination of class hierarchies and angst through the daily life and frustrations of a Christian mechanic. The director 'acknowledged that the film, which addresses India's minorities, is set in a Catholic Bombay milieu because at the time he lacked the courage to deal with Muslim issues'.[7] The film did not represent what the title promised. It hopped like an aimless tourist from one spot to another without direction. For a film with such a fiery title, the script was 'strangely somnambulistic', as Naseeruddin Shah, who played the title role, tersely but accurately remarked in his autobiography.

Nonetheless, the film became a talking point for its innovative title. However, Mirza had as much reason to get angry as *Albert Pinto...*—for the way he was treated by distributors. The film was completed in July 1980. Despite hosting forty 'trial' shows between August and December, he could sell the film in just two-and-a-quarter circuits: east India (West Bengal, Bihar, Assam, Orissa, and the North-east), Delhi-UP and one of the three sub-circuits in south India. The Bombay distributor backed out before signing the contract. He wanted to pay Rs 10,000 less than what had been agreed upon earlier.[8]

Eventually *Albert Pinto...* made modest profits. But as Shah wrote, 'There are probably more people who have heard the title than have actually seen the film.'

Much less talked about but certainly more thought-provoking was Mirza's *Mohan Joshi Haazir Ho* (1984). You could read a dozen newspaper articles on judicial delay in disposing of cases. Or you could watch the film to understand the plight of ordinary people who get trapped in such matters.

With *Salim Langde Pe Mat Ro* (1989) Mirza found a voice of his own. The film, produced by NFDC, shows how and why a young, urban, lower-class Muslim youth gets sucked into a life of crime and violence. Crime is the only way out for him to create an identity, and also a quick ticket to death. Actor Pawan Malhotra gave the right blend of braggadocio and vulnerability to the title role making *Salim Langde...,* a movie to remmeber.

Shyam Benegal

By the end of the 1970s, Shyam Benegal had moved away from realist hinterland tales (*Ankur, Nishant, Manthan*) in search of new cinematic frontiers. *Bhumika* (1977) was based on the bestselling autobiography of Marathi actress Hansa Wadkar. *Junoon* (1979), an unrealised love story between a much-married, middle-aged Pathan and a teenage Anglo-Indian girl set in the backdrop of the 1858 revolt, underlines this departure.

In the 1980s, the auteur made five Hindi movies, all reflecting his expanding canvas and shifting focus. Benegal explained how the change happened. 'I had made *Junoon* [1979] for Shashi Kapoor and he said, why don't you think of another subject? I wanted to do a contemporary Mahabharata. It was natural to imagine a battle between two industrial families who are cousins. In reality too, a battle was going on between two industrial families at the time. The timing seemed right.'[9]

The outcome was *Kalyug* (1981). In Benegal's nifty hands, the film feels like a game of human chess, except that the characters are neither black nor white, but grey. *Kalyug* builds up like a slow storm. When it ends, only the ruins remain. The film fetched the *Filmfare* Award for best movie.

Victor Banerjee, who played the role of Dhanraj, modelled on Duryodhan, recalled cheekily, 'The first lesson I learned [that holds true to this day] from working in *Kalyug* was that Bombay's stars only respected the authority of a director who knew his job and had acquired and earned international recognition at festivals for his work. They genuflected and served him with deference, obediently and diligently. An unknown actor who was on the verge of becoming a star, Raj Babbar, fell in line quietly and the superstar Rekha sat without any tantrums, all day long, day after day, for whenever she might be summoned for her scene.'[10]

Kalyug was followed by *Arohan* (*The Ascent*, certified in 1981), produced by West Bengal's Left Front government, an even gloomier tale of a tenant farmer (Hari Mondol) and his family. *Arohan* sought to explain the spiraling impact of land reforms and how the powerful landed gentry manipulates them at the expense of the underprivileged.

Om Puri in *Arohan*

Benegal, who had studied economics in Osmania University, reminisced how the film came to life. Buddhadev Bhattacharya, the state's I&B minister then, had artistic leanings and was also a well-known writer in Bengali. 'He said, "Why not go beyond documentaries and make a film that will look at the whole problem." They were looking at power relations in rural India.'[11] The film starts off with the certitude of a People's Democracy editorial but ends up being more nuanced. *Arohan* won the national award for best feature film in Hindi in 1982 but was released years later only in Bengal and Bihar.

In the late Seventies, *Bhumika* had underlined the musical side of Benegal's personality. The director further expanded on this aspect in *Mandi* (1983), a movie about life in a pretty little whorehouse—warts, rouges and all—and *Trikal* (1985), a complex inter-generational story of love and longing told through a Goan family of Portuguese origin. The movie fetched him the national award for best director. Both *Mandi* and *Trikal* were embellished by the sumptuous and apt compositions of Vanraj Bhatia.

The weary lives of the Pochampalli sari weavers found expression in *Susman* (1987). Some of them were award-winning master craftsmen but the profits went to the middlemen. The film's most notable performance came from Kulbhushan Kharbanda, who was excellent as the suave go-between guy.

Scriptwriter Shama Zaidi, who worked with Benegal in films such as *Mandi* and *Arohan* said, 'Benegal carries everyone along. He brings out the best in his team and challenges them at every point. For instance, many of the actors were given a lot of scope for improvisation in *Mandi*.'[12]

Actor Madan Jain, who performed a cameo in Benegal's *Kalyug* and had a meatier part in Nihalani's *Vijeta* said, 'Benegal gave you the big picture and contexualised what was happening. Things became easier for a performer. He also gave the actor a lot of liberty to interpret the scene. People like him or Nihalani made great films with little resources.'[13]

Shashi Kapoor

One of the less-acknowledged facts of new cinema is the role of Shashi Kapoor, the producer. The actor worked tirelessly in countless forgettable movies—his brother Raj Kapoor once called him a 'taxi'—only to invest money in sensitive cinema and the construction of Prithvi Theatre. Kapoor put his wallet where his heart was. Not many actors, directors or producers can make that claim.

He produced six movies in all. *Junoon* (1979), based on Ruskin Bond's *A Flight of Pigeons* was his first. And *Ajooba* (1994) was his last. But in the 1980s, he made four movies, which testify to his commitment to art cinema. *Kalyug* (1981), *36 Chowringhee Lane* (in English, 1981), *Vijeta* (1982) and *Utsav* (1984) are all benchmarks in Indian cinema.

Victor Banerjee, who worked in *Kalyug*, recalled: 'In all my years in films I never came across a more generous and caring producer than Shashi Kapoor. Part of it, I was informed, was due to the famous "Kapoor family" traditions that he maintained. But Shashi's genuine bonhomie and concern, not just about every aspect of the production, but for every little creature comfort of every actor and technician is something I was bowled over by.'[14]

Sai Paranjpye

Lucknow-born Sai Paranjpye brought another dimension to meaningful cinema of the 1980s. Her films captured a slice of urban India without directly engaging with ideology. Paranjpye's debut directorial feature, *Sparsh* (1980), was situated at the intersection of the diverse worlds of those who can see and those who cannot, and captured the psyche of the sightless better than most Hindi movies on the subject. The film, largely shot at Blind Relief Association in south Delhi, is a story of love and ego and a cry against the tyranny of sympathy.

The film was certified on 25 January 1980, but won the

national award for best actor for Naseeruddin Shah in 1979. *Sparsh* was commercially released, rather hesitantly, in Bombay in 1984 by producer Basu Bhattacharya. A frustrated Paranjpye later caricatured Bhattacharya in *Katha* (1983). The film's sly hare was named Basu. Over the years, though, *Sparsh* has travelled to a larger audience, first courtesy DVDs and then YouTube.

In popular memory, Paranjpye is remembered for *Chashme Buddoor* (1981), an unconventional but faithful look at college life in urban '80s India. The film brought a refreshing brand of young humour that school and college students could easily identify with. The characters played by Farooq Sheikh, Ravi Baswani and Rakesh Bedi could be spotted in many college hostels or nearabouts. And everybody wanted a Miss Chamko (Deepti Naval) in their lives. Even after four decades, its popularity endures, prompting a remake in 2013.

Comic actor Rakesh Bedi said, 'Sai was a good taskmaster and strong on convictions. But she allowed me some leeway for comedy. The *shers* [couplet] that you listen to in the film were all written by me.'[15]

Katha (1983) reworked Aesop's fable of the tortoise and the hare, locating the story in a Bombay chawl. Unlike the slums of Bombay cinema, Paranjpye's chawl—Salunke Chawl near Churchgate—isn't a grim place where the down-and-outstruggle each day of their lives, rather it thrums with humour and heart.

The tortoise (Naseeruddin Shah) is a golden-hearted do-gooder who's too bashful to express his fondness for the girl-next-door (Deepti Naval). The hare (Farooq Sheikh in a terrific crowd-pleasing turn) is a slick-talking hustler who charms and uses everyone, including Shah's object of adoration. In her autobiography, *A Patchwork Quilt*, Paranjpye revealed that both actors wanted to play the other role, insisting it suited them more. 'Finally I told them, guys, are you actors or what? Call it convincing or cajoling or bullying or whatever but it worked out well eventually.'

Hindi films generally favour moral endings. But in *Katha*, the bad doesn't get his just desserts. The hare manages to evade the law much like Gemini's *Mr Sampat*, a 1952 movie based on an R.K. Narayan story about the shenanigans of a smooth-talking cheat. But unlike *Mr Sampat*, *Katha* made money, which perhaps underlines India's shifting moral code in the 1980s.

Like many other top directors of that period, Paranjpye got attracted to TV. *Ados Pados* (1984) and *Chhote Bade* (1985) were pleasant but hardly memorable. Her next movie, *Disha*, would only come in 1990.

Ketan Mehta

Along with Nihalani, Ketan Mehta made the most contemporary and defiant Hindi films of the 1980s. Few Hindi feature films have captured student unrest like Mehta's *Holi* (1983). Mehta, who studied economics in college and was an FTII graduate, shot the film as part of a workshop with FTII students in Poona.

In its omphalos, *Holi* is a political film. The students, in their rather inchoate way, resist and rebel against the college authorities. Mehta employed sarcasm to mock the existing order and psychoanalysed sexual repression through bullying. Emotions such as joy, sadness, anger are easier to portray on celluloid. Restlessness of the mind is harder to project. But Mehta, whose outstanding debut *Bhavni Bhavai* (Gujarati, 1980) critically examined untouchability, used the moving camera to illustrate the edginess inside the students' heads. Jehangir Choudhury earned the national award for best cinematography. Future directors Amole Gupte (*Stanley Ka Dabba*) and Ashutosh Gowarikar (*Lagaan*) also acted in the film.

With a marquee ensemble—Smita Patil, Om Puri and Naseeruddin Shah—*Mirch Masala* (1987) got more attention than *Holi*. Set in British-ruled 1940s India, when a subedar was the king of his patch, the movie is a parable of power and its excesses. The subedar (Shah) covets Sonbai (Smita

Patil) and threatens to burn the village down if she doesn't acquiesce, while an entire village of able-bodied men cower before him. The Navsari-born director, with a fondness for folk, showed how power is hegemonic, how patriarchy burrows into our consciousness forcing even women to take anti-women calls. There's no one to stop the subedar, barring an aging factory watchman Abu Miyan (Om Puri) with a non-negotiable moral code. Abu personifies resistance and his resolve to battle empowers Sonbai and the other women to fight back.

The climactic scene is constructed like a duel in a Western. The soldiers hammer at the door of the shelter with a log while Abu Miyan finishes his namaz. The final shots, where chilli powder explodes in the subedar's eyes like a million atom bombs, are purgative and liberating. The performances are uniformly good, especially Patil as the woman of unflinching honour. But the pleasant surprise is Suresh Oberoi as the village headman. As a muscular male who succumbs like a mouse to authority, Oberoi took the national award for best supporting actor. Thereafter Mehta gradually adopted a more popular idiom for his works. *Hero Hiralal* (1988), his last feature of the 1980s, failed to either engage or impress.

Vijaya Mehta

Theatre and film personality Vijaya Mehta's *Rao Saheb* (1985) and *Pestonjee* (1988) are two finely grained, handcrafted gems. Both leave you with a sense of lingering regret. *Rao Saheb* (played by Anupam Kher) captured the tragedy of the 'half-modern' who remains a prisoner of tradition because he lacks the backbone to break free of the past. Director Mehta, who also acted in Benegal's *Kalyug* and Nihalani's *Party,* brought the right tenor of cheeriness to 'mawshi', the widowed aunt in the film. She won the national award for best supporting actress for *Rao Saheb,* a movie with little online footprint.

Pestonjee received the national award for best feature film in Hindi. The movie trawled through the lives of two Parsi friends—their bonding, their falling for the same girl, their different ways—even as it attempted to broad brush the so-called idiosyncracies of a community slowly vanishing with time.

Mehta once summed up the focus and intent of her work. 'What I have always found meaningful in my whole body of work is respect for life, respect for human beings. I like to look into relationships—between men or women—with each other, with life and try to identify the various finer nuances of existence,' she said.[16]

Mrinal Sen

The 1980s saw a mellowing of Mrinal Sen. The political filmmaker of the Seventies had morphed into a quiet interpreter of social pathologies. The outcome was a less angry and more meditative cinema. His movies in the Eighties reflect the wisdom of a sage who can see both sides. In an interview to wildlifefilms.com, Sen said, 'For the past few years instead of pointing my fingers at the enemy outside, I have been trying to see the enemy within me.'

The much-lauded *Khandhar* (1984) is an elegy on the cruelty of hope. Three friends on vacation spend a few days in a tumble-down mansion in rural Bengal. An interaction with a family living there—a blind old woman waiting for a man who had promised to marry her getting-too-old-for-marriage daughter—turns into a contemplative story on the possibilities of love that the self-constricted fail to reach out to. The ruins are an extension of their lives.

Khandhar was followed by the ambitious artistic failure, *Genesis* (1986), a proto-capitalism parable of need and greed. But Sen returned to form with *Ek Din Achanak* (1988), the story of a professor (Shreeram Lagoo) who leaves home one evening never to return. The film is knitted around his absence. The inward-looking and partially autobiographical film, produced by NFDC, tells us as much about the professor's family as the missing academic.

Mrinal Sen passed away on 30 December 2018.

Four Actors, Eight Characters

To many filmgoers in India, Hindi parallel cinema was synonymous with four faces: Smita Patil, Shabana Azmi, Naseeruddin Shah and Om Puri. The Fab Four were mega stars of a parallel universe. Their careers began in the 1970s. In the 1980s, they hit their prime, carrying an ISI-like stamp of quality acting. All had an overflowing shelf of awards. Barring Smita, all others were trained actors.

Naseeruddin Shah | *Sparsh*

Shah's blind principal Anirudh Parmar is the gold standard for anyone playing a visually challenged character. Parmar lives life without a trace of self-pity. He is self-sufficient, egoistic and sensitive. Shah got every gesture and attitude right.

Naseeruddin Shah | *Paar*

Shah brought a sincerity and simplicity to the Dalit labourer who crosses the swollen river with his pregnant wife, shepherding a herd of pigs. Shah's performance fetched him the national award for best actor and the Volpi Cup for best actor at Venice. No other Indian actor has earned that prize.

Om Puri | *Aakrosh*

The tribal Lavanya Bhikhu isn't dumb but has gone numb. In *Aakrosh*, Puri spoke with his haunting eyes and deafening silence, voicing the hidden history of a community exploited for centuries. 'It was a difficult role as he had hardly anything to say. It was mainly action and expressions. He had to essay all the emotions and angst on his face without articulating it and without overdoing the expressions,' said wife Nandita.[17] Shah called it Om's 'definitive film performance'. His acting got him the *Filmfare* award for best supporting actor and an offer from Satyajit Ray for the telefilm, *Sadgati*. Puri would also later receive the Karlovy Vary award for best actor for playing the complex cop in *Ardh Satya*.

Om Puri | *Arohan*

The Ambala-born actor played a landless farmer in the movie that few eventually saw. 'For days he would sit out in the sun, oiled and bare-bodied during shoots to get a tan so as to look natural,' recalled Nandita.[18] It was worth the investment. Puri received the national award for best actor.

Smita Patil | *Chakra*

Many thronged the theatres to watch her bathe in the open. But they went home thinking of Amma, the raw and real slum woman who sang to the melody of everyday life. Nihalani explained her creative process. 'She could internalise a role so perfectly that you would never see the planning and preparation that went into it,' he said.[19] The part got her both the national and *Filmfare* awards for best actress.

Smita Patil | *Mirch Masala*

Her eyes could start a forest fire in your heart or leave you scalded by the intensity of their anger. In *Mirch Masala*, Smita did both. The lascivious subedar has been turned on by her spit-fire act and wants her body. But he is not aware of her depths of dignity and her indomitable will to resist and fight. Smita made it a role to remember.

Shabana Azmi | *Arth*

She is drunk. In the party, she sees her husband with his lover. The confrontation that follows, despite shades of *Sahib Bibi Aur Ghulam*, shocked the audience. So did the film's end where she refuses a Prince Charming. Shabana carried the film, earning the national and *Filmfare* awards for best actress.

Shabana Azmi | *Khandhar*

For her part, Shabana lost the 12 kg, which she had put on for *Mandi*. She went on a diet and 'virtually starved' herself. But the film required more: an emotional transformation. In *Mandi*, she had played a loquacious courtesan. In *Khandhar*, she plays a rural woman of strength and quietude. She once said, 'I think *Khandhar* is the film in which I've made the least number of mistakes. Under Mrinal-*da's* capable direction I was able to invest Jamini with grace, dignity and immense beauty instead of interpreting her as a victim.'[20]

INTERVAL

THE BOX-OFFICE STORY

In the Eighties, the hit-flop ratio got increasingly skewed as the decade progressed. *Trade Guide's* 1980 records show that 21 per cent films earned profits. In business terminology, these films were in the A2, A1, A and +B category. About 32 per cent fell in the Good B and B category, which meant they recovered their costs. About 47 per cent or one out of two movies lost money (-B, C). The trend persisted the following year. In 1981, about 17 per cent films made money. Another 31 per cent made neither profit nor loss; 52 per cent lost money.

By 1988, the scenario had changed dramatically. A mere 10 per cent films earned profits. Only 7 per cent recovered their costs and an alarming 83 per cent flopped. The scenario remained equally dismal in 1989. Only 9 per cent films earned profits and just 11 per cent escaped without losses. A staggering 80 per cent films, or every four out of five movies, ended in the red.

In other words, hits dipped dramatically and filmmaking became a very risky business.

The key difference was that a huge number of break-even ventures—the thick band of movies which were neither winners nor losers—disappeared. Consequently, many small and medium-budget 'one-man army' producers were edged out of the industry.

The list of superhits and super flops reveals an absence of pattern. It is hard to explain why *Pyar Jhukta Nahin* hit the jackpot while many other similar yarns fell flat. The *Dacait* debacle again is a mystery of Hitchcockian proportions. There are dozens of such examples. With the benefit of hindsight one can say that telling an old story with a new twist and in an attention-grabbing way, backed by star power and good music, offered a better chance of box-office success than anything else.

Here's a compilation of the commercially successful films—**AIII (blockbuster), AII (superhit) and AI (hit)** in trade terminology—and flops in 1980-89. Only those films listed by both *Trade Guide* and *Film Information*, two prominent film business magazines, in the above-mentioned categories have been included. One must point out that both magazines differed on the ranking of several films. For example, *Trade Guide* gave an AII rating to *Insaf Ka Tarazu* but *Film Information* marked it only AI.

Superhits of the Decade

1980

Film: *Aasha* | Director: J. Om Prakash
Film: *Insaf Ka Tarazu* | Director: B.R. Chopra
Film: *Dostana* | Director: Raj Khosla
Comment: Only *Asha* received an AII rating from trade magazines, making it clearly the biggest hit of the year.

1981

Film: *Ek Duuje Ke* Liye | Director: K. Balachander
Film: *Laawaris* | Director: Prakash Mehra
Film: *Kranti* | Director: Manoj Kumar
Film: *Love Story* | Director: None named (for most of the film, Rahul Rawail)
Film: *Meri Aawaz Suno* | Director: Rajendra Singh Babu
Comment: Both trade magazines gave an AII rating to *Ek Duuje Ke Liye*, making it the biggest hit of the year. No other film received such a high rating.

1982

Film: *Vidhaata* | Director: Subhash Ghai
Film: *Namak Halaal* | Director: Prakash Mehra
Comment: No other film barring *Vidhaata* received a superhit rating from both trade magazines.

1983

Film: *Coolie* | Director: Manmohan Desai
Film: *Avtaar* | Director: Mohan Kumar
Film: *Andhaa Kaanoon* | Director: T. Rama Rao
Film: *Betaab* | Director: Rahul Rawail
Film: *Himmatwala* | Director: K. Raghavendra Rao
Comment: Both *Coolie* and *Avtaar* received superhit ratings.

1984

Film: *Chhota Chetan* | Director: Jijo Punnoose
Film: *Tohfa* | Director: K. Raghavendra Rao
Comment: *Chhota Chetan* (3D) was the smash hit of the year. *Trade Guide* gave it an AII rating (the only film to get so) while *Film Information* put it in the AI section.

1985

Film: *Ram Teri Ganga Maili* | Director: Raj Kapoor
Film: *Mard* | Director: Manmohan Desai
Film: *Pyar Jhukta Nahin* | Director: Vijay Sadanah
Comment: **Ram Teri Ganga Maili** received an AIII (blockbuster rating) from *Trade Guide*, the only film in the entire decade to reach that landmark.

1986

Film: *Karma* | Director: Subhash Ghai
Film: *Swarag Se Sunder* | Director: K. Bapaiah
Film: *Naam* | Director: Mahesh Bhatt
Film: *Nache Mayuri* | Director: T. Rama Rao
Film: *Nagina* | Director: Harmesh Malhotra
Comment: According to *Trade Guide*, *Karma* and *Swarag Se Sunder* were the two biggest hits (AII) of the year.

1987

Film: *Pratighaat* | Director: N. Chandra
Film: *Hukumat* | Director: Anil Sharma
Film: *Aag Hi Aag* | Director: Shibu Mitra
Comment: *Pratighaat* was the year's lone superhit, as per both magazines.

1988

Film: *Qayamat Se Qayamat Tak* | Director: Mansoor Khan
Film: *Tezaab* | Director: N. Chandra
Comment: *QSQT* pipped *Tezaab* as the year's biggest grosser.

1989

Film: *Ram Lakhan* | Director: Subhash Ghai
Film: *Maine Pyar Kiya* | Director: Sooraj Barjatya
Film: *Tridev* | Director: Rajiv Rai
Film: *Chandni* | Director: Yash Chopra
Comment: Both *Trade Guide* and *Film Information* gave AII to
only one film: *Ram Lakhan*

What Worked: Five Categories of Money-spinners

This is a categorisation of the same films according to themes.
In most cases, the genres overlapped. These categories broadly
indicate the kind of movies that the audience loved. Interestingly,
a close look at the flops reveals that it wasn't the storyline, but
the treatment that really mattered. The devil lay in the detail.

Love triangles: *Aasha* (1980), *Tohfa* (1984), *Chandni* (1989)

Young romance: *Ek Duuje Ke Liye* (1981), *Love Story* (1981), *Betaab*
(1983), *Qayamat Se Qayamat Tak* (1988), *Maine Pyar Kiya* (1989)

Action/drama/masala (Old style): *Dostana* (1980), *Laawaris* (1981),
Kranti (1981), *Namak Halaal* (1982), *Vidhaata* (1982), *Coolie*
(1983), *Mard* (1985), *Karma* (1986), *Naam* (1986), *Aag Hi Aag*
(1987), *Tezaab* (1988), *Ram Lakhan* (1989), *Tridev* (1989)

Action/drama/masala (New style, more earthy and violent): *Meri Aawaz Suno* (1981), *Andhaa Kaanoon* (1983), *Himmatwala* (1983), *Pratighaat* (1987), *Hukumat* (1987)

Romantic social/family drama: *Avtaar* (1983), *Ram Teri Ganga Maili* (1985), *Pyar Jhukta Nahin* (1985), *Swarag Se Sunder* (1986)

One of a kind: *Insaf Ka Tarazu* (sexual assault/revenge drama, 1980), *Chhota Chetan* (children/fantasy/3D, 1984), *Nache Mayuri* (inspirational, 1986), *Nagina* (romance/supernatural, 1986)

Big Losers

Here's a small collection from the huge of list of flops. Basis of selection: they were either produced by big banners or helmed by well-known directors or both.

1980

Film: *Shaan* | Director: Ramesh Sippy
Film: *The Burning Train* | Director: Ravi Chopra

1981

Film: *Professor Pyarelal* | Director: Brij
Film: *Krodhi* | Director: Subhash Ghai

1982

Film: *Deedar-e-Yaar* | Director: H.S. Rawail
Film: *Zamaane Ko Dikhana Hai* | Director: Nasir Hussain

1983

Film: *Razia Sultan* | Director: Kamal Amrohi
Film: *Romance* | Director: Ramanand Sagar

1984

Film: *Boxer* | Director: Raj N. Sippy
Film: *Manzil Manzil* | Director: Nasir Hussain

1985

Film: *Zamana* | Director: Ramesh Talwar

1986

Film: *Dharam Adhikari* | Director: K. Raghavendra Rao
Film: *Kasam* | Director: Umesh Mehra

1987

Film: *Dacait* | Director: Rahul Rawail

1988

Film: *Dayavan* | Director: Feroz Khan
Film: *Gangaa Jamunaa Saraswathi* | Director: Manmohan Desai

1989

Film: *Joshilaay* | Director: Sibte Hassan Rizvi
(Shekhar Kapur quit midway)
Film: *Jaadugar* | Director: Prakash Mehra
Film: *Toofan* | Director: Ketan Desai

This list may not be flawless. As a film-addicted youth during this period, I can vouch that some films did better than what the magazines say. My memory and experience, as well as Bob Christo's and Rishi Kapoor's accounts in their autobiographies, suggest that *Qurbani* was a roaring hit. The trade magazines disagree. *Trade Guide* put it as BB and *Film Information* as A, which means popular but not a biggie. Similarly, *Disco Dancer* was a bigger hit, at least in smaller towns, than what the film business mags report.

Again, in its 7 January 1984 issue, *Film Information* says that '*Nadiya Ke Paar* celebrated golden jubilee at eight stations and silver jubilee at twenty-two stations in UP, Bihar, MP, West Bengal and Assam. It has already completed seventy-five weeks at Jhankar, Allahabad.' In Vasundhara Cinema, Ranchi, the film celebrated golden jubilee, drawing a vast hinterland audience. Strangely, *Trade Guide* too puts it in the 'overflow' category, a modest success. Director Govind Moonis' work continues to be re-watched on YouTube where it has a staggering 175 million-plus million views. The influential film inspired a bunch of movies of similar flavour such as *Ghar Dwar* (1985), *Tulsi* (1985) and *Piya Milan* (1985). All were Sachin starrers and fetched decent profits.

One more point. The annual list of hits and flops was published in the first week of the year that followed. This means that the fate of films released in the last few weeks of the year wasn't fully decided yet, especially at a time when prints were limited and releases were often staggered in various territories. Broadly, though, the list strives to provide an accurate picture of a film's cash-counter kismet.

REEL 7

HOW THE SOUTH SHOOK
UP THE NORTH

In the 1980s, a bunch of producers and directors from south India barreled through the Bombay film market, introducing a novel style of storytelling and a new business culture of filmmaking. Their films entertained the Hindi film audience in a way they were not accustomed to. The critics wrote poisonous reviews. But the audience, even if they read them, did not seem to care. Thematically most of them were conveyor-belt movies, often forgotten even before they were over. Yet at a time when the industry was reeling under the ravages of VCR piracy, these films comforted producers and pleasured a huge number of filmgoers.

Many were remakes of Telugu hits, some reconstructed from Tamil blockbusters. These movies branched into two categories. The first can be described as the mainstream masala mix and best illustrated by the superhit *Himmatwala* (1983), helmed by K. Raghavendra Rao, or K. Bapaiah's *Mawaali* (also 1983). Both *Himmatwala* and *Mawaali* blended action, comedy and songs in a novel way for Hindi moviegoers.

The general template for a southern masala mix movie went

like this: Jeetendra-Sridevi or Jeetendra-Jaya Prada, sometimes both, with Kader Khan and Shakti Kapoor as comic villains. Asrani and Aruna Irani completed the guffaw quartet. To this, lyricist Indeevar's racy rhymes, Bappi Lahiri's bouncy tunes and Kader Khan's street-smart dialogues were sloshed together to create a steamy rasam. The plots were harder to believe than some of Donald Trump's statements. They could only be experienced, not explained. This was the general mould on which directors such as Raghavendra Rao and Bapaiah stencilled these films. Everything—sets, costumes, action, dances, scenes, characters—was unapologetically garish and in your face. The editing was often in fast-cutting mode.

The difference between these films and what was being dished out in Bombay was more in form than content. To use a much-used expression, it was old wine in a flashier bottle but with a sharper kick. It offered an instant gratification, which felt fresh and familiar at the same time.

These productions were distinct in their visual language from a Bombay-made film, even in the way the opening credits rolled out, often in maverick mauve and flamboyant fuchsia. Certain traits were distinctive. Sometimes the story defied logic even by Bombay cinema's existing low standards. In *Jaani Dost* (1983), a K. Raghavendra Rao flick, the storyline was like a crazy ball; it could go anywhere. Among other things, the movie had a chimp (in a double role) who dressed up in shiny red suits, blew birthday candles and quaffed red wine. It was the acme of inane.

The locales had a southern feel. 'The favourite location for Jeetendra films was the rural Rajamundary district. For song picturisation, the producers preferred to go to Ooty,' recalled K. Ravi Shankar, who directed the 1987 hit, *Sindoor*.[1] Not nudity but titillation was the name of the game. And it was done primarily via songs. A sari that blows off the body ('Oeee amma, oeee amma', *Mawaali*) or sexually suggestive moans and movements ('Maine tujhe chhua to tan jala', *Justice Chaudhury*) were some devices used to draw the predominantly male gaze.

Double-entendre dialogues were part of the package. In *Mawaali*, for instance, the character played by Shakti Kapoor says, '*Tumne meri phaadi thhi...pant, Ab main teri phadoonga... pant.*' A plain translation would go, 'You tore...my pants, now I will tear...your pants.' The meaningful pauses make it evident that the actor isn't talking about his trousers.

Titillation has always been integral to Hindi films, especially in B and C graders. But these productions managed to go risque even in big-budget films with top stars. In Bapaiah's *Maqsad*, the double entendre of Kader Khan matched Dada Kondke's.

Guess this riddle posed by Sridevi to Rajesh Khanna. '*Woh jaata thha, main bulati thhi, woh dalta tha, main roti thhi* (He was going, I called him, he put it in and I kept crying).' Answer: Bangle-seller. In turn, Rajesh Khanna quizzes Sridevi: '*Arora maroda, thook lagake ghuseda* (Twist and turn it, put your spit on it and shove it in).' Answer: Sui-dhaga (Threading the needle). The riddles kept the wolf whistles and catcalls going inside theatres.

Several downright misogynistic scenes were passed off as fun. In the opening scene of *Mawaali*, the hero makes a bunch of girls take off their clothes to pull their car. Little is shown on screen which probably allowed the scene to get past the censors.

Some dialogues made little sense but they often drew chuckles. *Himmatwala* had gems such as '*Yeh coat aur tie kya pahan liya, apne aapko Rajkot samajh baithe* (You think you have become Rajkot by wearing pants and coat).' And '*Humse uljhoge to tumhara Pathankot bana denge* (If you cross the line with me, I will make a Pathankot out of you).' Or, '*Tumhare dil ki baat sunkar humara dil Hyderabad ki tarah abaad ho gaya* (After hearing your feelings, my heart has become happy like Hyderabad).'

Dancing almost became mandatory for song picturisations. After years of running coyly around trees, onscreen lovers now pranced energetically in lush green fields. Those who didn't enjoy the choreography described the songs as 'PT lessons' but many loved them.

Silk Smitha

Silk Smitha was a rage in the South. But the dusky dancer made only a limited impact in Hindi films such as *Jaani Dost, Jeet Hamaari, Qaidi* and *Pataal Bhairavi*. She had a more fleshed-out part in *Sadma* but failed to impress.

The new breed of producers was not apologetic about their work, rather they flaunted its success. G.A. Seshagiri Rao, who produced *Himmatwala*, said, 'Some critics had criticised *Himmatwala*. So I gave a full-page ad in *The Times of India*, "*Himmatwala* is a film for Indian masses, not for intellectual idiots".'[2]

The combined impact of *Himmatwala, Mawaali* and the modestly successful *Justice Chaudhury*—remember the song 'Mama mia pom pom'—was immense. For a few years, Bombay filmmakers didn't know what hit them. Neither did the paying public.

The second category of films from the South was the socials. In the 1960s and '70s, family entertainers made by Madras-based Prasad Productions or AVM were magnets for middle-class married women. They offered comedy, drama and romance in a way that nobody—father, mother, sister, daughter-in-law or son—had to squirm or awkwardly look sideways.

In the southern dramas of the Fifties and Sixties, the family was fundamental to life and happiness. A plotting maternal uncle, a domineering mother-in-law, a fashion-conscious daughter-in-law or a wayward son would become a temporary antagonist before matters were resolved in the last reel.

Even in the early 1980s, South-based superhit 'family films' such as *Judaai*—directed by T. Rama Rao, starring Jeetendra and Rekha—maintained the familiar practice of providing 'clean' entertainment. *(For more details on Jeetendra's engagement with Southern productions see Reel 8)*

The mutated social dramas emerged a few years later with *Ghar Ek Mandir* (1984) and *Pyar Ka Mandir* (1988). The new films retained a conservative core. There was emphasis on traditional values where the family, especially a joint one, was still seen as a banyan tree. Plots were still braided around families fending off attacks from either the jealous outsider (an unscrupulous business rival, for instance) or the immoral insider (a rich, westernised bahu, who doesn't respect the elders).

But within the family-drama framework, several of these entertainers also offered healthy doses of ribald comedy, suggestive songs, titillating dances, and even graphic attempts at sexual assault. The difference between the conservative family drama and the mainstream commercial was blurred in these saucy socials. Yet they drew sizable family crowds.

In the money-spinner *Ghar Ek Mandir* (1984), a joint family of modest means but happy together, is torn asunder by a rich, arrogant and scheming daughter-in-law (Shoma Anand). Within the trappings of a family drama, the film had three action sequences, a prolonged rape attempt and several sexually suggestive songs.

Bapaiah's *Swarag Se Sunder* (1986), the only southern social to attain AII (superhit) status in the decade, was again about the trials and travails of 'an ideal happy family'. Early in the film, the heroine (Jaya Prada) says, '*Jiska Laxman [Mithun] jaisa devar ho, Ram [Jeetendra] jaisa pati ho, swarg se saman yeh ghar ho, mere liye yeh chhoti si duniya swarg se sundar hai.* (Anyone with a Laxman-like brother-in-law, Ram-like husband and a heaven-like home, for her this small world is better than heaven).' Gyandev Agnihotri, father of actor Apurva Agnihotri, wrote the film's screenplay.

The film had two extended fight scenes, including one with motorcycle stunts, and a few smutty dialogues. At one point, one of the characters played by Aruna Irani tells Asrani, '*Barsaat ka mausam aaya aur chala gaya. Mera badan aam ki tarah jalta raha* (The monsoon came and went and my body was left yearning like a mango).'

Production houses in the Eighties had figured out that even family dramas had to be calibrated by incorporating elements previously used only in masala films.

A sub-category was the family romantic dramas—these included *Maang Bharo Sajana* (1980) and *Ek Hi Bhool* (1981), both directed by T. Rama Rao, with Jeetendra and Rekha in lead roles. *Tohfa* was a significant film in this category. The physical sensuality of Sridevi in songs such as 'Pyar ka tohfa' and 'Gori tere roop rang ke' is a marked change in how the heroine is depicted in a film essentially targeted at a women-centric audience.

In southern films, the producer was king. He controlled the story selection, star cast, location, film promotion, exploitation of territories....The principle was simple: he who pays the piper calls the tune. 'Since the producer was investing the money, he should be the ultimate authority,' said G.A. Seshagiri Rao of Padmalaya Studios.[3] This was very different from the Bombay way of doing things where only a few top banners had clout. In most projects, the star was the centre of the universe.

Actor Raj Babbar, who acted in southern hits such as *Jeevan Dhaara* (1982), *Insaaf Ki Awaaz* (1986) and *Sansar* (1987), said the difference between North and South producers lay in their financial muscle.

He said, 'The southern producers were strong on finances. They would pay your hotel bills, pay your fees. In return they would expect bulk dates. You worked day and night, instead of shifts. Bombay had some strong producers. But most were mid-level producers who struggled to finish their films and pay you on time.'[4]

Comic actor Rakesh Bedi explained how he figured out a way to deal with mid-level producers in Bombay. 'My formula was: take 50 per cent before the shooting ends and 50 per cent before the dubbing.' In those days, dubbing was the last opportunity for actors to extract their dues from producers. If the producer dilly-dallied, Bedi would visit his office and ask how much he could pay. 'Some would say, I can pay this much, you forget the rest. I accepted that because if I didn't adjust, he wouldn't be considering me for his next film. It was a sort of goodwill debt he owed me.'[5]

In contrast South-based producers making Hindi films had stronger capital, and were consequently more organised and professional. Writer Kamlesh Pandey, who wrote the dialogues for producer D. Ramanaidu's money-making *Rakhwala* (1989), offered a first-hand insight into the working of a top South India production house.

He said, 'I was surprised to find that the best and the fastest Hindi typists of my script were not in Bombay but in Chennai! And they really looked after me! Their hospitality was amazing. I did not smoke or drink but there would always be a carton of imported cigarettes and bottles of imported whisky waiting in my hotel room! They would really spoil me. And whether it was their financial commitments or any other matter, they were real professionals. They paid well and they paid on time unlike Bombay film producers.'[6]

Since the payment was smooth, there were no date problems and films were canned faster. Director T. Rama Rao said, 'We took fifty days to complete a film. It was released in a maximum of six months. It would be distributed over three-four, or five months.'[7] *Himmatwala* was completed in three months.

In general, Bombay films had a far longer gestation period. *Jyoti Bane Jwala*, an in-house Jeetendra film directed by the superfast Dasari Narayana Rao, had the same storyline as Prakash Mehra's *Jwalamukhi*. Inevitably, there was a race to finish first. *Jyoti Bane Jwala* won by a distance, both in the timing of its release and the outcome. The film was among the top ten grossers of 1980. *Jwalamukhi*, with Shatrughan Sinha in the lead, reached the theatres six months later and disappeared like a corporator after elections.

Bombay stars appreciated and admired the southern way of working. Jeetendra, who worked in the maximum number of South-based productions, once said, 'Their films are made on time. There is so much discipline and they give us so much respect. I love working there.'[8]

Some were start-to-finish projects. In his autobiography, Rishi Kapoor recalled Rajesh Khanna telling him that *Maqsad* was wrapped up in eighteen days. A 1984 article said the southern film industry had a better 'work ethic' and 'cost consciousness'. It further said, 'The Hindi films made in the South, many of which are lavishly produced though, drastically cut non-productive costs, converting every rupee that is spent into high production values.'[9] An industry expert estimated in the same article that *Andhaa Kaanoon* and *Ek Duuje Ke Liye*, among the biggest southern successes in the all-India market, would have cost 'at least 30 per cent' more if they had been made in Bombay.

Amitabh Bachchan also illustrated the brisk and business-like approach. 'Often when I get down at the Madras airport, I'm driven straight to the studio where the shots are ready. The day's shooting is over—provided there is no work the next day—I am driven back to the airport where a man receives me with the boarding card ready. No hotel, no mixing of business with pleasure.'[10]

But amidst the technological and administrative competence, there was also a casualness of approach. And, one is not just

Mawaali (1983) was misspelt in Hindi in the
film's opening credits

referring to the spelling mistakes in the opening credits of
major hits such as *Mawaali* (1983) or *Insaaf Ki Awaaz* (1986).
Director K. Raghavendra Rao bluntly told a film magazine, 'All
my Hindi films don't have a [working] title because distributors
of different territories keep raising objections....As such my
Hindi film titles are easily interchangeable, *Himmatwala* could
have been *Naya Kadam* or *Kaamyaab* or *Hoshiyar*.'[11] Little
surprise, these films felt as disposable as diapers.

Producers preferred to make remakes of Telugu and Tamil
superhits because they had already passed the litmus test of
popular support, albeit in a smaller and distinct geographical
area. Director T. Rama Rao said, 'Most films I made in Hindi
were Telugu remakes. If it proved [to be a hit] we would be
very confident to produce it in Hindi.'[12]

Producer G.A. Seshagiri Rao echoed the same view. 'Most of
our films were made in Telugu. The successful ones, we remade
in Hindi. We wanted to make so many films and there was no
time to sit on [new] subjects for so many days.'[13]

South Indian filmmakers also understood the need to constantly provide something seemingly new to the audience. Bombay-based Veeru Devgan was the fightmaster in both *Himmatwala* and *Mawaali*. His work is often more inventive in southern productions—notably the fight sequences of Rajinikanth in *Andhaa Kaanoon*. In the 1980s, Devgan was action director in at least twenty southern productions.

Southern fight composers brought a new imagination and slickness to the filming of fight scenes. Watch how Anil Kapoor deftly balances himself on street carts, benches, pots and pans, and bottles while bashing up Gulshan Grover and Co. without putting his feet on the ground in the 1986 hit, *Insaaf Ki Awaaz* (thrills: Vijayan). Rajinikanth's kicks and snarls in *John Jani Janardhan* (thrills: Judo Rathnam) were distinctly different in the crowded bazaar of action films. Even Kamal Haasan's fight scenes in *Geraftaar* (fights: Judo Rathnam) and *Yeh To Kamaal Ho Gaya* (thrills: Kiruba, climax fight: Pappu Verma) stand out from the regular.

The link between South and North in cinema goes back to the first talkie, *Alam Ara* (1931), which was produced in Bombay. L.V. Prasad, who later became the founder of the respected Prasad Productions (PP), played a small part in the film.

But it was Gemini's blockbuster costume drama *Chandralekha* (1948), which set the ball rolling for South-based producers in search of a bigger market. In time, the two kids blowing the bugle became one of the most recognised banners of its time. Uday Shankar's *Kalpana* (1948), a joyful celebration of Indian classical dance, is one of the finest examples of North-South collaboration. Gemini again was the producer.

By the 1950s, Gemini, PP and AVM Productions had become respected brands in Hindi cinema, primarily known for 'clean family entertainment'. Action-adventure flicks such as Gemini's

Insaniyat or Pakshiraja Studio's *Azaad* were rare. 'In 1955, Dilip Kumar and Meena Kumari were flown south to make *Azaad*. The film was a knockout success—collecting Rs 8 lakh in those days, which was a feat. Its producer, S.M.S. Naidu was so overwhelmed that he never produced a film again.'[14]

Tamil Nadu CM M.G. Ramachandran receives a cheque of Rs 11,11,111 for Sri Lankan Tamils Relief Fund from Amitabh Bachchan at the *Coolie* premiere at Ega Cinema, Madras on 21 December 1983. (Photo Credit: *Film Information*)

Writer Kamlesh Pandey, who wrote the screenplay of producer A. Poornachandra Rao's *Chaalbaaz* (1989), recalled that in the olden days southern producers of Hindi films relied heavily on writers like Pandit Mukhram Sharma and Rajendra Krishan. 'These writers would decide the cast of the film, not the director or the producer,' he said.[15]

Sharma was the dialogue writer for Gemini Studios in *Gharana* (1961) and *Grahasti* (1963). He also collaborated with L.V. Prasad for *Daadi Maa* (1966), *Raja Aur Runk* (1968), *Jeene Ki Raah* (1969) and *Main Sunder Hoon* (1971), and with AVM Productions for *Do Kaliyaan* (1968). Rajendra Krishan was much sought after by AVM (*Bhai-Bhai*, 1956; *Chhaya*,

1961; *Pooja Ke Phool*, 1964), and by Vasu Films, notably in *Bharosa* (1963), *Khandan* (1965) and *Nai Roshni* (1967). 'Of course the remakes were not without problems but they were mostly about adapting south Indian customs for north Indian cinema,' said Pandey.[16]

Parallel comedy tracks were common in southern productions. Mehmood, Shubha Khote and Dhumal formed a riotous trio but often their antics were only loosely connected to the main plot. Pandey said, 'They had separate comedy writers who only wrote comedy scenes to be punched in the main track.'[17]

The first rumblings of a southern 'invasion' were heard in the early 1960s. Reviewing Prasad Productions' *Sasural* (1961), *The Times of India's* film critic wrote, '*Ghunghat, Bindiya, Nazrana* and now *Sasural*. The invasion from the South seems to be complete. Because, whatever be its artistic shortcomings, it cannot be denied that *Sasural* has got what it takes to be a big box-office hit.'[18]

But by 1974, South-based productions in Hindi had shrunk to single digits; L.V. Prasad's *Bidaai* (Jeetendra's comeback hit) and D. Ramanaidu's *Prem Nagar* (Rajesh Khanna's surprise success) were two of them. By the mid-1970s, both AVM and Gemini had lost sway. Others failed to make inroads. Film business data (1975-79) shows that only a handful of southern ventures such as *Julie* (1975), *Swarag Narak* (1978), *Amardeep* (1979), dubbed sex film *Man Ka Aangan* (1979) and director K. Vishwanath's tender musical *Sargam* (1979) minted money.

In 1980, South made a robust return with Jeetendra's *Jyoti Bane Jwala*. The film, produced at Annapurna Studios, Hyderabad and processed in Chennai, received an AI (hit) rating from *Trade Guide*.

Two southern socials, *Judaai* (Prasad Art, dialogues: Dr Rahi Masoom Reza) and *Maang Bharo Sajana* (Lakshmi Productions), both directed by T. Rama Rao, also kept the ticket clerks busy. Other movies such as producer B. Nagi Reddy's *Swayamvar* and director K. Raghavendra Rao's *Nishana* were moderately successful.

These successes may have renewed the enthusiasm of southern producers dreaming of an all-India market, and spurred the making of many more films. Of the five southern winners in 1980, Jeetendra was the hero in four—undoubtedly, the No. 1 Hindi filmstar for southern producers.

The investment zeal reached stratospheric heights after veteran producer L.V. Prasad's *Ek Duuje Ke Liye* (1981), a passionate and tragic love story, became a money-spinner. Director K. Balachander's film—released alongside *Love Story* that marked Kumar Gaurav's debut—drew repeated viewings among the young adult audience. Scenes like heroine Rati Agnihotri drinking the burnt remains of a photograph of her lover with her coffee or Kamal Haasan spinning a top on her washboard stomach became talking points.

Padmalaya Studios also struck gold the same year with the ultra-violent, vigilante *Meri Aawaz Suno* (1981), starring Jeetendra and Hema Malini. However, the production house became synonymous with another kind of movie. In 1983, it delivered *Himmatwala, Mawaali* and *Justice Chaudhury*—all Jeetendra starrers. To many critics and viewers, *Himmatwala* and *Mawaali* typify all that was wrong with Hindi cinema in the 1980s. But the impact of these movies is undeniable.

To understand their success, one needs to locate them in their time when VCR piracy ruled and the middle class had abandoned theatres. Movie halls were primarily the domain of young males from the underclass. Both movies provided likeable content for the new majority audience.

The Forgotten Forerunner

Director K. Raghavendra Rao's *Nishana* (1980), the tale of an elusive necklace, was a masochist's guilty pleasure. Made under the banner of Roja Pictures, the film was a remake of the NTR-Sridevi Telugu smash hit, *Vetagadu*, helmed by the same director and released the previous year. With Jeetendra and Poonam Dhillon in lead roles, the film was a middling moneymaker but became the prototype of many zany entertainers. Utpal Dutt's part was the forerunner to Kader Khan's comic villain in *Himmatwala*. The *Golmaal* actor spoke his lines (dialogue: Charandas Shokh) in rhyme: '*Kavita dekhne mein rooi hai, par chubhne mein sooi hai* (Kavita looks like cotton but stings like a needle).' Or, '*Tum achambhe mein khambhe ki tarah kyon khade ho* (Why are you standing in astonishment like a pillar)?'

The film's dress designer clothed Prem Chopra from top to bottom in a single strong colour like flaming red or vibrant violet. The film foresaw the future in other ways too. In the song 'Maine tujhe jeet liya', Poonam Dhillon wore the same clingy bejewelled clothes that later became famous after Sridevi put them on in *Tohfa's* 'Nainon mein sapna'.

However, a forerunner only serves as an advance warning. The tsunami finally came with *Himmatwala* in 1983. By the end of 1984, production houses based in Madras and Hyderabad had barrelled into the Hindi film market. In 1984, a whopping twenty-seven Hindi films were produced by South-based banners, signalling a large-scale entry of new capital.

Year 1985 was a blip after two years of southern comfort. No major hit came from Madras or Hyderabad that year. But in 1986, the South roared again delivering six of the year's top ten hits. Family drama *Swarag Se Sunder* was a monster hit. *Nache Mayuri*, the inspirational dance film based on the life of Sudha Chandran, was another runaway success. *Aakhree*

Raasta and *Insaaf Ki Awaaz* also yielded profits. Several other films were above-average earners: producer D. Ramanaidu's *Dilwaala* (Mithun), K. Bapaiah's *Muddat* (Mithun, Jaya Prada, Padmini Kolhapure), T. Rama Rao's *Dosti Dushmani* (Jeetendra, Rajinikanth, Rishi Kapoor) and *Sadaa Suhagan* (Jeetendra, Govinda, Rekha).

However, it would be fair to say that post 1986, the giant southern wave ebbed. *Kudrat Ka Kanoon* (1987), *Sindoor* (1987), *Watan Ke Rakhwale* (1987), *Pyar Ka Mandir* (1988) and *Rakhwala* (1989) made good money but the southern studios did not deliver any super-duper hit in the last three years of the decade, collections reported in a trade magazine show. Yet production continued at a good pace. In 1988, at least twenty Hindi films were directed by South-based directors.

K. Raghavendra Rao, T. Rama Rao and K. Bapaiah were the Southern trinity of the 1980s. Their special ingredient: a feel for the audience pulse. Each delivered more than half-a-dozen profit-making films. All of them helmed losers too. A few exceptions such as Subhash Ghai aside, their flop-hit ratio was far better than most of their competitors in the North or South.

The versatile T. Rama Rao started making Hindi films in his forties. Like a rapid-fire machine gun, he directed twenty-nine Hindi films—twenty-one in the 1980s—and found major success with *Judaai, Maang Bharo Sajana* and *Ek Hi Bhool*. As the decade progressed, he balanced his oeuvre between family yarns (*Sadaa Suhagan, Sansar, Jeevan Dhaara*), inspirational dramas (*Nache Mayuri*) and multistarrer action flicks (*Andhaa Kaanoon, Watan Ke Rakhwale, Insaf Ki Pukar*). *Nache Mayuri, Andhaa Kaanoon* and *Watan Ke Rakhwale* were resounding successes.

Actor Raj Babbar, who acted in *Sansar* and *Jeevan Dhaara*, said the director had a knack for aptly repurposing a Telugu film for a Hindi audience. 'He was very fast and would complete a film in twenty-five to thirty days. He delivered a high percentage of hits, which is what a producer wanted. He was a star among the southern directors who made films in Hindi,' he said.[19]

Sansar took a sympathetic look at the joint family. 'I grew up in a joint family,' T. Rama Rao explained.[20] *Judaai*, he said, gave a message that marriage isn't only about sex. 'People produce children who grow wings and fly away. Old people are left alone. Sometimes they are separated from each other. That is a very pathetic condition,' he said.[21] In the film, a couple separated for decades come together again. *Mujhe Insaaf Chahiye* took a progressive look at unwed motherhood. T. Rama Rao passed away on 20 April 2022.

K. Raghavendra Rao introduced himself to Hindi films with the controversial flop *Lok Parlok* (1979). He found success with *Nishana* (1980) and *Farz Aur Kaanoon* (1982) but went on to redefine entertainment and aesthetics with *Himmatwala* and *Tohfa*. However, he lost steam thereafter (*Mera Saathi, Hoshiyar, Dharam Adhikari*).

K. Bapaiah was more prolific than Raghavendra Rao in Hindi films and more versatile too. Bapaiah could dish out a *Mawaali* or a *Maqsad* but was also adept at family dramas, where he found greater success. Films such as *Ghar Ek Mandir, Swarag Se Sunder* and *Pyar Ka Mandir* were his big winners in the 1980s.

Producer-director Vimal Kumar, who produced the superhit *Dariya-dil* and directed *Jaisi Karni Waisi Bharnii*, said Bapaiah was a producer's director. 'If a producer says, I made a loss working with him, then he's lying. He was quick and worked as per the budget, and he charged reasonably. I paid Jeetu-*ji* Rs 20 lakh for *Ghar Sansar*, a modest success. I gave Bapaiah only Rs 4.5 lakh for the same film,' he said.[22]

Director K. Ravi Shankar (*Sindoor, Dariya-dil*) was the executive producer of *Ghar Ek Mandir* and *Swarag Se Sunder*. He recalled, 'K. Bapaiah was very down to earth, hardworking and focused. He always wore military-coloured shirts and pants to get into the mood for work. He was an early riser and very punctual.'[23]

Ek Duuje Ke Liye was the only major box-office winner for K. Balachander, who later received the Dadasaheb Phalke Award for his contribution to cinema in 2010. Among his other notable efforts was the vastly underrated *Zara Si Zindagi* (dialogues: Gulzar, 1983), a realistic take on the lives of three unemployed young men. Within the matrix of commercial cinema, *Ek Nai Paheli* (1984) again tackled a tricky topic: love can cross any generational barrier. Hema Malini was paired with Kamal Haasan and Raaj Kumar with Padmini Kolhapure. Both movies vanished like bubbles in water.

Dasari Narayana Rao (DNR) was a cult figure in Telugu films. Most of his Hindi films were either social dramas or action flicks. His 1978 film, *Swarag Narak*, did modest business. But *Jyoti Bane Jwala* (1980) was a box-office sensation. Hyper melodrama *Yeh Kaisa Insaf* (1980) broke even. But other films such as *Prem Tapasya*, *Yaadgaar* and *Asha Jyoti* tanked.

One of his most talked-about movies was *Aaj Ka M.L.A Ram Avtar* (1984), a political comedy starring Rajesh Khanna. The actor played a barber who becomes a proxy chief minister and then uses his guile to pay back the crafty politicos in their own coin. The film, especially Khanna's performance, received praise but failed to interest the audience.

Like several other southern directors, speed was DNR's forte. *Aaj Ka M.L.A Ram Avtar* was locked in a three-way race to the finish with Amitabh Bachchan's *Inquilaab* and Jeetendra's *Yeh Desh*. DNR was the first to complete the film. But all three flopped.

Dadasaheb Phalke winner K. Vishwanath, a giant of Telugu films, arrived with the winning *Sargam* (1979), the movie that introduced Jaya Prada to Bombay cinema. His movies were always a cut above the routine. *Jaag Utha Insan* was a poignant intercaste love story. But barring *Kaamchor* and *Sanjog*, his movies failed to excite the cash counters in the

1980s. Vishwanath passed away on 2 February 2023 at the age of ninety-two. Director Bapu found limited success with *Hum Paanch, Bezubaan* and *Prem Pratigyaa*, but a superhit eluded him.

Noted Tamil filmmaker Bharathiraja, who directed Sridevi in her flop Hindi debut *Solva Sawan* (1979), also helmed *Red Rose* (1980), a remake of the Kamal Haasan hit thriller, *Sigappu Rojakkal*. Despite good music and progressive themes, his other movies such as actor Kumar Gaurav's *Lovers* (1983) and the Sunny Deol-Poonam Dhillon starrer, *Saveray Wali Gaadi* (1986) all missed the mark, commercially as well as critically.

Producer-director K. Ravi Shankar was hugely successful during this period. He directed hits such as *Sindoor* and *Dariya-dil* and was the executive producer of box-office biggies *Ghar Ek Mandir* and *Swarag Se Sunder*, both family sagas.

Ghar Ek Mandir was produced by his father A. Krishnamoorthy. Ravi Shankar recounted how risk-taking paid off for the father-son duo. 'The movie cost Rs 60-70 lakh. When we decided to first release the film in Delhi-UP territory only rather than going for an all-India release, everybody said we are taking a big risk,' he recalled.[24]

'After the Delhi release of *Ghar Ek Mandir*, I went to a theatre in Worli to gauge the audience reaction on the first day, first show. There were only five people in the hall, including me. I saw a young couple in the empty hall. Normally young couples in empty auditoriums are not expected to concentrate on the film. But these two were almost oblivious of each other's presence and engrossed in the movie. After the movie, I gave a call to my dad and told him, "The movie has clicked",' he said.[25]

Padmalaya Studios, which produced at least twelve Hindi films in the 1980s, started their northern sojourn with *Takkar* (1980), a Jeetendra-Sanjeev Kumar flop. By 1983, they were the big boys of the circuit with *Himmatwala* and *Mawaali* under their belt. In fact, the studio became synonymous with southern masala movies of the era.

The banner used to be a three-man show. 'G. Hanumantha Rao was my brother. In some films, even in Telugu, he is the producer and I am the executive producer. In other films, the roles are reversed. After he passed away, I stopped making Hindi films,' said G.A. Seshagiri Rao.[26] Krishna, the hugely popular actor who passed away on 15 November 2022, completed the trinity.

Apart from Padmalaya, producer D. Ramanaidu's Suresh Films—*Tohfa* and *Maqsad* (both 1984), *Insaaf Ki Awaaz* (1986) and *Rakhwala* (1989)—was another exceptionally successful banner. 'He has displayed an inherent savvy that has put many veterans in the shade,' an article said about Ramanaidu.[27]

A. Poornachandra Rao (banner: Lakshmi Productions) was a colossus of the film trade. Also a communist leader, Rao displayed an openness to rope in north Indian directors. He teamed up with director Vijay Anand, then admittedly past his swaggering best, for *Ram Balram* (1980), a film that revived the *Sholay* pairing of Amitabh-Dharam without success. He also made the moderately successful *Chaalbaaz* (1989), a reworked *Seeta Aur Geeta*. But Poornachandra Rao's bigger hits were directed either by T. Rama Rao (*Ek Hi Bhool*, 1981; *Andhaa Kaanoon*, 1983; *Maang Bharo Sajana*, 1984) or Bhagyaraj (*Aakhree Raasta*, 1986).

The influx of southern films also opened the doors for heroines from Tamil and Telugu films. In the past, many leading ladies— from Vyjayanthimala to Padmini Kolhapure to Hema Malini— had ruled Hindi films. There were others who had ventured into Bombay waters—Padmini's sister Ragini, who acted opposite Ajit in the low-budget superhit adventure yarn, *Shikari*; B. Saroja Devi (*Sasural*); Jamuna (*Hamrahi, Milan*); Savitri (*Ganga Ki Lahren*), and Bharathi (*Ghar Ghar Ki Kahani, Hum Tum Aur Woh*).

In the 1980s, Sridevi became heroine No. 1, with Jaya Prada a popular second. Apart from these two, several heroines from the South acted in Hindi films with lesser degree of success, notably Madhavi (*Ek Duuje Ke Liye, Andhaa Kaanoon, Geraftaar, Loha, Pyar Ka Mandir, Kalyug Aur Ramayan*) and Swapna (*Ek Din Bahu Ka, Hukumat, Dacait, Aage Ki Soch*).

Male stars were a more complicated story. Barring Gemini Ganesan who delivered a couple of hits such as *Miss Mary*, others were unable to make headway. NTR's *Naya Aadmi* (1957) turned out to be a dud. Sivaji Ganesan presented *Rakhi* (1962), which earned Ashok Kumar a *Filmfare* best actor award, and made a special appearance as a patriot in *Dharti* (1970).

Kamal Haasan and Rajinikanth changed the picture dramatically. Both carved out larger success stories. In Bombay cinema, top heroes were generally moustache free. Facial hair in any form—beard or whiskers—was an exception, not the rule. Kamal Haasan broke that unwritten code successfully.

Hindi spoken with an accent was considered a turn-off those days. He rode over that seeming disability. The playback of both stars was often provided by S.P. Balasubrahmanyam, who sang with a pronounced accent. That many songs became a hit and so did Balasubrahmanyam was indicative of a more embracing North.

Kamal Haasan had all the ingredients in the thali that made a hero in the 1980s. He could dance and fight; as a bonus he could emote too. The actor found stardom and, consequently, fandom with *Ek Duuje Ke Liye*. 'Whether he is dancing, stunt-riding or brooding, his is a solid untricky acting. He squeezes all the juice out of the part without chewing up its rind,' wrote an overjoyed film reviewer.[28]

Kamal Haasan was the film's star centre. His impishness shone through in the song-and-dance sequence inside the lift, 'Mere jeevan saathi pyaar kiye jaa'. His impassioned dying, Ms Agnihotri in embrace, with angry waves lashing at the rocks got embossed in many a memory. Those who loved the movie saw it dozens of times. His guru K. Balachander told *Screen*,

'He is a director's delight. He is like wax. You can mould him any way you want and he adds something of his own and comes out with a beautiful performance every time. I am very proud of him.'[29]

His second film, *Sanam Teri Kasam*, directed by Narendra Bedi, had little to recommend itself barring R.D. Burman's music. But it worked. When asked in an interview why he acted in the film, Kamal Haasan said, 'Because of [the late director] Mr Narendra Bedi. When I asked for the story, he replied, "If you want a script, I can give it to you. But I am afraid, there's no story." He said it was going to be like a Nasir Hussain-Shammi Kapoor film. I was zapped by his frankness. Since I don't follow anyone's acting style or method, I don't mind doing anything as long as I am not repulsed. I can dance, cry, love, hate, roar, whimper, kung-fu.'[30]

Two of Kamal Haasan's best Hindi movies, *Sadma* (director: Balu Mahendra) and *Zara Si Zindagi* (director: K. Balachander) crashed. The last scene of *Sadma*, where he performs monkey tricks on a railway platform to make Sridevi recall her days of forgetting, still makes men and women cry. And he brought the right balance of frustration and barely controlled anger in the interview sequence in *Zara Si Zindagi*. You feel like shouting with him, 'Education down down, nepotism down down, democracy down down, Hindustan zindabad!'

He also over-emoted, a recurring feature, in Ramesh Sippy's ambitious movie, *Saagar*. But the *Filmfare* jury preferred that and gave him the best actor award. And while two of his action-comedy films—*Yeh To Kamaal Ho Gaya* and *Geraftaar*—were moderately successful, he also had a long list of flops: *Ek Nai Paheli*, *Yeh Desh*, *Yaadgaar*, *Karishmaa*. By 1986, Kamal Haasan had stopped doing Hindi films. He would return a decade later.

Bangalore-born Rajinikanth had a longer innings. With flaming eyes and flying fists, he arrived with *Andhaa Kaanoon* (1983) two years after Kamal Haasan. As an ingenious young man who keeps outmaneuvering his police officer sister

(Hema Malini), the quick-gun action star earned plenty of seetis and taalis, especially from front-stall crowds. In normal circumstances, the spotlight would have been firmly focused on the Tamil superstar hoping to create a Bombay dhamaka. But *Andhaa Kaanoon*, released in April 1983, was also among the first of Bachchan's films released after his serious injury on the sets of *Coolie*. Big B's extended cameo—long enough to fetch him a *Filmfare* best supporting actor nomination—hogged most of the headlines.

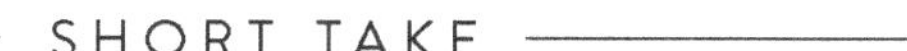

SHORT TAKE

Anant Nag

Kannada filmstar Anant Nag acted in several Hindi films in the 1970s and '80s. Among his notable films in the 1980s were Shyam Benegal's *Kalyug* and two supernatural flicks, Aruna-Vikas's *Gehrayee* and *Mangalsutra*.

This left Rajinikanth in a strange situation: he had delivered a hit but was unable to claim ownership. Little did he know that the peculiar predicament would keep happening in his unremarkable Hindi film career in the 1980s.

'I didn't expect to hit Bombay like a tidal wave. With *Andhaa Kaanoon*, I expected and got a good entry. *Jeet Hamaari* was okay, an average film. *Meri Adaalat* is doing better business,' said the son of a constable who had worked as a coolie and a bus conductor before getting into the movie business.[31]

In an interview to *Film Information* in 1984, Rajini said, 'I combine the histrionics of Sivaji Ganesan and the mannerism, to a certain extent, of Shatrughan Sinha. For the angry [young] man role I am influenced by Amitabh Bachchan.'[32]

Andhaa Kaanoon aside, only a handful of Rajinikanth movies really worked at the cash counters. And when they did, someone else always got the credit. In *Geraftaar* (1985), Rajinikanth made an electrifying 'special appearance', but Kamal Haasan and Big B had more central parts. Yet, when he threw a cigarette in the air and lit it with a bullet in the film, the audience whistled loud enough to interest producers and distributors.

In *Chaalbaaz* (1989), the spotlight was firmly on Sridevi in her 'Seeta Aur Geeta' double act. Big B and his 'Jumma chumma de de' chant, along with Kimi Katkar's cleavage, grabbed much of the eyeballs in *Hum* (1991). And in *Phool Bane Angaray* (1991), Rekha became the film's real hero after her husband (Rajinikanth) is bumped off. Perhaps 1980s Bombay cinema wasn't entirely convinced about the Tamil superstar's box-office potential.

His Hindi filmography includes a long list of embarrassing flicks that the hero himself may not remember: *Aaj Ka Dada, Mera Intaqam, Dosti Dushmani, Gair Kanooni, Tamacha, Zulm Ki Zanjeer* and *Insaniyat Ke Devta.*

While well-known directors such as Mukul Anand (*Hum*), K.C. Bokadia (*Phool Bane Angaray*), Pankaj Parashar (*Chaalbaaz*), and Ramesh Sippy (well past his prime in *Bhrashtachar*) gave him roles, Rajinikanth was always part of a larger package, a great 'add-on' to the overall commercial Hindi film thali. None of them presented him an author-backed role that maximised his expansive screen persona.

Southern directors did come up with more central parts: T. Rama Rao (*John Jaani Janardhan*), S.P.M. Raman (*Mera Intaqam*), Dasari Narayana Rao (*Wafadaar*), A.T. Raghu (*Meri Adaalat*), and D. Rajshekhar (*Gangvaa*). His triple role in *John Jani Janardhan*, especially his heavily stylised police inspector John A. Mendez, was totally paisa vasool. Even in the title role of *Gangvaa*, an innocent villager forced to become a dacoit, Rajini was impressive. Unfortunately, none of them became a superhit.

Delhi-based former film distributor Sanjay Mehta says

Kamal Haasan took his chances, made strong offbeat films. But Rajinikanth stuck to familiar themes. 'Ironically, Rajinikanth today has a bigger market in north India than in the 1980s.'[33]

There was plenty of cross-fertilisation in the film production business between the North and South in the 1980s. North Indian producers saw merit in using southern directors for their films. K. Vishwanath tried to offer a balance between the popular and the classy for producer Rakesh Roshan in *Kaamchor* and *Jaag Utha Insan*. Shabnam Kapoor roped in the prolific T. Rama Rao for *Watan Ke Rakhwale* and K. Bapaiah for *Pyar Ka Mandir*. Bapu's services were procured by producer Surendra Kapoor for *Hum Paanch*. Kannada director Kashinath was actor-producer Sujit Kumar's choice for the titillating *Anubhav*. K.C. Bokadia got Vijay Reddy for *Ganga Meri Maa*; Anil Rathi signed up K. Bapaiah for *Mard Ki Zabaan*.

There's more. Raj N. Sippy got noted Tamil film director-cinematographer Balu Mahendra for *Sadma*. Barkha Roy's *Karishmaa* and Mukul Roy's *Patita* were helmed by I.V. Sasi. Dasari Narayana Rao called the shots in *Jyoti Bane Jwala* for Jeetendra's home production. Producer Balubhai Shah's flop *Kahani Ek Chor Ki* was directed by S. Ramanathan.

The converse, too, happened at times. Producer S. Ramanathan's *Geraftaar* and A. Suryanarayana's *Hifazat* were both directed by Prayag Raj. A. Suryanarayana got Pankaj Parashar for *Chaalbaaz*. Vimal Kumar's *Dariya-dil* was remade in Telugu. Dasari Narayana Rao bought the film's rights.

REEL 8

SIX STARS—AND THREE OTHERS—WHO DEFINED THE DECADE

AMITABH BACHCHAN

Why the Eighties was Big B's most unpredictable decade

An injury that almost killed him, a whirlwind spell in politics and a rollercoaster of box-office biggies and bombs, the Eighties was the most volatile decade in the professional life of Amitabh Bachchan.

The decade started with three booming but predictable hits: *Dostana* (1980), *Laawaris* (1981) and *Namak Halaal* (1982). Then the unthinkable happened. An unintentional blow from fellow actor Puneet Issar felled him during *Coolie's* shooting on 26 July 1982. The stomach injury caused massive internal bleeding. For several weeks, Bachchan's life hung by the thinnest of threads. India prayed.

The injury became a national talking point. For many days, newspapers carried his health report on the front page. 'But like the superhero he often played in masala movies, Bachchan staged a remarkable recovery. *Coolie* became the biggest hit of 1983; the shot where he was injured was retained.'[1]

In his autobiography, Bachchan's *Coolie* co-star Rishi Kapoor recalled the day when Big B returned to shoot, six months after the injury at Reclamation Ground, Bombay. He said, 'Over one lakh people turned up for the shoot and local *dadas* had to be requisitioned for the *bandobast* as it was beyond the means of the police. I still remember the charged atmosphere every time Amitabh stepped out into the open and the crowd let out a roar, the likes of which I hadn't heard before. More than thirty years later, it still rings in my ear. It only reaffirmed what a huge star he was.'[2]

Actress Rameshwari recalled Jeetendra's wry observation: '*Koi kitna bhi haath paon maar le par* (Try as much as you can), Bachchan saheb is 1 to 10 and after that we are all 11, 12, 13.'[3]

Two years later on 31 October 1984, Prime Minister Indira Gandhi was assassinated by her bodyguards. As her elder son Rajiv Gandhi took over the reins of the Congress party, Bachchan impulsively jumped into electoral politics to boost his friend. He won handsomely from Allahabad but quit politics ingloriously, a Bofors-ed exit, and resigned from the Lok Sabha in 1987.

Despite the setbacks and the schisms, the Allahabad-born actor was the dominant star of the decade, especially during 1980-85. Yet it is equally true that the megastar slid into a difficult phase of his career thereafter. His films continued to garner the largest advance bookings and corner the maximum initials but they were unable to sustain the momentum. By the time the decade was over, he was like an emperor whose kingdom was being nibbled away.

In the Eighties, Bachchan primarily recycled the past. Raj N. Sippy's *Satte Pe Satta* (1982), inspired by Hollywood's *Seven Brides for Seven Brothers* (1954), was his only novel commercial film where he surprised the audience and his fans in a positive way. In an interview with Nasreen Munni Kabir, Javed Akhtar admitted that the writing duo had little new to offer to Amitabh. He said, 'After *Trishul* and *Don*, we failed as writers. We didn't do anything worthwhile...*Dostana* was a very big hit—at best it was a competent film...*Shaan, Dostana*—that's what we gave

Amitabh. Somewhere we lost that intensity and that quality.' Salim-Javed, who gave him his best lines, were past their prime and went separate ways in 1981.[4]

Ramesh Sippy's *Shakti* (1982), released after the split, was one of their better scripts. A father-son face-off where love and loathing are two sides of the same coin, *Shakti* was a casting coup. Dilip Kumar and Amitabh Bachchan matched histrionics for the first time. But the heavily publicised film only recovered its costs.

Apart from writer pair Salim-Javed, four directors were fundamental to the construction of the Bachchan mega brand: Prakash Mehra, Yash Chopra, Manmohan Desai and Hrishikesh Mukherjee. By the time the decade ended, barring Chopra, all had been reduced to has-beens. *Bemisal* (1982), Mukherjee's last film with Bachchan, barely recovered its cost. They never worked together after that. Even Chopra, the director of *Deewaar* and *Trishul*, found other actors to work with after the failure of *Silsila* (1981). The film meandered like a badly written poem amidst unprecedented hype. He too never directed a film with Big B again.

Both Mehra (*Laawaris, Namak Halaal, Sharaabi*) and Desai (*Coolie* and *Mard*) sought to tap Bachchan's versatility. Back in the late 1970s, the actor harnessed the Indo-Gangetic plains lingo to good effect in films such as *Don, Adalat* and *Ganga Ki Saugand*. Efforts were made to target region-specific audiences. Remember the scene in *Laawaris* where he pulls baddies out of smoke and abuses them in Telugu, Bengali, etc. In director Ravi Tandon's *Khud-Daar*, 'Angrezi mein kehte hain' channelised the same idea through a song. The dancers wore clothes to accentuate their state identity. In *Namak Halaal*, he employed the Haryanvi lingo.

By giving him acres of performing space, these movies maximised the star's charisma. Bachchan acknowledged in a 1982 interview, 'Putting it very basically, you're doing a [Marlon] Brando, a Burt Reynolds, a John Travolta and a Jerry Lewis—all in one.'[5] But the show was getting stale.

None of these box-office smashes took the Bachchan story forward. *Coolie* (dialogues: Kader Khan) and *Mard* (dialogues: Inder Raj Anand) were long essays in old masala. *Coolie* gained immensely from the accident. *Mard* made millions but it was essentially a Dara Singh buffet with a Michelin star. By 1986, Bachchan, the variety performer, had been mined empty. And it reflected in the collections.

Two southern productions did a better job at channelising his maturity. T. Rama Rao's *Andhaa Kaanoon* (1983) and K. Bhagyaraj's *Aakhree Raasta* (1986) understood that the Angry Young Man had grown up to be the Angry Middle-Aged Man. The elderly bearded avenger in *Andhaa Kaanoon* was the right fit for his age. The audience whistled and clapped every time the older Bachchan hoodwinked his younger self in *Aakhree Raasta*.

Anand's *Shahenshah* (1988) was Bachchan's last profit-making hurrah in the 1980s. To beat the piracy threat, the movie was released simultaneously in a record 300 cinema halls all over the country. In several cities, the film's advance booking opened twelve days before its release and tickets for all shows of the first week were sold out the very first day. Ismail Patel, manager, Navrang Theatre, Andheri, Bombay, said, 'The day we started selling tickets for *Shahenshah*, the theatre ground was packed with people. It was difficult to control the crowd. Finally, we had to call the police to help us maintain order... I believe tickets are being sold in black for Rs 50 and above, but we can't do anything about it.'[6] Tickets cost between Rs 5 and Rs 10 then.

At Ganesh cinema, Sri Ganganagar, the film opened a day before it was scheduled to be released, after the public learnt that the print had reached the town. They began to shout outside the cinema for a screening. The management had no option but to comply as even the police couldn't disperse the restless fans.[7]

Movie magazine said that 'after a long time, twenty prints of an Indian film were delivered for the overseas circuit. It is also the first time a Hindi film has been released on two video cassettes, which are being sold for more than Rs 500 per set. Reportedly, the buyer of domestic video rights paid approximately Rs 22 lakhs for the rights of *Shahenshah*, which is twice the amount paid for the rights of a film starring two heroes! And on distribution, he recovered as much as Rs 10 lakhs from one sponsor [Garware] alone.'[8]

Yet the movie (story: Jaya Bachchan) failed to sustain the initial hype. *Trade Guide* gave it an A rating alongside *Dariyadil* and *Pyar Ka Mandir*, but ranked it below *Tezaab* (AI) and *Qayamat Se Qayamat Tak* (AII), the major winners of the year.

——————————— SHORT TAKE ———————————

Mr Punctuality

Stories about Bachchan's punctuality abound. Director Ravi Tandon recalled, 'Once we were shooting the song, "Mach gaya shor saari nagri mein", for *Khud-Daar* at Chandivali studio. The shift timing had been changed the previous night from 7 a.m. to 9.30 a.m. But nobody bothered to tell Amitabh who came on time. 'When we arrived, we saw him watering the ground. Everybody was profusely apologetic. In such situations, heroes come down heavily on everybody around them. He just said, *"Chalo isi bahane mujhe paani dalne ka time mil gaya. Kaafi dhool udti hai. Yeh mitti mujhe bahut nuksaan karti hai* (This gave me a good opportunity to water the area. The dust hurts me a lot).'" Bachchan is asthmatic.[9]

Main Azaad Hoon (1988) at least walked a new line. Actor Tinnu Anand, maker of the modestly successful potboiler *Kaalia* (1981), interrogated the media's pursuit for sensationalism. The film was written by Javed Akhtar and inspired by Hollywood's *Meet John Doe*. Amitabh was miscast as a drifter turned crusader. He looked Amitabh, not the part, in a film that tried to be realistic.

Things got worse. Manmohan Desai's *Gangaa Jamunaa Saraswathi* (1988) and Prakash Mehra's *Jaadugar* (1989) flopped. *Toofan* (1989) disappeared faster than pistachios at a party. Bombay cinema's Hero No. 1 had to navigate a challenging 1990s—more lows than highs—before reasserting himself through Star TV's *Kaun Banega Crorepati* in 2000.

SRIDEVI

How a Himmatwali became bigger than the hero

If Hindi cinema is the opium of the masses, Sridevi was its biggest supplier in the 1980s. With a roll of her eyes and a shimmy of her hips, she became a stairway to heaven for millions of sweaty cinegoers in sweatier theatres. Across India, her photographs adorned autorickshaws, her posters hung in barber shops, and her poses provided amiable employment to calendar artists.

Who is the hero of *Nagina* or *Mr. India*? Who is the centre of attraction in *Chaalbaaz* or *Chandni*? In these films, made by established production houses, A-list heroes played supporting acts. These films revolved around her. And they were all runaway hits. Her clout can be judged by K.C. Bokadia's rare flop, *Main Tera Dushman* (1989), where Sridevi rescues hero Jackie Shroff from the clutches of the villain and delivers more punches than him in the fight scene that follows. She, not the 'hero' with facial hair, hacks down the villain (Anupam Kher). In an era when heroines were often effaced from the climax, Sridevi radically recast the gender script.

The 1980s were her most prolific years. She acted in a staggering 150-odd Tamil, Telugu and Hindi films in that period, roughly fifteen films a year. Many were forgettable but generally Sridevi managed to rise above the rubble. Like any good artiste, she was often better than the movie.

In Hindi films, Sridevi had first worked as a pre-teen in *Julie* (1975) but made her debut in Bharathiraja's *Solva Sawan* (1979). She triggered a tsunami with *Himmatwala* (1983). Producer G.A. Seshagiri Rao recalled that Jaya Prada had originally played the role of the bold and brassy daughter of a zamindar in the Telugu version. 'Bombay film industry wanted us to take Jaya Prada, not Sridevi. But we wanted to introduce someone new,' he said.[10]

There was nothing new or remarkable about the part or the film, which had traces of *The Taming of the Shrew*. But the public enjoyed her adipose-friendly voluptuousness and her easy dance movements. There was something paisa vasool about her that *Mawaali* (1983) and *Tohfa* (1984) further established. One of the most enduring images of 1980s Bombay cinema is Sridevi dressed like an apsara, sitting among rows and rows of copper vessels in *Tohfa*.

Many years later, Sridevi was asked if she was peeved by the tag 'Thunder Thighs', which gossip magazines used for her. She said, 'It [the tag] was given to me at the time of *Himmatwala*. I was very chubby then, I weighed 75 kg. At the time of *Chandni*, I lost weight and came down to 57 kg, which I think helped me a lot to improve my dancing.'[11]

What fresh ingredient did Sridevi bring to the table? Film critic Deepa Gahlot wrote, rather presciently, in January 1984, 'This girl has brought with her the oomph of Mumtaz, the discipline of the South, talent [*Sadma*] and charm entirely her own and joined the race for superstardom which she shows all signs of winning...'[12]

When the Eighties began, the Hindi film industry had two batches of heroines at work. Some had made their debuts in the early 1970s or earlier: Hema Malini, Zeenat Aman, Rekha, Parveen Babi and Reena Roy. Rekha was in her prime and pomp. Hema and Zeenat were still the prima donnas but, to use a golf analogy, in the back nine of their careers.

GenNow was Padmini Kolhapure, Rati Agnihotri, Poonam

Dhillon, Anita Raaj, Tina Munim, Amrita Singh and Kimi Katkar. All debuted on different dates but were poised to take the big leap.

But Sridevi overtook them all. Suffering Savitri in family dramas or fun girl in frothy entertainers, she could do them both. As producer G.A. Seshagiri Rao put it, 'Generally heroines were either performance-oriented or good-looking. Sridevi was a combination of both.'[13]

But above all, she could build an invisible bridge that dissipated the distance between the viewer and the performer.

At the end of 1984, columnist Ali wrote in *Screen*, 'People forgot the Sridevi of *Solva Sawan* and fell in love madly with the Sridevi of *Himmatwala, Mawaali, Maqsad, Sadma, Tohfa* and *Naya Kadam*. The love affair grew stronger with time. She was pronounced the No. 1 heroine and there were no two opinions—not even amongst the other younger heroines who were in the race.'[14]

Simply put, Sridevi brought in a fusion of elements that others couldn't. Her dance moves were marked by effortlessness, an uncontrollable energy and a sense of fun. In *Nagina*, there is a manic intensity in her no-holds-barred, choreographed battle with Amrish Puri. As the years passed by, Sridevi kept reinventing herself and offering something new. One had glimpsed her comic timing in the ribald *Masterji* (1985) but the star took it to another level in *Mr. India* (1987) and *Chaalbaaz* (1989). Her mimicking of Raaj Kumar and Charlie Chaplin are some of the most fun moments of 1980s Hindi cinema.

Fellow performer Rameshwari said, 'Amitabh Bachchan had the ability to make any ridiculous situation look convincing. Sridevi also had that ability. She could do anything. She had a hunger to do more, like Mr Bachchan.'[15]

In an interview, Sridevi once said that exposing body was unavoidable on the way up. 'Any artiste at the beginning of her career doesn't mind doing some bold scenes and wearing revealing clothes. That is necessary for glamour as well as for inching your way up. But slowly, one must give up these things and get into doing good roles.'[16]

A stylish romance, Yash Chopra's *Chandni* (1989) belonged to that category. The truth is Sridevi also put Chopra back in the list of A-plus directors. The film was his first major hit in the 1980s. With *Chandni*, Sridevi signed off the decade on a triumphant note, even though fresh competition was around the corner: Madhuri Dixit (*Tezaab*, 1988) and Juhi Chawla (*QSQT*, 1988). She was on top of her game, and at the very top when the Eighties ended.

JEETENDRA

Mr Reliable's secret sauce? Reliability

In the 1980s, Jeetendra was the safest box-office bet. He was the producer's Kamdhenu, the inexhaustible cash cow. His films, unlike Bachchan's, did not see desperate young men lunging at the ticket counters, unless the movie was a *Mawaali*. They generally drew a steady audience. In a decade when several southern production houses made large-scale investments and produced an assembly line of movies, the filmstar emerged as their most reliable blue-chip stock. The Bombay-based actor was such a frequent flier to Chennai and Hyderabad that he reportedly carried an open air-ticket in his shirt pocket all the time. During this period, he made more producers and distributors happy than any other star in Hindi films.

To arrive at this state of fiduciary grace, Jeetendra dumped his Gulzar-ish image of the Seventies created by *Parichay*, *Khushboo* and *Kinara*. He seemed to realise that serious, or even middle-of-the-road cinema, wasn't his cup of cutting chai. On the contrary, they had taken him away from his core fans. To woo them back, Jeetendra turned fully mercantile.

In the 1960s and '70s too, he had occasionally worked with banners based out of Madras. Now he raised his engagement with the South. 1980 became his breakthrough year. *Jyoti Bane*

Jwala (a home production directed by Dasari Narayana Rao) raked in big money. His biggest hit of the year, *Aasha*, though was directed by Bombay-based J. Om Prakash.

During 1980-1989, Jeetendra acted in about ninety Hindi films (excluding guest and special appearances), roughly nine a year. Of them, about 60 per cent were either made by southern-based banners or helmed by directors based out of Chennai or Hyderabad.

Broadly speaking, Jeetendra acted in three categories of southern films. The first was masala cinema (*Himmatwala*, *Mawaali*, *Maqsad*), which recast him in a new version of his older, dancing Jumping Jack avatar. A sub-category in the same format was the 'avenger' movies (*Jyoti Bane Jwala*, *Meri Aawaz Suno*, *Zakhmi Sher*), where he generally put on a beard for a toughie look. The second was the family romantic yarn (*Tohfa*, *Maang Bharo Sajana*). The third was the family social drama (*Sanjog*, *Swarag Se Sunder*, *Pyar Ka Mandir*, *Sindoor*).

Southern filmmakers loved him because he was disciplined, had no starry hang-ups, and readily followed the script and the director's orders. Director K. Ravi Shankar, who directed him in *Sindoor*, attested, 'Jeetendra used to report for shooting at 10 a.m. and finish shooting at 6.30, do the dubbing and then leave.'[17]

This was markedly different from several other Bombay stars, whose names were synonymous with egos, tantrums and coming late on the sets. Director T. Rama Rao remembered Jeetendra as a 'very cooperative actor' who 'mixed with the unit'. 'He ensured that business was done,' he said.[18]

Producer G.A. Seshagiri Rao of the famed Padmalaya films, who made about ten films with him described Jeetendra as a professional who 'understood all the business aspects of commercial cinema.'[19]

'When I moved to Hindi film production in the 1980s, I started our company with him. Almost fifteen days every month, he used to be with us in Hyderabad for either our film or some other film,' Seshagiri Rao said.[20]

The actor would directly negotiate his terms with the producer. 'We used to give him Bombay territory as fees. In the South, about 20 per cent of the cost was the hero's remuneration. *Meri Aawaz Suno* and *Himmatwala* cost Rs 1 crore,' Rao said.[21]

Jeetendra could seamlessly slip into the role of a college student, the middle-aged elder brother or the father. His main competitor was Rajesh Khanna, a better actor. But Khanna also had ego and obesity issues. Jeetendra was a better dancer and fitter than most of his contemporaries. Co-star Rameshwari remembered going to Vaishno Devi with him during the shooting of *Aasha*. 'My hairdresser was with me and we were panting during the climb. He had reached the top in a jiffy.'[22]

Shatrughan Sinha, his co-star in *Khudgarz*, laconically assessed: 'He was not a major star like Rajesh Khanna and Dharmendra. But he had charm and discipline. Producers signed him for his behaviour and for his audience.'[23]

What is less known, is Jeetendra's uncanny ability to judge a script. Rameshwari said, 'He had the ability to understand and evaluate a film's script. He could sense whether it could become a success. Many look at a script from the importance of their own roles. He didn't think like that.'[24]

But Jeetendra was guilty of excess. The scenario started changing from 1985 onwards. In the summer of 1986 film magazine *Madhuri* ran a cover story, 'Jitendra *ka dakshini samrajya dhah raha hai* (Jeetendra's southern empire is collapsing).' The magazine pointed out that in the past year and half, a series of Jeetendra solos had flopped: *Hoshiyar, Akalmand, Balidaan, Haisiyat, Sarfarosh, Mera Saathi, Aag Aur Shola, Singhasan, Zakhmi Sher* and *Kaamyaab*.

'His star value has gone down. And the market of the Hindi films produced down South has slumped. The "lucky" star has now become a "risky" star,' journalist Satish Jain wrote.[25]

'The films had the same storyline, the same scenes, the same dances. Jeetendra looked so typed in these movies that even watching a new film you felt you were watching something seen before,' he wryly observed.[26]

Amidst the barrage of flops, Jeetendra delivered a rare hit in 1986 with *Swarag Se Sunder*, albeit in tandem with Mithun Chakraborty, who walked away with the plaudits. The following year, he had another major winner, Bombay-based Rakesh Roshan's *Khudgarz* (1987), this time joining hands with Shatrughan Sinha, who excelled.

In 1988, films such as *Kanwarlal* and *Majboor*, among others, made early exits from theatres. Yet at the beginning of 1989, *Trade Guide* reported, 'The luckiest star today is Jeetendra. His punctuality, reputation and goodwill have ultimately come to his rescue and brought him renewed fortune. He has signed two dozen new films in two weeks in December.' Once a Jeetendra, always a Jeetendra.

―――――――― SHORT TAKE ――――――――

Jeetu's self-assessment

Director K. Ravi Shankar, who directed Jeetendra in *Sindoor*, recalled the actor had to deliver some emotional lines in a death scene. 'The first take was good but I felt he could push himself more. I asked for another take. He told me in front of a hundred people, "This is your first movie. You are wasting raw stock bought from [sic] your father's money. I can't do any better than this." I told him, I believe you can do much better. The next take was much better and to my satisfaction.'[27]

MITHUN CHAKRABORTY

How the dancing star changed dancing

Mithun Chakraborty wasn't just a hero; he was an idea whose time had come. He emerged when theatres were facing a video piracy crisis and the gentry had abandoned them. The new cinema demographics demanded a new star that non-gentry cinemagoers, in a larger majority than ever before, could root for. Mithun was their most representative idol.[28]

His entry marks an important break from the other darlings of the underclass. Dara Singh was the ultimate macho man whom the frontbenchers revered. Amitabh Bachchan had fanatical following among all classes. But his screen persona of a rebel did not tally with his public school background. In Mithun's case, the frontbenchers both loved and identified with him. Unlike Bachchan, he seemed to be one of them. Watching him was self-fantasy fulfilment.

But the actor had to walk through a minefield of perceived flaws. He was swarthy, considered a major drawback those days. His voice was too husky and his Hindi dialogue delivery wasn't the best in business. Director Deepak Bahry says objections were raised when Mithun was signed for *Tarana* (1979), a shehri babu-meets-bholi banjaran tale of songs and ardour. 'People said why have you taken him? Some industry people complained to Rajkumar [Barjatya] that he was dark....I had met him in Pali Hill and felt that *iss ladke mein kuch hai* (This boy has something special),' said Bahry, who also directed Mithun in *Hum Se Hai Zamana, Hum Se Badhkar Kaun* and other films.[29]

In an era when star sons were launched with fanfare, the national award-winning actor of *Mrigayaa* (1977) had to carve out his space inch by inch. A careful perusal of Mithun's filmography shows a slow upward curve, from bit roles to big parts, from B-minus to B and A-grade ventures.

In 1969, Mithun had left Kolkata after getting into trouble over his Naxal links. It took him ten years to find success.

Year 1979 was his breakthrough year with *Surakksha*, where he played the hyper-sexual spy, Gunmaster G-9, and Rajshri's *Tarana*.

Dancing and fighting were the twin bedrocks of Mithun's stardom, which came with B. Subhash's *Disco Dancer* (1982). The director recalled how the film happened. 'We were shooting the last scenes of *Taqdeer Ka Badshah* at the Sood Bungalow in Versova. Mithun looked depressed. *Unees Bees* had released that day and the initial reports were not good. [*The film did better in the weeks that followed.*] He was also dealing with some emotional issues with his first wife, Helena Luke.

'To lift his spirits, I told him, "Look I am going to make a film with you and you are going to be a big star." When he asked what film, I said, "Disco Dancer". I could immediately see a spark in his eyes when he heard the title. I told him the story and he got very excited. I told my PRO Jagdish Aurangbadkar to announce the film. "B. Subhash produces and directs Disco Dancer, music by Bappi Lahiri",' remembered Subhash.[30]

At this point, Babbar Subhash had a story but no screenplay. Till then he was known as a reasonably competent director but not a very successful one. This was his own production and he started the film with all the energy he could muster. 'I put up big sets. Shakti Samanta saw them and asked me, *"Tum itna paisa kahan se laaya hai* (Where have you got the money from)?" I told him, *"Shakti-da, yeh film ka kamaal hai".*'[31]

Disco Dancer cost Rs 42 lakh. Mithun's fees: Rs 3 lakh. The film celebrated golden jubilee. *Film Information* reported that at some cinemas in Calcutta, the audience forced the cinemas to repeat the title track. The magazine also noted, 'At some suburban cinemas, the restless cinegoers, who could not get tickets, resorted to explosive [*sic*] violence by blasting bombs.'[32]

'The movie changed the way Hindi films looked at dancing; but more importantly, it also changed the way people danced on the streets,' said Mithun.[33] For years, his hairstyle was among the most imitated.

In an interview, the actor acknowledged that he learnt a lot about dancing from John (no surname), an Afro-American, who saw him dancing in Calcutta's Blue Fox restaurant and took him under his wing. He said, 'It's said I copy John Travolta. Forget it. If I've been influenced by anyone, it's Elvis Presley. He used to be an expert at shaking the pelvis. I shake my pelvis in my own style and let me tell you it isn't easy. It's simple to shake the body but pelvis dancing, without making it vulgar, requires years of practice and skill.'[34]

In Russia, *Disco Dancer* touched a chord like *Awaara* had done nearly three decades earlier. Umesh Mehra, who directed Mithun in seven movies, recalled a couple of anecdotes. 'We were attending the Moscow Film Festival and staying in the huge Hotel Rossiya, which had over 3,000 rooms and corridors stretching a kilometre. As we walked in this high-security hotel, Mithun's female fans would jump out of the shadows just to touch him.[35]

'Then one morning after breakfast we saw Robert De Niro walking out of the hotel gates to the viewing rooms. We decided to get his autograph and started running after him. As we approached he turned around and his gaze shifted behind us. We two were after De Niro and about a hundred fans were after Mithun,' remembered Mehra, whose *Ashanti* (1982) was an important movie in the actor's career.[36]

Over the years *Disco Dancer's* fame has spread further. In Tokyo, there's a shrine to the *Disco Dancer*. In Egypt, people serenade Indian tourists by singing the movie's songs.[37]

The film raised Mithun's brand value. Former Delhi-based film distributor Sanjay Mehta said that Japanese electronics giant National Panasonic preferred to use big stars to promote their products those days. 'When Mithun endorsed their product in the Eighties, it meant he had arrived, he said.'[38]

Mithun struck unexpected gold in the romantic family drama, *Pyar Jhukta Nahin* (1985), a film refused by Rishi Kapoor. The film underlined Mithun as a versatile star who could deliver across genres. Director Jagdish Sadanah revealed in an interview how everyone felt that Mithun had been miscast as the father of a seven-year-old child, and revealed having problems selling the film. He said, 'We had held a trial for the Rajshris when the film was ten reels ready. After the trial, Kamal babu [Barjatya] came up to me to tell me how much he had liked my film but he said he was sorry he wouldn't like to buy my film...I reasoned with him that Rajshri's biggest hit with Mithun was *Tarana,* in which Mithun did neither any fighting nor any disco dancing. But Kamal babu was still unconvinced.'[39]

Gradually, Bombay biggies fell in line: Rakesh Roshan (*Jaag Utha Insan*), Manmohan Desai (*Gangaa Jamunaa Saraswathi*), Raj N. Sippy (*Boxer, Baazi*), to name a few, though none of these films worked.

Bigger successes came in the melodramatic southern socials: *Ghar Ek Mandir* (1984), *Swarag Se Sunder* (1986), *Parivaar* (1987) and *Pyar Ka Mandir* (1988). In *Swarag Se Sunder*, both Mithun and Jeetendra worked together. 'Mithun's dialogues earned far more applause in the theatre than Jeetendra's,' wrote film magazine *Madhuri*.[40] Action dramas such as *Ghulami* (1985), *Jaal* (1986), *Watan Ke Rakhwale* (1987) and *Daata* (1989), were some of his other hits in the decade.

Simi Garewal, who directed him in *Rukhsat* (1988), said Mithun's strength lay in his sheer physicality, a lean but powerful presence. 'This physicality manifested itself in his action scenes as well as his dances. I don't think he had any "weaknesses" as such. He was an all-round good actor with a star presence,' she said.[41]

In September 1983, *Screen* had reported that he had signed sixty films and was doling out dates of early 1985.[42] In January 1986, *Filmfare* ran a cover with the line: 'Hit-Man, The Busiest Star of 1986'. At the heart of his signing spree was perhaps a feeling of insecurity. There was a time when he had slept on pavements and paid Rs 50 for the space.

Between 1980 and '89, Mithun acted in a mind-boggling

120 films, as per IMDb records—a few engaging, the majority humdrum. In 1989, he had a staggering twenty releases. He once said, 'I do three kinds of films. One kind of movies I do only for money. Another I do only to satisfy myself. The third kind I do to please my fans.'[43]

One of the reasons Mithun managed to do so many films was, as director K. Ravi Shankar explained, his spontaneity as an actor. He 'never gave multiple takes to improve himself and waste others' time. He used to rehearse once or twice and generally gave a very good first take.'[44]

Vimal Kumar, who directed him in *Swarg Yahan Narak Yahan* (1991), echoed the view. 'Mithun was a one-take artiste. If we went to the second take due to a technical problem, his level would dip by 5-10 per cent. He had a sharp memory. He would say, "Vimal-*da scene sunao* (relate the scene)," while putting on his make-up. He would remember the dialogues. He was technically sound; he would know if the zoom or the trolley was late.'[45]

In times when losing ventures vastly outnumbered the profit-making ones, Mithun was a rare hero who could be unerringly counted upon to draw a sizeable audience in the first few weeks. In other words, he had a loyal fan base who watched a film just because it was a Mithun film. These fans were spread across India and mostly belonged to the economically backward class. They ensured that a Mithun film, even when it lost money, grossed a basic minimum at the ticket counters, much to the relief of distributors.

Distributor Mehta said the underclass identified with him. 'Titles like *Ustadi Ustad Se* (1982), *Kasam Paida Karne Wale Ki* (1984), *Charanon Ki Saugandh* (1984), *Hisaab Khoon Ka* (1989), *Garibon Ka Daata* (1989) leave no one in doubt who they were meant for. Even his dance steps reminded you of the common man dancing at festivals or weddings,' he said.[46]

The actor strived to improve his own brand. 'I've performed better [in *Dance Dance*] than I did in *Disco Dancer*. I was specially thrilled by the long shot during the climax, it lasts 168 feet. For the number, I added the moonwalk, the robot dance and added my own thing. Ordinary disco and breakdance are out, you have to be inventive to be "in",' he once said.[47] *Dance Dance* created a record, drawing full house in all fifty-six shows during the first two weeks at Triveni, Bangalore. Youngsters in the audience danced and showered coins during Mithun's dance numbers.[48]

In an interview with *Star & Style* magazine in 1984, his father Basanta Kumar Chakraborty said, 'Mithun always has been a model son. The one time I got disappointed with my son was when Mithun got involved with the Naxalites. At that time, the movement was sweeping through Calcutta and it was rumoured that Mithun was the gang leader. Young boys involved with the Naxalites were being rounded up by the police in Calcutta and I didn't want my son to be caught. That is when I asked Mithun to leave home, I wanted him out of Calcutta.' They didn't speak to each other for seven years.

But his son did him proud. Not many Naxalites went on to become a filmstar, a hotel baron, a Rajya Sabha MP from Trinamool, and now a BJP politico, all rolled into one. In the Nineties, he was also one of the country's highest income-tax payers.

SHORT TAKE

Mithun among Maoists

In 2006, when I visited Chhattisgarh's Dantewada district to report on the Maoist insurgency, a VCD seller at Giddam block told me, 'Only two actors are in demand here: Mithun and Emraan Hashmi.' Interestingly, Mithun acted in K.A. Abbas' *The Naxalites* (1980).

GOVINDA

Virar ka chokra, galiyon ka badshah

If Mithun was an idea whose time had come, Govinda was a child of the times. His pelvic thrusts perfectly fitted the disco tracks that had lost their freshness and energy by now but which Bombay filmmakers continued to insert faithfully into their scripts as if it was part of their muscle memory.

Dance directors scratched their heads to look for innovative ways to depict these songs In *Ilzaam* (1986), they literally hit the streets. Govinda grabbed the chance.

Dressed in flaming-red tights, glowing like a pinball machine and breakdancing to a new beat, the young actor broadcast his arrival loud and clear. In his introductory track, 'I am a street dancer', the jiving was as effortless as breathing. In the opening credits, Govinda's name figured after Shashi Kapoor, Shatrughan Sinha, Raj Kiran, Anita Raj and Neelam. But it was the new boy that the audience took home. Producer Pahlaj Nihalani's *Ilzaam* wasn't Govinda's first signing (*Tan-Badan*) or first release (*Love 86*). But it was this triumphant action-drama directed by Shibu Mitra that assured his future in tinsel town.

Govinda came from a family of actors. His Gujranwala-born father, Arun Kumar Ahuja, was a reasonably successful singer-actor in the 1940s. Known by the screen name, Aroon, his body of work includes Mehboob Khan's famous *Aurat* (1940). His Benaras-born mother, Nirmala Devi, was a semi-classical singer and actor. Together they formed the lead in *Savera* (1942) and *Sehra* (1948). *Sehra* was also produced by them, its fiasco forcing them to sell off their prized bungalow off Carter Road. The family fell on hard times when Arun's health started failing and his wife sang in concerts and radio stations to keep the kitchen fire burning.

At seventeen, Govinda watched John Travolta's disco-driven *Saturday Night Fever*. It transformed him. Dance became the driver of Govinda's life. He later said, 'I tried to dance like

Travolta. I was very raw, so I tried to get some polish from Saroj [Khan] and Vijay Oscar, although I kept my original style.'[49]

At this stage, Govinda lived in the faraway suburb of Virar. He flitted like a bumblebee from one producer's office to another in search of work. He once told video magazine *Lehren*, 'I shifted to my mama-*ji*'s residence in Khar since commuting to and fro from Virar would take three to four hours.'[50] But the tag, 'Virar ka chokra', remained.

Govinda had prepared a video portfolio of his work. However, he was hesitant to show the cassette to mama-ji because the latter was making an action film. 'But he liked the video so much that he changed the subject and signed me for my first film, *Tan-Badan*,' the actor said.[51]

He went on to sign twenty films before his first release. In January 1986, *Trade Guide* declared that Govinda was 'the

Govinda (Photo Credit: *Madhuri*)

new face of the year' even before the release of a single film. Director Esmayeel Shroff's *Love 86* was his first release—on Valentine's Day, 1986. Two weeks later came *Ilzaam*.

Director Shibu Mitra recalled being shown a dance video clip of Govinda and being captivated by his sense of rhythm. 'Later when we met in person I was not so impressed. He was short, compared to other stars of that time. But as I spoke with him, I could see a fire in his eyes and was more than impressed,' Mitra said.[52] Govinda is 171 cm tall, roughly five feet and eight inches.

Both Mithun and Govinda came from modest backgrounds. They have been often compared to each other. But there was an age gap between the two which ensured that they did not compete for each other's parts. When *Ilzaam* happened, Govinda was twenty-three, Mithun was thirty-six. Govinda had a film industry background; Mithun did not. Govinda found success with his first movie. Despite a national award, Mithun wallowed for years doing bit roles. Mithun acted in New Wave films, Govinda didn't.

That aside, there were quite a few stylistic similarities between the two. Both danced well. Both became darlings of the underclass audience. Together, they subalternised the Bombay hero on celluloid.

Both also signed dozens of forgettable movies in the early part of their careers. Producer-director Vimal Kumar, who collaborated with Govinda in eight movies, reminisced, 'When I gave him a cheque of Rs 1 lakh for *Dariya-dil*, he kept it in the mandir at his home. He had never seen [so much] money.'[53]

Dariya-dil (1988) had a triumphant run. 'The film was made for Rs 70 lakh and it grossed the same amount from the Delhi-UP territory, which I distributed myself. I had paid Govinda Rs 4 lakh for the film. By the time, *Jaisi Karni Waisi Bharnii* (1989) was made, his price had shot up. I paid him Rs 6 lakh.' Kumar said.[54]

Between 1986 and 1989, Govinda acted in forty movies. Many of them flopped but he had an impressive share of hits too: *Ilzaam, Khudgarz, Sindoor, Marte Dam Tak, Dariya-dil* and *Jaisi Karni Waisi Bharnii*. Few of these were solo hits though. He was often one of the several heroes, and in some cases, he even played third fiddle (*Ilzaam, Khudgarz*). Yet he left an impression.

Producers felt Govinda was good value for money. Like Mithun, he had a loyal fan base. Alongside senior heroes such as Jeetendra, Shashi Kapoor, Shatrughan Sinha or Raaj Kumar, he enhanced a film's saleability, especially in small towns. Several older heroes were below-average dancers. Govinda brought a special skill set to the table, best visible in *Ilzaam* ('I am a street dancer'), *Khudgarz* ('Main se meena se na saaki se') and *Marte Dam Tak* ('Naam se kya lena').

However, Govinda was notorious for being late on sets, an outcome of having signed too many films. Kumar explained, 'He was doing four shifts at a time. He used to exercise at 11 p.m. after his work was over. *Jo 11-12 baje exercise karega, woh soyega kab aur uthega kab*(Anyone who works out at 11-12 at night, when will he sleep or get up)? Govinda got dubbed as the most troublesome actor in Bombay. When I understood his problem, I adjusted accordingly. Otherwise I wouldn't have made any film with him.'[55]

What's less known, is Govinda's battle against depression. Vimal Kumar recalled, 'In his childhood, Govinda was suffering from a disease which I don't want to name. To get rid of it, he started taking sleeping pills. I noticed this when I was shooting *Jaisi Karni Waisi Bharnii*. I saw his make-up man give him something. I took it from him. It was Restal 5mg. I came to know that he was taking five-six pills every day.'[56] Among other things, Restal is used to control anxiety.

Govinda admitted to his mental health issues in a 2014 interview. 'I had a nervous breakdown twice and had to be hospitalised. Producers would be standing outside the hospital waiting for me. People are not sensitive or interested in your problems, they just want to do business with you. I have had a lot of tragedies in my house, so while I may have looked fit, inside I was going through a lot,' he said.[57]

He also said, 'Dilip Kumar sahab was the only person in the film industry who could understand my problem. He was sensitive and could see that I was not okay and advised me to do comedy and yoga. My comedy films started working and like he had said, to a large extent, comedy helped me get out of my emotional problems.'[58] Dilip Kumar had worked with Govinda in *Izzatdaar* (1990). After acting in *Devdas* (1955), Dilip Kumar too needed psychiatric counselling. A London doctor had advised him to do comedies.

In the 1980s, Govinda was not a finished product yet. The stylish, rat-a-chat David Dhawan comedies, which became his forte, weren't yet part of his repertoire. His best would come in the 1990s.

Both Mithun and Govinda deserve a closer look in cinema studies. They were not only self-made stars who overcame their disadvantages to become long-distance winners, but also a cultural phenomenon. They were 'galiyon ke badshah' in the true sense of the word.

REKHA

How Rekha waltzed through the decade

Rekha peaked in the Eighties. In a television interview with Simi Garewal, she detailed how Amitabh Bachchan played a major role in her improvement and evolution, beginning with *Do Anjaane* (1976). Rekha also revealed how she had never met anyone like Bachchan and how his professionalism affected her positively. Her improved comic timing was evident in *Mr. Natwarlal* (1979) where the two talk of love and buffaloes.

With director Hrishikesh Mukherjee's *Khubsoorat* (1980), Rekha created a new fan club. The audience, which cinema hall managers describe as 'gentry' or 'balcony class', loved her elfin but warm-hearted girl act in *Khubsoorat*. The movie gave her a permanent place in middle-class hearts and became a reference point in her career.

'When I did *Khubsoorat* everyone fought with Hrishikesh Mukherjee for taking me. His unit felt I wouldn't be able to do it. It was child's play,' she crowed later.[59] The performance got her the *Filmfare* award for best actress.

In *Judaai* (1980), her character spanned thirty celluloid years. Playing mother to Sachin Pilgaonkar, who was just three years younger to her, showed a growing commitment towards heftier roles. Her professionalism and sense of empathy were also evident in an interaction with Ramesh Talwar, who directed *Baseraa* (1981). In her biography, *Rekha: The Untold Story,* Yasser Usman writes that Talwar had used his allotted dates but some scenes involving her were yet to be shot. Rekha was scheduled to leave for Madras to dub for another film but promptly adjusted after coming to know of the director's problem. 'She said, "Okay, I will finish your work before leaving. Whether it finishes tonight at eight or tomorrow night at eight, I will finish all the work".'

Vinod Pandey, who directed her in *Ek Naya Rishta* (1988), praised Rekha's professionalism. 'She even drove with me to check out on the bungalow in Alibagh where the character she played was to live,' he said.[60]

Pandey vividly recalled how he managed to fix an appointment with her at lunch during a film's shooting, thanks to a second assistant who had worked in *Umrao Jaan*. After she acquiesced, it came down to fees. 'This was 1983. She was the biggest star those days charging about Rs 10-11 lakh. I told her, in half-jest, "Rekha is the finest actress in the country. And your fee should be Rs 50 lakhs. But can we please remove a zero?" She laughed and said, "I won't do that. But I will charge just Rs 7 lakh for the film".'[61] The film, with Raj Kiran and Rekha making an unlikely pair, was made for Rs 27 lakh. It flopped.

Unlike most mainstream stars of that time, male or female, Rekha showed a keenness to work both in parallel cinema (*Kalyug*, 1981 and *Vijeta*, 1982) and middle cinema (*Umrao Jaan*, 1982, *Utsav*, 1984 and *Ijaazat*, 1987). To her credit, she did these films when she was at the Everest of her career.

One of her most controlled performance came in Govind Nihalani's *Vijeta*. As a woman who chews on her hurt and never raises her voice in an unrelenting cold war with her husband, Rekha created a rare mother in Bombay cinema. In those image-conscious times, it would have taken a lot of guts to play a mother to an actor (Kunal Kapoor) who was twenty-three. Rekha was twenty-eight then.

Muzaffar Ali's *Umrao Jaan* (1981) is among her more memorable parts. The movie walks us through the chequered life and loves of a courtesan in nineteenth century Lucknow, a city of pleasure for the elite. '*Umrao Jaan* was vulnerable yet a survivor. To give soul to the character, I had to go through her eyes. I felt Rekha could do it,' said Ali.[62]

Rekha's acting is overshadowed by her visual gorgeousness. She was controversially preferred for the national award over the pitch-perfect Jennifer Kendal (English schoolteacher Violet Stoneham) in Aparna Sen's *36 Chowringhee Lane*. In a 1986 BBC London television interview to Krishan Gould, Rekha admitted that she didn't deserve it for *Umrao Jaan*. In Gulzar's much-admired but little-watched *Ijaazat* (1987), a love story of missed opportunities, Rekha sank her teeth into the role of an older women in love with a younger man.

Jaal (1986), *Sansar* (1987), *Insaaf Ki Awaaz* (1986) and *Biwi Ho To Aisi* (1988) were all successful. In all these films, her roles were central and she also received top billing in the opening credits. But the film that earned her larger attention was producer-director Rakesh Roshan's *Khoon Bhari Maang* (1988), which required her to transform from a simpleton to a glam girl. Rekha also got the *Filmfare* award for best actress. Her star appeal remained undiminished through the decade.

──────────── SHORT TAKE ────────────

Plan to kidnap Rekha thwarted

A bid to kidnap Rekha for a ransom of Rs 20 lakh was foiled by Bombay police in 1989. The idea was to waylay her on the road while she would be on her way to shooting or for her morning jog, *The Times of India* reported on 2 July that year.

KADER KHAN

The master dialogue-smith

A hit film in the 1980s was more likely to have Kader Khan's name than anyone else's. Between 1980 and 1989, he acted in a confounding 175-odd films and wrote the dialogues for nearly fifty. *Meri Aawaz Suno, Namak Halaal, Sharabi, Coolie, Himmatwala, Tohfa, Karma, Swarag Se Sunder* and *Ram Lakhan* were some of the major winners he engaged with.

He was immensely influential in his prime. 'I was once asked, which of the two camps (Manmohan Desai or Prakash Mehra) you belong to. I said, both are in my camp,' he once said on the show, *Ek Mulaqat Star Ke Saath*.

Kader Khan's dialogues were the bedrock of the southern masala movies (*Himmatwala, Mawaali, Maqsad* and the like). In a sense, he defined them. It was common to hear, '*Film mein Kader Khan ka dialogue hai*', which meant that the film would have the kind of lines that drew claps, whistles and showering of coins. Just as Shankar-Jaikishen's music was a big attraction for distributors in the 1960s, Kader Khan's dialogues elevated a film's market value, especially in smaller towns.

A master of both Urdu and Hindi, Khan's earthy dialogues were laced with sharp puns and easy alliterations. His lines could be rousing, funny, even make handkerchiefs wet. He could be ribald too. As a writer-actor, Kader Khan often reserved the funniest lines for himself.

Khan also had the gift of making the ludicrous sound amusing: '*Sarkar agar is gaon ke sar hain to main uska seeng hoon. Aur jo hamari baat nahi manta main use seeng marke Singapore bana deta hoon*' (*Himmatwala*, 1983). He could also write precise and powerful lines that endure in popular memory: '*Is thappad ki goonj suni tumne, ab is goonj ki goonj tumhe sunai degi*' (*Karma*, 1986). Big B's rollicking Vijay Merchant-Vijay Hazare and Wasim Raja-Wasim Bari monologues (*Namak Halaal*, 1982) were also penned by him.

The comic villain was an old idea in Hindi cinema. Character actors Radhakant, Jeevan, Kanhaiyalal did the part in the 1950s and '60s. Even Pran occasionally clowned around in negative roles. So did Utpal Dutt in *The Great Gambler* and *Nishana*. Kader Khan created Comic Villain 2.0. In *Insaaf Ki Awaaz*, he played Chaurangi Lal Domukhiya, a double-speaking politician, who always issues two contrary press statements on the same topic at the same time.

As a character actor, too, Kader Khan showed an admirable range. Khan could be mean (*Naseeb*), mean but funny (*Himmatwala*), downright funny (Dr Bhooljana in *Ghar Ek Mandir*), even the family's long-suffering patriarch (*Jaisi Karni Waisi Bharnii*). He brought an oddball flourish to his characters that always connected with the paying public.

Kader Khan passed away in Canada on 31 December 2018. His virtues were his own, his failings were those of the times.[63]

BHANU ATHAIYA

India's first Oscar winner

In the foreword to her autobiography, *The Art of Costume Design* (2010), British filmmaker Richard Attenborough wrote that it took him 'seventeen long years to set up *Gandhi*, my dream film' and 'just fifteen minutes' to make up his mind that Bhanu Athaiya was the right person for the job. The director of *Gandhi* was spot-on. Hindi cinema's finest costume designer became India's first Oscar winner, recreating early twentieth-century India through attire.

A gifted painter and a JJ School of Arts graduate, Athaiya worked in some of Bollywood's finest movies from the 1950s: *Shree 420, Sahib Bibi Aur Ghulam, Sangam, Guide* and *Waqt*. In the 1980s, the Kolhapur-born designer continued to impress with her range: *Insaf Ka Tarazu, Karz, Ek Duuje Ke Liye, Nikaah* and *Ram Teri Ganga Maili*. She was the one who dressed up Sridevi in chiffon saris in *Chandni*.

She worked for three more decades. It is sad and shameful that Athaiya didn't even receive a Padma Shri. In 2012, she returned the Oscar to its original owner, the Academy of Motion Pictures Arts and Sciences, Los Angeles. She said, 'If Tagore's Nobel medal could be stolen, what is the guarantee my trophy would be safe? In India, no one values such things and we lack a tradition of maintaining our heritage and things pertaining to our culture.'[64] She passed away on 15 October 2020.

SAROJ KHAN

Moves of the decade

Before the Eighties, choreography in Bombay cinema was dominated by men: P.L. Raj, Gopi Krishna, Badri Prasad, Kamal, Herman Benjamin, among others. Saroj Khan tossed aside the gender barriers of this male-dominated world. Blending sensuality with rhythm, she brought to celluloid a bunch of timeless jhatkas and mudras that are still aped at dance parties and wedding sangeets. She composed the signature moves that paved Madhuri Dixit's rise to stardom courtesy 'Ek do teen' (*Tezaab*). Her shimmies and shakes gave an extra dimension to Sridevi's iconic 'Hawa hawaai' (*Mr. India*), 'Yeh ladki' (*Chaalbaaz*), and the fuming snake dances of *Nagina*. No other choreographer, male or female, has bagged eight Filmfare awards.[65]

Her Punjabi-Sindhi parents, who named her Nirmala, had left Karachi for Bombay during Partition. The family lived in a one-room tenement in Mahim. A neighbour who ran a foodstall offered them the unsold leftovers. She worked as a child star (*Nazrana, Aagosh*), a group dancer ('Aaiyye meherbaan', *Howrah Bridge*), even trained as a nurse, before becoming an assistant to noted dance director B. Sohanlal, who taught her the nuances of choreography and with whom she shared a close relationship. She later married Sardar Roshan Khan.

Among those who backed her talent was producer-director

Subhash Ghai. 'It was not until Ghai's *Hero* [1983] that [Saroj] Khan became a name to be reckoned with,' says *Encyclopaedia of Hindi Cinema*. She enjoyed a thriving career till her death on 3 July 2020.

The Fate of Other Stars

Producers queued up for them. They signed films by the dozen, worked two-three-four shifts every day. In the 1980s, these were the other stars that magazines made a living out of and the audience dreamt of in Eastmancolor.

Dharmendra: In his prime, his soft face and tough body combo was irresistible to men, women and distributors. That was the Seventies. In the 1980s, the He-Man showed box-office vulnerability. After *The Burning Train, Aas Paas, Krodhi, Professor Pyarelal* and *Razia Sultan* tanked, Dharam was no longer garam. Thereafter, he abandoned romcoms and family dramas. J.P. Dutta's violent *Ghulami* (1985) put him back in the front seat. By 1987, he had rediscovered his mojo as a no-apologies action hero (*Hukumat, Aag Hi Aag, Loha, Insaniyat Ke Dushman, Watan Ke Rakhwale*). The title of one film summed up his new stock-in-trade: *Paap Ko Jalaa Kar Raakh Kar Doonga* (1989).

Hema Malini: The Dream Girl of the 1970s was now the veteran Dream Girl of the 1980s. The spark could still be seen in *Kranti, Satte Pe Satta* and *Andhaa Kaanoon* in the early 1980s but Kamal Amrohi's labour of love, *Razia Sultan* (1983), dealt a crushing blow to her prima donna status. Ms Malini continued to be seen in B-grade outlaw films (*Ramkali, Durgaa, Sitapur Ki Geeta*). Meaningful films like *Ek Chadar Maili Si* and *Rihaee* gave her a sliver of critical acclaim but the crown of heroine No. 1 was gone.

Rajesh Khanna: The ex-superstar arrested his precipitous slide with hit socials like *Thodisi Bewafaii* and *Aanchal*. Two money-spinners in 1983—*Avtaar* and *Souten*—made optimistic fans believe that this could be Rajesh Khanna 2.0. It turned out to be a false dawn. The southern dramas kept him busy but the growing number of flops meant Kaka was now into his also-ran days.

Zeenat Aman: She was a 'model' success but could she act? In the 1980s, Zeenat Aman tried. Her sensational turn as an avenging rape survivor in *Insaf Ka Tarazu* was lauded by critics and audience alike. *Dostana, Qurbani* and *Alibaba Aur 40 Chor* further enhanced her box-office ratings. But then as flops began to stalk her, the big banners moved away.

Shatrughan Sinha: The Patna-born actor added taste and tadka to crowded multistarrers (*Kranti* and *Naseeb*) and high-profile face-off flicks (*Dostana*) in the 1980s. Such felicity made him a sought-after star; he acted in about eighty-five films over the decade. Shotgun went through a relatively 'khamosh' patch in the mid-1980s before finding form again with *Ilzaam* (1986). A truckload of hits—*Aag Hi Aag, Khudgarz* (a compelling performance), *Loha, Insaniyat Ke Dushman* and *Khoon Bhari Maang*—kept him on the right track. Unlike most mainstream stars, he also flirted with parallel cinema, acting in Goutam Ghose's *Mahayatra*, and producing the well-intended but eventually unfulfilling coalmine drama, *Kalka* (1983).

Sanjeev Kumar: One of the decade's saddest moments was the death of Harihar Jariwala, better known as Sanjeev Kumar, in 1985. He was only forty-eight. His classy collaboration with Gulzar lasted till the very end with superhits like *Angoor* (1982) and the unforgettable *Namkeen* (1982). Even in the 1980s, Kumar brought vitality and quality to roles in *Khud-Daar* (1982), *Vidhaata* (1982) and *Hero* (1983). A rare actor-star, he left a vacuum impossible to fill.

Reena Roy: Through sheer hard work and talent, Ms Roy crawled her way from B-grade films to the apex. The Eighties were her best years when she paired with all A-list heroes barring Big B, and harvested a bundle of heroine-oriented hits, most notably *Aasha*. A good dancer, she acted in hits such as *Sanam Teri Kasam, Andhaa Kaanoon, Naukar Biwi Ka, Haathkadi, Ghulami* and more. Her marriage to Pakistani cricketer Mohsin Khan made her quit the field when she was still doing well.

Vinod Khanna: He left the glamour industry and became a glamorous resident of spiritual guru Rajneesh's Pune ashram. The actor became a seeker. Between 1983 and 1987, Khanna had one release. But the sexy sanyasi returned to the arc lights in 1987 with two mini-winners: *Insaaf* and *Satyamev Jayate*. Feroz Khan's expensive flop, *Dayavan*, and Yash Chopra's megahit romance, *Chandni*, were two noteworthy events in his second innings. But it was clear he wasn't going to be a challenger for the top slot again.

Parveen Babi: The Junagadh-born actor, whose chic elegance made her a poster girl for urbane glamour, remained a big-banner favourite in the 1980s (*Kranti, Khud-Daar, Mahaan, Rang Birangi, Ashanti*) before schizophrenia cruelly intervened in the second half of the 1980s.

Jaya Prada: *Tohfa, Mawaali, Maqsad* are synonymous with Sridevi. Many forget Jaya Prada was also a part of all these projects. A top-notch dancer, Jaya Prada made her mark in popular dramas such as *Sanjog, Sindoor* and *Swarag Se Sunder*. No heroine of her generation looked better in a sari or with tears in her eyes. Unfortunately, big commercial flops in Bombay— *Jaadugar, Gangaa Jamunaa Saraswathi*—arrested her progress.

Madhuri Dixit: She made her debut with *Abodh* (1984) but *Tezaab* (1988) created a new dancing queen. Two hero-oriented superhits in 1989, *Ram Lakhan* and *Tridev*, enhanced her status further. Madhuri would rule the 1990s.

The Bad Boys*

In the 1980s, villains became larger than life. They were terrorists and megalomaniacs. Shakaal (Kulbhushan Kharbanda), Dr Dang (Anupam Kher) and Mogambo (Amrish Puri) are three of the most remembered villains of the time. But nobody has forgotten the mean menace of *Ardh Satya's* Rama Shetty (Sadashiv Amrapurkar) either.

Puri emerged as the decade's bad guy No. 1. Amjad Khan was more good (*Qurbani*) than bad (*Himmatwala*). So was Danny Denzongpa who could be both upright (*Aitbaar*) and evil (*Andar Baahar, Kanoon Kya Karega*). Both also directed movies: *Chor Police* (Khan) and *Phir Wahi Raat* (Danny). Kader Khan and Shakti Kapoor blended comedy with villainy. So did Prem Chopra. Sadashiv Amrapurkar, Paresh Rawal, Gulshan Grover and Pran (less frequently) also kept the viewers uneasy. Kiran Kumar drew attention with *Tezaab's* Lotiya Pathan. Truth be told, we remember the villains more than the heroes of the Eighties.

---

*For more on the subject, read *Pure Evil...The Bad Boys of Bollywood* by Balaji Vittal.

REEL 9

RISING SONS AND PROMISING OUTSIDERS

Post-Independence India saw dynasties taking shape in the Bombay film industry, the Kapoors and the Mukherjis being two prime examples. What started as a trickle in the 1960s turned into a torrent in the 1980s.

By now, actors who had made it big in the 1950s and '60s had post-pubescent offspring. Their celluloid take-offs were carefully calibrated. The scripts were designed to bring out the best in their personality. The launch vehicles saw a blaze of publicity in film magazines and radio programmes.

Such unveilings came with a gender bias. No star daughter was launched with such publicity and fanfare into the big, bad world of cinema, though Bina (daughter of Pradeep Kumar), Sabeeha (daughter of Ameeta) and Preeti Ganguly (daughter of Ashok Kumar) did venture into the area.

Behind the scenes, it was the same story. The male offspring of top producers and directors stepped into their papas' shoes. Manmohan Desai's son Ketan and Nasir Hussain's Mansoor Khan came into the picture. B.R. Chopra's son Ravi was introduced in the multistarrer flop, *The Burning Train* (1980). Earlier, Raj N. Sippy was also launched in the family production, *Inkaar* (1977). Ravi Tandon produced and directed *Ek Main*

Aur Ek Tu (1986) for son Raj. He flopped but his sister Raveena became a star in the 1990s.

The star sons got multiple opportunities to boost their careers. Having tasted *la dolce vita* all through their lives, some lacked the drive of their parents. The audience also rebuffed them. They ended up being little stars rather than the superstars their parents had wanted them to be. Only Sunny Deol and Sanjay Dutt reached the top.

KUMAR GAURAV AND SANJAY DUTT

Two of an 'un'kind

Post *Bobby* (1973), no star son was launched as such a planned and manicured product as Kumar Gaurav in *Love Story* (1981). Film magazines published interviews, laid him out on the cover. Irreconcilable differences between producer (father Rajendra Kumar) and director (Rahul Rawail) led to more curiosity about the film. The stand-off ended with the director's name being omitted from the credits. Nonetheless, when the film, written by Mirza Brothers, was finally released, teenage girls found their vanilla of the month. Top banners chased him as if he was the last mango of the season.

Kumar Gaurav became the celluloid template that every famous actor of the 1950s and 1960s with a young male heir wanted to replicate. In the coming months and years, Sunil Dutt, Dharmendra, Dev Anand and Manoj Kumar prepared similar springboards for their sons. Breezy flicks peddling popcorn romance in scenic India, with sprightly songs invariably penned by Anand Bakshi and tuned by R.D. Burman, were formulated.

In the early race to the top, Gaurav was the galloping hare; Dutt more like a tortoise with brittle legs. Gaurav took the fast elevator. Dutt played snakes and ladders with life, his issues with drugs and girlfriends extensively documented in a biography and a biopic (*Sanju*, 2018).

Rocky (1981) hit choppy waters, barely recovering its cost.

Dutt, paired with then girlfriend Tina Munim, drew a mixed response. Some liked his droopy eyes and lean frame. Others felt he was on dope—and they were not wrong.

But as the decade entered the home stretch, Dutt found form and favour with Mahesh Bhatt's *Naam* (1986). 'Before Sanjay went to the de-addiction centre, he had heard [the story of] *Naam* and had quite liked it,' reminisced Bhatt. 'But he could see that it was far away from what he wanted to do. His father did not allow him to do a film with Kumar Gaurav. When he came back from the de-addiction clinic in the USA, he was completely hungry and his self-esteem charred. He wanted a place in the sun.'[1]

Naam, starring Sanjay and Gaurav, gave Bhatt his first major box-office winner. The film also became a redemption song for writer Salim, who hadn't delivered anything post separation with Javed. The industry chatter was that Salim didn't possess the minerals to make it on his own. *Naam* was his riposte.

Ironically, it was Kumar Gaurav who proactively ensured that the movie was made and Sanjay Dutt got the role, recalled Bhatt. He said, 'Kumar Gaurav took me to his father Rajendra Kumar. I pitched the story. After hearing it, Rajendra Kumar said, *"Yeh kahani to achchi hai, par yeh kahani to Sanjay Dutt ki hai. Tera role kitna bhi achcha ho, jo marta hai log usi ko yaad rakhenge. Kuchh aur banate hain.* (The story is good but it centres on Sanjay Dutt. The audience remembers the actor who dies in the film. So let us make something else.)" But Kumar Gaurav said, *"Yehi banayenge, nahi to kuchch aur nahi banayenge.* (We will make this or nothing else.) And I remember the grace with which the father said, *"Theek hai bhai to yehi banate hain* (Okay then. Let's do this)".'[2]

As Rajendra Kumar had predicted, Dutt walked away with the applause. And as he had envisaged, the movie didn't do much for Gaurav's career.

In Sanjay Dutt's biography, Yasser Usman writes how Dutt was launched in 'cosy club' style. Producer-director Amarjeet

(*Hum Dono, Teen Devian*), a Navketan insider who was married to Nargis's niece Rehana, played a key role in getting moneybags Gulshan Rai (*Johny Mera Naam, Deewaar*) on board.

'Favourite whisky in hand, Sunil called Sanjay and gushingly introduced him to the producer. Gulshan sized up Sanjay carefully. He went through the pictures of his training [screen test] and smiled. "Okay, done. I give you one crore rupees [for making the film]. Let's do Shri Ganesh. [Let's start.]." The film, *Rocky*, was to be made under Amarjeet's banner, Nalanda Productions, directed by Sunil Dutt and marketed as a father-son project.'[3] *Rocky* barely broke even. And it didn't help the Dutts.

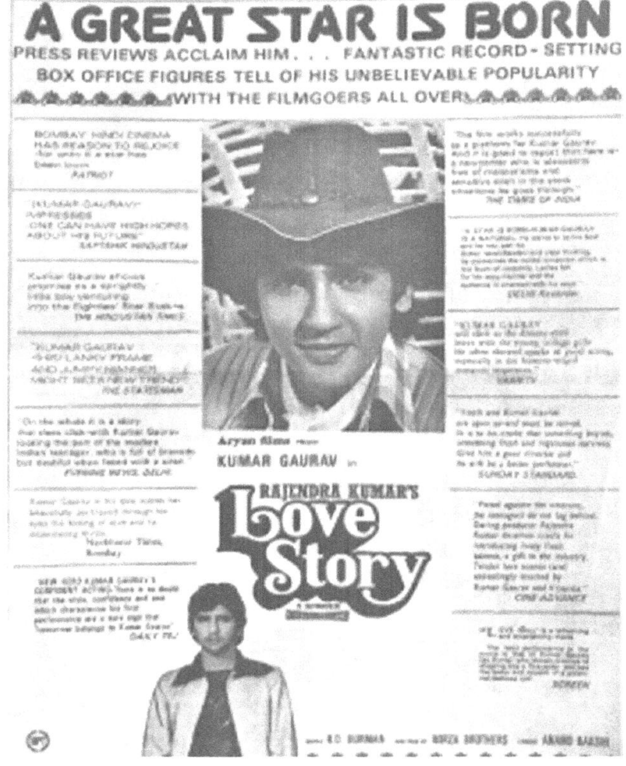

Kumar Gaurav's *Love Story* became a runaway success and made him a teenage heartthrob

On the other hand, the spectacular success of *Love Story* had created a different kind of problem for Gaurav. He had no idea what to choose or reject, although from all accounts, he wasn't the only one making the decisions. His second release was Tamil film director A.C. Trilokchander's *Teri Kasam*, a moneyed-girl-versus-middle-class-boy love story with regressive undertones. The family drama disappointed his fans who were expecting something trendier.

Here onwards, his career headed south. Big projects such as Biddu's *Star* (1983), Ramanand Sagar's *Romance* (1983), and his home production, *Lovers* (1983), directed by Bharathiraja fizzled out like damp crackers. *Star's* plot was fitted around the soundtrack, not vice versa. *Hum Hain Lajawab* (1984), *All Rounder* (1984) and *Ek Se Bhale Do* (1985) were essays in ennui. None of these films offered any freshness of theme or newness in storytelling.

Slowly his frustration reached a self-destructive point. Gaurav once said, 'When you're working with established names, they tend to treat you like a kid. I hate people who keep talking about their past glories and believe they're gods...There was this scene I was doing with this reputed director. Or at least he thinks he's reputed. I told him it was wrong and he said, "What do you know? You were born yesterday." I was so hurt. I abused him and walked off the sets. When the film failed, I felt secretly happy.'[4]

Only three Kumar Gaurav films were potentially promising. One of them was Jalal Agha's offbeat but frustrating film on drug problem, *Goonj*. The other two were Mahesh Bhatt movies: telefilm *Janam* (1985), which was shown to acclaim on DD, and *Naam* (1986).

Janam was produced by Mudra Videotech, a company owned by the Ambanis. It was made on a shoestring budget of Rs 7.82 lakh and completed in three months. 'Some actors wore their own clothes,' remembered Bhatt.[5] The story of an 'illegitimate' son trying to gain acceptance from his father had something raw and real—and not without reason. *Janam* was a brutal autobiographical movie by its director and an important film for its hero. The film underlined Gaurav's acting credentials in capital letters. Even today it remains the only film that he is remembered for as an actor. Bhatt said, 'Kumar Gaurav felt emotionally close to the film. It was his solo vehicle. He was a star after *Love Story* but already on the brink of oblivion after a succession of flops. The film re-established his faith in himself.'[6]

But *Janam* was only a telefilm. Kumar Gaurav kept waiting for the next hit which never happened. *Jurrat* (1989), a sacrilegious version of Brian De Palma's *The Untouchables*, didn't stand a chance under David Dhawan.

Bhatt felt that Kumar Gaurav was never consumed by the need to be in the performing arts. Writer-actor Akash Khurana offered a similar explanation. He said, 'He was an introvert who cherished his private, personal space and maybe subconsciously was a reluctant movie star.'[7]

The larger climate also went against Gaurav's teddy bear persona. Most of the 1980s was drowned in combats and stunts. Established romantic stars Rajesh Khanna (*Avtaar*) and Rishi Kapoor, too, found the going tough and had to find ways to stay relevant. Gaurav didn't fit into the southern masala or social dramas either. His self-confessed inability to dance also went against him in an era when jiving became *de riguer* for the hero. Unlike Dutt, who gradually improved as a dancer, he didn't.

Before finding his bearings briefly with *Naam*, Sanjay Dutt was regular fodder for the gossip magazines. He acted alongside thespians Dilip Kumar, Sanjeev Kumar and Shammi Kapoor in Subhash Ghai's *Vidhaata*, the biggest hit of 1982. Just like Kumar Gaurav got little credit for *Naam*, *Vidhaata* did not elevate Dutt's status, though it looked good on his resume.

The truth is that both Kumar Gaurav and Sanjay Dutt were overwhelmed by failures in the Eighties. Unlike Gaurav, Dutt did not have a single solo hit in the entire decade. Post *Naam*, Sanjay Dutt had seventeen releases between 1986 and 1989.

Even the movies helmed by top directors such as Raj N. Sippy (*Jeeva*), J.P. Dutta (the vastly underrated *Hathyar*), Mahesh Bhatt (*Kabzaa*), and Prakash Mehra (*Mohabbat Ke Dushman*) bombed.

But unlike Gaurav, Dutt stayed on course and gradually moved to an upward curve. When the 1980s drew to a close he was still a work in progress, but he had left his brother-in-law Kumar Gaurav behind.

SUNNY DEOL

'Sunny' Side Up

Like Dutt, Sunny Deol was a rare success story among star sons. Dharmendra's elder lad kick-started his career with a jubilee hit, *Betaab* (1983), and maintained a better momentum than the rest through the decade. The film, like any planned launch vehicle, presented him as an all-rounder who could emote, sing and fight. There were weaknesses too—his flat dialogue delivery, for instance. Like *Love Story* and *Rocky*, *Betaab* was elevated by R.D. Burman's melodies. Deol was paired with Amrita Singh, the daughter of Rukhsana Sultana, a close associate of Sanjay Gandhi during the Emergency.

The producers of *Betaab* put out an ad naming every theatre where the film was celebrating silver jubilee: Apsara (Bombay), Ritz (New Delhi), Odeon (Lucknow), Sheesh Mahal (Kanpur), Krishna (Amritsar), Pritam (Jalandhar), Kailash (Ludhiana), Apsara (Jammu) and Jyoti (Calcutta). Sadly, many of those movie halls are just memories now.

The director was Rahul Rawail, who finally had his name in the opening credits after being omitted from *Love Story*. Apart from the cash counters, critics also gave Deol a thumbs-up. Magazines described him as the most 'promising' star son. 'I don't want this label. It was given to me and it will go away with time. I'm trying to develop my own style as an actor. I'm not really like my dad,' he said in 1984.[8]

Post *Betaab*, Sunny focused more on young romance (*Sunny*, which was a flop) and the time-honoured love story *Sohni Mahiwal* (a success). Rawail's *Arjun* (1985) secured modest returns, except in Bombay and Hyderabad where the public loved it. But *Arjun* the first movie to bring out Deol's intensity and his ability to project restrained anger. 'He was smart enough to work with good directors such as Rahul Rawail and Rajkumar Santoshi,' said Shatrughan Sinha.[9]

J.P. Dutta's *Yateem* (1989) was another well-crafted movie that failed the audience test. *Joshilaay* (1989) was an underwhelming desi Western, shot lavishly in breathtaking Leh. But you couldn't have guessed the outcome when the director was Shekhar Kapur (he left midway), the writer was Javed Akhtar and the co-actors were Anil Kapoor, Sridevi and Meenakshi Seshadri. Yet the decade ended positively for Deol. In 1989, Rajiv Rai's *Tridev*, Sridevi-dominated *Chaalbaaz* and the muscular *Vardi* further improved his box-office biodata.

SUNEIL ANAND AND RAJIV KAPOOR

Hit fathers, flop sons

Most other sons failed to rise. Prominent among them was Suneil Anand, who was launched with fanfare by his father Dev Anand under home banner Navketan in *Anand Aur Anand* (1983). Zurich-born Suneil had learnt kung-fu from a master in Hong Kong and showed a felicity with dance moves.

'Mr Ratan Tata who headed CBS Records at the time took keen interest in its [music] launch,' said Suneil. Tata, along with Dev Anand and C.S. Dubey of CBS Records, 'jointly strategised for its promotion and release'.[10] The perky tracks were composed, once again, by R.D. Burman.

In his autobiography, Dev Anand gave A+ to his son's performance. 'Making his appearance on the screen for the first time, he performed admirably under my direction, looked boyishly charming and handsome, as I used to in my early days. He was very much in control of himself, and histrionically efficient whether he performed in scenes of light-hearted romance or in emotionally wrenching scenes,' he wrote.[11] Not many agreed with that assessment. The film flopped.

Appraising the film's fortunes, Suneil said, 'In my opinion, *Anand Aur Anand* was appreciated by our audiences. However, due to the offbeat nature of its screenplay, it was slow in taking off. Dad and I discussed nurturing the film for at least another two weeks and even spoke to our distributors about it at the time. However, cinemas didn't want to take risks that they thought may not be cost-effective because of the onslaught of forthcoming releases and pressures from TV viewership.'[12]

Suneil also played the lead in the forgotten *Main Tere Liye* (1988), directed by uncle Vijay Anand, and in the stylishly lensed *Car Thief* (1986), where he reconnected with *Love Story* heroine Vijeta Pandit. 'Presently I am working towards finishing my first Hollywood movie, 'Vagator Mixer', in which I play the lead and which I am also directing and co-producing,' Suneil said in 2020.[13] The film hasn't been released yet.

In the 1970s, Raj Kapoor had introduced two of his sons, Randhir Kapoor (*Kal, Aaj Aur Kal*) and Rishi Kapoor (*Bobby*) to movie audiences in home productions. His youngest, Chimpu, made his debut with *Ek Jaan Hain Hum* (1983) produced by F.C. Mehra's reputed Eagle Films.

If Rishi became a marathoner and Randhir a middle-distance runner, Rajiv barely broke into a sprint. This, despite making a positive impression in his debut movie. He oozed a natural flamboyance. Old-timers also spotted shades of uncle, Shammi Kapoor's brio in the exultant dance track, 'Dil chahe aasman pe'.

Director Lekh Tandon once recalled that Raj Kapoor had told him: 'This boy will make it big. From Prithviraj on he will be the best Kapoor.'[14] Papa Kapoor was as wide off the mark as Rajesh Khanna who had predicted that Vijay Arora (who crooned 'Chura liya hai' onscreen in *Yaadon Ki Baaraat*) could replace him.

Post *Ek Jaan Hain Hum*, Rajiv worked in a bunch of duds with reputed banners such as Nasir Hussain's *Zabardast* (1985) and Shomu Mukherjee's *Lover Boy* (1985). Even a double role in Toni's *Aasmaan* (1984), where he visibly relished playing the bad guy, didn't work.

It was left to Papa Kapoor to ensure that his youngest son received at least a footnote in Hindi cinema history. He played the lead in Raj Kapoor's blockbuster *Ram Teri Ganga Maili* (1985).

Rajiv Kapoor told a magazine once, '*Ram Teri Ganga Maili* has removed a big blot from my name. It has shown that given a good director and the right kind of note, I too, can deliver the goods and be accepted by the public in a very big way. I now have to my credit a film which is a bigger hit than that of the biggest stars, let alone those of the newcomers...But I am not really being flooded with offers the way I should have been after giving such a big hit. People say, "But *Ram Teri...* is Raj Kapoor's film".'[15] Critics found his performance 'poised and consistently credible'. Although the movie's female lead, Mandakini, profited more, its super success kept Chimpu in circulation.

In a first-rate biography of Hindi cinema's first family, *The Kapoors,* journalist Madhu Jain assessed that Rajiv was out of place at a time when action was Hindi filmdom's strongest currency. 'He was a throwback to the early Seventies, pre-Amitabh Bachchan era, and too early for the romantic family socials spawned after Sooraj Barjatya's *Maine Pyar Kiya*. Sadly, the son said to have Raj Kapoor's flair never really got a chance.'[16]

That's only partially true. Rajiv Kapoor did get his chances, at least a dozen of them. Quite a few were with top banners. How many newcomers get so many opportunities? When multistarrers such as *Zalzala* (1988), an inspired subversion of MacKenna's *Gold*, fell apart like a cheap Chinese clock, so did his career. Chimpu passed away following a massive heart attack in Mumbai on 9 February 2021. He was fifty-eight.

The Mehras who had launched Rajiv, also cast Nutan's son Mohnish Bahl as the lead in *Teri Baahon Mein* (1984), making him perhaps the skinniest topless hero in the history of Hindi cinema. The film, a terrifying copy of *The Blue Lagoon*, turned out to be a box-office blob. However, unlike some of the glory boys, Mohnish is still going strong in supporting roles in movies and TV shows. Hard work pays.

KUNAL AND KARAN

The two brothers

Shashi Kapoor's sons also made their debut in the 1980s. Neither was launched in an exclusive product by their father Shashi Kapoor, still in his prime as a star. Both ended with inglorious film careers.

Kunal Kapoor made his debut in Esmayeel Shroff's *Ahista Ahista* in 1981. He had a rich resonant voice but the audience didn't warm up to him. *Vijeta* (1982), directed by Govind Nihalani and produced by his father Shashi Kapoor, is the milestone movie of his brief career. As an aimless slacker who nurses a deep resentment against his father, Kunal was first rate in revealing the angst and self-doubts of an Air Force cadet. The boxing bout where he takes a lot of punishment and the series of horse jumps were intense pieces of physical acting that deserved an award. He had small parts in *Utsav* (1984) and *Trikal* (1985) too, but he found his calling later as an ad filmmaker.

His brother Karan made his debut in director Mukul Anand's lavishly mounted multistarrer, *Sultanat* (1986), looking distinctly uneasy while serenading beauty queen Juhi Chawla around the snowy mountains. As Bombay Dyeing's dream lover, Karan was the toast of the modelling world when he made his celluloid entry. His arrival as a hero is sociologically significant. Karan was more Kendal than Kapoor in skin tone and hair colour. He was the first foreign-looking hero in mainstream Hindi cinema. In the 1980s, it was a big moment.

Karan acknowledged much later, 'Cinema was haywire in the 1980s…in those days, commercial cinema wasn't inspiring. Also, I was too foreign looking. Very blonde. But I'm not blonde anymore. I [also] had a language problem. I felt my talent lay in photography, not movies.'[17]

He also acted in Raj N. Sippy's plebian anti-terrorism winner, *Loha* (1987), where he seemed to speak Hindi learnt in West Ham. He is colourfully introduced by Shatrughan Sinha as 'monkey brand, Bandar chhap, who looks like an Angrez but behaves like Changez.' Karan spoke about the reaction of his kids in the 2016 interview, 'They have seen clips of *Sultanat* and *Loha*. They laugh.'[18] Karan is now an award-winning photographer.

Manoj Kumar's son, Kunal Goswami, had a sorrier career. After his debut as a child actor in the blockbuster *Kranti* (1981), Kunal played the romantic lead in *Do Gulab* (1983) and *Ghungroo* (1983), which Prakash Mehra produced. Over the decade, he acted in a bunch of flops including the promising *Kalaakaar* (1983), where he played a down-and-out singer alongside Sridevi—remember the song, 'Neele neele ambar pe'— and *Ricky* (1986), a disastrous attempt to relaunch him.

The young actor, who was taller than Amitabh Bachchan, got another chance in director Ashim Samanta's *Aakhri Baazi* (1989), alongside Shatrughan Sinha and Govinda. This literally turned out to be his aakhri baazi, the last throw of the dice, in the Eighties. He got a couple of more chances as the decade changed. His luck didn't.

ANIL KAPOOR AND JACKIE SHROFF

Insider and outsider

Anil Kapoor's father, Surinder Kapoor, started out as a secretary to Geeta Bali, produced a bunch of C-grade films (*Tarzan Comes to Delhi*, 1965) before tasting a modicum of success with Rajesh Khanna's *Shehzada* (1972). A bunch of flops followed before he struck gold with *Hum Paanch* (1980). One of Anil's first lead roles happened in the home production, *Woh 7 Din* (1983).

In his generation of lead actors in mainstream cinema, Anil stood out for a variety of reasons. He was a rare young actor who also seemed interested in building a varied resume. In both *Woh 7 Din* (director Bapu's remake of Tamil film *Antha Ezhu Natkal*) and *Mashaal* (1984), he effectively matched histrionics with Naseeruddin Shah and Dilip Kumar.

Early in his career, he also acted in M.S. Sathyu's ode to urban naxalism, *Kahan Kahan Se Guzar Gaya*, which was held over for years and released only in 1986. 'KKSGG is Anil's first Hindi film. He wanted to work with me and that is how he landed the part. He was adequate for the anti-hero part,' said Sathyu.[19]

<hr>

SHORT TAKE

A model decade

The drizzle of models started in the 1970s, with Zeenat Aman, Parveen Babi and Kabir Bedi joining movies. By the Eighties, it had turned into a deluge. Suresh Oberoi, Deepak Parashar, Jackie Shroff, Ardhendu Bose, Karan Kapoor, Tina Munim, Kimi Katkar, Juhi Chawla, Sonu Walia, Kitu Gidwani, Sangeeta Bijlani, Nisha Singh and many more endorsed products before they turned to films with varying degrees of success.

<hr>

Anil was more than adequate in Basu Chatterjee's moderately successful *Saheb* (1984), where he played a footballer who sacrifices his career to help his family, and in the inter-caste love story, *Chameli Ki Shaadi* (1986). He also received all-round appreciation for K. Vishwanath's *Eeshwar* (1989), a remake of the Telugu hit, *Swathi Muthyam*, framed around the life of a malice-free simpleton.

The actor said in early 1989, 'During its entire making I was a vegetarian. Don't ask me if that's method acting because I don't know what method is. I tried to think like a saint, if evil thoughts came to my mind, I shooed them off. I abstained from any physical relationship. I became a monk because the character had to be played with purity.'[20] This commitment to craft made him stand above and apart from his contemporaries and helped him emerge as a long-distance runner.

Anil's career soared post 1985. *Karma* (1986), *Tezaab* (1988) and *Ram Lakhan* (1989) were superhits. *Insaaf Ki Awaaz* (1987), *Mr. India* (1987) and *Rakhwala* (1988) were other notable winners. In most of them, the credit was shared but his stock shot up nonetheless.

Anil Kapoor and Jackie Shroff made a lesser version of the Amitabh-Shashi or Amitabh-Vinod pairs. The two shared something in common: a moustache. Whiskers had become rare in Hindi cinema after the era of Raj Kapoor, Pradeep Kumar and Kishore Kumar. Raaj Kumar was an exception. The young duo made facial hair acceptable for GenNow leading men, much like the heroes of southern cinema.

Anil-Jackie collaborated in *Andar Baahar* (1984), a rip-off of the Hollywood hit, *48 Hours*. Kapoor came off better as a smart-talking crook than Jackie's constipated cop. They worked again in Rajiv Rai's *Yudh* (1985). Kapoor was a scene-stealer in *Karma* and *Ram Lakhan*, where he relished playing the 'one two ka four' crook. But Jackie, too, earned plaudits as Ram, the sober police officer in *Ram Lakhan*.

Both Anil and Jackie also made their moolah in southern productions. Kapoor's *Insaaf Ki Awaaz* and *Rakhwala* were produced by the formidable D. Ramanaidu. Jackie's southern success came in *Aaj Ka Daur*, directed by K Bapaiah.

In the early careers of both Anil and Jackie, Subhash Ghai was fundamental. Apart from his two biggest hits, *Karma* and *Ram Lakhan*, Ghai also cast Anil in the lead role of a lawyer in *Meri Jung* (1985). Jackie got his big break in Subhash

Ghai's *Hero* after playing Shakti Kapoor's nicotine-friendly sidekick in Dev Anand's *Swami Dada* (1982), a box-office turkey. Nonetheless, in many interviews, Jackie acknowledged that it was Dev *saab's* magic touch that worked for him.

Ghai marketed Jackie with double-page posters in *Screen* magazine. But before the shooting, the actor suffered a major motorcycle accident. Jackie lost two teeth but managed to hide the accident's seriousness from Ghai. Shroff told Anupam Kher in a television interview, 'When the film did not run for three weeks, Subhash-*ji* called me and said, "Get ready to model again, *teri picture to chali nahi* (your film flopped)." But after that, "*itni chali ki utri nahi* (It turned out to be such a big hit that it never went off the theatres)".'[21]

Perhaps it was written. Jackie was born in a one-room, 10x10 Bombay chawl; his father was a Gujarati astrologer, his mother came from Central Asia. He grew up in poverty, but in a family bonded by love. His mother sold saris and utensils for the family. His seventeen-year-old brother drowned before his eyes when he was ten. The incident left an abiding scar in his heart. He worked briefly in a travel agency before becoming a model by chance, which led to his career in movies.

After *Hero's* super success, his collaboration with Ghai continued. Both *Karma* and *Ram Lakhan* showed his growing maturity as an actor. His best performance came in Vidhu Vinod Chopra's *Parinda* (1989). As an underworld criminal torn and trapped between his brother, whom he is attached to like second skin, and the mafia don whom he owes unswerving loyalty to, Jackie delivered a straight-from-the-gut performance. The film earned him his first *Filmfare* award for best actor. Another film where he got noticed for his acting was Mahesh Bhatt's *Kaash* (1987), a marital-squabble yarn.

Jackie's success is also significant because he was arguably the first male model to make a successful transition as hero in Hindi cinema. Others flirted with success too—Deepak Parashar and Suresh Oberoi, to name just two. But neither became a durable star.

A Star from West Uttar Pradesh

Raj Babbar was the first actor from National School of Drama (1972-75) who made it big in mainstream Bombay cinema. The Agra-born and Tundla-bred actor, who came from a middle-class family of railway employees, became a familiar name in the Delhi theatre scene, acting in *Mitti Ki Gaadi* and other plays.

In 1977, he became the winner of the United Producers' Talent Contest, which technically meant that the caucus was committed to make films with him. Then irony stepped into his life. For the next two years, none of the United Producers started their projects. The consortium included the likes of B.R. Chopra, Subodh Mukherji, F.C. Mehra, Devendra Goel and Shakti Samanta.

Hope floated again after Javed Akhtar saw him perform in the play, *Nadir Shah*, in Delhi. The next day he was introduced to a bunch of Bombay bigwigs who had all come to attend a film festival: Salim, Ramesh Sippy, Yash Chopra and others. '*Bhai Javed saab tumhari bahut tariff kar rahe the* (Javed *saab* was praising you a lot),' Salim told him. He was called for a screen test to Bombay. 'It was my first flight and my first stay at a five-star hotel. I took the screen test at [Ramesh] Sippy's office where I also met G.P. Sippy. My screen test was lensed by Nariman Irani,' recalled Babbar.[22]

He was given a sheet of dialogue to speak. 'After the screen test, I was asked to wait. I learnt that Dilip *saab* had also seen the rushes and approved it. I was asked to go back to Delhi. "We will call you a week before the muhurat," they said.'[23]

The call never came. On the contrary, Babbar saw an announcement in *Screen*, 'Dilip Kumar and Amitabh Bachchan in *Shakti*', in early January 1978. Babbar had been tested, approved and dumped.

'I was broken inside. But I kept silent. When I went back for theatre work in Delhi, people would make fun. "*Haan bhai* star," they would say. But I composed myself,' he said.[24]

The same year, producer Satyendra Pal Chaudhary (*Hera Pheri, Sharaabi*) saw him act in a DD television play, *Ek Phool Ka Patjhar*. Chaudhary was a friend of Prakash Mehra and they were producing a film together. Babbar was asked to meet Mehra at New Delhi's capacious Hotel Ashok. In the evening he was invited for a party where Mehra was interacting with film journalists. When asked about the cast of his next film, Mehra said he was thinking of a Delhi actor, Raj Babbar.

'On hearing this, I immediately stepped back. I had already downed three to four pegs. *Free ka daaru peene ka shauk tha. Ek jhatka sa laga. Meri sab utar gayee.* (I was fond of free booze. I got a shock and instantly sobered up),' the actor reminisced.[25]

Babbar was aware of the heartbreaking distance between the cup and the lip. When he met Mehra the next day and he offered him work, he extracted a promise from the producer-director to arrange his accommodation for a year. Babbar remembered, 'I told him I needed a place to stay in Bombay for a year and I would be going on 1 January 1979. At home, I sold my Bajaj scooter for Rs 6,000 in the black market and gave the money to my wife Nadira, telling her to use Rs 500 every month. There was some tension at home over my decision but I had decided to give it a shot for one year.'[26]

The film with Mehra did not materialise immediately but Babbar had a place to stay and struggle. The first movie he shot for was *Chan Pardesi* (1981), the award-winning Punjabi film alongside Rama Vij. The first Hindi film he faced the camera for was Lekh Tandon's *Sharda* (1981), but B.R. Chopra's *Insaf Ka Tarazu* (1980) was released first.

The film became a surprise superhit; suddenly, Raj Babbar was red-hot property. 'I always say—because I feel it—that my parents gave me my name, Raj Babbar. But Chopra *saab* gave me recognition and identity as Raj Babbar. He is not my godfather. He is my father,' the actor said.[27] Eager to cash in, other biggies from the United Producers cabal now burst into action. 'But I received only Rs 10,000 for those movies,' he revealed.[28]

The three biggest hits of his career—*Insaf Ka Tarazu, Nikaah* (1982) and *Aaj Ki Awaz* (1984, inspired by *Death Wish*)—were all produced and directed by the Chopras; the first two by B.R., the third by Ravi, his son. The three films needed him to project three different personalities—a rapist industrialist (*Insaf Ka Tarazu*), a poet (*Nikaah*) and a vigilante killer (*Aaj Ki Awaz*). Like a perfectly kneaded dough, Babbar rose to the occasion every time. Despite playing the villain in *Insaf Ka Tarazu*, he easily shook off the negative image, much like Shatrughan Sinha in the 1970s.

As an actor, Babbar also commanded attention as the flamboyant dacoit in *Umrao Jaan*, a coal miner in *Kalka*, a diffident industrialist scion in Shyam Benegal's *Kalyug* and a conscientious contract killer in *Andha Yudh*.

But noteworthy parts were rare. Between 1980 and 1989, Babbar waltzed through 110 films, a majority in lead roles. Most solos were losers. Producer Tahir Hussain's *Dulha Bikta Hai*, was an exception. The film was released in Bombay in January 1982 and declared a flop. 'The film was released subsequently in the North and it went on to become an incredibly big hit.'[29]

Babbar had a clear understanding of his status within the industry. He said, 'There were A-grade stars like Amitabh, Dharmendra, Rajesh Khanna and Jeetendra. Then there were the star sons. Many producers couldn't afford them. I belonged to a lower category of stars. With me even medium-budget producers were happy. I never stopped a film because an instalment was delayed. That's why I survived so long.'[30]

AAMIR, SALMAN, SHAH RUKH

Khan they become major stars?

The three Khans tiptoed into Hindi films in the late 1980s. Aamir was the first of the trio to figure in the opening credits; first as a child artiste in *Yaadon Ki Baaraat* (1973) and then in a cameo in Ketan Mehta's *Holi* (1984), where he used his real name, Aamir Hussain.

Aamir's producer father Tahir Hussain had struggled for decades delivering more damp squibs than winners. Tahir's elder brother Nasir Hussain, with a bigger banner and a bouquet of hits under his belt, gave his nephew the break he needed.

The movie and its young star arrived amidst hype. A few weeks after *Qayamat Se Qayamat Tak* was released in 1988, *Movie* magazine ran an interview with a glowing introduction and headline, 'Will this Khan create Qayamat?' After the movie became a hit, they even got Aamir to write an article on how the audience had reacted to the new star by sending him to report on himself from outside a theatre.

But it seemed the critics had spoken too soon, when his follow-up films such as Aditya Bhattacharya's stylishly lensed dark thriller *Raakh* (1989) and B. Subhash's formulaic *Love Love Love* (1989) tumbled.

In fact, *Tum Mere Ho*, which was directed by his father Tahir and his first release of 1990, also fared below expectations. Director Indra Kumar's *Dil* (1990) rescued and revived him. It was a long bumpy journey before he became the star that he was initially predicted to be.

A few months after Aamir's blockbuster *QSQT*, Salman made his debut with director J.K. Bihari's *Biwi Ho To Aisi* (1988). In the opening credits, his name came after every other major actor, though the makers were decent enough to add the word 'Introducing' before his name, alongside Renu Arya, the film's heroine. The film, presented by K.C. Bokadia and revolving around Rekha, was a middling success.

Sooraj Barjatya's *Maine Pyar Kiya* (1989) relaunched his career and changed his life. The film showcased and maximised Salman's appealing face and appetising body. He seemed to exude a rare blend of innocence, charm and confidence that gave him the option of playing both romantic and action parts.

Unlike Salman and Aamir, outsider Shah Rukh went through the grind of teleserials (*Dil Dariya*, *Fauji*, Aziz Mirza's *Circus* and Mani Kaul's *Idiot*) and telemovies (*In Which Annie Gives It Those Ones*) before landing the lead role in director Raj Kanwar's *Deewana* (1992). Of the three Khans, Shah Rukh was the only real outsider in the industry.

REEL 10

MOVERS AND MOGULS:
TOP AND FLOP FILMMAKERS OF
THE 1980s

The hierarchy of producers and directors in mainstream Hindi cinema changed radically during the decade. Many top directors, who started their careers in the 1970s or earlier, delivered a major hit in the first half of the decade. Thereafter they were on shaky ground. Post 1986, a new breed of filmmakers more attuned to the time, seized the moment. The old-timers continued to produce and direct movies for another decade or more, even delivering the occasional hit. But they ceased to be the demigods of distributors. They didn't burn out but simply faded away.

PRAKASH MEHRA AND MANMOHAN DESAI

Lions in autumn

They shaped popular Hindi cinema of the 1970s. Mehra's *Zanjeer* (1973) ignited Amitabh Bachchan's stuttering career. Desai's *Amar Akbar Anthony* (1977) showcased him as a one-man variety show. The duo was the prime mover—along with writers Salim-Javed and director Yash Chopra—in the construction of the Bachchan megabrand.

The 1980s started promisingly for the Bijnore-born Mehra. *Laawaris* (1981) and *Namak Halaal* (1982) drew queues longer than a goods train. *Sharaabi* (1984) was received the same way. These films leaned heavily on Big B's larger-than-life persona and charisma. Each had at least one rip-roaring comic scene. For instance, his stand-up comic act in *Namak Halaal*—'When Vijay Merchant and Vijay Hazare were at the crease' followed by his 'Wasim Bari and Wasim Raja were at the crease'. Or, his '*Moochhein hon to Nathulaal jaisi*' quip in *Sharaabi* (dialogue: Kader Khan). From Big B's cross-dressing act in 'Mere angane mein' (*Laawaris*) to the marathon 'Pag ghunghroo baandh' (*Namak Halaal*), the tracks became the talk of the town.

Mehra, who started out as a lyricist, lost form after that. A brief rift with his star didn't help the producer-director's cause either. He was to direct *Godman*, a film announced at Bombay's Holiday Inn by Hollywood's Frank Yandolino. The title role was supposed to be played by Robert Di Nero, Al Pacino or Dustin Hoffman.[1] Nothing materialised.

Instead, he ended up dispensing three consecutive duds—*Muqaddar Ka Faisla* (1987), *Mohabbat Ke Dushman* (1988) and *Jaadugar* (1989). The flopping of *Jaadugar* had deeper import. It was the first time that the Bachchan-Mehra combo had served a turkey after hitting bullseye six times. Mehra never made a hit film again.

Like Mehra, Manmohan Desai too roared into the decade with *Naseeb* (1981), a furiously entertaining multistarrer. Unperturbed by the *Desh Premee* (1981) setback, he followed it up with two monster hits: *Coolie* (1983) and *Mard* (1985). Prayag Raj wrote the story of all these films.

But one could see from a furlong that the director, once described as the Man with the Midas touch, was running out of ideas. A long-winded drama, *Coolie* profited from the publicity after Bachchan's near-fatal injury on its set. The idea to freeze the shot belonged to V. Gopalakrishnan (popularly known as Gopal Babu), general manager of Rajshri Pictures, Bombay.[2] The film, with a rare Muslim protagonist in a mainstream film and loaded with religious references, became a box-office sensation. 'Burqawalis have patronised *Coolie* in a big way,' Desai said.[3]

Mard (1985) blended anti-colonial masala with elements derived from Shakespeare's *The Taming of the Shrew*. Animals were integral to Desai's blockbusters. Falcons played key supporting acts in *Dharam-Veer* and *Coolie*. *Mard's* (dialogue: Inder Raj Anand) acting entourage included a dog and a horse, features incorporated from C-grade costume dramas of the 1960s. *Mard* was the last successful charge of the Bachchan-Desai brigade. Interestingly, in the summer of 1984, Smita Patil told *India Today*, presciently, 'Mehra and Desai may be very good. But things are changing faster than they can change.'[4]

Desai's *Gangaa Jamunaa Saraswathi* (1988) is inarguably the most painstaking product of an illustrious career. He never directed a winner again. By the time the Eighties ended, both Mehra and Desai had lost their mojo and their place at the top.

RAJ KHOSLA AND RAMESH SIPPY

Fallen maestros

A singer for All India Radio in his earlier days, Raj Khosla had built up a standout resume in Bombay cinema, ranging from *C.I.D* (1956) to *Woh Kaun Thi?* (1964) to *Mera Gaon Mera Desh* (1971). The Ludhiana-born director was the all-rounder equivalent of Kapil Dev in Hindi cinema, a master of genres like Vijay Anand.

Like Desai and Mehra, the decade started purposefully for Khosla. Producer Yash Johar's *Dostana* (1980) triumphed at the box office. But then the hits ran dry like water taps in a desert town: *Do Premee, Daasi, Teri Maang Sitaron Se Bhar Doon, Maati Maangey Khoon, Sunny, Mera Dost Mera Dushman,* and *Naqab*. Even his most ardent fans shook their heads in disappointment. Where was the maker of *Kala Pani* and *Do Raaste*? Raj Khosla died in 1991.

A generation younger to him, Ramesh Sippy directed the box-office marvel *Sholay* (1975), among the most culturally influential Hindi films of all time. Three of the four films that Sippy made in the Eighties generated unprecedented chatter. *Shaan* (1980), released five years after *Sholay*, was expected to repeat *Sholay's* success.

The film was lavishly produced, heavily promoted. Sippy once said, 'The movie grew bigger as I made it, it grew and grew. It encompasses everything that a city has to offer. The five-star hotels, skyscrapers, the slums, the big crime organisations, the loves, hatreds, sentiments and the eternal jokes.'[5]

Sholay was set in the outback, amidst rocks and horses. For *Shaan*, Sippy shifted the terrain to the megacity and an underwater workstation. Gadgets replaced guns. Cast in the mould of a Bond villain, Shakaal (Kulbhushan Kharbanda) was less talkative and more tech-friendly than Gabbar (Amjad Khan), but equally fiendish. Ace cinematographer S.M. Anwar recalled, 'The film required a lot of varied camerawork. We had underwater photography for crocodile sequences as well as aerial shots for the helicopter sequences. It was totally James Bond level.'[6]

Shaan became a victim of its own hype. The film had a posse of stars, a lively soundtrack and exotic locales. The killing of DSP Shiv Kumar (Sunil Dutt) from an airborne helicopter was carried out on a beach in Somerset. But the film, trade magazines reported, failed to recover its estimated Rs 5-crore expense.

Another Salim-Javed film, *Shakti* (1982), again spawned huge curiosity. Father-son face-offs have often been plugged as the movie's highlight, notably in *Mughal-E-Azam*. The Dilip Kumar-Amitabh Bachchan showdown was played up in magazines. The actors delivered. But there seemed to be something amiss, like an ache you can't put a finger on. The film barely broke even but remains one of Sippy's best.

When *Saagar* (1985) was launched in the early 1980s, it was promoted as Dimple Kapadia's comeback movie. Like her debut film *Bobby*, she was paired with Rishi Kapoor. Kamal

Haasan, fresh from his *Ek Duuje Ke Liye* (1981) triumph, was the third angle in the love triangle.

The 186-minute love epic carried the stamp of a Ramesh Sippy film: polished production values, above-average performances, chartbusting tracks. But, unlike *Shaan* and *Shakti*, the script tasted like a reheated, stale leftover. The film, written by Javed Akhtar, was all cliché and no heart.

Thereafter Sippy fell off the A-list, *Bhrashtachar* (1989) a testament to his freefall. The slide continued in the 1990s. But before that, unlike the others, he found a second wind on television with *Buniyaad* (1986), the inter-generational saga of Master Haveliram (Alok Nath), Lajoji (Anita Kanwar) and their progeny, which enraptured north Indian viewers and is fondly remembered to this day. Haveliram's sister was played by Kiran Juneja, who became Sippy's wife.

HRISHIKESH MUKHERJEE, BASU CHATTERJEE AND GULZAR

Trapped in the middle

The three directors began their independent careers in different decades. But they shared a tenuous association of sensibility. Both Hrishikesh Mukherjee and Gulzar were assistants to auteur Bimal Roy. Basu Chatterjee assisted Basu Bhattacharya, who in turn had assisted Roy.

For an entire generation, watching their films was like leafing through a family photograph album. The stories they told offered a fluid combination of role models and ideal constructs. They were not only filled with characters you could identify with but also ones you wished to be. At a time when action and melodrama was tinsel town's strongest currency, they raged against the tide. But once video piracy led to the gentry's large-scale abandonment of theatres, these eloquent essayists of middle cinema lost their core viewership.

Hrishi-*da* made a fecund start to the 1980s with *Khubsoorat* (story: D.N. Mukherjee, dialogues: Gulzar), a sly but heartwarming manifesto against discipline and order. *Bemisal* (1982) repeated the Amitabh-Rakhee-Vinod Mehra trio of *Jurmana* (1979) but changed the star who wins the woman's heart and hand.

The feel-good comedies released in rapid succession during the same period—*Naram Garam* (1981), *Rang Birangi* (1983), *Kisi Se Na Kehna* (1983)—had familiar, easy-going humour but many could see the jokes wearing thin and the style getting dated. All these films carried a subterranean social message and didn't do badly—they are part of the Amazon Prime package now—but lacked standout quality.

Post 1984, Hrishi-*da* slipped further from public favour, best exemplified by *Jhooti* (1985), another *Khubsoorat*-like film with Rekha again as lead. *Namumkin* (1988), his first murder mystery after *Buddha Mil Gaya* (1971), was a mess. Like many other directors of the time, he sought refuge in television (*Talaash, Rishte*) before making another flop feature ten years later: *Jhoot Bole Kauwa Kaate* (1998).

Ajmer-born Basu Chatterjee was the most prolific of the lot. *Apne Paraye* (1980), a Bengal hinterland courtyard drama based on Saratchandra's *Nishkriti,* and *Shaukeen* (1982), the story of three aging men in search of adult fun, saw him back in winning form after a string of flops in the late 1970s. But subsequent films such as *Pasand Apni Apni, Lakhon Ki Baat* and *Chameli Ki Shaadi,* a progressive poke at caste hierarchy, fell flat. So did *Ek Ruka Hua Faisla,* a photostat copy of Hollywood's *12 Angry Men.* Chatterjee, who had started his career with the arthouse *Sara Akash* (1969), also made the hard-hitting *Kamla Ki Maut* (1989), where the suicide of an unmarried pregnant girl impacts the lives of the entire neighbourhood. But it barely got a theatrical release.

Basu Chatterjee had analysed his own plight in a 1996 interview: 'In the absence of TV and video, the films made in the '70s and '80s did better. My films had good audience response and some even branded me "a balcony class" filmmaker. Today the same class is not keen on going to the theatres. Even if the late Bimal Roy were to make films today it would be a difficult situation. That is the reason even followers of Roy—Hrishi-*da* and Gulzar—had a tough time with their later films.'[7]

Gulzar started the decade with the riotous *Angoor* (1982), which was based on Shakespeare's *Comedy of Errors* and a remake of Bimal Roy's *Do Dooni Chaar*. But tough times loomed ahead. *Namkeen* (1982), a sensitive story exploring the hearts of four women and their relationship with an itinerant truck driver, quietly perished like an unseen wild flower. So did *Ijaazat* (1988), a love story of lost chances, despite the sensitive music (R.D. Burman) and the stars (Rekha, Naseer). '*Libaas* [1988], a radically different look at the eternal love triangle, was produced by Lata Mangeshkar. But the film didn't even get a theatrical release. The failure of *Libaas* to reach the theatre was a huge setback for Gulzar,' wrote film journalist Saibal Chatterjee.[8] 'All of us had worked really hard for the film,' recalled Raj Babbar wistfully, who starred with Naseeruddin Shah and Shabana Azmi in the film.[9]

Both Gulzar and Basu Chatterjee were rescued by television. Gulzar's teleserial on the nineteenth-century Urdu poet Mirza Ghalib is a gem. Basu Chatterjee presented India's first consumer awareness serial, *Rajani*. He served hidden pearls of Indian literature in *Darpan* and turned Manohar Shyam Joshi's rustic and witty *Netaji Kahin* into an immensely engaging series (*Kakaji Kahin*) on kasbah politics.

Basu Bhattacharya's *Teesri Kasam* (1966) and *Uski Kahani* (1966) were forerunners of the New Wave cinema. His *Anubhav* (1971) and *Aavishkar* (1975) explored marriage woes. In the 1980s, Bhattacharya continued to conduct endoscopies of marital pathologies. *Griha Pravesh*, like *Sparsh* (which was produced by Bhattacharya) was certified in 1977 but released in 1980 (as per *Trade Guide*). The film, starring Sanjeev Kumar, Sharmila Tagore and Sarika, scored both with the critics and the janta. But it was a sign of the times that his next movie, *Panchvati* (1986), came six years later and barely found space in the theatres. Filmmakers like him were pushed to a corner during the decade. In the 1970s, as director, Bhattacharya had seven releases; in the Eighties, only two.

His impact can be seen in Madhusudan's self-consciously titled, *Trikon Ka Chautha Kon* (certified in 1983, released in 1986), which captured south and central Delhi in vivid, identifiable detail. The slowburn marital trilogy carries a distinct resemblance to Bhattacharya's films.

SHORT TAKE

Do you know?

V. Shantaram produced and directed his last film, *Jhanjhaar*, in 1987. He was eighty-five then. His grandson Sushant Ray and Padmini Kolhapure were the lead actors.

SUBHASH GHAI AND B. SUBHASH

The showman and the hitman

Few filmmakers understood the changing political, social and technological landscape of India better than Ghai, the failed actor (*Gumrah*) who became the red-hot director of pacy action-thrillers like *Kalicharan* and *Vishwanath* in the 1970s.

In the 1980s, Ghai got bigger and glitzier. His villains became larger than life, notably Dr Dang of *Karma* (1986). The sets were flamboyant; even muhurats were lavish affairs. For *Ram Lakhan* (1989), eighty rooms of Lonavla's luxurious Fariyas Holiday Resort were booked for a daylong celebration attended by top artistes, distributors, producers and directors. Even the music release functions were grand. Raj Kapoor was the original Showman. This was the New Showman at work.

Not all Ghai films seduced the audience. *Karz* (1980) and *Meri Jung* (1985) were modest triumphs; *Krodhi* (1981) only angered the distributors. But no other director conjured three 'super-duper' hits at a time when runaway successes were rarer than clothes in porn: *Vidhaata* (1982), *Karma* (1986) and *Ram Lakhan* (1989). *Hero* (1983), which launched Jackie Shroff in a leading role, was also a smash hit.

What made Ghai stand out from most of his peers was that he often wrote his own stories (*Hero, Karma, Ram Lakhan*), sometimes also the dialogue (*Krodhi*) and screenplay. He was the complete helmsman of his movies. Like Hitchcock, he also made fleeting appearances in his own films.

A distinct awareness of evolving market forces kept the Nagpur-born director ahead in the game. He understood the present and had a vision for the future. His emphasis on visual gloss was an effective method to counter piracy. His Eighties films were roughly three hours long and shot in 70mm, which meant the full frame and the entire movie couldn't be captured on VHS tapes. Watching them on video left the viewer dissatisfied.

Ghai also monetised his films' music and maximised its market potential like few had done before. He had a knack for creating song-related controversies that worked to his benefit. *Vidhaata's* double-entendre folksy track, 'Saat saheliyan khadi khadi (Seven friends standing)', would have swelled Dada Kondke's chest with pride.

Ghai's less famous namesake was master of another kind of movie. Ghai started small but graduated to A grade. B (B for Babbar) Subhash made medium-budget films and stayed that way. But the Delhi-born director delivered a whopping five winners in the 1980s: *Disco Dancer* (1982), *Kasam Paida Karne Wale Ki* (1983), *Aandhi-Toofan* (1984), *Tarzan* (1985) and *Dance Dance* (1987). Eminent writer Dr Rahi Masoom Reza (*Aadha Gaon*) wrote the dialogues for all.

Disco Dancer was seminal. Many filmmakers before B. Subhash had profited by incorporating a disco track. He knitted a movie around the songs which were choreographed by the prolific Suresh Bhatt. Disco tracks were fundamental to *Kasam Paida Karne Wale Ki* and *Dance Dance*, both fronted by his favourite hero, Mithun Chakraborty.

Disco Dancer—Muhurat Picture (Photo Credit: B. Subhash)

Film Information and *Trade Guide* described *Disco Dancer* as a minor hit. The movie received unflattering reviews from *The Times of India*: 'Not one fleeting glimpse is provided into the pop world that the title promised so tantalisingly.'[10] The public felt differently. One recalls the front-stall audience dancing in the aisles, a few matching Mithun step for step.

In erstwhile USSR, *Disco Dancer* acquired iconic status alongside four other Indian films: *Awara* (1951), *Shree 420* (1955), *Mother India* (1957), and *Seeta Aur Geeta* (1972).[11]

Film academic Elena Igorevna Doroshenko wrote, 'In the same way that *Seeta Aur Geeta* became a metaphor for India in the 1970s, *Disco Dancer* (1982) came to represent the Indian culture of the 1980s in the former USSR...Younger viewers, who enjoyed the film, looked for Western trends in fashion and music and the female audience, in particular, adored Mithun Chakraborty.'[12]

B. Subhash vividly remembered the day the film was shown

at Moscow's Mir theatre. 'The film wasn't dubbed, there were no subtitles. But the reaction was the same that I got in India. The title song was clapped by everyone in the theatre. I was overwhelmed. Few directors would have experienced what I did that day. You climb Mount Everest only once. *Disco Dancer* was my Everest,' he recalled.[13]

'Mithun, Bappi and me—all three of us got success together. Bappi became a king in Madras after that,' he said.[14]

Decades later, the film's popularity endures. 'When I went to Russia recently, I was expecting my fans to be around forty to forty-five years of age. But the girls who surrounded me were nineteen to twenty years old. Obviously, the mothers had passed on the movie's legacy,' Mithun said in 2010.[15]

─────────────── SHORT TAKE ───────────────

Strange pairings

In *Dance Dance*, Smita Patil is married to Shakti Kapoor. In *Mulzim*, Ranjeet plays Hema Malini's husband.

Dance Dance muhurat picture. Amirsh Puri, Smita Patil and Bappi Lahiri are no longer with us. (Photo Credit: B. Subhash)

Tarzan (1985) was another talked-about film of its time. C-grade Bombay cinema had always been obsessed with *Tarzan*. At least a dozen *Tarzan* films were made in the 1960s and 1970s, notably *Tarzan Comes to Delhi* (Dara Singh) and *Tarzan 303* (featuring Asian gold medal-winning wrestler Chandgi Ram).

Subhash elevated the production quality of his venture with a talented ensemble: cinematographer (Radhu Karmakar), dialogues (Dr Rahi Masoom Reza) and music (Bappi Lahiri). For a generation of young adult film watchers, Kimi Katkar in a red wraparound introducing the uninitiated Tarzan (Hemant Birje) to the pleasures of the mating game, while crooning 'Tarzan My Tarzan', is a pin-up moment of the mind. Trade magazines ranked *Tarzan* as a bigger hit than *Disco Dancer*.

At one point, Subhash's stock was so high that Aamir Khan, then a one-film sensation, visited his office and told him, 'My uncle [senior filmmaker Nasir Hussain] has told me, "*Yeh film sign kar ke aao* (Go and sign this film)."'[16]

The film was *Love Love Love* (1989), the rare occasion when Subhash went wrong in the 1980s. 'I made one mistake which I realised later. There was one sequence where the hero [Aamir Khan] gets beaten up. Some things happen in real-life but don't look nice on screen,' he said.[17]

N. CHANDRA, ANIL SHARMA AND SHIBU MITRA

Three shades of violence

N. Chandra grew up on the shanty side of Bombay. 'There were only poor people around me: my friends, my relatives. We only heard about places like Napean Sea and Warden Road,' he once disclosed. Chandra also briefly peddled smuggled goods such as 'stretchlon pant pieces'.[18]

Then, Chandrashekhar Narvekar (his full name) became a cog in the great wheel of Bombay cinema. He started out as a clapper boy and graduated to assisting Gulzar for ten years and Bapu for five. He idolised Vijay Anand and described himself as 'the director's Eklavya.' He later became an editor and directed his debut feature, *Ankush*, made for Rs 12 lakh.

'From the beginning, I had the passion to produce and direct a film. That's why when I started out as a director with *Ankush*, I had produced it as well, though jointly. I had sold my house, wife's jewellery and valuables. I knew that one gets ten times his investment if he makes a worthy product,' he told a film magazine.[19]

The story of four unemployed young men—Nana Patekar in a powerhouse performance—offered an identifiable and indelible portrait of Bombay's restless underclass localities where violence is embedded in life. In an interview, Chandra once said that *Ankush* was the result of his personal experiences. 'I have been brought up in a slum-like area of Worli and have myself seen gang fights and *dadagiri*. There were two murders that I still remember. In one case, red chilli powder was blown into the eyes of the victim and as the blinded *dada* waved his Rampuri knife helplessly, he was stabbed by the rival *dada*,' he said. 'In the other instance, a *dada* was walking on the road when suddenly a handful of men, with their faces covered, descended on him with swords and hacked him to pieces. Both incidents took place in broad daylight and I've used these sequences in my film.'[20]

Actor Madan Jain, who got top billing in the film's opening credits, ahead of Patekar, said, 'The film became successful because it was very relevant at the time. The audience could identify with the film.'[21]

Chandra's follow-up flick, *Pratighaat* (1987) was a more in-your-face vigilante movie, this time with a female protagonist, who is disrobed in public. A remake of the Telugu hit, *Pratighatna*, the film was produced by Ramoji Rao and distributed by Rajshri pictures.

In the cathartic climax, the protagonist hacks down the antagonist (Charan Raj). Sujata Mehta, who was paid Rs 41,000 to play the lead role of Laxmi, said, 'If you go through the list of films released those days, *Pratighaat* stands out. It was neither fully commercial nor art. It was a unique film and a women-oriented film. No character is as dynamic as Laxmi. It was about *naari-shakti*.'[22]

Pratighaat was released in March 1987, at a time when the Ram Janambhoomi movement was slowly gathering steam. In his book, *Sex in Cinema,* Fareed Kazmi provided a counterpoint saying that the film, filled with references to Hindu mythology, fed into political Hindutva's ideological core. *Trade Guide* ranked *Pratighaat* as 1987's top hit.

The atavistic grittiness of *Ankush* and *Pratighaat* inspired several similar low-budget films such as Dilip Shankar's surprise hit *Kaalchakra* (1988), and Dayal Nihalani's grim *Andhaa Yudh* (1988).

The edge that Chandra enjoyed over his peers came from his life experiences. But after two films, that know-how had exhausted itself. Chandra's *Tezaab* (1988) came with the catchline, 'A violent love story'. But it lacked the director's signature. The passion felt manufactured. *Tezaab* was N. Chandra lite. The film rode on the perky 'Ek do teen', which Madhuri Dixit enlivened. The dance became the film's lighting rod and turned Dixit into a hot-selling star. But the director fell off his perch in the 1990s.

Like N. Chandra, Anil Sharma feasted on violence. But his idea of savagery was markedly different. *Pratighaat's* warped intensity told us something about the times— the enmeshing of the lumpen with

Anil Sharma directed *Hukumat,* a superhit in 1987 (Photo Credit: Anil Sharma)

the political class. There was a method to Chandra's madness. In Sharma's *Hukumat*, madness was the method. There was no coherence of narrative. One moment the entire town is scared of the goons, the other minute the entire town is beating them up, with no plausible, even pulp explanation, as to how. The dialogues were coarse. *'Teri biwi baanjh nahi hai, tu hi napunsak hai* (Your wife isn't barren, you are infertile).' But the high-decibel, hyper-violent movie—children are gunned down in one scene—became a humongous hit.

Hukumat provided an insight into Sharma's astute social observation skills. When only twenty-two, he had directed *Shradhanjali* (1981), a modest success. This was followed by *Bandhan Kuchchey Dhaagon Ka* (1983), which found appreciation but no audience. 'Bigger and better directors than me didn't know what to make. I made the larger-than-life *Hukumat* in that backdrop. It was like creating a T20 match during the time of Tests. *Public ko mazaa aa gaya,*' recalled Sharma, who was twenty-five during the release of *Hukumat.*[23]

The Mathura-born director's movie was perhaps the first big-star venture where storytelling and aesthetics were consciously aimed at pleasing the young male in the front stall and rear stall, rather than the more expensive ticket holders. But the housefull boards placed outside theatres for weeks meant the balcony tickets were also sold out.

Sharma explained, 'I thought the masses are the only ones coming to the theatre, the gentry is watching videos at home. Why should I make films for the gentry, who watch it free at home? I should make films for those who pay and watch at the theatres.'[24]

Hukumat also cleverly pressed the bellybutton of the public mood. A villainish cop was named Javed Miandad, the Pakistani cricketer who had struck a heartbreaking six against India in an ODI game in 1987. 'He was my favourite cricketer. But I used that role to vent my anger. The character gets his head shaved. *Bachpana tha* (I was being childish),' he said.[25]

With *Hukumat*, Sharma latched on to the action gravy

train. His next, *Elaan-E-Jung*, was on similar lines, though only a modest success. But he would earn higher dividends with *Tahalka* (1992) and find a permanent place in the Hindi film pantheon with *Gadar: Ek Prem Katha* (2000).

Shibu Mitra was far more prolific than both Chandra and Sharma. Like N. Chandra, he was an editor by training. He, too, had assisted a stalwart of middle cinema: Basu Chatterjee. And like Chandra, his cinema had no similarities with his mentor.

A master of low-budget action yarns in the 1970s, Mitra directed an incredible twenty-three movies between 1980 and 1989. Quite a few were bustling bandit flicks. *(Also see the section on dacoits)*. He formed a steady and successful team with producer S.K. Kapur *(Shankar Dada, Sitapur Ki Geeta)* and Pahlaj Nihalani *(Ilzaam, Aag Hi Aag* and *Paap Ki Duniya)*.

Kapur's son Manmohan recollected that Mitra needed only a few retakes and never wasted raw stock. 'He was good at editing too. And he could work within a budget. He never exploited a producer. Rather, he was a producer's director. He made a film with us every year: *Durgaa, Raja Aur Rana, Maan Gaye Ustaad, Insaaf Main Karoonga, Sitapur Ki Geeta*,' said Manmohan, a producer himself.[26]

But it was with Pahlaj Nihalani, who became a controversial CBFC boss later, that Mitra delivered his biggest hits: *Ilzaam* and *Aag Hi Aag*. *Ilzaam* pitchforked Govinda into the limelight. *Aag Hi Aag* introduced Chunky Panday in the superhit dacoit drama. Both films had screenplay and story by the versatile Ram Kelkar.

Saleem A. Khan of the writer pair Faiz-Saleem lauded Mitra's ability to milk a celluloid scene. Saleem said, 'He knew how to bring a twist to the tale before the interval and how to add punch to the climax. He had the ability to select the right material—just like Rajkumar Kohli. I have worked with various directors, including T. Rama Rao, but I thought he was the best.'[27] Among the most prolific writer duos of the 1980s, Faiz-Saleem's works include *Ilzaam* (scenario) and *Aag Hi Aag* (dialogue).

MAHESH BHATT, SHEKHAR KAPUR
AND RAHUL RAWAIL

The insurgent, the maverick and the whiz kid

Bombay-born Mahesh Bhatt announced himself with a series of commercial turkeys (*Manzilein Aur Bhi Hain, Vishwasghaat, Naya Daur*) in the 1970s and built a reputation for driving his producers to the footpath. In the 1980s, he finally found what he was looking for.

In the past, filmmakers like Guru Dutt had weaved in autobiographical elements in films like *Kaagaz Ke Phool* (1959). Nobody had mined his own life like Bhatt in *Arth* (1982), *Janam* (1985) and *Daddy* (1989).

Arth was how his first marriage, which ended in divorce, had panned out from the perspective of his wife. In the end, the protagonist not only walks out of the union but also refuses the hand of a Prince Charming. She prefers to be her own person. In the book, *Mother Maiden Mistress*, Shabana Azmi recounted how the character she played had evolved in the eyes of the viewer. She said, 'Twenty years after the film was released I was invited to the Smithsonian Institute in Washington for a retrospective of my films and was amazed to find that *Arth* still resonates with audiences across the globe. What has changed over the years is the attitude of the men—today they are less hostile and more empathetic to my character and the film.'[28]

Janam was about him getting recognised as his father's son. Mahesh's father Nanabhai Bhatt was famous for his fantasy-adventure films (*Zimbo Comes to Town*). His mother was a Gujarati Shia Muslim. He said, 'The status of my mother being an illegitimate wife of my father was concealed. Anything that you are ashamed of has a great narrative in its core. From his side, my father tried to give our family a relationship status. Yet there were angularities. Making *Janam* was revisiting all this anguish.'[29] Ditto for *Daddy* (1989), where the protagonist battles alcoholism just like Bhatt himself. *Saaransh* (1985) wasn't autobiographical but had the same intensity, which became the hologram of his movies.

These films gave him an identity and name as a sensible filmmaker whose films were neither Left-leaning art nor feel-good middle. In a sense, he birthed personal cinema.

Bhatt spoke about his battle with private demons that led to the making of *Arth*. 'I started making the kind of films they wanted me to make. My potboilers were disastrous. I was at the end of my tether. There was the end of a fairytale marriage with my childhood beloved. I had an affair with Parveen Babi who cracked up before me. She went into dust. For me, *Arth* was a rising,' he said.[30]

The film wasn't easy to sell. Bhatt narrates how sheer happenstance led to the movie's release. Delhi distributor Raj Chopra was in Bombay and had missed his Indian Airlines flight. He had time to kill and was shown a film that nobody was willing to buy.

'He came out shaking. "What a film!" he said. Those days they used to operate through a broker who was taken aback because when a distributor breaks into superlatives, the chances of lowering the price goes for a toss. He asked the broker for his cheque book and signed for Rs 6 lakhs, a generous amount those days. I couldn't believe what had happened! He was a big distributor who used to buy Manoj Kumar films. When a moneybag like him showed implicit faith in *Arth*, the word went around the trade like wildfire. The rest is history,' Bhatt recalled.[31]

More serendipity lay in store. Bhatt came across Hrishikesh Mukherjee by chance. 'Hrishi-*da* told me that he had heard *Arth* was a good film and asked me to send the film for national awards. I said, "*Dada*, the last date for submission is gone." Hrishi-*da* said, "Just send it. I am the chairman of the awards committee." The film won three national awards: for best actress [Shabana Azmi], best music [Jagjit Singh] and best editing [Keshav Hirani],' the director remembered.[32]

The process of making *Saaransh*, which followed *Arth*, had actually started earlier. Bhatt had signed a three-film deal with the Barjatyas. The 1970s films made by Rajshri were gentle stories of gentle people who received gentle setbacks in life that were gently sorted out by the sixteenth reel. Bhatt promised something different. '"We saw a hunger in your eyes. Which is why we decided to go with you," Rajkumar Barjatya told me later,' Bhatt said.[33]

Saaransh was a tricky movie for Rajshri. The movie confronted death and faith. Bhatt had a major difference of opinion with Rajshri's patriarch Tarachand Barjatya, referred to as Seth-*ji*, on the ending. 'The movie said there's no rebirth. All you have is this life. This went against Seth-*ji*'s beliefs. There was a deadlock. Ultimately, Rajkumar Bartjatya gently stepped in and requested his father to let me go ahead with the film,' the director said.[34] The film certified Anupam Kher as an actor of merit.

Writer-actor Akash Khurana, who acted in *Saaransh*, remembered Bhatt's intensity on the sets. He said, 'His gut level understanding of a scene's emotional quotient and communicating it to actors with unwavering concentration and immediacy brought it very close to a rehearsal experience in theatre.'[35]

With *Naam* (1986), Bhatt struck gold. The following year he said, 'I think with *Arth, Saaransh, Janam* and *Naam*, I found the tune, the lyric. And that is my own. I struggled for fifteen years to find my own lyric, my own tune. I will sing this tune till people get tired of it one day and discard it for another tune.'[36]

Naam marked the elevation of director Mahesh Bhatt, the return of Salim (the other half of Javed) as a premium scriptwriter and the rise of Sanjay Dutt who outshone his brother-in-law Kumar Gaurav in an author-backed role.

Bhatt gave a lot of credit to Salim for the film's success. 'He wrote the script of *Naam* with great feeling. We used to discuss the script, we used to argue—not for a moment, but till both of us were convinced about something. We would see each other's viewpoint,' the director said.[37]

Naam recast Bhatt as a frontline director of mainstream Bombay cinema, a man who, finally, could be trusted with the financier's money. It didn't matter that *Kaash* (1987), *Thikana* (1987) and *Kabzaa* (1988), all flopped. Bigger triumphs and turkeys would follow in the coming decades.

Like Bhatt, Shekhar Kapur married artistic merit with commercial viability. The 70s flop actor of *Jaan Haazir Hai* and *Toote Khilone* found his voice and moorings behind the camera. Kapur made only two movies in the 1980s but left a wider imprint than those who made a dozen.

Masoom (1983), inspired by Eric Segal's *Man, Woman and Child*, milked middle-class tear ducts in a cultured way. A family drama lightly spiced to suit the subtle taste of a convent-educated, urban middle-class, it found a wider pulse. The ending—acceptance of the 'love' child—made the middle-class feel morally good about itself, even though most might have acted otherwise in real life.

In Bombay cinema, child artistes were often made to speak and behave like adults. The debutant director extracted natural performances from the three child artistes: Jugal Hansraj, Urmila Matondkar and Aradhana Shrivastav.

In an interview to *The Times of India* in 1987, Kapur said, 'In *Masoom*, my audience was my immediate contemporaries. I wanted to show other filmmakers that I was capable of directing, too. I'd realised that there was a market for films that were somewhere between Yash Chopra and Shyam Benegal. You have to be true to life and, at the same time, have an element of fantasy. You have to raise your story above the mundane.'

Mr. India (1987), too, overflowed with child actors. Kapur's gift for getting credible performances out of them is evident in a film that should have been titled 'Miss India'. The film rode on Sridevi's flamboyant energy, Laxmikant-Pyarelal's (L-P) boisterous tunes, Amrish Puri's outrageousness—'*Mogambo khush hua* (Mogambo is happy)' is dialogue No. 1 of the 1980s—and the not-so-novel idea of an invisible hero.

Kapur also shot extensively for the curry Western, *Joshilaay* (1989), but quit midway following differences with producer Sibte Hassan Rizvi, whose name adorned the opening credits.

But *Masoom* and *Mr. India* set the tone for his defining movie, *Bandit Queen* (1994), which ultimately paved his path to Hollywood (*Elizabeth*, 1998).

Rahul Rawail was hailed as the next big thing in Bombay cinema in the early 1980s. The son of director H.S. Rawail (*Mere Mehboob*, *Laila Majnu*) had assisted Raj Kapoor in *Mera Naam Joker* and *Bobby* in the 1970s before branching out on his own. Gossip magazines went to town over his bitter falling out with producer Rajendra Kumar over *Love Story* (1981). His name isn't there in the credits. The buzz went that he went to extremes as a taskmaster. In an interview to *Star & Style* in 1985, Rawail said that he had taken as many as 100 to 150 takes for a single shot. 'For one shot of Vijeta just looking over her shoulder, I took more than 100 takes,' he said.

Even the flopping of the hilarious *Biwi-O-Biwi* (1981) didn't affect his stature. Rawail played a key role in shaping the early career of Sunny Deol with *Betaab* (1983), *Arjun* (1985) and *Dacait* (1987), all written by Javed Akhtar. He was the first to harness and harvest Deol's coiled rage. Unfortunately, *Dacait* flopped. Thereafter Rawail, too, lost his way with *Samundar* (1987), a pretty but ultimately vacuous action-romance. But he remained one of the most important directors of the early Eighties.

MANSOOR KHAN AND SOORAJ BARJATYA

Hot kids on the block

Beginning with *Tumsa Nahin Dekha* (1957), Nasir Hussain had perfected the song-and-dance routine. But in the tricky 1980s, he couldn't find his box-office feet. *Zamaane Ko Dikhana Hai*

(1981), *Manzil Manzil* (1984) and *Zabardast* (1985) showed his formula was past its expiry date.

It was time to pass on the baton to his Hyderabad-born son Mansoor Khan, a scholastic vagabond who went to IIT, Bombay, Cornell University and MIT, Boston without ever completing a course. What he learnt in these places was probably a new way of looking at life. In his debut film, Mansoor brought in a freshness of approach and farm-fresh young stars: Juhi Chawla and Aamir Khan. R.D. Burman, the driving force behind the banner's many triumphs, was dumped for the young Anand-Milind, sons of composer Chitragupt.

Within the format of a conventional formula, Mansoor's *Qayamat Se Qayamat Tak* (1988) created believable characters who reacted to situations in identifiable ways. The young lovers trapped between two warring families didn't have the courage to face their parents, but loved each other passionately enough to run away. Elopement doesn't always end well in real life; even more so in the 1980s. Many in the audience understood the lovers' plight, as they had in *Ek Duuje Ke Liye*.

The tragic romance, which felt new and now without being so, brought the college-going crowd back to the theatres in droves. A news magazine gushed, 'Aamir Khan, 23, has become something of a teenage phenomenon, the dreamboat of a new generation, to whom Amitabh Bachchan is well, more like dad.'[38] 'Papa kehte hain' became the song of the year and remains a favourite at college farewells.

Mansoor, who received the *Filmfare* award for best director, tried to explain the success. '...I think people were waiting for a film that spoke with honesty, rather than style. Then we also consciously worked to ensure that the story was well written and the characters clearly etched...So we looked at small things like making the character of the hero vulnerable, honest and simple. At that time, the tendency was to make the hero invincible. Somehow people had started thinking that people liked to see this, but I didn't believe in that.'[39]

Over the years, *QSQT* acquired an iconic status. But its influence and impact is overrated. A look at the movies that proved successful in subsequent years reaffirms that little changed in terms of public taste or producers' predilections. Nonetheless, *QSQT* will be remembered as a courageous movie that triumphed despite sailing against the wind.

Like Mansoor Khan, Sooraj Barjatya restored the family banner's pride and financial health. The Barjatyas, who owned the banner Rajshri, ran a successful film distribution network. They started producing films with *Aarti* (1962), followed by *Dosti* (1964) and *Jeevan Mrityu* (1970), all mega hits.

In the 1970s, they decided to make economy films without stars, after a reportedly bad experience in *Jeevan Mrityu*. Soon Rajshri became a trusted brand for clean films that launched a dozen new faces. They didn't just make movies; they also showed an alternative way of making profitable movies. *Geet Gaata Chal* (1975), *Chitchor* (1976), *Tapasya* (1976), *Dulhan Wahi Jo Piya Man Bhaaye* (1977) and *Ankhiyon Ke Jharokhon Se* (1978) were all major winners. These films were markedly different from the southern family melodramas, or anything else created in Bombay. The bad guy, an indispensable part of Hindi films, was noticeably absent. Barring circumstance, there was no villain.

In 1979, Rajshri became a retail store of *shakahari* (vegetarian) socials, producing a staggering eight films. Of them, *Tarana* (Mithun and Ranjeeta) and *Sawan Ko Aane Do* (Arun Govil and Zarina Wahab) were hits. Among the flops was *Sunayana*, a pathetic copy of Charlie Chaplin's *City Lights*.

But in the Eighties, the house of Rajshri became vulnerable to the winds to change. In 1980, *Manokaamnaa, Maan Abhiman, Payal Ki Jhankaar* managed to recover costs but *Ek Baar Kaho* (inspired by *Come September*) didn't. Hits like *Nadiya Ke Paar* (1982), often mistaken as a Bhojpuri film, were exceptions.

In 1984, the reliable Rajshri was dragged down by a clump of debacles: Madhuri Dixit's debut film *Abodh, Rakta Bandhan*,

Phulwari. Stung by the reverses, Rajshri stopped making films after *Babul* (1986).

Maine Pyar Kiya (1989) gave the production house its first in-house director. Sooraj was only twenty-four, a few months older than the film's hero, Salman Khan. What *QSQT* gave to Aamir, *Maine Pyar Kiya* bestowed to Salman Khan: stardom.

With *Maine Pyar Kiya*, Sooraj partially reset the template of a happy family saga. Unlike earlier Rajshri movies, which were smaller in length than the usual Hindi films, his movies were long-drawn dramas. *MPK* was 173 minutes long; *Chitchor* (1976) finished in 105 minutes. Earlier films were low-key dramas. Sooraj raised the decibel. *MPK* cost over Rs 1.5 crore, staggeringly high by Rajshri standards.

From the outset, songs were fundamental to Sooraj's idea of movies. *MPK* had eleven songs, too many by 1980s Hindi film standards. But the audience loved them. The film became a runaway success. Sooraj had created Rajshri 2.0. In the coming years, the Sooraj-Salman partnership would blossom and conjure a megahit (*Hum Aapke Hain Koun..!*, 1994), which had fourteen songs!

RAJ KAPOOR, B.R. CHOPRA AND YASH CHOPRA

Golden (jubilee) veterans

Among the old-timers, Peshawar-born Raj Kapoor was the only producer-director who effortlessly sailed through the 1980s. In fact, his last four films as a director—*Bobby* (1973), *Satyam Shivam Sundaram* (1978), *Prem Rog* (1982) and *Ram Teri Ganga Maili* (1985)—all ran till the posters peeled off the theatre walls.

Prem Rog was a hesitant but ultimately socially progressive love story between a widow in a wealthy, feudal family and a likeable young man patronised by them. *Ram Teri Ganga Maili* (dialogue/screenplay: K.K. Singh) was the megahit of the decade, earning an AIII ranking (blockbuster) as per *Trade*

Guide. *RTGM* was a major feather in Kapoor's cap. Not for its commercial success or artistic merits but because the film validated the veteran director's ability to sense the public pulse at a time when younger, and allegedly smarter, directors were dispensing flops. He was sixty-one when the film released.

Nearly three hours long (178 minutes), *RTGM* was a cross between youthful romance and high-wattage drama with a pair of wet nipples thrown in. An innocent mountain girl falls for a young man from the city who loves and leaves her. Her travails to find him in the city formed a larger part of the drama. The movie created a stereotypical binary of innocent hill folk versus devious city slickers. The holy river's journey from the verdant mountains to the polluted plains became the metaphor to illustrate the point. When Kapoor passed away in 1988, he was still on top of his game. Not many directors—Yash Chopra being an exception—can claim such an exalted status.

A post-graduate in English literature, Yash's elder brother B.R. Chopra had the remarkable ability to engage with delicate social issues and walk away with cash and commendation. In a long career spanning more than six decades, the journalist-turned-filmmaker unfurled a slew of movies over a sweep of themes. *Ek Hi Raasta*, starring Ashok Kumar, Sunil Dutt and Meena Kumari, dealt with widow remarriage. *Naya Daur* was a plea for humanising industrialisation. *Gumrah* explored infidelity.

His low-budget quickie, *Insaf Ka Tarazu* (1980), was a major gamble because the film also had a new hero (the wooden Deepak Parashar) and a new villain (the mesmerising Raj Babbar). At a time when Zeenat Aman was primarily cast in vacuous glamdoll parts, he gave her the meaty role of a rape survivor who guns down the offender. The film, written by journalist Shabd Kumar (who also penned *Aaj Ki Awaz*), became a jubilee hit. Both Zeenat and Raj won awards.

Film scholar Fareed Kazmi wrote, 'The importance of *Insaf Ka Tarazu* lies in the fact that perhaps never before there has been such an overtly aggressive female protagonist who not only physically liquidates her tormentor, but also in a clever display of semantics, redraws the terrain so that the accused becomes the accuser and the judge the accused.'[40]

True. But there was also a voyeuristic relish in the way the camera captured the sexual assaults. The movie can also be read as a sexploitative flick in the garb of women's empowerment—like *Lipstick*, the C-grade Hollywood film it copied from. *Insaf Ka Tarazu* was a bold film but not entirely honest about its objective.

Nikaah (1982) navigated the position of women in the context of the Muslim personal law. The writer Dr Achala Nagar recalled how she came to write the film. She said, 'A news item of Sanjay Khan and Zeenat Aman's divorce and a possible remarriage had been published in the film magazine *Mayapuri*. The story stuck in my mind. Those days I also came to know about triple talaq. I found the idea of divorce, just by pronouncing talaq three times, regressive. A Muslim friend further helped me understand how a remarriage between a divorced couple after triple talaq wasn't possible unless she had married and divorced another man and had consummated [the] marriage with him.'[41]

Achala Nagar, also daughter of noted Hindi litterateur Amritlal Nagar, explained how the title was arrived at. The film's original title 'Talaq' was booked by another producer. He requested B.R. Chopra to opt for another name, which he did: 'Talaq Talaq Talaq'. 'However, actor Iftekar pointed out that he cannot even tell his wife the name of the film's title, "Talaq Talaq Talaq", which in any case was negative. That's how a more positive word, "Nikaah" was selected,' she said.[42]

The film got drawn into a major controversy. 'Posters were put out in Muslim-dominated areas of Bombay urging Muslims not to see the film because it was "anti-Islamic." Dr Rahi Masoom Reza, Hasan Kamal and others came forward and organised the film's special show. Several maulvis saw it, approved and issued a fatwa in favour of the movie. Later I learnt thirty-four cases were filed against the film,' Nagar said.[43] The movie was a mega hit, drawing Muslim families like a magnet.

Even *Tawaif* (1985), a reworking of *Sadhna* (1958), was a mini success. The film broke free from conventions. Film historians Ira Bhaskar and Richard Allen wrote, 'In films where the fallen woman is a rival to the woman of the home for the hero's love, such as *Benazir* (1964) or *Mirza Ghalib* (1954), it is always the fallen woman who must sacrifice her love to the woman of virtue and thereby attain virtue herself by acknowledging her fallen condition...However, remarkably in *Tawaif*, the terms of her sacrifice are reversed. It is the middle-class woman of virtue Qainat [Poonam Dhillon], who sacrifices her love for the hero and redeems the prostitute.'[44]

But after the failure of spy thriller *Awam* (1987), the director moved towards the small screen and attained cult success with *Mahabharat* (1988-90). He passed away in 2008.

The Eighties was the roughest decade for B.R.'s younger brother, Yash, one of Bombay cinema's most versatile directors. The hits dried up and Yash struggled to find his mojo. In the 1970s, Salim-Javed and Amitabh Bachchan (*Deewaar*, *Trishul* and *Kaala Patthar*) were fundamental to his films. In the early 1980s, the Lahore-born director parted ways with both. Salim-Javed themselves went separate ways in 1981. Bachchan went out of favour after a fiasco called *Silsila* (1981), dubbed by gossip mags as 'Silly-sila'. *Mashaal* (1984) was written by Javed, and despite a stunning performance by Anil Kapoor, didn't work either. *Faasle* (1985) bombed. *Vijay* (1988) fared better but lacked the Yash Chopra stamp.

It seems that the director was unsure of the material he was working with for most of the Eighties. He packed these films with stars while trying to blend young romance with high drama. He was finally rescued by Sridevi, Switzerland and chiffon sarees in *Chandni* (1989); Bhanu Athaiya being the dress designer. The mature love triangle, with dialogues by Sagar Sarhadi (*Kabhi Kabhie*, 1976) scorched the cash counters. In time, Yash Chopra would morph into a master of romance and keep painting the celluloid with different shades of love till his sudden death in 2012. Dengue was the cause.

JIJO PUNNOOSE AND HARMESH MALHOTRA

Unlikely winners

What's common between Jijo Punnoose and Harmesh Malhotra? Nothing. Except that the two directors from different generations and different geographies crafted two of the biggest surprises of the decade.

Chhota Chetan, 1984's monster hit, left the industry flabbergasted. A dubbed Hindi version of the Malayalam fantasy flick, *My Dear Kuttichathan*, which was released the same year, the film's USP was its use of 3D technology. The audience was knocked out by the novel special effects. Director Jijo Punnoose said, 'The movie was sans major stars, at half the length but double the budget of a standard feature film. *Kuttichathan* cost Rs 40 lakhs.'[45]

Jijo, who belongs to the pioneering Kerala-based Navodaya Studio family, had earlier directed *Padayottam* (1982), a 70mm film with six-track stereo sound. He got interested in 3D imaging by reading optical physics textbooks in school and college, and later learnt the science behind stereoscopy in California.

As part of the film's preparation, Jijo and colleague Mathew Paul undertook 'study tours' to meet prominent people and understand how an Indian children's fantasy film should be. Among those they met were Anant Pai (*Amar Chitra Katha*) in Bombay and writers Paul Zacharia and Punathil Kunjabdulla.[46]

For the production of their 3D film, Navodaya adopted the 35mm, single filmstrip stereovision system, enlisting the services of its creator Chris Condon, an optical physicist and lensmaker in Hollywood.

The film arrived at the peak of the video piracy boom. Since the 3D technology couldn't be duplicated properly on VHS, the film retained its freshness for the bigger screen.

To beat the pirates, producers queued up to make 3D films. In its 1984 year-ending issue, *Screen* posed the question, 'Will 1985 be the year of 3D?' Not many such films were completed though. Raj N. Sippy directed *Shiva Ka Insaaf*. The Ramsay brothers' horror movie *Saamri* was a middling success, but *Shiva* was a modest failure. The 3D fever soon ebbed.

(I recall watching Shiva Ka Insaaf *at Ranchi's Sujata Cinema. Everyone was given a pair of 3D glasses to wear. People soon forgot the rumours that the glasses caused conjunctivitis and the theatre was filled with laughter and gasps. The audience tried to touch the plate of laddoos or nervously shifted in their seats trying to avoid a vehicle coming their way.)*

Unlike the young Punnoose, Harmesh Malhotra was a well-experienced industry hand when he hit the jackpot with *Nagina* (1986), the story of a shape-shifting snake in love with a man.

Agra-born Malhotra had arrived in Bombay hoping to be a composer, but by the 1970s had built a decent biodata (*Gaddaar, Patthar Aur Payal*) as producer-director while exhibiting a flair for absorbing storytelling.

His first movie of the decade, *Choron Ki Baaraat* (1980), assembled a cluster of crooks to tell an engaging yarn. But thereafter, Malhotra doled out duds like *Aapas Ki Baat* (1981), which was extensively shot in Delhi, and the mystery *Raaz* (1983), or break-even flicks like *Poonam* (1983) and *Phaansi Ke Baad* (1985).

Then he decided to make *Nagina*. His wife Manju Malhotra recalled, 'Writer Jagmohan Kapoor's story was lying with him for four years. But he was wondering whether to make a film or not. That's because the subject was different from the kind of films he had made. I told him, we should experiment. *Nagina* was an experiment that succeeded.'[47]

Sridevi was the movie's spine and shine. Intrestingly, in an interview, Harmesh said that he had first thought of casting Jaya Prada. '...I thought she was beautiful and had lovely eyes. But when I narrated the subject to her she did not identify with it at all. Then I met Sridevi on the sets of Subhash Ghai's *Karma* and I asked her to spare some time to listen to a story. She gave me one hour and when I completed the narrative she just turned to her mother and said, "Mummy I am doing this role."'[48]

Nagina was released on 14 November 1986, shortly after the end of the biggest strike in the history of the Hindi film industry. It became a box-office sensation. In some small centres of Bihar, the film recorded over-capacity collections, as people did not mind seeing the film standing on their feet rather than going home after seeing the housefull board.[49]

'We celebrated the film's silver jubilee at Hotel Sea Rock in Bombay. It became a platinum [seventy-five weeks] jubilee hit,' Manju said.[50]

Nagina (dialogues: Dr Achala Nagar) helped Malhotra survive the Eighties. The film has outlived its creator in popular culture. Over three decades later, Sridevi's venomous dance continues to colonise popular imagination. Interestingly, the female dance has been largely appropriated by males at weddings. In Bihar, *naagin* dance sessions are commonplace at marriage events. On YouTube, paunchy geriatric men can be seen frolicking to the sound of an imaginary *been* even in Pakistan.

Later, he produced and directed another hit, *Dulhe Raja* (1998), with Govinda at his rollicking best. He passed away in 2005.

MOHAN KUMAR AND VIJAY SADANAH

Sailing against the wind

Producer-director Mohan Kumar, another successful director of the 1970s like Malhotra, had his moment under the sun with *Avtaar* (1983), which became a distributor's dream. Writer

Mushtaq Jalili's story of a self-respecting mechanic who prefers to live life on his own terms rather than surrender to the demands of his uncaring sons and daughters-in-law touched a guilty chord among the audience.

Avtaar voiced the concerns of the above fifty at a time when the much-venerated joint family was breaking up slowly, like a glacier, and aging parents were left to fend for themselves in urban India. For once a movie did not make the senior citizens an object of pity but gave them spunk, made them fight back. Their independence was valued and celebrated. Rajesh Khanna invested the role with heft and theatrics, making it one of the most remembered performances in his post-superstar career.

Like *Avtaar*, *Pyar Jhukta Nahin's* (1985) box-office conquest was as surprising as India's ODI World Cup triumph in 1983. Love stories (with a bratty kid thrown in) and inter-class dramas were standard fare in Bombay cinema. But this Mithun-Padmini Kolhapure movie by director Vijay Sadanah (*Sau Din Saas Ke*, 1980) befuddled the pundits. Rishi Kapoor divulged in his autobiography that he had refused the movie! And Rajshri had preferred not to distribute it! The movie, *Trade Guide* wrote, ended up doing as much business as Manmohan Desai's *Mard*. Sadanah didn't even come close to making another money-making flick. His post-*Pyar Jhukta Nahin* washouts include *Adhikar* (1986) and *Aulad* (1987).

MANOJ KUMAR, FEROZ KHAN, SANJAY KHAN AND RAKESH ROSHAN

Actors as directors

Manoj Kumar's anti-colonial saga, *Kranti* (1981), literally created a box-office revolution. The expensive and expansive multistarrer, which had Kumar's imprint in every frame, was lifted by a commanding performance by Dilip Kumar. Shatrughan Sinha's boisterous performance was loved by the audience. L-P tunes added to the film's saleability. At some theatres, the three-hour movie was shown non-stop day and night. The film celebrated dozens of silver jubilees, even in places where most films ran a few weeks.

Strangely, the actor sleepwalked through the rest of the decade. His effort to launch his brother Rajeev Goswami with *Painter Babu* (1983) misfired. Kumar also acted in super duds like *Santosh* (1989) and finally came out with the much-awaited but totally outdated *Clerk* the same year. The film showcasing Pakistani stars—the Rampur-born Mohammad Ali and Zeba Ali—was a titanic flop. The decade ended badly for Mr Bharat.

The Eighties behaved similarly with his contemporary Feroz Khan. When he took to directing in the 1970s, Feroz went for a cocktail of glamour and action as evidenced in *Apradh* and *Dharmatma*. *Qurbani* (1980) was his most ambitious project. Both *Film Information* and *Trade Guide* gave the slick and sexually charged thriller a modest rating. In sharp contrast, Rishi Kapoor writes in his autobiography that the film's huge collections put Subhash Ghai's *Karz* on the backfoot. Kapoor was pinning a lot of hope on *Karz* and consequently sank into 'depression'.[51]

(My own memories of the film are closer to Kapoor's. I remember travelling 50 km by train to watch the film in Patna Saheb at a packed theatre. I bought the ticket from a scalper.)

Khan followed up with the drug-laced *Janbaaz* (1986), which fared below expectations. But the audience showed little mercy to his imposing *Dayavan* (1988), a remake of the Tamil superhit *Nayakan*. Vinod Khanna's brave performance couldn't match Kamal Haasan's original turn. Feroz's brother Sanjay Khan made the dubiously 'tax-free' *Abdullah* (1980) and the fast-paced *Kala Dhanda Goray Log* (1986). Their youngest brother Akbar Khan produced, directed and acted in the much-delayed flop *Haadsaa* (1983).

Unlike Kumar and the Khans, fellow actor Rakesh Roshan blossomed as a director. Roshan started by picking up plots from English novels and mini TV series and converting them into desi winners. *Khudgarz* (1987) gathered material from Jeffrey Archer's *Kane and Abel*. *Khoon Bhari Maang* (1988) was chiselled out of the mini TV series, *Return to Eden* (1983). Roshan's next, *Kala Bazaar* (1989), was a success as well. The son-in-law of director-producer J. Om Prakash became a bigger director in the decades that followed, especially after producing a home-bred star in Hrithik Roshan (*Kaho Naa... Pyaar Hai* and the *Krrish* series).

─────────── SHORT TAKE ───────────

Arati and Simi

Women directors were rare in 1980s commercial Hindi films. Two exceptions: Arati Bhattacharya (*Maashuka*, 1987) and Simi Garewal (*Rukhsat*, 1988). Both movies flopped.

Arati Bhattacharya also acted in Satyajit Ray's *Jana Aranya* and became the first woman director of Bhojpuri films with *Dagabaz Balma* (1988) (Photo Credit: Arati Bhattacharya)

RAJ N. SIPPY, MUKUL ANAND, UMESH MEHRA AND PANKAJ PARASHAR

Young guns

At a time when the big Bombay directors were losing steam, a bunch of young colts born and bred in Bombay, with Hollywood scripts as their Bible, marked their debut in the 1980s. Their films had the smarts and were largely city-centric. These directors—touted as Bombay cinema's GenNext—were not comfortable with the sentimental sister, the weepy mother, the weary patriarch on the brink of a heart attack and other stock-in-trade characters of popular cinema. They were not comfortable with songs either, an inseparable ingredient of mainstream Hindi masala. But at a time when about 60 per cent of the collections came from the B and C class centres, the non-cosmopolitan towns, they were forced to incorporate elements—a parallel comedy track, a mujra or a disco, a duet or two—to please another set of audience. They were different, though not necessarily better than the others.

Raj N. Sippy had assisted Gulzar but his cinematic vision was vastly different from the director-lyricist. Raj preferred thrillers. What he shared with his guru was a love for foreign templates. Some of Gulzar's finest movies in the 1970s such as *Parichay* (*The Sound of Music*) and *Koshish* (*Happiness of Us Alone*) had their creative roots in foreign films. Sippy's debut flick, *Inkaar* (1977), was inspired by Akira Kurosawa's *High and Low*. The much-loved *Satte Pe Satta* (1982) was reinterpreted from *Seven Brides for Seven Brothers*. The super flop *Boxer* (1984) took elements from *Rocky*. *Andar Baahar* (1984) was a straight lift from *48 Hours*.

Sippy once said, brashly, 'Even the Indian constitution was adapted from other countries. So why can't I adapt a few foreign films to suit my purpose.'[52] With *Shiva Ka Insaaf*, he became the first director in north India to experiment with 3D technology. If nothing else, Sippy was prolific. During 1980-89, he directed fourteen movies.

Changing popular taste made him change his locales and subjects. *Jeeva* (1986) dabbled with old-fashioned banditry. *Satyamev Jayate* (1987) recycled the good old cop movie. Sippy stooped to conquer with *Loha* (1987), a movie riddled with over-the-top villains and melodramatic male bonding. He signed off the decade with two resounding losers: *Mahaadev* (1989) and *Shehzaade* (1989).

Before he died in his prime at forty-five, Mukul Anand made *Hum* (1991) and *Khuda Gawah* (1992), cementing his reputation as a savvy director with an eye for the visually dazzling. But in the 1980s, he was still struggling to Indianise his stories. Like Sippy, he too shopped abroad for stories. And he looked more at ease doing the songless *Kanoon Kya Karega* (1984), which had shades of the original *Cape Fear* (1962). *Aitbaar* (1985) had its roots in *Dial M for Murder*. Anand also made the flop costume spectacle *Sultanat* (Juhi Chawla's debut, 1986) and the humdrum *Main Balwaan* (1986) before he landed his first modest success, *Insaaf* (1987), the movie that ended Vinod Khanna's *sanyaas* from cinema.

Both Raj N. Sippy and Mukul Anand were much-discussed directors of their time. Film magazines saw them as harbingers of a nascent new Bombay cinema. And while it can be safely suggested that both were agents of change, at least in terms of stylised storytelling, they couldn't be the change makers they were expected to be. The fault wasn't theirs entirely, it lay in the 'system' that wasn't ready for a switch. It was only when the multiplex reached critical mass in another two decades that their kind of films became routine.

Umesh Mehra (Eagle Films) was a shade different from both. He came to prominence with the hit, *Alibaba Aur 40 Chor*, an Indo-Soviet co-production. Till then, foreign collaborations such as K.A. Abbas's *Pardesi* (USSR again, 1957) and *Subah-O-Sham* (Indo-Iranian film, 1972) had disappeared like bubbles in water.

Alibaba Aur 40 Chor got underway after Eagle Films helped in shooting a film, *Sunrise Over the Ganges*, for a USSR film company in 1975. Mehra recalled. 'The experience was excellent for all. It was decided during the 1976 Tashkent Film Festival that a co-production would be announced between Eagle Films and Sovin Films.'[53]

Umesh's father, well-known producer F.C. Mehra led a delegation of almost sixty stars and filmmakers, including Yash Chopra and Gulzar to the Soviet Union. Unfortunately, no script was agreed upon and the directors flew back to India. Before heading back, the Mehras met the Sovin Films bosses at Moscow where F.C. suggested *Alibaba*. Everyone agreed. 'When the Sovin people asked, but your directors have returned to India, who will direct the film, F.C. pointed to me and said, "Umesh Mehra"!'[54] The film, co-presented by Eagle Films and Uzbek Films (USSR), was jointly directed by Latif Faiziyev and Mehra.

The film's making was a fascinating clash of cultures of two different schools of filmmaking. 'I am from a commercial filmmaking school where we answer to the box office. And for them the most important issue was toeing the line laid out by the Soviet thinkers,' said Mehra.[55]

The script was laboured over for two years. 'Every step was a struggle. They were not agreeable to the casting of Dharmendra, as they wanted *Alibaba* to be played by an eighteen-year-old. For us the stars were [an] absolute necessity!...However once we established a level of trust things became good; the wonderful cave was a creation of the technical team from their side...The film remains as one of the top five grossers in the Soviet Union and much loved even today,' Mehra said.[56]

Mehra's oeuvre underlines a willingness to change gears and stories. He made the action-packed *Ashanti* (1982), *Teri Baahon Mein* (1984, a copy of *The Blue Lagoon*), a traditional love story (*Sohni Mahiwal*, 1984) and the knottily plotted *Jaal* (1986), which had one of the most imaginative opening credits you will ever see. Apart from *Teri Baahon Mein*, all fared well. *Sohni Mahiwal* was another Indo-Soviet co-production with Faiziyev and Mehra again jointly credited as directors.

But his bull run was halted when three adrenaline-rush movies, *Avinash*, much-touted *Kasam* and *Guru*, crashed. Mehra found success again with *Vardi* (1989) and *Mujrim* (1989), and had enough gas left in the tank to navigate the Nineties with his *Khiladi* series.

The fourth in the rat pack was Pankaj Parashar. His modestly successful *Ab Aayega Mazaa* (1984) and the modestly unsuccessful *Peechha Karro* (1986) exuded a sense of zaniness. But Parashar, who had a penchant for unusual camera angles, came into his own with *Jalwa* (1987), a trendily lensed crime thriller on the illegal narcotics trade in Goa. Naseeruddin Shah underwent a metamorphosis building his biceps. Parashar said, 'When I took Naseer for *Jalwa*, everybody thought I was mad— he was "not a hero and has not done any successful commercial movie". But I needed a good actor.'[57] Heroine Archana Puran Singh danced like a dervish. And Remo Fernandes delivered his first footstomper, 'Dekho dekho, yeh hai jalwa'.

But Parashar's runaway winner was *Chaalbaaz* (1989), a reworked *Seeta Aur Geeta*, with Sridevi as the new Hema Malini. Yet the director is more fondly remembered for the DD teleserial, *Karamchand*, with the carrot-nibbling detective (Pankaj Kapur) and his assistant Kitty (Susmita Mukherjee). 'Shut up Kitty!' is one of the most remembered lines in that era.

—————————— SHORT TAKE ——————————

Do watch if you find a good print

1. *Dhanwan*
2. *Misaal*
3. *Pushpak*

The first two are written by the vastly underrated Mirza Brothers. The third is a silent movie. They are a cut above the rest in terms of mainstream entertainment.

RAJKUMAR KOHLI AND J.P. DUTTA

Multistarrer makers

If any producer-director owned the word 'multistarrer' in Bombay cinema, it was Rajkumar Kohli. The director leapt into public consciousness with *Nagin* (1976) and *Jaani Dushman* (1979), two of the biggest assemblages of stars in the history of Hindi cinema.

The Lahore-born filmmaker continued in the same merry vein in the 1980s. For *Badle Ki Aag* (1982) and *Raaj Tilak* (1984), Kohli roped in stars as if they were available on discount at a retail store. He was certainly a genius at managing dates and egos in an era when most top actors signed at least thirty films and often worked in three shifts. Both films were a modest success. However, it was Dharmendra's comedy in *Naukar Biwi Ka* (1984)—with a far smaller cast—that hit the right button.

As the tenor of action films changed in the mid-'80s, so did Kohli. The Kohli of *Jaani Dushman* was unrecognisable in *Insaniyat Ke Dushman*, which landed in serious censor trouble for its hyper violence (*See section on censors*). It worked nonetheless. However, the '80s ended badly for Kohli with *Saazish* (1988), *Inteqam* (1988) and *Bees Saal Baad* (1989). And it stayed that way. He is the oldest surviving producer-director of his era.

Bombay-born J.P. Dutta came a generation after Kohli. In Dutta, we see a gift for desert aesthetics. Technically able, Dutta turned sandy Rajasthan's barrenness into a fetching landscape. The camels, the palaces, men with proud moustaches, sun-soaked women with hesitant gestures—we see it all. But we see the social warts too. The son of well-known film director-writer O.P. Dutta (*Pyaar Ki Jeet*, 1948) also contextualised the violence inherent in the social feudal order of the western state.

Sujata Mehta, who was pitch-perfect in a negative role in Dutta's *Yateem*, said, 'J.P. *saab* was a fantastic director. His framing, way of explaining shots to actors, his takes—

everything was lovely. He was short-tempered too—though he never shouted at me. He was very particular about location and enjoyed outdoor shooting. And he loved actors without makeup. He took his own time to shoot.'[58]

In 1989, three well-crafted action dramas—*Hathyar, Yateem* and *Batwara*—all came undone. *Hathyar* was one of the early gangland films that felt more real than fantastic. Both *Yateem* and *Batwara* were immaculately mounted. With passing years, these movies have gathered a decent reputation and audience on cable TV and online, a tribute to the director's skills. In the 1990s, Dutta moved to war movies; *Border* (1997) being the most watched.

J. OM PRAKASH, RAVI TANDON, LEKH TANDON AND BRIJ

Struggling in a new world

In 1961, producer J. Om Prakash found success with Rajendra Kumar's *Aas Ka Panchhi*. The Sialkot-born filmmaker, who later also turned director, stuck with the letter 'A' for the rest of his career. *Aasha* (1980), his biggest hit of the decade, was a timid *ménage a trois* involving a singer (Reena Roy), a truck driver (Jeetendra) and his wife (Rameshwari). 'Sheesha ho ya dil ho' (singer: Lata) was one of the hit songs of the year. 'Even today, I hear, J. Om Prakash-*ji* gets royalty cheques for the songs,' Rameshwari said in a 2018 interview.[59]

But success, deserted Om Prakash thereafter, even though he stuck to 'A': *Aas Paas* (1981), *Apna Bana Lo* (1982), *Arpan* (1983), the mini hit *Aakhir Kyon?* (1985) and *Aap Ke Saath* (1986). Like many others, he switched to fists-and-fight movies such as *Bhagwaan Dada* (1986) and *Agnee* (1988). And like many others, he failed. J. Om Prakash passed away in 2019.

Agra-born Ravi Tandon, who rose to prominence in the 1970s directing taut thrillers such as *Anhonee, Majboor* and *Khel Khel Mein*, lost his identity in the 1980s. The decade started promisingly enough for him with two hits, *Waqt Ki Deewar* (1981) and *Khud-Daar* (1982), though they lack his signature. But the rest of the decade was abysmal: *Aan Aur Shaan* (1984), *Rahi Badal Gaye* (1985), *Jawaab* (1985), *Bond 303* (1985), *Ek Main Aur Ek Tu* (1986), *Albela* (1987), *Nazrana* (1987). Like many others, he seemed to be directing films that he didn't have full control over. He breathed his last on 11 February 2022.

Lekh Tandon, whose romcom *Professor* (1962) drew the best out of Shammi Kapoor and whose *Dulhan Wahi Jo Piya Man Bhaaye* (1977) brought families in droves to theatres, also had an eventful Eighties. He directed *Ek Baar Kaho* (1980) and *Doosri Dulhan* (1983), both a notch better than average entertainers of the era. But the maudlin *Sharda* (1981) and *Agar Tum Na Hote* (1983) drew more audiences. Overall, like the other Tandon, he struggled to find his feet in the latter half of the decade. However, his TV show *Dil Dariya* (1988) boasts an important trivia. It had Shah Rukh Khan in one of his earliest roles. Lekh Tandon passed away in 2017.

In the 1960s and '70s, Brij (Sadanah) emerged as a top-notch director displaying a flair for crime thrillers and hybrid crime-comedies. Films such as *Yeh Raat Phir Na Aaygi* (1966), *Night in London* (1967), the iconic *Victoria No 203* (1972) and *Chori Mera Kaam* (1975) testified to his talent, and became his signature. But Brij lost form in the 1980s. *Bombay 405 Miles* (1980), *Professor Pyarelal* (1981), *Taqdeer* (1983), *Oonche Log* (1985) and *Mardon Wali Baat* (1988) all fared tepidly. Sponsored by Topaz, an early case of product endorsement in a movie, *Professor Pyarelal* (1981) was an ambitious flop. On 21 October 1990, Brij shot his wife, former heroine Sayeeda Khan and his daughter, Namrata, then turned the .32 Smith and Wesson on himself. His son, Kamal Sadanah survived with injuries and went on to become a hero achieving moderate success in the 1990s.

ESMAYEEL SHROFF AND K.C. BOKADIA

The Outsiders

Kurnool-born Esmayeel Shroff emerged on the scene when he helmed an unlikely success, *Thodisi Bewafaii* (1980). The movie established Rajesh Khanna and Shabana Azmi as a dependable combo in family dramas. An important ingredient in *Thodisi Bewafaii* was Shroff's ability to extract a restrained performance from Khanna, no mean feat in his heyday of mannerisms. When Shroff also drew a controlled act from Raaj Kumar, perhaps a tougher task, in the youthful *Bulundi* (1981), his reputation soared like a blue-chip share.

After the flopping of *Jhutha Sach* (1984), Shroff, who had a fine ear for music, altered course. As exemplified by the careers of several others directors, his output in the second half of the 1980s is vastly different from the first. The later films lack poise, a key trait in his earlier movies, which could be a possible reason why he enjoyed a healthy run. Both *Love 86* (1986, one of Govinda's early films) and *Suryaa* (1989, his second venture with Raaj Kumar after *Bulundi*) prolonged his career to the 1990s.

Confident of his craft, Shroff never hesitated to work with newcomers. *Thodisi Bewafaii* was also the debut film of Sushant Ray, the grandson of the great V. Shantaram. Ray was paired with Padmini Kolhapure, then in transition from a child artiste to a heroine. She also acted in *Ahista Ahista* (1981), alongside debutant Kunal Kapoor. *Love 86*, released on Valentine's Day, was the first release of Govinda although *Tan-Badan* was the first film he had signed up for. Not many remember that Shroff directed two early Salman Khan movies: *Nischaiy* (with Vinod Khanna, 1992) and *Majhdhaar* (1996). Shroff also had a keen ear for music and lyrics.[60] His films were often enriched by Khayyam's tender melodies that continue to be played on retro radio shows. He passed away on 26 October 2022.

The 1980s also threw up a small bunch of filmmakers who

understood the pulse of the changing times and modelled their material around audience tastes. Rajasthan-born K.C. Bokadia was one of them. He became the super-debutant producer with *Pyar Jhukta Nahin* (1985). The success of *Teri Meherbaniyan* (1985), the story of a vigilante dog, and *Jawab Hum Denge* (1987) encouraged him to direct *Kudrat Ka Kanoon* (1987), another superhit. In the 1990s, he became one of the most successful directors of the film industry.

DEV, VIJAY AND CHETAN

Three brothers, no Anand

The Anand brothers, important signposts in the progress of Hindi cinema, were still in the game but unable to deal a winning hand in the Eighties. Actor-producer-director Dev Anand continued to make films on fresh subjects but failed to find the popular pulse. *Lootmaar* (terrorism, 1980), *Swami Dada* (godman, 1982), *Anand Aur Anand* (1984), *Hum Naujawan* (wayward youth, 1986), *Sachche Ka Bolbala* (journalism, 1989)—all had disappointing runs.

His son Suneil Anand said, 'Dad had a penchant for making films on contemporary subjects. He took inspiration from news events and the trends of the time. They were in a sense the motifs...*Swami Dada* was inspired by the character of godman Dhirendra Brahmachari and some notorious Indian gangland figures of the time. *Sachche Ka Bolbala's* central theme revolved around a daring and forthright editor of a leading newspaper. Dad sometimes wanted to play personalities of the most talked-about people of the day. Stories were developed around that character.'[61]

But his Midas touch with newcomers continued. Jackie Shroff who had a bit role in *Swami Dada*, and Tabu who acted as a juvenile in *Hum Naujawan*, went on to become stars.

Dev's younger brother, actor-director Vijay Anand, one of Hindi cinema's all-time finest, was frustrated by a couple of big-budget, big-star flops: *Ram Balram* (1980) and *Rajput* (1982), neither of which came close to his best work. Viewing them, one got the feeling that his heart was not in these projects, much like the Raj Khosla films of this decade. What had happened to the director of *Guide* (1965), *Teesri Manzil* (1966) and *Johny Mera Naam* (1970)? The fall continued with *Main Tere Liye* (1988), where he directed nephew Suneil Anand.

Chetan Anand's ambitious reincarnation multistarrer, *Kudrat* (1981), overshot its budget and suffered losses. Like his brother, the maker of classics such as *Neecha Nagar* (1946) and *Haqeeqat* (1964) went through a bad patch. *Hum Rahe Na Hum* (1984) and *Hathon Ki Lakeeren* (1988) neither made money nor added to his fame.

Chetan, the eldest of the three brothers, breathed his last in 1997. Vijay Anand died in 2004. Dev Anand passed away in 2011.

VINOD PANDE AND VIDHU VINOD CHOPRA

The two Vinods

In the late Seventies, ad-man Vinod Pande, doubling up as a newsreader at the BBC London, wrote a script inspired by an article on the loneliness of Dimple Kapadia, then wedded to fading superstar Rajesh Khanna. The film, *Ek Baar Phir* (1980), also directed by Pande, was about a married woman's freedom of choice and the possibility of finding love and life beyond the husband. The brave movie, which launched Suresh Oberoi and Deepti Naval, fetched healthy dough and kick-started Pande's career in Bombay.

Pande seemed to be heading for Bombay's big league with *Star* (1982), which had two of the hottest properties in the industry then: music director Biddu of 'Aap jaisa koi' (*Qurbani*) fame and Kumar Gaurav (*Love Story*).

But the film nosedived. Pande recalled, 'Biddu had no sense of screenplay. He would walk into my home in Juhu—his boots making sound, tak tak tak—and plead, "Please don't keep any emotion." *Star* was a big mistake on my part. The only consolation was that Jeetendra's film, *Deedar-e-Yaar* was a bigger flop. People used to say, "*Deedar-e-Yaar se better hai.*"[62]

The same year, *Yeh Nazdeekiyan* (1982), a relationship triangle with Marc Zuber, Shabana and Parveen Babi was released to better reviews. The film, despite suggestive posters, sank. Pande fired two bigger blanks: *Ek Naya Rishta* (1986) and *Sach* (1989). Interestingly, *Sach* now has an impressive eight million views on YouTube.

In the Eighties, Srinagar-born and FTII-trained Vidhu Vinod wrote and directed *Sazaye Maut* (1981), *Khamosh* (1986) and *Parinda* (1989)—all thrillers but each distinct from the other, like spinners Bedi, Chandra and Prasanna. *Sazaye Maut* was a self-conscious, lazy-burn murder mystery. It was nerve jangling in places, but also ineptly written in parts. Brimful of neat little ideas, *Khamosh* was a Hitchcockian whodunit shot in Pahalgam. '[But] nobody bought the film for one or two years...*Khamosh* I released myself,' the director complained during a conversation at the Jio Mami film festival in 2015.

Parinda was among the first underworld yarns told with a dash of realism, a precursor to the likes of *Is Raat Ki Subah Nahin* and *Satya*. In *Parinda*, we also find his movement towards more ambitious and bigger films. In the film, Vidhu Vinod finally added Chopra to his name. Mega success would come to him primarily as a producer more than two decades later.

Rest of Bengal Brigade: Also on the Backfoot

From New Theatres to Bombay Talkies to Filmistan, Bengali directors were prime movers in the growth and evolution of Bombay cinema. Bimal Roy, Nitin Bose, Amiya Chakraborty, Asit Sen, Biren Nag, Phani Majumdar and others were known for their sensitive bhadralok films.

In the first three decades after Independence, directors such as Subodh Mukerji, Shakti Samanta, Pramod Chakravorty, Satyen Bose, and Dulal Guha became A-listers in Bombay. Samanta and Chakravorty also engaged with the thriller and action genres. The 1980s witnessed their slow fall.

Subodh Mukerji, who created his own brand of fun formula films typified by *Junglee* (1961), directed two flops: the multistarrer *Teesri Aankh* (1982) and the comic *Ulta Seedha* (1985).

The hits also dried up for Pramod Chakravorty, maker of superhits like *Love in Tokyo* (1966) and *Jugnu* (1973). The Eighties began promisingly enough with *Jyoti* (1981), which was based on the Bengali novel and film, *Swayamsiddha*. This was followed by the haggard *Nastik* (1983), a rare Bachchan flop. Like many other veterans of his ilk, he never conjured up a hit again. The bilingual *Jagir* (1984) recovered its cost but not *Shatru* (1986), another bilingual and an Indo-Bangladesh production. Celebrated Bangladeshi actress Shabana Siddique worked in the film. Chakki-*da* also made two forgettable Akshay Kumar movies in the 1990s before breathing his last in 2004.

Director Anil Ganguly is best remembered for the amiable romantic drama, *Kora Kagaz* (1974), which was based on the Bengali film, *Saat Pake Bandha*. He started the 1980s with the rural melodrama, *Aanchal* (1980), a middling success. Romantic comedy *Agreement*, with singer Shailendra Singh and Rekha in the lead, also worked. His shining moment came with family-football drama *Saaheb* (1985), a remake of the Bengali hit starring Tapas Paul, who later became a Trinamool MP and passed away in 2020. The Hindi version featured Anil Kapoor and Amrita Singh. But even Ganguly lost his footing as the decade petered out. *Pyar Ke Kabil* (1987), *Sadak Chhap* (1987) and *Mera Yaar Mera Dushman* (1987) were un-Ganguly films that failed to generate either curiosity or crowds.

Burdwan-born Shakti Samanta established himself as one of the most reputed and reliable directors of mainstream Hindi cinema in the 1960s (*Kashmir Ki Kali, An Evening in Paris*).

His *Aradhana* (1969) and *Kati Patang* (1971), to name just two, spurred Rajesh Khanna to superstardom.

In the 1980s, Samanta backpedaled to survive. Romantic thriller *Barsaat Ki Ek Raat* (1981), with Big B in the lead, made money after his flop murder mystery *Khwab* (1980), partly lifted from Hollywood's *A Place In The Sun* (1951). It was described by one of its lead actors Naseeruddin Shah as 'pure cat-vomit'. Further setbacks were in store: *Ayaash* (1982), *Awaaz* (1984), bilingual *Aar Paar* (with Bangladeshi heroine Rozina, 1985) and *Alag Alag* (1985). His son Ashim began his career with the moderate success of *Aamne Saamne* (Mithun in a double role), before being pegged back by duds: *Main Awara Hoon* (1983), *Palay Khan* (1986) and *Aakhri Baazi* (1989). Dulal Guha, who made the lovable *Dushmun* (1971) and the amiable revenge drama *Pratiggya* (1975), also found the going tough. Murder-mystery (*Dhuan*, 1981), romantic drama (*Do Dishayen*, 1982), reformist hinterland tale (*Mera Karam Mera Dharam*, 1987) or family social (*Sagar Sangam*, 1988), nothing seemed to work for him.

Purnea-born Satyen Bose, who directed unforgettables such as *Chalti Ka Naam Gaadi* (1958), *Dosti* (1964) and *Jeevan Mrityu* (1970), could only deliver three average performers: *Bin Maa Ke Bachche* (1980), *Payal Ki Jhankaar* (1980), *Tumhare Bina* (1982), and a dud, *Woh Din Aayega* (1987). Like many others, the versatile director with a felicity for progressive emotional dramas got lost in the labyrinth-like decade.

Hiren Nag, maker of two cherished young romances, *Geet Gaata Chal* and *Ankhiyon Ke Jharokhon Se* in the 1970s, also lost his way with *Maan Abhiman* (1980), *Saajan Mere Main Saajan Ki* (1980), *Aakhri Mujra* (1981) and Madhuri Dixit's debut film, *Abodh* (1984). These films were more refined than the average Eighties fare but made little impact critically and commericially.

REEL 11

ALSO STARRING: DACOITS AND DEVOTIONALS; SUSPENSE AND SEX MOVIES

The smaller genres of Hindi cinema are subterranean indicators of social tastes at a certain moment of time. In them, you find the industry's hidden history and the public's secret yearnings.

Dacoits

Bad boys had many vocations in post-Independence Hindi cinema. They turned up as despicable moneylenders, rapacious zamindars, oily profiteers, smugglers masquerading as nightclub owners, and obese politicians with obscene smiles. Each was a familiar face of vice and crime. Add *baaghi* (rebel) of the *bihadh* (ravines) hugging the Chambal, to that list.

For decades, the ravines and forests of Madhya Pradesh, Uttar Pradesh and Rajasthan were home to the brigand. Carrying guns was part of the local culture. Revenge earned respect. The *baaghi* was idolised. The saying went: *Jaako bairi jinda hai, taako jeeno dhikkar* (Your life is meaningless, if your enemy is alive). Outlaws were hot news in local newspapers and widely written about in pulp magazines. Journalist Tarun Kumar Bhaduri's book, *Abhishapta Chambal* (in Bengali), profiled the most feared dacoits in meticulous detail. He was also Jaya Bhaduri's father. The name of the blood-soaked river inspired many titles: *Chambal Ki Raani* (1979), *Chambal Ki Kassam* (1980), *Chambal Ke Daku* (1982), *Chambal Ka Badshah* (1986). Some of the legendary *baaghis*—Maan Singh, Sultana Daku and Putli Bai—had film titles named after them by opportunistic Bollywood.

The dacoit movies were considered safe bets by distributors in B and C class centres, roughly translated as the small towns, kasbahs and mofussils. Even flops would be guaranteed of a basic return, which would cut down on losses. Men with double-barrelled guns slung over their shoulders, riding shiny horses, was always a rousing sight for those with a yen for reel action. In real-life, dacoits seldom rode horses.

The exploration of banditry as a social problem was rare in Bombay cinema. Within the matrix of commercial movies, *Mujhe Jeene Do* (1963) and *Ganga Jamuna* (1961) were relatively serious ventures. Basu Bhattacharya's *Daaku* (1975), based on Punjabi writer Amrita Pritam's work, was largely unfulfilling.

The boondocks brigands were both heroes and villains depending on the script. In *Mera Gaon Mera Desh* (1971) or *Sholay* (1975), the outlaws were profiles in evil. In others, they were idolised. In the latter, they were Robin Hoods who robbed the rich to help the disadvantaged. They married off their daughters, arranged for their dowry and saved them from predators, including cops. The scripts justified their bloodlust. The mujra song was standard in such movies. These were films of familiarity and sameness. The mostly male viewer went to watch a certain plot unfold in a certain way and got exactly what he had envisaged in return.

In the 1960s and 1970s, Dara Singh, Feroz Khan, Sunil Dutt and Vinod Khanna figured frequently in such projects. In the 1980s, Mahendra Sandhu became a familiar face in such medium-budget encounters, notably *Paanch Qaidi* (1981), *Jwaala Daku* (1983), *Mujjhe Vachan Do* (1983) to name a few. Sandhu, the original 'Agent Vinod', also produced the last-named film.

The 1980s saw a continuum of the 1970s, especially in terms of the genre's plot development. Most dacoit films were revenge dramas and treated in a certain way. In this era of lost and found, several films—*Ganga Aur Suraj* (1980), *Lahoo Pukarega* (1980), *Khoon Aur Paani* (1981), to name just three—were plotted around the most favoured theme of the time: brothers separated by circumstances and poised on either side of law.

Several dacoit films also offered a parallel urban track (*Aag Hi Aag, Jeeva, Maa ki Saugandh,* to name three). Such settings—one half city-centric, the other hinterland-oriented— helped please two different sets of audiences.

Many well-known directors helmed standard dacoit dramas with modest or indifferent results: Writer-director Akhtar-ul-Iman (*Lahoo Pukarega,* 1980), Chand (*Khoon Aur Paani* and *Kasam Bhawani Ki,* both 1981), Narendra Bedi (*Insaan* and *Kachche Heere,* 1982, both fared well), Raj N. Sippy (*Jeeva,* 1986), Brij (*Mardon Wali Baat,* 1988, echoes of *Sholay*), Raj Khosla (*Maati Maangey Khoon,* which had Ghulam Ali's 'Aawargi' song, 1984, and *Mera Dost Mera Dushman,* 1987) and Rajkumar Kohli's multistarrer (*Badle Ki Aag,* 1982). Some others were S. Kalidas of *Half Ticket* fame (*Ek Daku Saher Mein,* 1985), Satpal (*Chunaoti,* 1980 and *Do Waqt Ki Roti,* 1988), Vinod Talwar (*Sindoor Aur Bandook,* 1989).

SHORT TAKE

Curry Western

Narendra Bedi's raging hit *Khote Sikkay* (1974) gave a new angle to the indigenous genre: a curry Western where the avenger wore a cowboy hat. Like Clint Eastwood in *High Plains Drifter,* Feroz Khan played a man with no name. Khan wore similar attire in *Khote Sikkay*'s sequel *Kachche Heere* and *Chunaoti.*

J.P. Dutta's films on dacoits were more cerebral. Within the framework of commercial cinema, Dutta invested *Ghulami* (1985), *Batwara* (1989) and *Yateem* (1989) with a measure of contemporary realism. His films located the outlaw's social origins as a logical corollary to the iniquitous and unjust feudal order. *Ghulami* bared the exploitative aspect of casteism. 'The scene where the hero's mother rushes into the villain's house to save her son without taking off her slippers, and is then humiliated by being forced to put slippers on her head and walk out, led to riots in several cities in Rajasthan.'[1]

A bleak realism runs through *Yateem*, a complicated cop-bandit tale around adoption. Sujata Mehta earned a *Filmfare* award nomination for her role of a woman who's sexually attracted to her stepson in the film. Mehta said, 'I asked J.P. *saab* why he chose me. He had seen me in a Gujarati play where I played a sweet newly-married wife. He said he wanted someone whom people cannot imagine in a negative role.'[2]

Rahul Rawail's well-made flop, *Dacait* (1987), also walked the same line. The film promised a sliver of seriousness in a mainstream way: how police bullets find their way to dacoits and how the trader-cop-landlord axis of exploitation in rural India operates.

Among the genre's most prolific directors was Shibu Mitra. *Paanch Qaidi* (1981, the cast included, hold it, Girish Karnad), *Mujjhe Vachan Do* (1983), *Sitapur Ki Geeta* (1987) and *Aakhri Ghulam* (1989) were all modestly entertaining and moderately successful.

Mitra's *Aag Hi Aag* (1988) was the genre's big-ticket winner. Produced by Pahlaj Nihalani, the movie was nearly three hours long. Nobody seemed to mind. Writer Ram Kelkar's story displayed a thematic consistency and was packed with high-testosterone face-offs between its main characters (Dharmendra-Danny, Chunky Panday-Shotgun Sinha), making it a formidable combo of action and emotion. Dharmendra was compelling in a well-delineated role. '*Aag Hi Aag* was a dacoit film with a romantic-emotional angle,' said Saleem of Faiz-Saleem fame, who wrote the film.[3]

Producer-director Sultan Ahmed was another specialist of the genre. Lucknow-born Ahmed had assisted K. Asif (*Mughal-E-Azam*). His films were leisurely paced, lavishly shot and generally hosted well-etched characters (*Heera*, 1973; *Ganga Ki Saugand*, 1978). Lensed in the desert with plenty of 'horse power' and helicopter thrills, *Dharam Kanta* (1982) was among the genre's biggest multistarrers. Raaj Kumar, Waheeda Rehman, Rajesh Khanna, Jeetendra, Reena Roy, Sulakshana Pandit and Amjad Khan acted in this 'brothers separated from parents' flick. Mithun Chakraborty-led *Daata* (1989) also fared well but the movie marks a distinct fall in Ahmed's creative standards. The film has over fifty million views on YouTube now.

In the Eighties, Shyam (sometimes spelt 'Sham') Ralhan, brother of the noted filmmaker O.P. Ralhan (*Phool Aur Patthar*), also directed three dacoit films: *Jeeo Aur Jeene Do* (1982), *Ganga Meri Maa* (1983) and *Ramkali* (1987). *Jeeo Aur Jeene Do* (Jeetendra), a blend of high drama and hardy action, was a major hit of 1982.

In 1984, Rajinikanth played the title role of *Gangvaa*, a rare dacoit venture by a southern producer (B.S. Dwarakish). The tale of an innocent villager forced into banditry, the film's surprise ending could have affected its fortunes.

Ironically, some run-of-the-mill dacoit movies hit bullseye. Rajendra Kumar's glory days in mushy sentimentals were long gone but he registered a mini triumph with director Kewal Sharma's *Badla Aur Balidan* (1980).

Director Ram Maheshwary (*Kaajal, Neel Kamal*) ventured into dacoit territory with *Chambal Ki Kassam* (1980). The audience enjoyed the flamboyant face-off between Raaj Kumar and Shatrughan Sinha, both known for robust dialogue delivery. Khayyam's melodious 'Simti hui yeh ghadiyan' was a bonus.

When Real-life Dacoits Acted in a Bombay Movie

US-based businessman L.S. Chima created a buzz in Bombay's film world when he roped in two former outlaws, Madho Singh and Mohar Singh, to play themselves on celluloid. The two had quit banditry in 1972 following an appeal by reformist leader Jayaprakash Narayan.

Chambal Ke Daku (1982) was a unique experiment. Till then, no known convict of such 'stature' had done a major film role. Madho Singh once had a Rs 1.5 lakh reward on his head and Mohar Singh, Rs 2 lakh. Javed Khan, who played the male lead, joked, 'When the producers announced that they would go to Chambal and shoot with them, a lot of established heroes said they didn't have dates.'[4]

One of Bombay's top models of the time, Javed Khan was the face of the Only Vimal campaign. *Chambal Ke Daku* was the first film he signed. 'Lanky and over six feet tall, Madho Singh's eyes were bloodshot because he was drunk most of the time,' said Khan.[5] Mohar Singh had a heavy moustache. Both were extremely intimidating.

Khan met Madho Singh after reaching Navjeevan Shivir, a sort of open jail for surrendered dacoits, which had been set up in Mungaoli in the Chambal region. Madho Singh was initially very polite with him. But his attitude changed the moment he saw him dressed in a police uniform for the shooting.

'Madho Singh looked at me with such a crazy look in his eyes that it sent a chill down my spine. I told myself, this man was so humble a few minutes back and he has changed completely,' recalled Khan.[6]

What followed was even stranger. The first scene was of a shootout between the dacoits and the cops. The junior artistes playing the cops had toy guns and fake bullets. But Madho Singh had a real gun. The district superintendent of police told Khan later that due to their violent past, dacoits like Madho Singh were permitted to keep their guns for their own defence.

In the scene, Madho Singh, who was referred to as Masterji, was to aim his gun at Khan. 'I remembered the wild look and asked the fight director to check the guns, especially of Masterji. They found out there was a real bullet in Madho Singh's gun. When asked, the ex-dacoit said, "I would have fired the real bullets, *par inko bacha deta*," meaning he wouldn't have shot me. I thanked my stars. The action director told him, "Master-*ji filmon mein aisa nahi hota hai*," and changed the bullets.'[7] The film turned out to be a mini success.

Incidentally, Madho Singh was also a qawwali singer and a performing magician. Later Mohar Singh rode into the world of politics and contested state elections. Madho Singh died in 1991 and Mohar Singh in 2020.

Female Dacoit Movies: Avenging Angels on Horseback

Back in 1972, *Putlibai*, named after the real-life famous dancer-turned-dacoit, was a cult success in small towns. The film's qawwalis are popular to this day.

In the early 1980s, real-life bandit queen (*dasyu rani*, in Hindi) Phoolan Devi was at the peak of her prowess. The infamous Behmai massacre in 1981 made her a poster girl for notoriety. The re-emergence of avenging women on horseback on the silver screen can be directly attributed to the banner headlines she earned.

The dubbed *Daku Rani Himmatwali* (1984) found box-office serendipity. Directed by K.S. Reddy and starring Kavitha and Vijayalalitha, the film was hyperdramatic, probably a plus for its core audience. From Fearless Nadia to Hema Malini, women brandishing whips have always been popular in Hindi cinema. *Daku Rani Himmatwali* had a hysterical laugh and wielded both a gun and whip. The distributors also laughed their way to the bank.

More women outlaw movies arrived shortly. In these films, traditional gender roles were reversed. The male star took a rare backseat. Director Ashok Roy's *Kahani Phoolvati Ki* (1985) was a spurious attempt at cashing in on the life of Phoolan Devi. Rita Bhaduri played the title role. The 1960s star Joy Mukherji made his debut as a bad guy. The film was earlier titled 'Kahani Phoolan Ki'. Then Roy received a letter, warning that he 'will have to face dire consequences if she was misprojected in the film.'[8] He sprinted with alacrity to change the film's name. The film received a thumbs-up from the paying public.

Sham Ralhan's *Ramkali* (1985, Hema Malini in the title role) also earned handsome dividends. Spurred by the success, Ms Malini then acted in *Sitapur Ki Geeta* (1987), a clever title pun on her old superhit, *Seeta Aur Geeta* (1972). In these films, Shatrughan Sinha and Rajesh Khanna played second fiddle to her. Similarly in *Daku Hasina* (1987), the focus was on Zeenat Aman, not the male star Rakesh Roshan.

Dacoit films seem to have had a longer shelf life than anticipated. All these films have been watched by millions online. Sridevi-led *Sherni* (1988) flopped when released but has garnered over twenty million views on YouTube. Writer-director Raju Saigal's *Saat Bijliyaan* (1988) attempted a desi gender twist to *The Magnificent Seven*. Tina Munim, Kajal Kiran and Shoma Anand were the lead performers, and Raj Kiran the maniacal villain with tobacco-stained teeth. Trade reports show *Daku Bijlee* (1986) was relished in Delhi and Uttar Pradesh and *Dilruba Tangewali* (1987), with Sripradha in the title role, across India.

Devotionals: Faithful Following

Since the silent era, devotional movies have enjoyed a steady output in Bombay's cinema bazaar. Some of the biggest landmarks in Indian cinema are owned by the genre. The first Indian film, *Raja Harishchandra*, was a mythological. The first film to be banned by the British government, the deceptively political *Bhakta Vidur*, was a mythological. *Ram Rajya*, the only Indian feature film seen by Mahatma Gandhi, was a devotional.

In these religio-centric films, the opening credits were put out in Hindi, not English, which was the general norm. These movies about gods, goddesses, saints, and noble men and women who by their karma were worthy of reverence, were a complete ecosystem. They had their own star directors, actors and music composers. Trilok Kapoor, Manhar Desai and Mahipal were major stars in such films in the 1950s and 1960s. Mainstream star Bharat Bhushan also acted in several devotionals and even received the *Filmfare* award for best actor in *Shri Chaitanya Mahaprabhu*.

In 1975, the genre got a major boost when producer Satnam Rohra's *Jai Santoshi Maa* hit the jackpot. India was stunned as cinema theatres morphed into temporary temples. Sociologists and box-office pundits were left wondering how the story of a little-known goddess became such a ginormous success.

The convent-educated urbanite may have scoffed at it but the genre enjoyed a faithful following. Its importance can be judged from one remarkable piece of trivia: The titles of at least twenty-five films made in the first sixty years of Hindi talkies (1931-91) carried the word 'Sati'. Director Shantilal Soni made a name for himself making *naag* (snake) movies in the 1960s: *Naag Devta, Naag Jyoti, Naag Mandir*.

Explaining the genre's presence and popularity, film historian Firoze Rangoonwala wrote that the 'the ideal characters of Ramayana, as interpreted by Valmiki and Tulsidas, have provided an endless source of films showing good fighting and destroying evil in its worst form. They have also justified the qualities of duty, sacrifice, chastity, tolerance et al, being virtues as practised by a vast majority of people whether voluntarily or enforced by circumstances.' He also pointed out that 'by and large these themes have been treated in a crude, melodramatic, pseudo-devout fashion'.[9]

These movies attracted more women than several other genres. Movie watching was still controlled by the family patriarch in large parts of India. Only movies promoting healthy family values or religious thoughts were deemed fit for female consumption. The devotionals fitted the bill.

No *dharmik* film rose to the same exalted status in the Eighties. Roughly twenty-five devotionals were released in 1980-89. Year 1981 was the most prolific period for the genre with ten films, two of them dubbed.

Ashish Kumar (*Jai Santoshi Maa*), Biswajit and Arun Govil were the most productively divine faces in this era. Kanan Kaushal, heroine of *Jai Santoshi Maa*, was among the most in-demand heroines along with Rita Bhaduri. Pandit R. Priyadarshi, who had scripted *Jai Santoshi Maa* and a host of other devotionals, continued to be the genre's star writer. Ravindra Jain, C. Arjun and Chitragupt were the sought-after composers.

South-based production houses generally avoided making Hindi devotionals. So did the big Bombay stars. Director K. Bapaiah's *Pataal Bhairavi* (1985), with Jeetendra and Jaya Prada, was more an adventure yarn than a devotional. Perhaps, they were spooked by the failure—also temporary banning—of director T. Rama Rao's controversial *Lok Parlok* (1979).

Films with southern superstars N.T. Rama Rao and Gemini Ganeshan were also dubbed in Hindi. Gemini's *Shri Maata Tere Roop Anek* (1982) was helmed by the renowned K.S. Gopalkrishna and, interestingly, included trick photography by noted cinematographer-director Ravikant Nagaich (*Farz*, *Surakksha*).

Special-effects genius Babubhai Mistry was among the most wanted directors of the genre. In these films, trick photography played a major role because divine miracles and saintly wonders were imperative to the storyline. Mistry was a master of the craft. In the 1980s, he was at the twilight of an illustrious career. The films he directed were *Mahabali Hanuman* (1981), *Sati Naag Kanya* (1983), *Sant Ravidas Ki Amar Kahani* (1983). *Sampoorna Mahabharat* (1983) was dubbed from Gujarati.

Mistry's *Mahabali Hanuman* was a late charge from an

aging pack. The film was produced by Homi Wadia, a legend in the genre of fantasies and devotionals. John Cawas, once the hero in movies starring Fearless Nadia, was involved in the production. He was *nirman sutradhar*, the opening credits said. The screenplay, special effects and direction were attributed to Mistry.

Rakesh Pandey (*Sara Akash*) played the male lead. Kavita Kiran, the name probably inspired by Kajal Kiran, was the heroine. As in many other films, Dara Singh played the title role of *Mahabali Hanuman*. Another wrestling star, Hercules, also acted in the film.

In 1986, Hindi film magazine *Madhuri* ran a story headlined, '*Kya dharmik filmon ka zamana lautega* (Will the good times return for religious movies)?' where the writer lamented the absence of lyricists such as Bharat Vyas and Pradeep, who brought a degree of authenticity to the songs.

This, however, wasn't accurate. Both Pradeep and Vyas were writing regularly even in the 1980s. Pradeep wrote the songs for *Karwa Chouth* (1980) and Shantilal Soni's *Sati Aur Bhagwan* (1981), and Vyas for *Sant Gyaneshwar* (1981), *Sati Sita Lav Kush* (1983), and *Krishna Krishna* (1987). Most of these films failed to please their core audience. The returns were feeble.

Where films failed, television succeeded. Two television serials on DD—Ramanand Sagar's *Ramayan* and B.R. Chopra's *Mahabharat*—became a national addiction. The first episode of *Ramayan* was shown on DD on 25 January 1987. It lasted seventy-eight episodes. *Mahabharat* started on 2 October 1988. It wasn't just the pious, practically everyone with access to television at home or in the neighbourhood watched the series. *Ramayan* and *Mahabharat* showed that devotionals still had a market but it had to be tapped the right way.

Trade magazine statistics show that *Badrinath Dham* (1980), *Gangadham* (Arun Govil, 1980), *Jai Baba Baidyanath* (Biswajit, 1981), *Sampoorna Santoshi Maa Ki Mahima* (1981), *Teri Pooja Kare Sansaar* (1985) fared reasonably well. But unlike the TV serials, their audience was restricted to the religiously inclined.

Badrinath Dham was produced and directed by Ashish Kumar, the hero of *Jai Santoshi Maa*, and packed with the biggest names of the genre: Mahipal, Anita Guha, Bharat Bhushan, Manhar Desai, S.N. Tripathi and Trilok Kapoor.

Jai Karoli Maa (1988), directed by Ram Pahwa and starring Arun Govil, Alka Nupoor and Bharat Bhushan in the lead roles, was a surprise success, especially in smaller centres. Karoli Maa (Kaila Devi) is a popular deity in Rajasthan. It is obvious that Ramanand Sagar wanted to cash in on Govil's virtuous image, earned from regular appearances in devotionals. With *Ramayan*, Govil's face became synonymous with Ram and was peddled in photo frames even in the 2019 Ardh Kumbh mela.

Interestingly, *Jai Baba Amarnath* (1983) was directed by B.R. Ishara (*Chetna*), better known for putting sex on the Hindi cinema menu.

A socially significant devotional of this era was *Sant Ravidas Ki Amar Kahani*. The fifteenth-century saint is venerated by Dalits in many parts of north India, especially Punjab. According to sociologist Ronki Ram, 'Sant Ravidas unleashed a frontal attack on the long tradition of social oppression and untouchability. He, therefore, is regarded as a messiah of the downtrodden. They revere him as devoutly as Hindus revere their Gods and Goddesses, and Sikhs their Gurus.'[10]

The film was directed by Babubhai Mistry. Little is known about Roshan Lal, the producer. The film had Ashish Kumar in the title role. The title song, written by Uday Khanna (also co-producer), went: '*Jab tak hai aakash mein suraj, Ganga mein hai pani, amar rahegi dharti par Ravidas ki amar zubani, Ravidas ki amar kahani*' (singer: Jaspal Singh, music: Chitragupt). The film made a strong statement against untouchability. '*Har koi apne janm se nahi, apne karm se pehchana jaata hai* (Everyone is recognised by his deeds, not by his birth)', went one of the closing dialogues.

A small number of films, aimed at devout Muslim viewers, were also produced during the decade. *Khwaja Ki Diwani*

(1981), *Fajr-E-Islam* (1981), and *Madine Ki Galian* (1981) did okay business. *Bismillah Ki Barkat* (1983) was a moderate success. One of the film's highlights was Nusrat Fateh Ali Khan's qawwali, 'Yaad unki rahe dil mein' (composer: Iqbal Qureshi). One might recall that Manmohan Desai's superhit *Coolie*, with key Muslim characters, also had several scenes of religious significance.

Supernatural/Horror: Thrills and Chills

In 1977, Ravikant Nagaich's *Jadu Tona* hit the screens at a time when Hollywood films such as *The Exorcist* (1973) and *The Omen* (1976) had created major interest in the imitation-inclined Bombay film industry.

But the genre developed a constituency and a distinct identity only when the Ramsays started making supernatural films regularly in the 1980s. Through them, the industry discovered that a sizeable audience will pay to get spooked.

In these horror films, you expected the expected. Women in white nighties inevitably crooned songs of rebirth and longing. Murderous monsters chased screaming visitors through deserted hallways. The bathtub was a favourite indoor location for getting murdered on windy nights, the victim occasionally in the middle of a bubble bath.

Today's viewers might think these technologically tacky movies evoked lurid delight than real fright. But in less demanding times, ghoulish tales of the uncanny spooked an entire generation. Such movies would be screened at grindhouse theatres but box-office records show they often enjoyed decent returns. Everyone went home happy, especially distributors and young men with a craving for a scare.

Ramsays, the Hauntsmen

They were prolific in the early 1980s. *Hotel, Guest House* and *Dahshat* haunted the theatres in 1981. Their biggest hit, as per trade magazines, was *Purana Mandir* (1984), a ghoulish tale of a devil-worshipping, sexual fiend named Saamri, who seemed to possess a license to kill and chill. The brothers also stayed in tune with the times. Following the blockbuster success of the dubbed 3D film, *Chhota Chetan*, they tried their hand at the industry's latest fad. Result: *Saamri* (3D, 1985), another small success. *Veerana* (1986), a perennial favourite on cable TV, has an awesome 100 million views on YouTube.

The Ramsays were an anglicised version of Ramsinghani. F.U. Ramsay, a Sindhi from Karachi, migrated to Bombay during the Partition. He dabbled in film production (*Rustom Sohrab*) but his seven sons developed a taste for horror. Unabashed fans of the human bloodhound Dracula and the fiendish Frankenstein, they learnt the craft of cinema from Joseph V. Mascelli's book, *The Five C's of Cinematography*.[11]

The brothers specialised in different aspects of filmmaking; hence costs were low enough to make selling easy. Tulsi, who passed away in 2018, and Shyam, who died a year later, were the helmsmen. 'Directed by Tulsi Ramsay and Shyam Ramsay' was a familiar sight in the opening credits. Kiran was the sound recordist, Gangu the cameraman and Kumar the writer. Arjun assisted in direction, wrote and edited too. Keshu produced, directed and lensed. Together they converted the genre into a family business and a saleable brand in the Bombay cinema industry. As Delhi-based film distributor-cum-exhibitor Sanjay Ghai pithily said, 'Like Maruti in cars, the Ramsays were a trademark in horror films.'[12]

The Ramsays hit pay dirt with *Do Gaz Zameen Ke Neeche* (1972), a murder mystery masquerading as a horror flick. The movie was shot in forty days on a budget of Rs 3.5 lakh. The seven brothers and their wives drove to Mahabaleshwar and rented eight rooms in a government guest house for Rs 12 per day. The shooting took place on location on borrowed cameras.[13] The film earned Rs 45 lakh, a staggering amount considering the investment made. In 1978, they delivered *Darwaza*, a true-blue monster movie with a down-and-out Anil Dhawan that set the basic template of their work. In the Eighties, they grew bigger.

Tulsi and Shyam constructed the grand visual template of what became a standard Ramsay horror: aging mansions, angry bats, foggy cemeteries, monsters with rolling eyes and anxious background music. The demons usually emerged from a derelict grave or from a chained coffin kept in a basement. Huge, ugly and unsteady creatures of the dark, they were brought to life by men who worshipped Satan and darkness. They had unlimited sexual powers. In the end, good always triumphed over evil with a little help from God's tool, usually a *trishul* (trident), a spear with Om written on it or a cross that pierced the beast's heart.

SHORT TAKE

Who were the monsters?

The monsters were the actual stars of the 'creature horror' films. Two big-unit actors fitted the part. Anirudh Agarwal (*Purana Mandir*, *Saamri* and *Bandh Darwaza*) had the height of an NBA basketballer and was built like a heavyweight boxer. A civil engineer from Dehradun, he remains the most recognisable blood-sucking beast in Hindi horror. His face, as Amborish Roychoudhary rightly observed in his book, *In a Cult Of Their Own*, brings to mind the Great Khali, the wrestler-entertainer who also found success in Hollywood. Shamshuddin (*Tahkhana*, *Khooni Mahal*, and *Veerana*) also became a familiar fiend. In the 1980s, the blood-thirsty ogre became the USP of horror films, most notably in *Veerana* and *Purana Mandir*.

Several horror movies were indigenised versions of Hollywood hits. The central character of *Dahshat* (1981), a deranged Dr Vishal (Om Shivpuri), is loosely modelled on H.G. Wells'

Dr Moreau. Vishal uses animal blood to treat human beings. His wife (Nadira) injects him with the same, turning him into a beast when enraged. The reasonably slick *Guest House* (1981) borrowed the idea of a disembodied hand from *Dr. Terror's House of Horrors* (1965). Vinod Talwar's *Wohi Bhayanak Raat*, by his own admission, was based on *Fright Night*. Producer K.M. Bhakri recalled that his brother, director Mohan Bhakri's *Kabrastan* (1988) was also based on a Hollywood film.

The Ramsay horrors blended laughter with fear. Comedians such as Rajendra Nath and Satish Shah were regulars. Rajendra Nath seemed to relish playing the horror writer on a honeymoon in *Guest House*, though some of the credit should go to the wise-cracking dialogue writer (Omar Khayyam Saharanpuri). Satish Shah's parody of old hits drew guffaws in *Purani Haveli* (1989). The horror-comedy template was imitated by others.

Several spooky flicks such as *Dahshat, Hotel* and *Purana Mandir* also had pleasing music, a rather unexpected bonus. Even suspense thrillers such as *Saboot* and *Sannata* had agreeable tracks. Lyricist Amit Khanna recalled, 'The Ramsays did not interfere with the creative process and gave the music director and me the freedom to do our work.'[14]

The musical aspect of the Ramsay films hasn't been focused upon. The music, sometimes by the now-forgotten Ajeet Singh (*Tahkhana, Purana Mandir, Purani Haveli*), makes them stand out in the pantheon of the global fear factory. The blending of terror and gore with hummable tracks contributed to the uniqueness of Bombay cinema horror.

The Bhakris

Like the Ramsays, the Bhakris also came from Pakistan. They, too, helped the genre expand in the 1980s and '90s. Gujranwala-born Mulk Raj Bhakri had produced films such as *Guest House* and *Taxi 555* in the 1950s. His brother Lekhraj Bhakri had directed two early Manoj Kumar starrers, *Honeymoon* and *Banarasi Thug*, in the 1960s.

Mohan Bhakri, son of Mulk Raj, was the writer-director of scare flicks such as *Cheekh* (1985), *Khooni Mahal* (1987), *Kabrastan* (1988) and *Khooni Murda* (1989). Mohan also worked for outside banners, making films such as *Sau Saal Baad* (1989).

The Bhakris, too, converted horror into a family affair. Mohan's brother K.M. (Krishna Mohan) Bhakri produced *Cheekh* and *Khooni Murda*. Cousin Arvind Bhakri was a regular cinematographer for the unit.

Mohan Bhakri had directed a hit Punjabi film, *Jatti* (1980). His suspense thriller *Apradhi Kaun?* (1980) also fetched decent returns. Producer K.M. Bhakri said, 'But when Mohan saw the Ramsays making money with horror, he decided to follow suit. He used to watch videos of Hollywood horror films, take ideas and sequences from them. He was also encouraged by distributors to take that route.'[15]

Model-turned hero Javed Khan, who played the lead in several Bhakri films such as *Kabrastan*, remembered Mohan Bhakri's penchant for incorporating scenes from Hollywood films. 'We couldn't match the special effects. But people still tell me they enjoyed those films,' said Khan.[16]

Like the Ramsays, the Bhakris belonged to the frugal school of filmmaking. Costs were lower than camera angles in dance scenes. Made for a mere Rs 18 lakh, *Cheekh* was heroine Dipika Chikhalia's debut venture. She had some steamy scenes in the film. K.M. Bhakri recalled, 'When she signed up for Sita in Ramanand Sagar's *Ramayan*, some journalists came asking for those photos. But Dipika had already requested me not to give them anything, so I refused them outright.'[17] Dipika later joined BJP and won the Lok Sabha seat from Baroda in 1991.

Raza Murad, Madan Puri and Rajendra Nath were regulars in the Bhakri movies. So were composers Nadeem-Shravan, yet to hit their stride.

Among Mohan Bhakri's biggest successes was *Kabrastan* (1988). Javed Khan, who now runs an acting academy in his hometown Bhopal, said, 'The devil possesses me and I start killing people. It became the film's novelty. People didn't expect me in the role.'[18]

He also recalled how the system worked: 'I never got more than Rs 75,000 for a horror film. Even that amount was never fully paid. There were no contracts. The amount agreed upon was never delivered. The common line was: "*Agley film mein dekh lenge* (We will see in the next film)." It was a relationship based on mutual need.'[19]

Another director who joined the bandwagon was Delhi-born Vinod Talwar. He had an interesting story to narrate about how he joined the horror bandwagon. Talwar said, 'I produced a Punjabi film, *Ishq Nimana*, which did well. I then signed Sanjay Dutt for a Hindi movie, but stopped getting dates after his *Jaan Ki Baazi* [1985] became a moderate success. I had no interest in horror films but writer Dharam Vir Ram [*Cobra, Patton Ki Baazi*] told me, "Make a horror film, you will not need a hero then".' Talwar had learnt filmcraft assisting his maternal uncle O.P. Ralhan (*Phool Aur Patthar, Talash*) in *Paapi*.[20]

The advice helped. *Raat Ke Andhere Mein* (1987), a murder mystery with a faux supernatural theme, was completed in eight months. Talwar said distributors kept asking him to make more horror movies, the low-budget flavour of the season. 'So I made *Wohi Bhayanak Raat* (1989), which was inspired by *Fright Night*. The movie again did well. I made a few more horror films in the 1990s,' he said.[21]

Even director B.R. Ishara tried his hand at the supernatural. *Woh Phir Aayegi* (1988) had a high-profile cast: Rajesh Khanna, Farah and Moon Moon Sen. But the movie only horrified the distributors.

Arthouse Horror

Gehrayee (1980) came closest to arthouse horror in the 1980s. The film stood out because it wasn't located in an abandoned haveli or a smoky graveyard. Part of the film was shot in Bangalore's Cubbon Park, the tall aging trees acting as scary props.

Made by the talented husband-wife director duo Aruna-Vikas, the film was about a young girl who gets possessed by a spirit. In her autobiography, *Freedom,* Arunaraje Patil admitted that the runaway success of *The Exorcist* prompted them to make the movie. Getting renowned playwright Vijay Tendulkar on board was a coup.

Padmini Kolhapure was the lead protagonist. She spoke in Jalal Agha's voice when controlled by the spirit. Amrish Puri played the tantrik. 'He was so threatening and evil in the film that when Steven Spielberg was casting for *Indiana Jones and The Temple of Doom,* the reference we sent of Amrish's performance and look in *Gehrayee* was bang on and landed him the role,' she wrote.[22]

A nude scene involving Padmini and Amrish Puri drew frenzied media attention. Patil explained how the scene was filmed. 'I had used my mustard-coloured shawl, fixed halter-style with a ribbon to fully cover her from the front so that even if a little bit of the shawl was visible, it blended with the fire in front of her. Her long hair covered most of her back—the nude effect was simulated.'[23]

The film received mouthwatering publicity after Kolhapure kissed the visiting Prince Charles on his cheek. The promos went, 'See the girl who kissed Prince Charles in *Gehrayee.*' The film recovered its costs.

Rebirth Yarns

In 1980, two big-budget films, Subhash Ghai's *Karz* (1980, inspired by *The Reincarnation of Peter Proud*) and Chetan Anand's *Kudrat* (1980), were based on *punar janam.* Both were lavishly shot and elevated by good music. But neither of them did as well as expected.

The Snake-woman

The shape-shifting snake-woman bred another supernatural sub-genre. In the 1970s, Reena Roy played the seductive serpent in the super-flop movie, *Milap* (1972), and the box-office biggie, *Nagin* (1976). The genre got a second wind with Harmesh Malhotra's box-office sensation *Nagina* (1986), a romantic family drama with the supernatural element as its USP.

One way of measuring a film's long-term impact is by the number of imitations it spawns. *Nagina* sprouted a bunch of clones: *Badla Nagin Ka* (dubbed, 1987), *Nagin Aur Nagina* (dubbed, 1988), *Nagin Ke Do Dushman* (dubbed, 1989), and *Tu Nagin Main Sapera* (1989). Malhotra, too, went for a sequel, *Nigahen* (1989), but lightning did not strike twice.

Nache Nagin Gali Gali (1989), starring Nitish Bhardwaj of *Krishna* fame and Meenakshi Seshadri, also earned profits. The movie also led to a Punjabi remake, *Nache Nagina*, which reportedly became a superhit in Pakistan.[24] However, websites show the name as 'Nachey Nagin'. The idea of a snake-woman has found a new life on new-millennium television too. *Naagin* (2015) is a popular serial.

SHORT TAKE

With love from Madras

Director B. Vijay's *Mangalsutra* (1981) was a rare Hindi horror made in Madras. A remake of the Kannada superhit, *Naa Ninna Bidalare* (1979), it had Anant Nag and Rekha in the lead roles, with Prema Narayan playing the evil spirit who is finally silenced by the divine trishul.

Wahem (1987) starred Suresh Oberoi and Sangeeta Naik (*Nukkad*, TV) and was described as 'India's first stunning sexiest marital horror, murder mystery.' Only the unfortunate few saw it. Vishal Bharadwaj's gave the music for one song, 'Saat phere', among his early film songs as a composer.

Murder Mysteries

In the 1960s, suspense flicks like *Bees Saal Baad* (1962), *Woh Kaun Thi?* (1964), *Gumnaam* (1965), *Teesri Manzil* (1966) and *Humraaz* (1967), became major box-office winners. One of the key reasons for the genre's success then was its ability to integrate the standard Bombay thali of enchanting melodies and slapstick comedy within the matrix of a smart murder mystery. A-list directors such as Raj Khosla and Vijay Anand were in fine fettle and added to the genre's quality.

The 1980s too saw a glut of murder mysteries but most of them lost money. The yarns of deception and intrigue in this decade too often had catchy, if not captivating, music. *Phir Wahi Raat* (1980), *Ghunghroo Ki Awaaz* (1981), *Aitbaar* (1985) to name a few, had enchanting tracks. But the box-office shows the public was more interested in fists and guns than taut stories filled with suspense and songs.

Among the most discussed films in the genre was southern director Bharathiraja's adult flop, *Red Rose* (1980), a remake of Tamil hit *Sigappu Rosakkal* (1978), with Rajesh Khanna replacing Kamal Haasan in the Hindi version. The actor invested the part of a psychopath with a suitcase of neatly tailored suits and a truckload of mannerisms. Few were impressed.

Actor Danny's Hindi directorial debut, *Phir Wahi Raat* (1980), fared relatively better. Starring Rajesh Khanna and Kim (then Danny's girlfriend) in lead roles, the tale of a young woman troubled by nightmares, was let down by the scrawny suspense. Most whodunit regulars could guess the killer before the interval.

Writer-director Ved Rahi's *Kali Ghata* (1980) had a more carefully hidden villain but it didn't help the film's cause.

Even seasoned director Raghunath Jhalani's *Jal Mahal* (1980) produced a surprise antagonist in the climax. But the film, shot in the palaces of Rajasthan, was a letdown.

Harmesh Malhotra's *Raaz* (1981), written by the extremely talented Ravi Kapoor (*Gaddaar, Patthar Aur Payal, Ashanti, Loha*) was an offbeat thriller starring Raj Babbar (in a mysterious role) and Sulakshana Pandit. The film had a fairly absorbing first half but lost momentum and the plot after the banta break.

Some whudunits were shot in scenic locales. Jug Mundra's *Suraag* (1982) was lavishly shot in the United States with a pipe-smoking Sanjeev Kumar adding flair. Director Anil Ganguly's *Kaun? Kaisey??* (1983) was lensed in panoramic Shimla. Mithun was the investigating cop in this occasionally absorbing tale. In Hrishikesh Mukherjee's *Namumkin* (1988), largely shot in Canada with local technicians, an aging bridegroom commits suicide on his wedding night. The film is among the director's weaker efforts.

Mukul Anand's stylish *Aitbaar*, a xeroxed copy of Hitchcock's *Dial M for Murder*, had a leisurely crafted and utterly gripping sequence where a hired killer (Sharat Saxena) comes to murder the protagonist (Dimple Kapadia).

A taut psychological thriller, Ketan Anand's *Shart* (1986) explored the twisted mind of a serial killer, who hates sex workers. Boosted by powerful performances from Naseeruddin Shah and Shabana Azmi, this intermittently riveting film went largely unwatched.

Director Zafar Hai's *The Perfect Murder* (1988) was lovingly and innovatively filmed the streets of Bombay, better than most filmmakers based in the city. Naseeruddin Shah played Inspector Ghote of the famous detective series by H.R. Keating. Swedish actor Stellan Skarsgård was his companion.

Plot No 5 (1981) was a casting coup: Uttam Kumar, Amol Palekar, Sarika and Amjad Khan. The storyline—a string of murders of young girls connected to a house on Plot No 5—was neatly fashioned but shoddily released after the death of Uttam

Kumar, the superstar of Bengali movies; it failed to create even a ripple.

The Ramsays, too, were murder-mystery specialists. The brothers rustled up a cluster of watchable flicks such as *Saboot*, *Sannata* and *Telephone*, though bigger rewards came in the horror genre. *Saboot*, the best of the lot, was immensely watchable with a wonderfully surprising denouement.

The Bhakris had their own share of edgy thrillers, such as Mohan Bhakri's *Apradhi Kaun?* The excited producers advertised in a trade magazine that the film was made in only thirty-seven shifts with just thirty-seven rolls. The film was sold for Rs 3 lakh in Bombay and within five months had fetched Rs 7 lakh, they claimed.

Arthouse Whodunit

Vidhu Vinod's *Khamosh* (1985) was the most wickedly compelling whodunit of the 1980s. The film was shot in Kashmir's Pahalgam district, just a few years before the Valley echoed with the cries of *'Azaadi, Azaadi'*. The songless film is about a series of murders that occurs during the shooting of a sleaze flick, 'Aakhri Khoon'. Even today when the killer's identity is finally revealed in an unnerving climax, it draws gasps of collective shock from most viewers.

Vidhu Vinod—also the film's story and scenario writer—had the *crème de la crème* of offbeat cinema and theatre assisting him with the script and dialogues: Saeed Mirza, Sudhir Mishra, Kundan Shah and Ranjit Kapoor. Some of the brightest future stars of parallel cinema (Pawan Malhotra, for instance) were doing bit roles here.

The murder sequences were designed to scare, and they did. Like the film's warped killer, the director seemed to relish the murders. The killings were filmed like scenes of romance. The scene where Shabana goes to the houseboat to fetch a scarf was as creepy as it gets. The houseboat climax was nerve-wracking and the way the killer pronounced 'Shabana' in a mean, soft whisper, drew gasps from the audience.

The movie was rated 'Good B' by *Trade Guide*, which roughly translates into modest profits.

Sex Films

In the 1980s, 'Jawani' was the most commonly used word in titles of Hindi films of a certain kind. The word simply means adulthood in Urdu but for producers, it also opened every available door to adult imagination.

These movies were prominently advertised in trade magazines. Posters, generally of underclad young couples in various stages of coitus, were prominently splashed across cities and towns, arousing curiosity and attracting attention. Social conservatives would write letters to the editor, bemoaning the trend.

Such films would have crowd-pulling punchlines such as 'Sex is not a lesson; it is an experience' (film: *Anubhav*). Shekhar Suman's *Kharidar* was advertised with dialogues such as *'Bachche to koi bhi paida kar sakta hai chanda / magar ladkiyan paida karna taaki tera dhanda chalu rahega.'*

In the imagination of the common public, these movies loomed much larger than the queues outside theatres indicated. Generally attracting young male viewers, sex films were shown in the seedier cinemas. Women were practically non-existent among the audience. Such films enjoyed a steady clientele in early morning or late-night shows. They were like oxygen to theatres that had fallen on hard times. A few reels of XXX-rated films were often stealthily inserted in such films. Authorities, palms suitably greased, would look the other way.

'Jawani' was used as the root word to which anything could be added to spice up its meaning and, in turn, lure the viewer to the theatre. Between 1986 and 1989, fifteen Hindi films (some dubbed from Malayalam) used 'Jawani' in their titles: *Jawani Ki Kahani, Jawani Ke Jalwe, Nashilee Jawani, Kachchi Jawani, Bhatakti Jawani, Jawani Ki Pyas, Junglee Jawani* and more.

There was a reason why certain Malayalam films became a favourite of small distributors. In 1979, director I.V. Sasi's *Man Ka Aangan*, dubbed from the Malayalam hit, *Vadakakku Oru Hridayam*, became a surprise box-office sensation. The film unleashed a trend of sex films, some dubbed.

Sex films were ubiquitous in the 1980s

During 1986-1989, at least twenty-nine films with a healthy dose of titillating dialogues and sex scenes made it past the censors. The movies which made money were *Garbh Gyan*, *Pashu Sangram* (1982), *Prem Rahasya* (1982), *Yeh Hai Aurat* (1984), *Jism Ka Rishta* (1989) and *Jawani 16 Saal Ki* (1989). The most profitable was *Jawani Ki Kahani* (1986), a faux film on sex education in universities and raising public awareness about family planning. Among those who acted in the film were Vijay Arora, a happening hero of the 1970s, and Nylex Nalini, the name allegedly inspired by Silk Smitha. *Yeh Hai Aurat* (dubbed, 1984) was an even bigger success.

Well-known stars generally shied away from such films but there were exceptions. Vikram (*Julie, Swami*) performed in *Jawani Ki Bhool. Anubhav* starred Shekhar Suman, Richa Sharma and Padmini Kolhapure. Tina Munim and Alok Nath acted out a couple of hot scenes in *Kam-Agni*. Gajendra Chauhan, who later became FTII chairman, was a voyeur in *Khuli Khidki,* which had some bold and bawdy scenes.

———— SHORT TAKE ————

Dada Kondke's ribald comedies often landed into censor trouble. *Tere Mere Beech Mein* (1984) managed to recover costs. *Andheri Raat Mein Diya Tere Haath Mein* (1986), a title that brought smiles as much for its ingenuity as for the double entendre, was a bigger success. But his other Hindi films— *Aage Ki Soch* (1988) and *Khol De Meri Zuban* (1989)—missed the mark. Describing him as the 'sultan of smut', *The Times of India* film critic Khalid Mohamad wrote in his review that *Aage Ki Soch* 'does to the art of filmmaking what the bombs did to Hiroshima and Nagasaki'.

Secret Agents and Karate Choppers

Sixties Bombay cinema had a yen for secret agents modelled on James Bond, which translated into their felicity with guns, gadgets and gals. They tried to save the country from '*desh ke dushman*' who were both '*videshi taqat*' (often Chinese) and desi quislings. Stealing scientific secrets—usually an indigenously developed formula related to atomic or nuclear energy, which would change the fortunes of India—was a running theme. Small and major stars—from Randhawa and Sailesh Kumar to Jeetendra, Biswajit, Dharmendra and Mithun—tried their hand at these desi Bond ventures.

Director-cinematographer Ravikant Nagaich will be remembered for gifting Hindi cinema with two secret agents: Secret Agent 116 (*Farz*, 1967) and Gunmaster G9 (*Surakksha*, 1979). These films are the first hits in the careers of Jeetendra and Mithun. Deepak Bahry's *Agent Vinod* (1977), the lone solo success of Mahendra Sandhu, was reprised in 2012.

In 1981, Nagaich rolled out G9's second edition, *Wardat*, where the villain wants to rule the planet by controlling an artificial army of locusts. At a time when there's persistent conversation among scientists on engineered viruses, the movie was more prescient than anyone would have thought. G9 had become a popular brand and, with Mithun's rising currency, could have become a popular franchise, but sadly for its fans that never happened.

Raksha (1982, Nagaich-Jeetendra combo again) was about atomic energy theft. The opening credits were a straight lift from the Bond franchise. The Asian Games gold medallist for discus throw, Praveen Kumar, played a desi Jaws (Richard Kiel in *The Spy Who Loved Me*), metallic teeth and all. The film flopped. Undeterred, Jeetendra joined hands with director Ravi Tandon to bring out *Bond 303* (1985), where mini grenades were hidden in shoe heels. Sub-par special effects and a shoddy script combined to make the film a low point in Tandon's bright career.

Shatrughan Sinha and Sanjeev Kumar also played secret agents, whom everybody seemed to know, in Feroz Chinoy's pedestrian *Bad Aur Badnaam* (1984).

B.R. Chopra's *Awam* (1987) was a spy espionage thriller with Rajesh Khanna playing an army intelligence-wing captain. The film borrowed elements from the real-life Coomar Narain (1985) and Larkins (1983) cases.

Thanks to Bruce Lee, martial arts became popular among a section of youth in the 1970s. His posters were put up in college hostels. Martial arts coaching classes sprouted across India. Black belt became a term of respect.

Bollywood saw an opening. Ravikant Nagaich's *Morchha* (1980) was the best of the martial arts movies. Ravi Behl (of TV show *Boogie Woogie* fame) was hugely impressive as the nunchaku-wielding thirteen-year-old in search of his parents' killers. The movie was dedicated to 'the man who inspired us all: Bruce Lee'. One song was also dedicated to the guru. For the record, the movie was released four years before Hollywood's *The Karate Kid* (1984).

The lone bright spark in director Batra Mohinder's *Cobra* (1980) was debutant Ardhendu Bose, nephew of Subhash Chandra Bose, who looked at home in the karate sequences and might have enjoyed a longer career but for his westernised looks, which also extended to his diction.

Karate (1983) was Deb Mukerji's love child. The Mukerji family scion wrote the film's story and screenplay. He also acted, produced and directed the movie which had Mithun in another karate-chopping avatar. Mukerji himself wielded a mean nunchaku. The same year came *Agent 123*, a dubbed kid flick with three young karate-trained teens. Both films, surprisingly, recovered their costs.

REEL 12

DISCO OUTBREAK AND UNSUNG CLASSICS

Disco struck Bombay cinema like a viral fever in the early 1980s. Swinging strobe lights, loose-limbed dancers, shimmery outfits, and hysterical synth-driven rhythms—the disco song was obligatory in the mainstream movie. Even a vegan family romance like *Saajan Mere Main Saajan Ki* (1980) found a way to incorporate a disco number. Ashok Kumar, then approaching sixty, and Shashikala, touching fifty, jived and crooned 'Hi honey' at a night club. The song was peddled as the film's special attraction. Horror films (*Hotel*) and murder mysteries (*Sannata*) couldn't do without them either. It was almost as if a film wouldn't get censor clearance without a couple of shake-and-rattle tracks.

Disco came out of the West in the 1970s. The online Merriam-Webster dictionary describes it as a 'style of dance music... characterised by hypnotic rhythm, repetitive lyrics, and electronically produced sounds'. John Travolta bopped his way to millions of hearts and dollars in *Saturday Night Fever* (1977). The growth of disco coincided with the birth of MTV in 1981, which fundamentally changed the way the global young consumed popular music.

Till now, music was primarily about listening. Now songs also became about watching. Music videos rose to prominence in due course. The beat became as important, if not more crucial than the melody. Words were often drowned by the electronic beat. Looking back *The Economist* wrote in December 2020 how the Yamaha DX7 synthesiser single-handedly influenced the world of electro-pop in the 1980s.

In Bombay cinema, the first disco track to make a mass impact was 'Aap jaisa koi' from Feroz Khan's *Qurbani* (1980). Khan got London-based composer Biddu to record a song for him. The composer was unknown to most Indians but had carved out a name for himself with floorscorchers like 'Kung fu fighting' (Carl Douglas, 1974) and 'Dance little lady dance' (Tina Charles, 1976).

In his autobiography, *Made in India*, Biddu said that he knew little Hindi, having forgotten most of what he had learnt at Bishop Cotton School, Bangalore. But language was no

Composer Biddu's 'Aap jaisa koi' from *Qurbani*
kick-started the disco boom in Hindi films in the 1980s.
(Photo Credit: *The Pioneer*)

barrier in this case. He wrote, 'I had a catchy introductory riff played on the sitar; I used syn drums, which had never been used in a song before. The syn drum made a sound not unlike my name. It went "bidoo" every time you hit it and I double-tracked Nazia's [Hassan] voice to give it some oomph. Once again, I used a rhythm box with a Latin beat to give it a hip-swaying groove. "Aap jaisa koi meri zindagi mein aaye," she sang, her voice sounding young and sexy as the song came alive.'[1]

'Aap jaisa koi', lensed on Zeenat Aman, sounded novel and proved contagious. The song bossed the airwaves, bellowed out of loudspeakers at street corners and was endlessly swayed to. Even bandmasters found a way to play it in wedding processions. It finished fourth in the wildly popular radio countdown show, *Binaca Geetmala's* (*BGM*) annual charts in 1980. Nazia even got the *Filmfare's* best female singer award! And the syn drum was employed a hundred times over.

The hot-selling *Qurbani* track ushered in the disco age in Bombay cinema. Another chart climber, 'Hari Om Hari' (*Pyaara Dushman*, 1980) also joined the party. The song was a xeroxed version of 'One way ticket' by British band, Eruption (1978).

Of course, the disco sound was not completely alien to Bombay cinema before the Eighties. Several 'inspired' tracks in Nasir Hussain's box-office smash hit, *Hum Kisise Kum Naheen* (1977), especially those used in the song-and-dance competition scene, could be categorised as disco numbers.

Lahiri's compositions in *College Girl* (1978), *Shikshaa* (1979) and *Surakksha* (1979) had already given the audience a foretaste of the things to come. Just watch the hot-stepping 'Tum jo bhi ho aaj dil do' from *Surakksha*. Power-packed tracks such as 'Yaari hai phoolon se meri yaari hai' (*Shikshaa*, 1979) and 'Mausam hai gaane ka' (*Surakksha*, 1979) were shot on city streets but could well have been filmed in a disco.

But it needs a blockbuster to start a trend. That's what 'Aap jaisa koi' did. It kick-started Hindi cinema's disco song industry. A series of non-film disco albums were released around the same time. Cashing in on composer Biddu's insta-popularity, HMV brought out *Disco Deewane* (1981) with songs crooned by the teenage sister-brother sensation, Nazia and Zoheb Hassan. The album went gold in twenty-four hours and platinum in three weeks. As per HMV ads of the time, platinum disc meant that 2,00,000 LPs and cassettes had been sold. Gold translated to 1,00,000 LPs and cassettes being snapped up.[2]

Soon non-film disco became the musical snack of the season. Runa Laila and Bappi Lahiri's *Superuna*; Sharon Prabhakar's *Chal Disco Chal*; Mahendra Kapoor, Canadian singer Musarrat and Boney M's *M3*, Babla's *Disco Dandiya* and Preeti Sagar's *Heartbeat* were some other disco-centred albums of this period. The Agha sisters—Salma and Sabina—brought out a Hindi version of ABBA hits.

In Bombay, directors, dance directors, lyricists and composers were forced to introduce something novel in the disco track in what soon became an overused genre of music. A railway station set was constructed for 'Disco Station' (*Haathkadi*, 1982). The song was integral to the film's climax. Composer Rajesh Roshan gave a sitar twist to *Khud-Daar*'s 'Disco 82'. In *Saaheb's* (1985) 'Yaar bina chain kahan re', the night streets became a 'disco' setting.

Disco gave rise to a bunch of female singers with muscle in their voices. Usha Iyer nee Uthup's sensual huskiness, which first came into chart-busting prominence in *Hare Rama Hare Krishna* (1971), sprouted new shoots in the 1980s: Sharon Prabhakar, Alisha Chinoy and Anette Pinto. These voices, brimming with vitality and power, were the forerunners of the more sinewy voices that emerged in the 1990s and the new millennium: Jaspinder Narula, Sunidhi Chauhan and many more. In those conservative times, however, their voices were mostly filmed on dancers, and seldom on major heroines.

Born in Bombay and settled in Calcutta, Usha voiced the smash hit 'Rambha ho ho' (film: *Armaan*, 1981), which ranked third in *Binaca Geetmala's* annual hit parade. Her verve also found suitable outlets in 'Aowwa aowwa' (*Disco Dancer*, 1982), 'Pyaar mein jeena, pyaar mein marna, pyaar se lena hai uska nam, Radhey Shyam' (*Do Ustad*, 1984), 'Aaa main gulbadan, main hoon chaman, beautiful, sundaram' (*Locket*, 1984), and many more.

She, however, made bigger news for an unmusical courtroom drama in 1983; Jatin Chakraborty, the PWD minister in Jyoti Basu's Left Front government in West Bengal, being on the other side. Chakraborty described her performances as, '*apasanskriti*' (anti-culture), which was destroying the youth of Bengal. She was stopped from performing at government-run venues. The minister's young supporters even tried to disrupt one of her concerts.

Uthup filed a defamation suit. Underlining everyone's right to song and dance, the Calcutta High Court ruled in her favour. The judgment even made news abroad. In its 4 September 1983 issue, the *New York Times* headlined an article, 'Marxist leader fails to silence Indian singer.'

Sharon Prabhakar's 'Haan meri jaisi haseena ka dil yahan jise mil jaaye' (*Armaan*, 1981), inspired by Dr Hook's 'When you're in love', became a runaway success. Her urbane intonation created the perfect stew of melody and desire in 'Pyar chalke halke halke' (*Sumbandh*, 1982). She also acted and sang in M.S. Sathyu's *Kahan Kahan Se Guzar Gaya*.

Ahmedabad-born Alisha Chinoy's sumptuous voice found a suitable platform in 'Tarzan My Tarzan' (*Tarzan*, 1985). The footstomper rose to *BGM's* song No. 2 the following year. 'Zoo zoo zoobie zoobie' (*Dance Dance*, 1987) has a combined seventy million YouTube hits now.

Kalpana Iyer was the dancing queen of the era. If you close your eyes and think of a disco song, she is the first face that flashes before your eyes. Some of the bestselling tracks of the era—'Hari Om Hari' (*Pyaara Dushman*), 'Tu mujhe jaan se bhi pyaara hai' (*Wardat*), 'Haan meri jaisi haseena' (*Armaan*), 'Aowwa aowwa' (*Disco Dancer*)—were filmed on her. The foot-thumping 'Rambha ho ho' (*Armaan*, with Prema Narayan in company) had a disco-friendly beat but was filmed outdoors in a carnival. Even today her dances feel trendy. Later, Iyer worked as a hospitality hostess in Dubai.

Among the male singers, Vijay Benedict, and to a lesser extent Nandu Bhende, became a disco specialist in Mithun movies. Allahabad-bred Benedict burst into limelight with the title song of B. Subhash's *Disco Dancer* (1982). His energetic rendition of 'I am a Disco Dancer' matched the song's rhythm and aura. Over the next few years, Benedict continued to deliver hot-sellers especially in B. Subhash movies such as *Kasam Paida Karne Wale Ki* (1984) and *Dance Dance* (1987). He became a gospel singer later.

Disco Dancer's music magnified the appeal of the genre, bringing it to the forefront in Hindi films. What was just an item song until then had become the subject of a movie. *Disco Dancer* has become iconic like Raj Kapoor's *Awara*, especially in Russia and China, where people continue to sing and jive to its songs in music talent contests. At least ten separate Russian dance videos of 'Jimmy Jimmy Jimmy aaja aaja aaja' (singer: Parvati Khan) are available on YouTube. So are videos made in Georgia (over 7.3 million views), Belarus, Mongolia and other countries. The song, has also become a part of the original score in Adam Sandler's *You Don't Mess With The Zohan*. By the way, 'Jimmy Jimmy's' original tune can be traced to 'T'es OK, T'es Bath' (1980) of French pop duo Ottawan. 'Krishna dharti pe aaja tu' (singer: Nandu Bhende), an unabashed lift from Tielman Brothers' 'Jesus, won't you come back to earth', was another winner.

Dancing in Hindi films can be broken up into two categories: indoors and outdoors. Till the 1980s, an overwhelming majority of indoor songs which required dancing were either performed in nightclubs or kothas. In either case, women dancers were the central performers. Disco facilitated the parallel rise of male dancers and assisted the ascent of Mithun and Govinda as stars.

Disco also spurred the rise of the revelry tracks. As journalist-lyricist Hasan Kamal said, 'There are two kinds of songs. Some you listen in a crowd and enjoy. Others you listen in solitude. The songs of solitude have a larger shelf life. The number of such songs has dramatically gone down. In the 1980s, the music of gatherings picked strength.'[3]

L-P Still Unbeatable

Despite the disco craze, old hand Laxmikant-Pyarelal (L-P) stayed way ahead of their competitors in the 1980s. They were the preferred composers of A-list directors such as Subhash Ghai, Manoj Kumar, Manmohan Desai and many top southern production houses. And they seldom let them down.

A collated list of top twenty songs from *BGM's* annual countdown shows from 1980-1989 (20 x 10 = 200 songs) shows, L-P leading the list with seventy-six songs. Bappi Lahiri furnished thirty-four and R.D. Burman twenty-nine. Except in 1983 and 1984, when Bappi rustled up more hits than them, the duo stayed on top in the world of Hindi film music.

Popular music was defined by quantity, not quality, in the 1980s. As per IMDb data, L-P gave music to 193 films in the 1980s, roughly an astonishing nineteen films every year. Their success can be attributed to their ability to deliver tunes to suit changing demands. Subhash Ghai's disco-propelled *Karz* (1980) was a challenge for L-P, who despite their pop-driven numbers in *Night in London* (1967) weren't the preferred choice for

Western tracks. The music was a suitable riposte to the doubting Thomases. 'Om Shanti Om' was the second biggest hit of 1980 after *Sargam's* (1979) 'Dafliwale dafli baja' (also L-P), the year's song No 1 on *BGM*. Not many knew then that 'Om Shanti Om' was pilfered from Caribbean singer Lord Shorty's 1978 track of the same name.

Versatility was L-P forte. The fertile duo stacked up hits for weepy family dramas (*Prem Rog*), youthful romances (*Ek Duuje Ke Liye*), romantic family dramas (*Pyar Jhukta Nahin*), thrillers-romance (*Hero, Karz*). They produced chartbusters in multistarrers like *Kranti, Naseeb, Coolie* and *Karma* where the focus was on violence, not violins. Laxmikant-Pyarelal had a tune for every occasion.

The twosome was also in demand among the South-based producers, producing a bagful of winning scores in *Ek Duuje Ke Liye, Ghar Ek Mandir, Sanjog* (which had the 1986 *BGM* topper, Lata's 'Yashoda ka Nandlala'), and many more.

Director K. Ravi Shankar (*Sindoor*) said, 'I would attribute part of *Sindoor's* success, to L-P's music. The song, 'Patjhar saawan basant bahar', is played four times in the film. If that song was a bore, the film would have bombed.'[4]

When given the opportunity, the duo also displayed their proficiency with the classical. 'Megha re megha re' (*Pyaasa Sawan*, 1981) was based on raag Charukesh. Director K. Vishwanath's *Sur Sangam* (1985) was a feast of raag-based melodies sung by the renowned Banaras gharana singers, Sajan Mishra-Rajan Mishra. Even Girish Karnad's *Utsav*, which recreated fifth century BC India, had melodies and instruments to match the era, such as raag Bibhas-based 'Saanjh dhale gagan taley' and the award-winning 'Man kyon behka'.

Lyricist Hasan Kamal, who worked with L-P in *Batwara, Hathyar* and *Yateem* (all J.P. Dutta movies), highlighted another facet that gave them the edge. He said, 'Nobody matched Pyarelal's calibre as a music arranger in the industry. Both were also lucky to find a lyricist like Anand Bakshi who gelled with them so completely.'[5]

In her autobiography, *Freedom*, film director Arunaraje Patil (Aruna-Vikas) acknowledged the role of Pyarelal's background music in creating the eerie atmosphere in the supernatural *Gehrayee*. The veteran music director used Tibetan singing bowls and employed a visiting musician from the United States who had the ability to 'produce strange guttural sounds from his throat that...sounded like they were from an alien world'.

RD Blues

For R.D. Burman, the '80s began on a promising note. The singer-composer's cool and catchy tunes contributed hugely to the success of debutants Kumar Gaurav (*Love Story*) and Sunny Deol (*Betaab*). Unfortunately, many films brimming with fetching tracks faltered at the box office: *Harjaee* (1981) *Yeh Vaada Raha* (1982), *Romance* (1983), *Lovers* (1983), *Sunny* (1984), *Manzil Manzil* (1984), *Sitamgar* (1985), *Saveray Wali Gaadi* (1986), to name a few.

Two gorgeous melodies embellished *Parinda* (1989): 'Pyar ke mod pe' and 'Tumse milkar'. *Ijaazat* (1988) brought national awards to Gulzar (lyrics) and Asha Bhosle (singer). Regarded as classics today, songs like 'Mera kuchh saaman' and 'Katra kara' never vaulted to the charts when first released. That, in brief, was R.D.'s tragedy. His best compositions didn't fetch him rewards. It is a tribute to the composer that these songs continue to be played with abandon on FM channels and their orchestration seems as fresh as it sounded nearly forty years ago. Modern and timeless, they have led to a reassessment of his work.

Hasan Kamal, who worked with R.D. in *Mazdoor* and *Siyasat*, said that he heard L-P saying once that if they valued or respected any of their contemporaries, it was R.D. He recalled, 'When I worked with R.D. Burman, his career was on a downward spiral. The fact that he was not doing well used to reflect in his attitude. He would often lose his temper. If I reached late for a recording, he wouldn't show his displeasure to me, but start scolding his assistant Sapan Chakravarty.'[6]

That is not to overlook the fact that, like other members of his tribe, R.D. also gave patchy music in dozens of forgettable films in this era—*Ganga Meri Maa* (1983), *Bheema* (1984), *Farishta* (1984), *Aar Paar* (1985), *Mardon Wali Baat* (1988), *Mil Gayee Manzil Mujhe* (1989), to name a few. Several top banners and long-time associates—Nasir Hussain (*QSQT*) and Dev Anand (*Sachche Ka Bolbala*), to name just two—dumped him. The *Binaca Geetmala* charts his fall from commercial grace. Between 1986 and 1989, R.D. had only three tracks among the Top 20 hits in the year-end list.

In their award-winning book, *R.D. Burman: The Man, The Music*, Anirudha Bhattacharjee and Balaji Vittal write that Pancham was told by the peerless Salil Chaudhary to be more selective about films. It doesn't seem he listened. R.D. gave music to 138 films between 1980 and 1989, roughly fourteen films every year. Bappi and L-P supplied music for more movies in the 1980s. But there was an important difference. L-P were a team of two. And Bappi was fresher and hungrier.

Disco Dancing with Bappi

Nobody understood the disco sound better than Bappi Lahiri. And nobody made India dance to his tune like him. It wouldn't be an exaggeration to say that his music massified dancing on the streets. In the Eighties alone, the composer-singer provided the score for an eye-popping 230 films, including a few in Bengali, to become the most industrious and prolific music director of the decade.

Here's a startling fact: In 1985, he gave music to thirty-three movies—thirty Hindi, two Bengali and one Tamil—which means a film released every twelve days! *Trade Guide* editor B.K. Adarsh wrote that Bappi Lahiri once signed thirty films in thirty days. 'He was the king in Madras. He used to do four to five recordings a day,' recalled film director B. Subhash.[7]

In a cover story for *Madhuri* magazine in 1986, well-known film journalist Vinod Tiwary described Bappi as a workaholic who preferred to spend more time at the recording studio or doing music shows than resting at home. Even if he reached home by eleven or twelve at night and found a producer waiting for him, Bappi would not only talk to him but also start a music sitting with him.[8]

Critics carped that Bappi's music lacked originality and longevity. But the music director saw that as a sign of changing times. He once told *Film Information*, 'In the old days, our films had a slow tempo. Also, lesser number of films were produced. Today we have fast kind of films made at a comparatively faster pace. Since we provide fast music at a faster pace, the sustenance power of a tune, howsoever good, has diminished to quite an extent. This leads to the wrong notion that today's songs do not linger on in one's mind because they lack melody.'[9]

Bappi's name was almost mandatory in the opening credits of southern masalas, notably in the box-office winners of director K. Raghavendra Rao and K. Bapaiah. The fortunes of *Himmatwala, Mawaali, Maqsad,* and *Tohfa* were propelled by his bouncy compositions. Director K. Ravi Shankar described 1980s as a Bappi phase. 'He ruled the southern market,' he said.[10]

The composer was in demand among Bombay directors too, notably Prakash Mehra and Basu Chatterjee. His music in *Disco Dancer, Namak Halaal* and *Sharaabi* were worth the weight of the gold chains he wore. *Namak Halaal's* 'Pag ghungroo baandh', including the opening orchestral passage, was nearly twelve minutes long. The composer's love for electronic sound as well as new instruments such as the bokodor, which imitated the human voice, kept him in fine fettle through the jiving times.

Bappi was born in Jalpaiguri, the north Bengal town. His parents were practitioners of Indian classical music; his mother the first woman music director in Bengali films. He learnt tabla from the legendary Samta Prasad. He had made his debut as a music director with *Nanha Shikari* in 1973 and found limited success with *Chalte Chalte* (1976), arguably his best score. But he worked his way up dishing out hit music even in low-budget films such as *Wardat* ('Tu mujhe jaan se bhi pyaara hai,' 1981). Even his disco superhits such as 'Hari Om Hari' (*Pyaara Dushman*), 'Rambha ho ho' (*Armaan*), 'Pyaar chhalke halke halke' (*Sumbandh*) weren't exactly from A-list movies.

He surprised critics with his surefooted folksy tunes in *Apne Paraye* (1980). 'Shyam rang ranga re', where he employed the Bengal percussion instrument khol, has the meditative feel of a Chaitanya kirtan. 'Gao mere mann' carries the smell of ponds, banana leaves and nineteenth-century Bengal. *Apne Paraye* wasn't an exception; it underlined Bappi's proficiency with folk music, just as he had underscored his familiarity with the classical in *Aangan Ki Kali* (1979).[11] In the 1980s, Bappi created noteworthy melodies in several other small-budget films such as *Ek Baar Kaho* (1980) and *Sheeshey Ka Ghar* (1984).

'He had sound knowledge of Indian music. People don't believe me when I tell them that the song "Kisi nazar ko tera intezaar aaj bhi hai" [*Aitbaar*] was composed by him,' said lyricist Hasan Kamal.[12]

The composer, who was once part of R.D. Burman's unit, established his musical identity with *Disco Dancer*. Film director B. Subhash recalled, 'He could sing, play and compose. He was a complete music man. Interestingly, Bappi would play the worst tunes first during a session. Then he would gradually pull out his better tunes.'[13]

Bappi was often accused of plagiarising tunes. The composer didn't deny the charge. His view was: Everybody steals. He once told *Madhuri* film magazine, 'All great musicians of the past that we don't tire of praising have also used foreign tunes. In their times, people travelling abroad wasn't a common thing. There were no cassettes. People praised them thinking they were original. If you want, I could give examples. But I am not doing so because I don't think it is wrong. Every artiste is inspired by something. He gets a thought from somewhere in his head. What's wrong in hearing a tune and creating a composition based on it? Even today many famous music directors are doing the same.'[14]

He wasn't wrong. A visit to the websiteitwofs.com, which lists plagiarised tunes in Hindi films, underlines what Bappi said.[15] Even the old masters would occasionally lift or get 'inspired' by foreign tunes. But it is undeniable that Bappi was more regular in filching foreign tunes. He even used foreign tunes for background music. In a chase sequence in *Dance Dance* (1985), you can hear the famous theme of *Chariots of Fire* (1981). In another scene, the composer used the haunting background score of *Picnic At Hanging Rock* (1975).

Sometimes he also copied tunes from indigenous classics. The song, 'Roshan roshan' (singer: Kishore Kumar-Asha Bhosle, lyrics: Kaifi Azmi, film: *Hum Rahe Na Hum*, 1984) was borrowed from Rabindranath Tagore's, 'Purono sei diner kotha'. Again, 'Chanda dekhe chanda' (film: *Jhooti*, 1985) incorporated elements from 'Aami tomay joto', another Tagore composition.

Bappi-*da* passed away on 17 February 2022. He was sixty-nine. The glowing tributes that followed underlined that his music was far more durable and influential than what many critics had predicted.

They Too Left their Mark

Rajesh Roshan (*Julie*, 1975) was among the most inventive and experimental composers in the 1980s. A regular in his brother, Rakesh Roshan's productions (*Kaamchor, Khoon Bhari Maang, Khudgarz*), he composed the vastly popular music of Amitabh Bachchan starrers *Yaarana* (1981) and *Khud-Daar* (1982). His intelligence shone through even in his interpretation of the Tagore composition, 'Tomar holo shuru', which became 'Choo kar mere man ko'. 'Angrezi mein kehte hain' (singers: Lata-Kishore, lyrics: Majrooh) was *BGM's* No 1 song of 1982. His creative talent is best demonstrated in the melodies of *Man Pasand* (lyrics: Amit Khanna): 'Sa Re Ga Ma Pa Ma Ga Re Sa' (Lata-Kishore), 'Main akela hi apne dhoon' (Kishore), 'Hothon pe geet jaage' (Lata), 'Logon ka dil agar' (Rafi).

Veterans Kalyanji-Anandji (*Qurbani, Laawaris, Vidhaata, Jaanbaz, Kalyug Aur Ramayan* and *Tridev*) and young blood Anu Malik (*Sohni Mahiwal, Ek Jaan Hain Hum, Toofan*) also remained amiably employed in the 1980s.

SHORT TAKE

Did you know?

'Y.O.G.A' was a chartbuster from *Haadsaa* (singer: Amit Kumar, lyrics: M.G. Hashmat, music: Kalyanji-Anandji), long before the wellness art from ancient India was eulogised and promoted by the central government.

It is often argued that it was a bad decade for good music and courteous poetry in Hindi films. That's doesn't hold true for most part of the decade. Much of this argument derives its strength from songs that became popular and have since been forgotten. The contrary view is equally strong. For instance, in the early 1980s, Khayyam produced dulcet melodies in films such as *Umrao Jaan, Bazaar, Thodisi Bewafaii, Dard* and *Ek Naya Rishta*, among others, which are hummed to this day.

Here are some more examples from mainstream movies: Shiv-Hari (*Silsila, Chandni*), Ravindra Jain (*Ram Teri Ganga Maili*), Anand Milind (*Qayamat Se Qayamat Tak*), Raamlaxman (*Maine Pyar Kiya*), Usha Khanna (*Souten*), Uttam-Jagdish (*Waaris*), Babul Bose (*Jeena Teri Gali Mein*), Ravi (*Nikaah*),

Naushad (*Dharam Kanta*), Kuldeep Singh (*Saath Saath, Arth, Ankush, Dhat Tere Ki*), Rajkamal (*Chashme Buddoor*). Songs from these films forged a happy marriage between melody and market. Even today, they don't feel dated. Not many know that *Arth-Saath Saath* is one of the most successful combo cassette ever.

However, many other top-notch compositions were forgotten because their albums and cassettes were neither widely promoted nor easily available. Even radio stations did not give them adequate playtime.

The Eighties were also enlivened by the first-rate compositions of Jaidev (*Trikon Ka Chautha Kon, Ankahee, Jumbish*), Hridaynath Mangeshkar (*Chakra, Subhah*), Kanu Roy (*Sparsh, Griha Pravesh*), Vanraj Bhatia (*Hip Hip Hurray, Mandi, Tamas, Kalyug*), Ajit Varman (*Aakrosh, Vijeta, Saaransh*), Jagjit Singh (*Prem Geet, Raavan, Tum Laut Aao*), Raghunath Seth (*Ek Baar Phir*), and Ilaiyaraaja (*Sadma*). Songs from these films always brought you closer to the radio. Many of these hidden treasures have got an afterlife on YouTube.

The era also saw Udaipur-born Dhrupad maestro Ustaad Zia Fariduddin Dagar provide the score for Mani Kaul's *Satah Se Uthata Aadmi* (1980), where music harmonised the text and the characters. Ustad Ghulam Mustafa Khan, who received the Padma Vibhushan in 2018, struck the right notes in Muzaffar Ali's *Aagaman* (1982). He passed away on 17 January 2021. Poornadas Baul, the great baul singer, composed and sang for Shyam Benegal's *Arohan*.

Ajit Varman and Vanraj Bhatia

The work of Ajit Varman and Vanraj Bhatia merits a longer assessment because they are two of the most under-appreciated composers from the Eighties.

Varman's minimalist compositions effortlessly captured the troubled, dark moments in *Aakrosh* and *Saaransh*. Mahesh Bhatt, who directed *Saaransh* said, 'For the song "Andhiyara gehraya soonapan ghir aaya" [*Saaransh*], I told him, your reference is the chant, *"Buddham sharanam gachhami"*. That's the tune's bedrock. If you listen to the song carefully, you will find a deep silence in the composition. Few music directors could have touched its core.'[16] That reflective, questioning quality which Bhatt talks about is again evident in 'Maa bolo kab tak yun hi chalna hai' (*Wasta*, 1989), an introspective, little-heard track.

'Har ghadi dhal rahi', again *Saaransh*, can easily be placed among the best ten songs of the 1980s. Varman maximised Amit Kumar's huskiness and matched the sensitive metaphors of Vasant Dev, who won the national award for best lyrics for this film.

Unlike many music directors, Varman arranged his own music. Background score was his forte. In several scenes in *Aakrosh*, the music created a sense of foreboding without ever being overbearing. Director Govind Nihalani remembered one such instance. 'I had seen some Japanese films and suggested the use of koto, a traditional stringed instrument, in a scene. He said, we can opt for the sarod to create the same effect. And he did it with his own arrangement,' Nihalani said.[17] Most films that Varman worked for had tight budgets. Nihalani said he could make rich and nuanced music within the constraints. 'He always wanted to do something fresh. That was inherent in his nature,' the director said.[18]

Varman, who loved playing the drums and bongo, also gave music for Nihalani's *Vijeta*, which was embellished by the composer's meditative compositions. 'Man anand anand chayo', based on 'Raag Ahir Bhairav' and sung by Asha Bhosle and Satyasheel Deshpande, is a perfect example. 'Asha loved the tune and congratulated him,' recalled Nihalani.[19]

That he could do routine mainstream stuff with equal elan is evident in Mirza Brothers' *Misaal* (1985), where he conjured with the friskiest of tunes, 'Aao na bahon mein chale aao na'. Varman passed away in 2016.

The masterly Vanraj Bhatia began his film career with Shyam Benegal in the 1970s and provided the score in most of his movies. In Benegal's films, the background track and theme music are braided with the larger narrative. Bhatia, who had trained under the great French composer and conductor Nadia Boulanger in Paris, was always equal to the task.

The Bombay-born composer, who also taught music briefly at Delhi University, brought several new facets to Hindi films. 'He was probably the only Indian composer who understood harmony,' said Benegal.[20]

Background music in Hindi films is largely demonstrative. It matches the mood to the action. It does not complement a scene, but illustrates it. '...Vanraj was different. He understood that if the film is one arc, the music is another. They complement and complete each other. He and I would discuss the concept, what I wanted. His own mind worked in divergent ways. He could sense the pace of my films,' the director said.[21]

Benegal further explained, 'The concept of thematic score of a film came with Satyajit Ray. Like *Pather Panchali* (music: Ravi Shankar) has a theme. Vanraj brought it to Hindi movies, when he started working with me. I thought of this concept and he wholeheartedly accepted it.'[22] *Trikal* (1985) was shot in Goa. The music of the place is a blend of Indian and Portuguese influences. Goan music also has a strong north Indian classical tradition. Bhatia's background in the form of themes—'Title Theme', 'Maria's Theme', 'Leon's Theme'—welded these varying facets.

Bhatia's mastery over the background score earned him a national award for best music direction in Govind Nihalani's telefilm, *Tamas* (1987). *Kalyug* (1981), a modern take on Mahabharata, also had a moody background score. The film's only song, 'Kya hai tera gham bata' (lyrics: Balwant Tandon, singer: Preeti Sagar), is a regular nightclub track but Bhatia uses hurtling drums, screeching violins and a persistent chorus to construct an atmosphere missing from other songs in the same genre. In *Mandi* (1981), he excelled in the mujra compositions: 'Shamsheer bhare na maang ghazab' (lyrics: Bahadur Shah Zafar) and 'Zabaane badalte hain' (lyrics: Mir Taqi Mir).

Outside Benegal's films, Bhatia excelled when given a chance. His two compositions in Prakash Jha's *Hip Hip Hurray* (1984): the inspiring 'Ek subah ek mod par' and the introspective 'Jab kabhi mudh kar dekhta hoon main' are among the most under-appreciated songs of its time. The composer's background score is among the film's attractions. This includes the whistling background melody, suggesting the young protagonist's 'Summer of 42' style infatuation with his schoolteacher. Vanraj Bhatia died on 7 May 2021. He was ninety-three.

For Your Personal Playlist:
Fifty Super Songs That Never Hit the Charts

Here's an eclectic and eccentric list of songs to prove the point that the decade produced its share of unforgettable music. Many obvious choices from films such as *Bazaar, Saath Saath, Arth, Umrao Jaan,* and *Ijaazat* have been deliberately omitted to provide a more expansive list of notable but less heard melodies of this period. The list also underlines the staggering range of lyricists and singers who were given space in Hindi films.

1980

Chakra

'Oobi hui aankhon mein tooti hui neend hai'
(singer: Bhupinder; lyrics: Madhosh Bilgrami;
music: Hridaynath Mangeshkar)

Griha Pravesh

'Zindagi phoolon phoolon ki tarah mehki rahe'
(singer: Bhupinder; lyrics: Gulzar; music: Kanu Roy)

Aakrosh

'Saans mein dard hai'
(singer: Madhuri Purandare; lyrics: Suryabhanu Gupt;
music: Ajit Varman)

Ek Baar Phir

'Jaane yeh mujhko kya ho raha'
(singer: Bhupinder; lyrics: Vinod Pande; music: Raghunath Seth)

Ek Baar Kaho

'Chaar din ki zindagi'
(singer: Yesudas; lyrics: Maya Govind; music: Bappi Lahiri)

1981

Dhanwan

'Yeh aankhen dekh kar'
(singers: Lata-Suresh Wadkar; lyrics: Sahir Ludhianvi;
music: Hridaynath Mangeshkar)

Shradhanjali

'Jaane kyun aisa lagta hai'
(singers: Bhupinder-Asha; lyrics: Anjaan; music: Hemant Bhosle)

Kanoon Aur Mujrim

'Sham rangeen hui hai tere aanchal ki tarah'
(singer: Suresh Wadkar; lyrics: Ahmed Wasi; music: C. Arjun)

Daasi

'Piya bin jiya naahi laage'
(singer: Bhupinder; lyrics and music: Ravindra Jain)

Mangalsutra

'Raat banoo main aur chand bano tum'
(singer: Bhupinder-Asha; lyrics: Nida Fazli, music; R.D. Burman)

Chashme Buddoor

'Kahan se aaye badra ghulta jaaye kajra'
(singers: Yesudas-Haimanti Shukla; lyrics: Indu Jain; music: Rajkamal)

'Kali ghodi dwar khadi'
(singer: Yesudas; lyrics: Indu Jain; music: Rajkamal)

1982

Dil... Akhir Dil Hai

'Jab se dekha hai tumhe, aisa lagta hai'
(singers: Lata-Suresh Wadkar; lyrics: Nida Fazli; music: Khayyam)

Angoor

'Roz roz daali daali'
(singer: Asha Bhosle; lyrics: Gulzar; music: R.D. Burman)

Namkeen

'Raah pe rehte hain'
(singer: Kishore Kumar; lyrics: Gulzar; music: R.D. Burman)
'Phir se aayo badra bidesi'
(singer: Asha Bhosle; lyrics: Gulzar; music: R.D. Burman

Bedard

'Zindagi tum mera saath dena'
(singer: Bhupinder; lyrics: Naqsh Lyallpuri; music; Kanti Kiran)

Kalka

'Bidesiya re'
(singers: Jagjit Singh, C. Anand Kumar, Ghanshyam Vaswani,
Vinod Sehgal, Ashok Khosla; lyrics: Madhosh Bilgrami, Dinesh;
music: Jagjit Singh)

1983

Nishaan

'Lehron ki tarah yaadein'
(singer: Kishore Kumar; lyrics: Gulshan Bawra; music: Rajesh Roshan)

Rang Birangi

'O Mriganayani o Chandramukhi'
(singers: Faiyyaz, Dr Vasantrao Deshpande; lyrics: Kaka Hathrasi;
music: R.D. Burman)

Sadma

'Surmai ankiyon mein nanha munna'
(singer: Yesudas; lyrics: Gulzar; music: Ilaiyaraaja)

Shubh Kaamna

'Baagon mein khile hain kaise kaise phulwa'
(singers: Asha, S.P. Balasubrahmanyam; lyrics: Anjaan;
music: R.D. Burman)

Dhat Tere Ki

'Is waqt ke paon mein kanta koi chubh jaye'
(singers: Ashok Khosla, Asha Bhosle; lyrics: Sayeed Qadri;
music: Kuldeep Singh)

Mandi

'Shamsheer bhare na maang ghazab'
(singer: Preeti Sagar; lyrics: Bahadur Shah Zafar;
music: Vanraj Bhatia)

Be-Aabroo

'Pyaase naina pyaasa man'
(singer: Dilraj Kaur; lyrics: Zafar Rahi; music; Ajay Swami)

1984

Ankahee

'Raghuvar tum to meri laaj'
(singer: Bhimsen Joshi; lyrics: Goswami Tulsidas; music: Jaidev)
'Thumak thumak pag dhumak kunj'
(singer: Bhimsen Joshi; lyrics: traditional; music: Jaidev)

Sparsh

'Khaali pyaala dhundhla darpan'
(singer; Sulakshana Pandit; lyrics: Indu Jain; music: Kanu Roy)

Sunny

'Jaane kya baat hai'
(singer: Lata; lyrics: Anand Bakshi; music: R.D. Burman)

Hip Hip Hurray
'Jab kabhi mud kar dekhta hoon main'
(singers: Bhupinder-Asha; lyrics: Gulzar; music: Vanraj Bhatia)

Aagaman
'Nisaar main teri galiyon pe ae watan ke jahan'
(singer-composer: Ustad Ghulam Mustafa Khan;
lyrics: Faiz Ahmed Faiz)

Saaransh
'Dhal rahi har ghadi shaam hai zindagi'
(singer: Amit Kumar; lyrics: Vasant Dev; music: Ajit Varman)
'Andhiyara gehraya, soonapan phir aya'
(singer: Bhupinder; lyrics: Vasant Dev; music: Ajit Varman)

Nadaniyan
'Dil ki khamoshiyo se baat na kar'
(singer: Hariharan; lyrics Sardar Anjum; music: Sumitra Lahiri)

1985

Sitamgar
'Pyaar jab na kiya zindagi ne kabhi'
(singer: Kishore Kumar; lyrics: Majrooh; music: R.D. Burman)

Aitbaar
'Aawaz di aaj ik nazar ne'
(singer: Bhupinder; lyrics: Hasan Kamal; music: Bappi Lahiri)
'Kisi nazar ko tera interzaar aaj bhi hai'
(singer: Bhupinder; lyrics: Hasan Kamal; music: Bappi Lahiri)

Sur Sangam
'Jaoon tore charan kamal par vaari'
(singers: Rajan Mishra, Saajan Mishra, Lata; lyrics: Vasant Dev;
music: L-P)
'Dhanya bhag seva ka avsar paaya'
(singers: Rajan Mishra, Saajan Mishra, Kavita Krishnamurthy;
lyrics: Vasant Dev; music: L-P)

1986

Ankush

'Itni shakti humein dena data'
(singers: Sushma Shretha, Pushpa Paghdhare; lyrics: Abhilash;
music: Kuldeep Singh)

Saveray Wali Gaadi

'Din pyaar ke'
(singer: Lata Mangeshkar; lyrics: Majrooh; music: R.D. Burman)

Ek Pal

'Zara dheere zara dheema'
(singers: Bhupinder Singh, Bhupen Hazarika, Haimanti Shukla,
Usha Mangeshkar; lyrics: Gulzar; music: R.D. Burman)

Trikon Ka Chautha Kon

'Kiya piya pe kya jadoo'
(singer: Chhaya Ganguly; lyrics: Mahadevi Verma/Maya Govind;
music: Jaidev)

Anjuman

'Kab yaad mein tera saath nahi'
(singers: Khayyam-Jagjit Kaur; lyrics: Faiz Ahmed Faiz;
music: Khayyam)

1987

Vali-e-Azam

'Mere shareek-e-safar ab era khuda hafeez'
(singers: Hemlata-Talat Mahmood; lyrics: Ahmed Wasi;
music: Chitragupt)

1988

Akhri Muqabla

'Zindagi kya kanta hai ya phool'
(singer: Kishore Kumar; music: Usha Khanna)

Ek Naya Rishta

'Jise samjhe they afsana kal tak'
(singers: Bhupinder-Lata; lyrics: Nida Fazli; music: Khayyam)

Akarshan

'Mausam ka takaza hai'
(singers; Ajeet Singh-Kavita Krishnamurthy; lyrics: Rajesh Johri;
music: Ajeet Singh)

Susman (The Essence)

'Jheeni jheeni beeni chadariya'
(singer: Sangeet Martand Pandit Jasraj; lyrics: Sant Kabir;
music: Sharang Dev)

1989

Parinda

'Pyar ke mod pe'
(singer: Asha Bhosle; lyrics: Khurshid Halluri; music: R.D. Burman)

---

*The year of a film's release and the year of its songs making it to
Binaca Geetmala's annual chart may differ. Sometimes the songs were
released much ahead of the film. And sometimes the songs became
hits the following year. This was true especially of films, which were
released in November and December.

REEL 13

WHEN LAMBA RHYMED WITH KHAMBHA

'*Ladki nahi hai tu lakdi ka khambha hai / Bak bak mat kar nak tera lamba hai* (You are not a girl but a wooden pole / Don't blabber, your nose is long)'. For many, this teasing track from *Himmatwala* (1983) is emblematic of the state of lyrics in 1980s Hindi cinema.

This wasn't the first time that a Hindi film number had indulged in asinine rhyming. But now they proliferated like pests after a monsoon rain. *Himmatwala* alone had three such tracks: 'Taki ho taki, taki taki taki re' and 'Wah wah wah khel shuru ho gaya' were the other two.

Fortified by their success, the lyricist Indeevar (also spelt as Indivar and Indiwar in many films), a noted Hindi poet, produced a deluge of such playful and senseless doggerels in *Mawaali* (1983), *Maqsad* (1983), *Justice Chaudhury* (1983), *Tohfa* (1984) and dozens of movies made by South-based producers. *Mawaali's* '*Char baar marenge, ek baar ginenge, aise nahi chhodhenge, daant tera todenge* (Will hit you four times and count one / Won't leave you like this, will break your teeth)' is an eloquent example. A race to the bottom had begun.

The Eighties also saw an eruption of lurid lyrics. Naughty—even mildly risqué—songs were always part of the Hindi cinema menu. Now the numbers multiplied. Some were sexually suggestive, others downright lewd. Lyricist Javed Akhtar said that the 1980s and early '90s were 'a terrible period' for Hindi film songs. The situation had deteriorated so much that even 'light-hearted songs started sounding like classical poetry', he pointed out. 'There was a drop in aesthetic and literary values. Songs with double-meaning lyrics, bordering on obscenity, vulgarity and crossing all lines of decency had come into fashion.'[1]

Fellow lyricist Hasan Kamal succinctly summed up the larger impact. In the 1980s, it 'became accepted that cheap songs do well', he said.[2]

'Saat saheliyan khadi khadi' (lyrics: Anand Bakshi; *Vidhaata*, 1982) was one of the trendsetters in the 'double meaning' song genre. The folk song was reworked by Bakshi in the Subhash Ghai hit. In the song, a girl explains why one shouldn't marry a doctor, or a driver, or a postman, etc. One of the stanzas goes, '*Arrey doctor ki biwi na banna kabhi, na banna kabhi, raat bhar mua sone na de, injection lagaye ghadi ghadi* (Don't become a doctor's wife because he won't let you sleep all night and keep giving you injections)'. No prizes for guessing what the injection stood for!

The titillating track finished sixth in the 1983 *Binaca Geetmala* annual countdown show but was far more discussed than the top five. 'Saat saheliyan' was the forerunner to 'Choli ke peechche kya hai' (*Khalnayak*, 1993; another Subhash Ghai film).

Even family dramas bowed to the mood of the times. *Ghar Ek Mandir* (1984) had the suggestive smash hit by Anand Bakshi: '*Doctor babu, der na karna jaldi laga de sui, oouui* (Dear doctor, don't delay, please insert the needle, ouuch).' In case one missed the innuendo, the heroine pointed out specifically where the needle should be injected.

Superhit Marathi filmmaker Dada Kondke entered Hindi cinema with his inimitable indigenous brand of raunchy sex comedy in *Tere Mere Beech Mein* (1984). One of the stanzas in the song 'Roop tera sundar maar dala' (lyrics: Rajesh Majumdar) goes, '*Tu hai meri gaiya, main doodhwala, phoot bada aaya mujhe doodhnewala.* (You are my cow, I am your milkman, go away I won't let you milk me).'

Double-meaning songs were the norm in his films. Sample this: '*Tere ghade mein bol meri raani, petrol daaloon ya kuen ka paani / Jhatka na de matka phootega jaani, dheere dheere chhod pipe ka paani*' (lyrics: Bal Kishan Puri; *Andheri Raat Mein Diya Tere Haath Mein,* 1986). The translation roughly goes: 'What should I insert in your vessel, my darling? Petrol or water drawn from a well / Don't thrust hard, the vessel will break, release the water slowly from your pipe.'

But beyond the ribald Kondke comedies, several big-budget masala movies also included songs laced with suggestive phrases and sounds generally associated with coital pleasure. In *Maqsad* (1984; lyrics: Indeevar), Rajesh Khanna and Sridevi dance to the song, '*Garmi hai, kahan hai, sanson mein / Toofan hai, kahan hai, seene mein / Tu pyaar ki barsat kar, ubalne laga hai badan, abba amma abba amma abba amma aa, ee, ooo aa* (Where is the heat? On my breath. Where is the storm? In my heart. You shower me with love. My body is boiling. Followed by sensual moans of *abba…amma*).'

Hasan Kamal himself wrote the double-meaning mujra track, 'Khali pili pyar se mera hoga nahi bhala' (*Aitbaar,* 1985). In the folksy lyrics, the dancer asks a *thanedar* to get a *ganna* (sugarcane) which both can suck *(Main bhi choosungi, tu bhi choosega).* Such examples abound in dozens.

Lucknow-born Maya Govind (*Ek Baar Kaho, Rang Birangi*), who taught Hindi, music and history in school before coming to Bombay, held the producers responsible for the state of affairs. She said, 'The songwriter is the least to be blamed for it. He or she was made to write lyrics of a certain kind. They would say, "*Is tarah se nahin, is tarah se kar dijiye* (Don't do it like this, but like this)." Even if the words were mild, dance directors added suggestive movements leaving nothing to imagination. And this happened in consonance with the director and the producer.'[3]

Bappi Lahiri, too, admitted that many songs composed by him contained double-meaning lyrics but blamed the producers. 'If a producer is looking for risqué numbers, he is going to ask the songwriter to write something on those lines. The composer only provides the tune,' he said.[4]

In a conversation with Nasreen Munni Kabir, songwriter Javed Akhtar said that he withdrew from some films after he 'heard the song situation'.[5]

Indeevar

In this season of the inane, Indeevar thrived. In the 1960s and '70s, he had stitched a fruitful partnership with Kalyanji-Anandji, writing songs such as the poetic 'Chandan sa badan chanchal chitwan' (*Saraswatichandra*) and the philosophical 'Zindagi ka safar, hai yeh kaisa safar' (*Safar*). But in the 1980s, he realised that the kind of films he was working for required lyrics in tune with the larger ecosystem of the script. Consequently, he came up with easy hooklines, which were the right fit for his 'partner-in-crime' Bappi's rhythms, such as 'Mama mia pom pom' (*Justice Chaudhury*, 1983) and 'Devi o baby tu ban ja meri biwi' (*Maqsad*, 1984). Lyrics like these defined the Eighties music, casting a long, impactful shadow.

However, Indeevar also displayed his dormant sensitive side when presented with an opportunity: 'Hothon se chhoo lo tum' (*Prem Geet*, 1981), 'Tujh sang preet lagayee sajna' (*Kaamchor*, 1982) and 'Neele neele ambar pe' (*Kalaakaar*, 1982). But most film music lovers remember him for his frisky songs of this era. In fact, his name became a synonym for mindless lyrics.

IMDb records show Indeevar wrote for 267 films over a staggering forty-eight years: 1951-1999. Of them, 116 or 43 per cent films were released between 1980 and 1989. In the six years between 1984 and 1989, he engaged with an astonishing eighty-seven films, roughly fourteen every year. In other words, he jotted about one-third of all songs of his career in just six years. Between 1980 and 1989, thirty-two songs authored by him finished among the Top 20 tracks in *Binaca Geetmala's* annual show. In 1986 and 1988, he finished with the highest number of songs among the Top 20: five.

During this period, apart from Bappi, he also wrote bestsellers for other composers: 'Julie Julie' (*Jeete Hain Shaan Se*; music: Anu Malik), 'Zindagi ka naam dosti' (*Khudgarz*; music: Rajesh Roshan), 'Ek to kam zindagani' (*Janbaaz*; music: Kalyanji-Anandji).

Anand Bakshi

Indeevar grabbed the spotlight. But nobody came close to Anand Bakshi in terms of delivering chartbusters. Between 1980 and 1989, sixty-nine Anand Bakshi songs found their way to the Top 20. In 1980, Bakshi's name figured in ten songs among the Top 20 hits of that year. The next year, he went even better—eleven—meaning that he wrote more hits than all other lyricists in Bombay.

Karz (1980), *Love Story* (1981), *Ek Duuje Ke Liye* (1981), *Vidhaata* (1982), *Betaab* (1983), *Coolie* (1983), *Hero* (1983), *Karma* (1986), *Naam* (1986), *Ram Lakhan* (1989), *Chandni* (1989)—some of the biggest hits of the 1980s had one name in common: Anand Bakshi.

A frequent collaborator with Laxmikant-Pyarelal and R.D. Burman, Rawalpindi-born Bakshi made songwriting appear as easy as drinking tea. Accessibility was his forte. He brought a simple conversational style to lyric writing. But most of his songs in the Eighties were like fast food: consume and forget.

Anjaan and Majrooh

After Bakshi and Indeevar, Anjaan was an honorable third in penning chart-toppers. Anjaan, who came from Banaras, had a felicity with the lingo of the Indo-Gangetic plains, reflected in 'Khai ke paan Banaraswala' (*Don*, 1978). In the Eighties, he wrote a cache of superhits such as 'Hari Om Hari' (*Pyaara Dushmun*), 'Pag ghunghroo baandh' (*Namak Halaal*), 'Jimmy Jimmy' (*Disco Dancer*), 'I am a Disco Dancer' (*Disco Dancer*), 'Yashoda ka Nandlala' (*Sanjog*)—the biggest hit of 1986—and many more.

The evergreen Majrooh Sultanpuri had forged an early marriage between poetic beauty and box-office necessity. In the 1980s, he continued to write runaway winners. His 'Angreji mein kehte hain' (*Khud-Daar*, 1982) showed he had mastered the language of the time. He was nearing seventy when he wrote, 'Papa kehte hain' (*Qayamat Se Qayamat Tak*, 1988), now the anthem of farewell parties. It was also *Binaca Geetmala's* Song of the Year in 1988. The song underlined his ability to absorb the mood of the times and create a texture in words to illustrate it.

Speak, Poetry

Ditties and double-meaning songs are engraved in popular memory, shaping public perception of film songs from that era. But 1980s Bombay cinema also offered plenty of outstanding poetry which has been either overlooked or under-addressed.

Gulzar

The 1980s were not a fertile period for Gulzar, the film director. But for songwriter Gulzar, it was springtime. In the 1970s, he wrote about languid winter afternoons spent soaking the sun and stars walking the streets after rain, thereby bringing a range of fresh metaphors to songwriting. In the 1980s, he continued to search for newer shades of mysteries of the human heart. Gulzar chiselled a contemporary language of looking: the women in his songs are not objects of the male gaze. They are neither over-idealised nor coveted. He looks at them as part of an imperfect rhythm that every man-woman relationship dances to. The poet seemed to be carrying a seismograph in his heart that allowed him to track every tremor evident in the songs of *Ijaazat, Namkeen, Sitam* and *Baseraa.*

'Aye zindagi gale lagale' (*Sadma*) bared the helplessness of one-sided love. The song didn't create any ripples when first released but gradually became a cult track for lovers of a certain disposition. 'Jab kabhi mud kar dekhta hoon main' (*Hip Hip Hurray*) is a tender lament on a relationship past its expiry date.

The writer-director wrote songs for nineteen films; an average of two per year. But unlike the 1970s when many songs penned by him cruised to the charts, the Eighties were more subdued. During the entire decade, he just had two hits in *BGM's* annual Top 20 charts: 'Lakdi ki kaathi' (*Masoom*) and the now-forgotten title track of *Jeeva*, 'Dil pukare jeeva re jeeva'.

But the decade was bountiful for him in another way. Gulzar got the best lyricist *Filmfare* award on four occasions in the 1980s, more than any other songwriter in the decade. In 1980, he received it for 'Aaanewala pal' (*Golmaal*), and for the 'Hazaar rahein mud ke dekhin' (*Thodisi Bewafaii*) the following year. 'Tujhse naraaz nahi zindagi' (*Masoom*) and 'Mera kuchh saaman' (*Ijaazat*), competing with 'Ek do teen' (*Tezaab*) and 'Papa kehte hain' (*QSQT*), got the award in 1989.

Vasant Dev and Indu Jain

Vasant Dev was a finely grained lyricist whose works went largely unnoticed like eddies in a stream. Dev, who taught Hindi literature in Bombay's Parle College, wrote for Govind Nihalani (*Aakrosh*, 1980; *Vijeta*, 1982), Girish Karnad (*Utsav*, 1984), Mahesh Bhatt (*Saaransh*, 1984) and K. Vishwanath (*Sur Sangam*, 1985). There are no cliches in Dev's lyrics. The metaphors are fresh and precise. In *Saaransh's* stunning evocative track, 'Dhal rahi har ghadi shaam hai zindagi', he writes, *'Bhatke hue panchhi ki raat hai zindagi* (Life is like the night of a bird that cannot find its home)', a singular summation of the protagonist's life, which is like a dark tunnel. There is subtle eroticism in 'Man kyun behka re behka aadhi raat ko' (*Utsav*), a rare Lata-Asha duet, for which he won a *Filmfare* award. He also received a national award for best lyricist for *Saaransh*. 'Andhiyara gehraya, soonapan phir aaya' is another classic.

Hindi poet Indu Jain also found the right words for director Sai Paranjpye's *Chashme Buddoor* (1981), *Katha* (1983) and *Sparsh* (1984). Jain, who taught Hindi in Delhi University for over three decades, wrote the contrasting 'Khaali pyaala dundhla darpan' and 'Pyaala chhalka ujla darpan', both in *Sparsh*, to explain the shifting mindscape of a visually impaired man in agony and love. In *Chashme Buddoor*, her classical Hindi vocabulary—'Kahan se aaye badra' and 'Kaali ghodi dwar khadi'—gives a certain gravitas to the light comedy. She probably became the first lyric writer to use the French word for love, *la amour*, in the zany bonding track: *'Pyaar lagawat pranay mohabbat prem geet ya love l'amour...'*

—————— SHORT TAKE ——————

The last hurrah

The decade also witnessed a final flourish of several senior lyricists. Celebrated poet Sahir Ludhianvi breathed his last on 25 October 1980. His qawwali, 'Pal do pal ka saath hamara' (*The Burning Train*; music: R.D. Burman; 1979) turned out to be an ironic forecast. Hasrat Jaipuri enjoyed a late waltz in *Ram Teri Ganga Maili* (1985); 'Sun sahiba sun' was *Binaca Geetmala*'s No. 1 song of 1985. Veteran S.H. Bihari came up trumps in *Pyar Jhukta Nahin* (1985) and *Teri Meherbaniyan* (1985). Asad Bhopali left an imprint with *Maine Pyar Kiya* (1989). Kaifi Azmi wrote the meaningful and evocative tracks of *Arth*, *Yeh Nazdeekiyan*, *Razia Sultan* and *Bhavna*.

Hasan Kamal, Nida Fazli and Shahryar

The trio represented a break from the earlier generation of Urdu poets in the way they framed their alphabets and thoughts on love and society. A favourite at mushairas, Nida Fazli (1938-2016) invested a quality to the songs of *Red Rose*, *Harjaee*, *Ahista Ahista* and *Ek Naya Rishta*. His couplet, '*Kabhi kisi ko mukammal jahan nahin milta / Kahin zameen to kahin aasman nahi milta*' (*Ahista Ahista*), has become an everyday phrase to articulate the imperfect human condition of modern times.

Journalist-poet Hasan Kamal earned two *Filmfare* awards for his songs in *Nikaah* (the despondent 'Dil ke armaan') and *Aaj Ki Awaz* (the fiery title track). The popularity of his sensitive, word-perfect ghazal, 'Dil ke armaan aansuon mein beh gaye', showed that there was still space for substance.

A noted poet of his generation, Shahryar taught Urdu at Aligarh Muslim University. He first drew the industry's attention with his agonising ode to urban alienation, 'Seene mein jalan' (music: Jaidev) for Muzaffar Ali's *Gaman* (1978). In Muzaffar Ali's *Umrao Jaan* (1981), his ghazals were mostly filmed as mujras and they help the audience navigate the voices and noises in the protagonist's head. To help him ease into the world of *Umrao Jaan*, Muzaffar Ali invited Shahryar to stay in his ancestral house in Kotwara for several months. It helped the poet imbibe the spirit of the protagonist.[6] His verse again found a perfect match in Khayyam's minimalist compositions in *Anjuman* (1986).

Javed Akhtar and Santosh Anand

After splitting up with writing partner Salim Khan, Javed Akhtar gradually transformed from a storyteller to a lyricist and found reasonable success. His verse seldom rose to the levels of outstanding poetry but he generally produced clean and engaging songs. 'Yeh kahan aa gaye hum' (*Silsila*, his debut as a lyricist) and 'Tumko dekha to yeh khayal aaya' (*Saath Saath*) are above par tracks without being outstanding in terms of artistic merit.

Akhtar also showed a knack for finding smart hooklines on which to hang his rhymes. In *Arjun*, he framed a riddle where the desperate unemployed hero answers 'naukri' to every query, much like in *Shree 420* (1955). He turned an abacus lesson, 'Ek do teen', into a superhit song in *Tezaab*. 'Mamaiya kero kero kero mama' (*Arjun*) and 'Hawa Hawaai' (*Mr. India*) also highlight how easily he had found the omphalos of public taste.

Poet Santosh Anand, who worked as a librarian in Delhi, forged a rewarding association with Manoj Kumar in the 1970s (*Purab Aur Paschim, Shor*, and *Roti, Kapada Aur Makaan*). He again had a brief but impressive run in the 1980s, especially in the films of Manoj Kumar and Raj Kapoor. 'Zindagi ki na toote ladi' (*Kranti*) was the second biggest hit of 1981. 'Main na bhoolunga' (*Roti, Kapada Aur Makaan*) had fetched him a *Filmfare* award for best lyricist in 1975. A second award came in Raj Kapoor's *Prem Rog* for 'Mohabbat hai kya cheez'. He also authored the much-appreciated ode to rain clouds, 'Megha re megha re' (*Pyaasa Sawan*). The composers, invariably, were Laxmikant-Pyarelal.

'My understanding with Laxmikant was perfect. He once told me, "I was born to compose. You were born to write songs." We even made songs on the telephone,' Anand said.[7] Anand was born in the western UP town of Sikanderabad and used to be a major crowd-puller at kavi sammelans in his prime. In 2019, his words, 'Ek pyar ka nagma hai', hurtled railway platform singer Ranu Mondal to instant fame.

—————————— SHORT TAKE ——————————

Words from history

In the 1980s, New Wave filmmakers like Shyam Benegal found musical inspiration in the past. Benegal's *Susman* and *Mandi* sourced lyrics from medieval poet Sant Kabir. In *Mandi*, he tapped into the fertile heritage of nineteenth century ghazals by masters Mir Taqi Mir and Bahadur Shah Zafar. Amol Palekar's *Ankahee* also found meaning and affliation in the poetry of Kabir and Goswami Tulsidas.

Yogesh and Amit Khanna

In 1970s India, Yogesh's philosophical lyrics uplifted middle-of-the-road cinema (*Rajnigandha, Anand*). With a gift for the perfect word to express hesitant ardour, he became the enduring courier of men and women who couldn't glibly articulate their feelings. In the 1980s, Yogesh continued in the same vein as the preferred lyricist of Basu Chatterjee and Hrishikesh Mukherjee. 'Gao mere man' (*Apne Paraye*) and 'Jab bhi koi kangna bole' (*Shaukeen*) showed he was still in touch with his elegant and pre-dominantly Hindi poetic side. 'In the 1980s, there was still some scope to write good songs,' said Yogesh.[8] But as the decade wore on, the demand for his gentle verse fell, a sign of the times. 'Lucknow born, he carried grace in his personal life and poetry,' fellow lyricist Amit Khanna said of Yogesh who passed away in 2020.[9]

A graduate of the Capital's St Stephen's College, Khanna started out in the 1970s (*Des Pardes, Swami, Baton Baton Mein*), often writing lyrics for Navketan Productions, Ramsay Brothers and Basu Chatterjee. Khanna was also among those who broke free from the overused metaphors of '*hawa, phool, kaante*', opting for a new idiom that was more in tune with the urban, modern listeners. He also wrote for Basu Chatterjee's *Hamari Bahu Alka*, a 'pure' Hindi song, 'Prem ki kya hai sun paribhasha, sundar sapne, madhur abhilasha.' Two of his more popular songs in the Eighties were 'Sa Re Ga Ma Pa Ma Ga Re Sa' (*Man Pasand*, 1980) and 'Jab chhaye mera jadoo' (*Lootmaar*, 1980). He later won the national award for his lyrics in *Bhairavi* (1996).

Lyricist Amit Khanna collaborated well with Bappi Lahiri and Rajesh Roshan. (Photo Credit: Amit Khanna)

The rise of ghazals in non-filmi popular music in the late 1970s encouraged several producers and directors to insert well-known ghazals and nazms in their films which underlines the multiple spaces that the 1980s offered to men of letters in Hindi cinema.

Director Basu Bhattacharya included Kafil Azar's nazm made famous by Jagjit Singh, 'Baat niklegi to phir door talak jayegi' in *Griha Pravesh* (1980). Pakistani ghazal singer Ghulam Ali became a favourite for background tracks. In director Raj Khosla's fierce but unrealised hinterland drama, *Maati Maangey Khoon* (1984), Pakistani poet Mohsin Naqvi's ghazal 'Aawargi' (singer: Ghulam Ali) served as the backdrop to Shotgun Sinha walking through the forlorn fields.

Another ghazal sung by Ali, 'Chupke chupke raat din aansoo bahana yaad hai' (lyrics: Hasrat Mohani), played in the background as the drunk and depressed protagonist stares vacuously in B.R. Chopra's *Nikaah* (1983). A freedom fighter, Mohani is known to have coined the slogan, 'Inquilab Zindabad'. In Buddhadev Dasgupta's *Andhi Gali* (1984), another ghazal sung by Ali, 'Kiya hai pyar jise humne zindagi ki tarah' (lyrics:

Qateel Shifai) can be faintly heard as Kulbhushan Kharbanda and Deepti Naval visit their new flat. Director Rajat Rakshit's *Yahan Wahan* (1984) made use of husband-wife duo Rajendra Mehta-Neena Mehta's signature song, 'Tajmahal mein aa jana' (lyrics: Prem Warbartani).

There are more examples. Sudarshan Faakir's ode to childhood, 'Yeh daulat bhi leh lo, yeh shohrat bhi lelo', was immortalised by Jagjit Singh in his album, *The Latest and the Best*, as 'Kagaz Ki Kashti'. The nazm found its way into Kumar Gaurav's uneven *Aaj* (1987), with Kumar Gaurav lip-synching the song to his sister, Smita Patil. The Ferozepur-born poet also wrote all the songs for *Raavan* (1984), which were composed by Jagjit Singh. The most popular was the brooding 'Hum to yoon apni zindagi se mile ajnabee jaise ajnabee se mile'. In *Trikon Ka Chautha Kon*, Jaidev set renowned Hindi poetess Mahadevi Verma's words to music.

Pakistani Marxist poet Faiz Ahmed Faiz's 'Kab yaad mein tera saath nahi' found its way in Muzaffar Ali's *Anjuman* (1986), a rare duet sung by composer Khayyam and his wife, Jagjit Kaur. Faiz's rebel poetry was used as the leitmotif in the opening scene of Muzaffar Ali's *Aagaman* (1984), 'Nisaar main teri galiyon pe ae watan ke jahan'. M.S. Sathyu's *Kahan Kahan Se Guzar Gaya* (1986) also hosted a Faiz ghazal sung by Krishna Dhar and composed by Ustaad Bahadur Khan. The gentler side of communist poet Makhdoom Moinuddin's verse was used in both *Mandi* ('Ishq ke sholay') and Sagar Sarhadi's *Bazaar* ('Phir chhidi raat').

Hindi film music in the 1980s, therefore, was rich in both music and lyrics. Some of these tracks have been forgotten and need to be resurrected and reintroduced to new music lovers.

The Eighties started badly for male singers. Mohammed Rafi died of a cardiac arrest on 31 July 1980. He was only fifty-five.

Relegated to the background after Kishore Kumar started ruling the charts in the post-*Aradhana* (1969) world, Rafi had made a strong comeback in 1977 with *Laila Majnu*, *Hum Kisi Se Kum Nahin*, *Dharam-Veer* and *Amar Akbar Anthony*.

He had seven duets among *Binaca Geetmala's* Top 20 songs of 1980, with one solo ('Hum to chale pardes', 1980; *Sargam*). Song No. 1 of the year was 'Dafliwale dafli baja', a Lata-Rafi duet, again from *Sargam* (1979). For several years after his death, his songs kept appearing in countdown shows.

Attack of the Clones

The death of Rafi and Mukesh, who had passed away following a heart attack in Detroit on 27 August 1976, created a void in the world of male singers. In an ecosystem that was generally wary of experimenting, the hunt for clones began. Singers like Anwar (*Janta Hawaldar*), whose voice belonged to the same school, were already there. But in the next few years, Shabbir Kumar and Mohd Aziz emerged as the top replacement singers. Their voices were underlined by an absence of elegance but possessed a certain earthiness that made them hugely popular among the masses.

Shabbir had grown up performing on stage in Baroda. In an interview to *Dharamyug* magazine, he said, 'After Rafi *saab* passed away, I was called to Bombay to do a show, *Ek Shaam Rafi Ke Naam*. After the success of that programme, my struggle began in Bombay. Manmohan Desai gave me my first film song in *Coolie*.'[10]

All seven songs in *Coolie* (1983) were sung by Shabbir Kumar—two solos and five duets, including the street sonnet, 'Accident ho gaya rabba rabba' (lyrics: Anand Bakshi; music: L-P). He further ensconced himself on the charts with 'Jab hum jawan honge' (*Betaab*, 1983), 'Yaad teri aayegi' (*Ek Jaan Hain Hum*, 1983) and 'Sun Rubia' with Asha (*Mard*, 1985). *Pyar Jhukta Nahin* (1985), where he sang the maudlin 'Tumse milkar na jaane kyun', was another proud feather in his cap.

Mohd Aziz, also known as Munna Aziz, arrived on the scene shortly after Shabbir. Aziz, born and bred in Kolkata, struggled before Anu Malik gave him his big break in *Mard* (1985). 'I used to live as a paying guest. It was seven in the morning and I was sleeping when someone woke up me and said, *"Tumhari taqdeer khul gayee hai, tum Amitabh ke liye gaane wale ho* (You are in luck, you are singing for Amitabh)"...*Phir apna kaam chal nikla* (I was in business after that),' he said in a TV interview years later.[11] Aziz commanded attention with his confident delivery of the title track in director Manmohan Desai's blockbuster, along with the hit duet, 'Hum to tamboo mein bamboo', with Asha Bhosle.

His career took another giant leap when he sang the mournful chart-topper, 'Duniya mein kitna gham hai, mera gham kitna kam hai' in *Amrit* (1986). The song finished at No. 2—jointly with Alisha Chinoy's 'Tarzan My Tarzan'—in 1986 and highlighted his expansive range. Soon he was singing for other biggies such as Subhash Ghai (*Karma, Meri Jung*) and Rakesh Roshan (*Khudgarz*). Backed by top music directors such as Laxmikant-Pyarelal, Aziz gave playback for most major stars of the era: Amitabh Bachchan, Mithun Chakraborty, Anil Kapoor and Govinda.

In 1989, Subhash Ghai's *Ram Lakhan* gave India the tapori classic, 'Ae ji o ji loji suno ji', which went on to become the *BGM's* song of the year. Aziz enlivened this frisky track in a manner that had frontbenchers dancing in the aisles. In his prime, Aziz was a hugely popular singer. His concerts always attracted huge audiences. Like his guru Rafi, he died of a heart attack in 2018. He was sixty-four.

That there's a thin line between stardom and stardust, the career of Ashok Khare, another Rafi clone, shows. Khare's rendition of 'Mehfil hai meri yeh tanhaiyan' (*Partner*, 1982) and 'Dil ki is dehleez tak' (*Kabhie Ajnabi The*, 1985) makes you wonder why more composers didn't try him.

Kishore No. 1

Statistics collated from the Top 20 hits of *Binaca Geetmala* during 1980-89 show that Kishore Kumar was by far the most popular male singer of the decade. He notched up fifty-two Top 20 hits, solos and duets included. His two closest rivals, Shabbir Kumar and Mohd Aziz, registered less than half the number, eighteen and seventeen respectively, in 1980-89.

Kishore Kumar received five of the eight *Filmfare* awards for best male singer in the Eighties. No awards were given out in 1987 and 1988. The songs were: 'Hazaar rahein mud ke dekhin' (*Thodisi Bewafaii*), 'Pag ghunghroo' (*Namak Halaal*), the title track of *Agar Tum Na Hote*, 'Manzilein apni jagah hain' (*Sharaabi*) and 'Saagar kinare' (*Saagar*).

However, some songs betray signs of tiredness and aging in his voice. While Kishore's rendition remained energetic as ever, the youthful effervescence synonymous with the singer appeared to be slipping away. He was still the preferred voice of the older generation such as Rishi Kapoor, Rajesh Khanna and Jeetendra. But as the decade progressed, Amitabh Bachchan opted for other singers, too, such as Mohd Aziz in *Mard* and Shabbir Kumar in *Coolie*. Like Rafi and Mukesh, Kishore Kumar also died of a heart attack. He was only fifty-eight.

Yesudas and SPB

In the 1970s, Yesudas became the first male singer from South India to make major inroads in Hindi films. In the 1980s, his classically adept voice continued to bring both quality and variety to Hindi film songs. Among his classier numbers were 'Char din ki zindagi' (*Ek Baar Kaho*, 1980), 'Ae mere udaas man' (*Maan Abhiman*, 1980), 'Kahaan se aaye badra' (with Haimanti Shukla; *Chashme Buddoor*, 1981) and the raag Pilu-based 'Surmai ankiyon mein nanha munna' (*Sadma*, 1983).

However, S.P. Balasubrahmanyam, who idolised Rafi, emerged as the most popular male singer from South in the

1980s. With a voice that climbed the notes as fluidly as an eagle soars in the sky, S.P. gave his biggest hits in Kamal Haasan's debut flick in Hindi, *Ek Duuje Ke Liye* (1981). *Binaca Geetmala's* 1981 annual show had two Top 10 numbers by S.P.: Raag Shivranjani-based 'Tere mere beech mein' (with Lata, No. 5) and the frisky 'Mere jeevan saathi' (with Anuradha Paudwal, No. 8). He continued to do the playback for Kamal Haasan (*Yeh To Kamaal Ho Gaya, Saagar*) and sang frequently in southern Hindi productions.

A versatile singer, SPB delivered hits in Jeetendra's *Ek Hi Bhool* ('Hey Raju, Hey Daddy' with Rajeshwari) and Salman Khan's first biggie, *Maine Pyar Kiya* ('Dil deewana bin sajna ke' and 'Kabutar ja ja ja'). The superhit tracks made him the voice of Salman Khan in the early 1990s. He passed away on 25 September 2020.

Suresh Wadkar and Amit Kumar

Suresh Wadkar maintained a steady and reliable presence throughout the 1980s without ever taking the charts by storm like Aziz. The Bombay-born singer, who grew up in the mill area near Delisle Road, drew attention with composer Jaidev's melancholic classic, 'Seene mein jalan' (*Gaman*, 1979). Wadkar's voice amplified the song's sadness and gave it the soul it needed. His biggest hits, though, were more pedestrian tracks like 'Chal chameli bagh mein mewa khilaoonga' (with Lata, *Krodhi*, 1981) or 'Main hoon prem rogi' (with Lata, *Prem Rog*, 1982).

He once said, 'I got my identity after *Prem Rog* was released in 1982. It happened owing to Laxmikant-Pyarelal. But the credit for establishing me as a singer in the industry goes to Ravindra Jain, who gave me my first song in *Paheli* [in] 1977.'[12]

Wadkar brought a certain polish and nuance to singing, cultivated by years of classical training as exemplified in 'Saanjh dhale gagan tale' (*Utsav*, 1984). His adaptability can be seen in 'Aye zindagi gale laga le' (*Sadma*, 1983), 'Dekho yeh kaun aaya'

(*Saveray Wali Gaadi*, 1986), and the street-singer's declaration of ardour, 'Goron ki na kaalon ki, duniya hai dilwalon ki' (*Disco Dancer*, 1982).

Singer Suresh Wadkar brought a touch of class and gravitas in the Eighties. (Photo Credit: Suresh Wadkar)

Unlike some of the more successful singers of his time, Wadkar was not a clone. Duets such as 'Megha re megha re' (with Lata; *Pyaasa Sawan*, 1981), 'Khamosh sa afsana' (with Lata; *Libaas*, 1988) and 'Tumse milke aisa lagaa tumse milke' (with Lata; *Parinda*, 1989) reveal his comfort with both higher and lower notes.

He told a magazine, 'The singers who came after me are busier and that's due to one reason, I sing in my own voice. Mohd Rafi is my ideal and I am his fan. But I don't copy him. That's why I am getting fewer songs than those who copy him such as Shabbir Kumar and Mohd Aziz...I don't like copying. This is my personal view.'[13]

Amit Kumar was often compared with his father Kishore Kumar and even accused of being his shadow. The accusation was both unfair and inaccurate. Amit's bouncy style resembled his father's but the voice was distinctly his own. Taking off from the 1970s when he delivered the earnest 'Bade achche lagte' (*Balika Badhu*, 1976) and several other hits, Amit started promisingly in the 1980s with Kumar Gaurav's *Love Story*.

The film became one of the biggest hits of 1981. Gaurav became hot property. So did Amit Kumar as his playback. In the years that followed, Gaurav went in a free fall. Music was the saving grace in *Teri Kasam* and the two notable duds, *Romance* and *Lovers*—with music by the luckless R.D. Burman and songs crooned by Amit. He was especially impressive in the lower notes as exemplified in songs such as 'Yeh zameen ga rahi hai' (*Teri Kasam*, 1982) and 'Zamaane mein sabse purani' (*Lovers*, 1983).

Like Kumar Gaurav, Amit Kumar's career went on a downward spiral in the mid-1980s. Notable duets like 'Roz roz ankhon taley' (with Asha), an R.D.-Gulzar creation in *Jeeva* (1986), were rare. Composer Ajit Varman showed unwavering faith in Amit and gave him two of his most unforgettable tracks: 'Har ghadi dhal rahi' (*Saaransh*, 1984) and 'Ma Bolo' in the little-known *Wasta* (1989), which recreated the Varman and Vasant Dev combo of *Saaransh*. 'Har ghadi dhal rahi', which starts with a slow movement of violins like a Western symphony, makes rich use of Amit's huskiness.

In 1988, Amit Kumar flew back on the charts with hits in *Tezaab* ('Ek do teen'), following it up with *Tridev's* (1989) 'Tirchhi topi wale' (with Sapna Mukherjee; lyrics: Anand Bakshi; music: Kalyanji-Anandji). But overall he remained an underutilised, unfulfilled promise.

Bhupinder

Amritsar-born Bhupinder Singh brought a touch of class and classical to mainstream Hindi film singing in the 1970s and '80s. The music teacher's son, who grew up in Delhi, was taken to Bombay by composer Madan Mohan. He had a baptism by fire singing alongside greats such as Mohd Rafi, Manna Dey, Talat Mahmood in the pining soldiers' track, 'Hoke majboor mujhe' (*Haqeeqat*, 1964).

Critics praised his sober and distinctive voice and easy control over difficult notes, noticeable in songs like the raag Yaman Kalyan-based 'Beeti na beetai raina' in *Parichay* (1972). Gradually, Bhupinder became the perfect fit for background songs reflecting ache and angst. His rich reflective voice added depth and gave soul to every song he sang. And while many of them did not climb the charts, they always felt like sincere companions of solitude and suitable accessories for the broken-hearted: 'Karoge yaad to har baat yaad aayegi' (*Bazaar*), 'Kabhi kisi to muqammal jahan nahi milta' (*Ahista Ahista*), 'Ahl-e-dil yun hi' (*Dard*), 'Zindagi phoolon ki nahi' (*Griha Pravesh*), 'Jaane yeh mujhko kya ho raha hai' (*Ek Baar Phir*). He also sang some outstanding duets such as 'Raat banoo main aur chand bano tum' (*Mangalsutra*), 'Kisi nazar ko tera' (*Aitbaar*) and 'Aawaz di hai aaj ik nazar ne' (*Aitbaar*).

His biggest hits came in *Masoom* ('Huzoor is kadar bhi', with Suresh Wadkar) and in *Satte Pe Satta* where he sang two uncharacteristic group fun songs: the title track and the feel-good 'Zindagi mil ke bitaenge'. He later branched out as a ghazal singer with Bangladesh-born wife Mitali Mukherjee.[14] Bhupinder died of colon cancer on 18 July 2022. He was eighty-two.

Nitin Mukesh and Shailendra Singh

Nitin Mukesh and Shailendra Singh were two other prominent playbacks of the time. Nitin's oeuvre and vocal range was limited but he had an astonishing strike rate of hits ('Zindagi ki na toote ladi'; *Kranti*, 1981) and ('Zindagi ka naam dosti'; *Khudgarz*, 1987).

In the Eighties, Bombay-born Shailendra Singh was frequently used for male-bonding tracks in films like *Chashme Buddoor*,

Hum Paanch, *Arjun* and *Coolie* ('Lambuji-Tinguji'). His best solos and duets came in *Agreement* (where he also played the male lead opposite Rekha), *Saagar* ('Jaane do naa', with Asha Bhosle) and in two Nasir Hussain films, *Zamaane Ko Dikhana Hai* and *Manzil Manzil*. But he remained a fringe player in a market dominated by Kishore, Shabbir and Aziz.

New Kids on the Block

The Eighties marked the entry of three male singers who would dominate the Hindi film music world in the 1990s: Kumar Sanu, Udit Narayan and Abhijeet.

Kanpur-born Abhijeet caught notice singing peppy tracks such as 'Prem doot aaya' (*Mujhe Insaaf Chahiye*) and 'Main awara hi sahi' (*Anand Aur Anand*). Composer Rajesh Roshan gave Udit Narayan his break in *Unees Bees* (1980) and *Sannata* (1982); 'Sun jaane jaan' with Alka Yagnik was a pleasant duet. His jackpot moment came with *Qayamat Se Qayamat Tak* (1988). 'Papa kehte hain' became the song of the year.

Kumar Sanu, whose voice had distinct shades of Kishore Kumar, started out as Sanu Bhattacharya. He was rechristened as Kumar Sanu by Kalyanji-Anandji. He struggled through the 1980s singing in films such as *Yeh Desh* (1984) and *Hero Hiralal* (1988). He got his big break in *Jaadugar* (1989) where he sang three numbers. But the songs didn't work, neither did the film. Sanu lorded over the 1990s, winning five *Filmfare* awards in a row. Another Kishore clone, Vinod Rathod, also made his debut in the 1980s.

Mangeshkar Sisters Dominate

The story of the female singers was more of continuity than departure. The Mangeshkar sisters, especially Lata and Asha, continued to rule in the Eighties. They took the lioness' share of the hits and the awards.

Male or female, Lata was the most popular singer of the

decade. Of the Top 20 songs each year (1980-89) on *Binaca Geetmala*, Lata had fifty-seven hits, solos and duets included. In six out of ten years, she had more hits than all other female singers put together. In 1985, ten out of the twenty top songs of the year belonged to her. The playful bhajan 'Yashoda ka Nandlala' has over 38 million views on YouTube. At the same time, she also sang the sensual 'Dooriyaan sab mita do' (*Saboot*).

A closer look shows that she was the preferred singer of most composers. And she remained a perfect fit for heroines of any age. Lata was sixty when she sang 'Dil deewana bin sajna ke' for twenty-year-old Bhagyashree in *Maine Pyar Kiya*.

Three tracks from *Subah* (1983) demand a more detailed attention. Lata is flawless in the 'Chand roza zindagi' and in the intricate 'Khile the kal jo gulab laakhon'. In the incomparable 'Tum aasha vishwas hamare', a morning hymn which you can sing at a temple or a school's morning assembly prayer, Lata's soaring rendition has the clarity of a bell and the power of a devotee. This faith-strengthening bhajan shows how great film music can feel like a spiritual union with the Creator. The superlative singer passed away on 6 February 2022. She was ninety-two.

In terms of hits, Asha Bhosle finished second best to her *didi* but this was a creatively fecund period for her. With her voice, a heady mix of allure and abandon, she was on top of her game winning two national awards for *Umrao Jaan* and *Ijaazat*.

Bhosle was preferred by Bappi Lahiri for perky duets in southern-produced movies. She sang the finest of ghazals (*Umrao Jaan*, 1980) and even outperformed the powerpuff girls—Usha Uthup, Sharon Prabhakar, Alisha Chinoy—in their comfort zones. Asha's 'Disco Station' (*Haathkadi*, 1982) or 'Jab chhaye mera jadoo' (*Lootmaar*, 1980) are benchmarks in the sub-genre.

The 1980s saw the rise of a new bunch of female singers, who belonged to the Lata school. Anuradha Paudwal, who started in the '70s, got a national award for 'Mera man baje mridang' in *Utsav*. Alka Yagnik sang 1981's topper, 'Mere angne mein tumhara kya kaam hai', but had to wait till *Tezaab's* 'Ek do teen' (1988) to find another blockbuster.

Salma Agha's weepy solo, 'Dil ke armaan ansuaon mein beh gaye' (*Nikaah*), became her calling card. The London-bred daughter of a Pakistani businessman got a *Filmfare* award for the song.

Nazia Hassan hit the music industry like a tsunami with 'Aap jaisa koi' (*Qurbani*, 1980) and followed it up with the non-filmi bestseller *Disco Deewane* (1981) and *Star* (1982) before fading away. Her 'Boom Boom' was one of the few highlights of *Star* (1982), the shabby musical that composer Biddu produced and squandered money on. Few remember, though, that she also sang in *Ilzaam*, *Dilwaala* and *Main Balwaan*—all under the prolific baton of Bappi Lahiri—in the Eighties.

Some other female singers from another side of the border also made a guest appearance. Sabina Yasmin of Bangladesh (now wedded to Bengal urban folk singer Kabir Suman) sang in *Aar Paar* (1985) for R.D. Burman while her countrymate Runa Laila crooned for Bappi Lahiri in *Yaadgaar* (1984). Laila, one might recall, had also sung in *Gharaonda* and *Ek Se Badh Kar Ek* in the 1970s.

Kavita Krishnamurthy hit the high notes with 'Hawa hawaai' (*Mr. India*) and the songs of *Chaalbaaz* ('Na jaane kahan se' with Amit Kumar). The versatile S. Janaki also performed a slew of Hindi hits such as 'Yaar bina chain kahan re' (with Bappi Lahiri; *Saaheb*, 1985), 'Sun rubia' (with Shabbir Kumar and Sharon Prabhakar; *Mard*, 1985) and 'Gori ka saajan saajan ki gori' (with Mohd Aziz; *Aakhree Raasta*, 1986). Sapna Mukherjee's zippiness earned her plaudits in tracks like 'Tirchhi topi wale'. Sadhna Sargam proved her all-rounder skills in two Kalyanji-Anandji compositions, 'Neele neele ambar pe' (*Kalaakaar*, 1983) and 'Har kisi ko nahi milta' (*Janbaaz*, 1986), two stylistically different numbers.

Boom Time for Ghazal Singers

The 1980s were a busy time for ghazal singers in Hindi films. Jagjit Singh was the most in demand amongst them. Jagjit, who was born in Sri Ganganagar in north Rajasthan, sang and composed music for *Prem Geet*, *Arth* (with wife Chitra), and *Raavan*. Among other singers of the genre, Anup Jalota soared with 'Solah baras ki baali umar ko salaam', composed by Laxmikant-Pyarelal in *Ek Duuje Ke Liye* (1981), and to a lesser extent with 'Kisi ka dil jo todega' (*Qatl*, 1986). But the songs of Talat Aziz have proved to be more enduring: 'Phir chhidi raat baat phoolon ki' (*Bazaar*, 1982), 'Zindagi jab bhi tere bazm mein bulati hai humein' (*Umrao Jaan*, 1980) and 'Aina mujhse meri' (*Daddy*, 1989).

Pankaj Udhas delivered the biggest hit of 1986, 'Chitthi aayi hai' (*Naam*). The song was a geet, not a ghazal.

Peenaz Masani sang for *Hamari Bahu Alka*, *Katha* (one of the voices in the fun-filled, inquisitive track, 'Kaun aaya'), and Dev Anand's *Hum Naujawan* ('You are my darling', with Kishore Kumar). Masani's high-pitched rendition of poet Salauddin Parvez's ghazal, 'Koi purani magar sansani si saajish ho', offsets the lower notes of Bhupinder in this forlorn but masterly Jaidev composition for *Jumbish* (1986). Chitra Singh also sang for husband-composer Jagjit in several films. Jagjit-Chitra also sang for Bappi Lahiri in *Bhavna* (1984). The poignant duet, 'Mere dil mein tu hai dil ki dawa kya karoon', was penned by Kaifi Azmi. Rajkumar Rizvi gave poignancy to *Anokha Mod's* (1985) 'Aas kisi ki na toote' (music: S.D. Kashyap).

Jalota also composed for films but was unable to capture the spirit of a film score. *Patton Ki Baazi* (1986) didn't work despite his fetching rendition of 'Aakhri baar tere husn ko' (lyrics: Maya Govind). *Tohfa Mohabbat Ka* (1988) added little to his popularity or prestige.

Udhas rehashed his popular composition, 'Tum na mano haqeekat hai' (*Aurat Pair Ki Juti Nahi*, 1985), and again the wildly popular 'Mohey aayee na jag se laaj' (*Ek Hi Maqsad*, 1988). He also gave the music for *Agnidaah* (1985). But like Jalota, he couldn't reinvent himself as a successful tunesmith.

Actors on Song

Amitabh Bachchan | 'Mere angne mein tumhara kya kaam hai' (*Laawaris*, 1981); 'Chal chal mere bhai' (*Naseeb*, 1981); 'Padosan apni murgi ko rakhna sambhaal' (*Jaadugar*, 1989); 'Baahar mein hai problem' (*Toofan*, 1989)

Amjad Khan | 'Khat pe khatmal' (with Deven Verma; *Josh*, 1981)

Anil Kapoor | Title track of *Chameli Ki Shaadi* (1986)

Deven Verma | 'Bol beta bol paisa gol' (*Chhupa Chhuppi*, 1981)

Govinda | 'Jawan jawan o jawan', a copy of the famous Hasan Jahangir hit, 'Hawa hawa' (*Billoo Baadshah*, 1989)

Kamal Haasan | 'Ek dafa ek jungle thha' (*Sadma*, 1983)

Mithun Chakraborty | 'Kal se chhodh doonga main sharab, aaj mujhe peene de' (*Ilaaka*, 1989)

Rekha | 'Kaida kaida aakhir faida' (*Khubsoorat*, 1980)

Naseeruddin Shah | 'Dil chura le jo mera' (*Tajurba*, 1981)

Shatrughan Sinha | 'Teri chachi bulldozer' (*Naram Garam*, 1981)

Shabana Azmi | 'Gulab jism ka yun nahi khila hoga' (with Bhupinder; *Anjuman*, 1986).

Smita Patil | 'Chandi ki roti' (*Raavan*, 1984)

REEL 14

LITERATURE, DOWRY, JOURNALISM AND CASTE INEQUITY

Ever since movies in India got talking with *Alam Ara* (1931), literature and Hindi cinema have been uneasy but inseparable bedfellows. Works of Tagore, Premchand and Shakespeare, to name just three formidable men of letters, found their way to celluloid with debatable degrees of quality and success.

Contrary to popular perception, the Eighties decade too was a fecund period for literary adaptations. Both serious and popular literature, primarily from Marathi, Bengali, Hindi, Urdu and English languages, became a constant source for moviemaking. Films were also made from Malayalam, Tamil, Punjabi, Gujarati, Rajasthani, even Sanskrit, classics. That many of them did not meet with commercial success is another story.

Bengali writer Samaresh Basu and Marathi playwright Jaywant Dalvi were among the most filmed litterateurs of the decade. Among the directors, Gulzar, Govind Nihalani, Mrinal Sen and Basu Chatterjee were the most prolific interpreters of literary work.

Hindi

Director Mani Kaul's *Satah Se Uthata Aadmi* (1980) was an artistic success even though the experimental film wasn't easy to process. The film sought to recreate the poetic inner world of Gajanan Madhav Muktibodh through his letters and poems. Muktibodh sculpted a new modernist, avant-garde idiom of Hindi poetry. Like a lost city rediscovered, his reputation blossomed after his death in 1964 and his poetry collection, *Chand Ka Muh Tedha Hai,* was feted as a masterpiece.

The film has an unfinished, dream-like quality. It is like looking at a painting and walking in sleep at the same time. 'Kaul's images could make you meditate,' said M.K. Raina, who acted in the film.[1] Now available free on the internet, the film had garnered over 20,000 views by November 2022.

Satah Se Uthata Aadmi, financed by the Madhya Pradesh Kala Parishad, had a puny budget and was shot in various MP towns: Bhopal, Ujjain, Mandu, Raipur and Rajnandgaon. Poet Ashok Vajpeyi, who once headed the institution, was the film's producer.

Hindi writer and Sahitya Akademi award winner, Mridula Garg's short story, *Mera* (Mine), was adapted by producer-director Bhimsain (*Gharaonda, Doooriyan*) for *Tum Laut Aao* (1983). The movie, with Kavita Chaudhary (of *Udaan* teleserial fame) playing the protagonist, was little seen, lesser heard.

Mera told the story of a working woman whose husband doesn't want her to get pregnant because he intends to migrate to the US. Despite protests from all fronts, she decides to bear the child.

What irked Calcutta-born Garg was that the director had taken serious liberties with the plot. In an interview to *Saptahik Hindustan* magazine after the release of the film, she said, 'The film has destroyed the fundamental world view of my story. The director Bhimsain himself had said in 1984 that the merit of the story lay in showing that the woman of today has found her persona and is willing to take crucial decisions.'

But the film ignored this. Unlike the novel which validated her agency, the woman who refuses to get an abortion to honour the wishes of her husband and family, dies during childbirth.

'It was, as if, she was being punished for her independence,' recalled the writer, who was paid Rs 30,000 for the film.[2]

There were stronger cases of writers clashing with the producer. Mannu Bhandari's wildly popular novel, *Aapka Bunty*, became the centre of a major controversy that landed in court. The novel, which related the plight of a nine-year-old boy whose parents are divorced, was released with the title, *Samay Ki Dhaara* (1986). The film was produced by Dharmendra Goyal and directed by noted filmmaker of Odiya films, Sisir Misra, who had also helmed *Bheegi Palkein* (1982) and *Billoo Baadshah* (1989) in Hindi.

Rachana Yadav, daughter of noted litterateurs Mannu Bhandari and Rajendra Yadav, recalled: 'I was sent by my mother to Bombay after she received a phone call from one of the stars in the film that they were putting in too much commercial element. I saw the shooting at a hired bungalow. After the shoot, the star who had called my mother told me, "Please ask your mother to get more involved in the shooting. Probably some significant changes are being made in the script which may not be very good for the film".'[3]

'My mother was very unhappy with the development and later filed a case in court. *Aapka Bunty* was very close to her heart. It was the novel that got people talking about her,' said Yadav, now managing director of literary magazine *Hans*.[4] Garg too felt that *Samay Ki Dhaara* veered away from the book and developed its own story. 'It was nothing more than a masala movie,' she said.[5] The case was settled out of court. The film was a minor success.

Earlier, two of Bhandari's stories had been filmed by Basu Chatterjee: *Yahi Sach Hai* (*Rajnigandha*, 1974) and *Ekhane Aakash Neyi* (*Jeena Yahan*, 1979). Yadav said, 'She enjoyed a very good equation with Basu-*da*. They interacted closely also for *Swami* (1977), in which she wrote the dialogues. 'At one time Basu-*da* also showed interest in making *Aapka Bunty*. But since his expertise lay in making light, humorous films, my mother felt that maybe she should work with someone else on a serious subject like *Bunty*. Later, Basu-*da* used to tease her saying, you refused to give me the film, now see what's happening.'[6] Bhandari passed away on 15 November 2021.

Woh Phir Nahi Aaye, Bhagwati Charan Verma's searing novel on the human tragedy of Partition and the cruel choices it forced on common people, became a movie of the same name, helmed by debutant director Joginder Shelly (not to be confused with the director of the 1970s cult-basement flick, *Rangakhush*).

Woh Phir Nahi Aaye (1981) isn't available on the net or DVD. But at the time of its release, it was the subject of a perceptive article by journalist Girija Rajendran who praised the movie and criticised the critics for their inability to appreciate a movie that is neither angry Left nor feel-good middle-of-the-road.

Rajendran wrote in *The Times of India* that Shelly revealed, 'The inherent ability to tell a tale in a style intelligible to the hoi-polloi. It is Shelly's singular achievement that he has accomplished the feat by giving full play to the talents of three of the sadly neglected talents of our commercial cinema: Jalal Agha, Dinesh Thakur and Rita Bhaduri.' The film, originally named 'Shyamala', took a long time to complete. Some films deserve a relook and a reassessment. *Woh Phir Nahi Aaye* is one of them.

Prakash Jha's *Damul*, wrenched out of Hindi litterateur Shaival's story, attracted far more attention. The writer recalled that he had published some poems on the infamous 1981 Biharsharif communal riots in *Dharamyug* magazine. Shaival said, 'Prakash Jha had read those poems and asked my permission to use them in his documentary, *Faces After the Storm*. I sent my acquiescence by post. That's how we came to know each other.'[7]

Later, Shaival sent him the synopsis of a story in two pages and requested that if he made a film, it should be named *Damul*. He said, 'The film was based on my story, *Kalsutra*.

Before writing the story I had worked for about two-and-half years on *panha* (man-made famine). Part of the research was first published as reportage in *Ravivar* and later became the source of my story, *Kalsutra*. I worked with the director for three years on its script and dialogues. I was with him during the shooting, editing and dubbing.'[8] Rarely a film's writer is allowed such close engagement with the film; in *Damul's* case, the outcome was stunning.

The man-woman relationship was also explored through literature. Basu Bhattacharya's *Panchvati* (1986), based on writer Kusum Ansal's novel *Ek Aur Panchwati,* walked the same line. But the Akbar Khan-Deepti Naval film found few takers.

———————————— SHORT TAKE ————————————

Popular pulp

Popular Hindi literature also found its way to celluloid in a more robust fashion. Romance writer Gulshan Nanda's novels had become box-office biggies in the late 1960s and early 1970s: *Neel Kamal, Khilona* and *Daag. Kati Patang* (1971) helped shape Rajesh Khanna's image as a romantic star. Several Nanda stories were also filmed in the 1980s, notably *Bade Dil Wala* (1983), *Palay Khan* (1986) and *Nazrana* (1987), but without success.

Marathi

Playwright Mahesh Eklunchwar's Marathi works formed the basis of both Ketan Mehta's *Holi* and Govind Nihalani's *Party*. He also played a Naxalite in Nihalani's *Aakrosh* (1980). Eklunchwar, who taught English in a Nagpur college, says Nihalani was a regular theatregoer and had seen his work.

'We got to know each other through Satyadev Dubey and

then became friends. He had read and seen *Party* and liked it. When he asked if he could make a film on it, there was no reason to say no. Mehta came over to Nagpur and expressed his desire to make a film on *Holi* and I said yes,' he said.[9]

The reason for him agreeing to the request, he said, was the curiosity to see 'how the texts, which are written for theatre would work in a different medium'.[10]

Rabindra Dhanraj's *Chakra* was based on Marathi novelist and playwright Jaywant Dalvi's work. Dalvi worked as an assistant editor in Marathi newspapers, *Prabhat* and *Lokmanya*. He became the most filmed Marathi writer of the decade.

Director Mohan Kaura's *Mahananda* (released in 1987) was also written by Dalvi. An elegiac account of forbidden love and lingering regrets, the film critically examined the devdasi system. Director Vijaya Mehta's *Rao Saheb* (1988), adapted from Dalvi's play *Barrister* underlined the gap between what the liberals preached and what they were unable to practise in early twentieth century.

Govind Nihalani's *Ardh Satya* was constructed from S.D. Panwalkar's short story, *Surya*. Amol Palekar's *Ankahee* was based on Sahitya Akademi-winning C.T. Khanolkar's play, *Kaleya Tasmai Namaha*. Sai Paranjype's *Katha* had its origins in S.G. Sathye's play, *Sasa aani Kasav* (Hare and Tortoise). Playwright Vijay Tendulkar was also closely involved in writing screenplays for Nihalani (*Aakrosh, Ardh Satya* and *Aaghat*), Jagmohan Mundhra's *Kamla* (1985) and Aruna-Vikas's *Gehrayee.*

Bengali

Samaresh Basu was the most filmed litterateur in 1980s Hindi cinema. Dhaka-born Basu lived life and its ironies on the streets and wrote a staggering 100 novels and 200 short stories. His work attracted directors as diverse as Gulzar (*Namkeen*, 1982), Basu Chatterjee (*Shaukeen*, 1981), Goutam Ghose (*Paar*, 1984) and Mrinal Sen (*Genesis*, 1986). The films, too, are as different from each other as Narendra Modi is from Russi Mody.

Namkeen was based on his short story, *Akal Bosonto,* the story of a man and four women, each as distinct from the other as sweet is from sour and bitter from bland. Yet their lives are knitted together like stitches in a quilt. Basu got a *Filmfare* award for best story. Goutam Ghose's stark and minimalist *Paar* captured the essence of Basu's story, *Paari,* the triumph of human spirit against all odds. *Shaukeen,* a story of three old men in search of adult fun, was culled out of Samaresh Basu's short story, *Ram Naam Kewalam,* and marked director Basu Chatterjee's return to form after a string of flops. Mrinal Sen's ambitious failure *Genesis* was again filmed on Basu's work on isolation and exploitation.

Some other Hindi films recreated from Bengali literature during this decade were:

***Apne Paraye* (1980):** Basu Chatterjee's second stab at Saratchandra after the sensitive and successful *Swami* (1977). Based on the novel *Nishkriti,* the family drama took a caring look at courtyard politics in hinterland Bengal and was a critical and commercial success.

***Shama* (1981):** Noted Bengali writer Jarasandha (real name: Charu Chandra Chakraborty), also the writer of Bimal Roy's *Bandini,* authored the story. Kader Khan, largely known for his snappy and indelicate dialogues in masala movies, produced a movie contrary to his oeuvre. The Girish Karnad-Shabana Azmi starrer was set in the years before and after Independence and sedately told the travails of a Muslim aristocratic family. It fared reasonably well.

***Hamari Bahu Alka* (1982):** Basu Chatterjee's shoddily crafted film had its roots in Manoj Basu's *Nishi Kutumbo.*

***Ayaash* (1982):** Producer-director Shakti Samanta used novelist Bimal Mitra's story and employed Hindi writer Kamleshwar for the dialogues. But the story of a decadent landlord in Bengal didn't sit well on screen.

Khandhar (1984): Benaras-born writer Premendra Mitra persistently investigated the dark crevices of the human psyche. Mrinal Sen's *Khandhar* was based on his *Telenapota Abishkar*.

Sheesha (1986): Based on Shankar's novel, *Man Samman*. A rare film on sexual harassment in the workplace, the film had an unusual cast: Mithun Chakraborty, Moon Moon Sen and Mallika Sarabhai. At least in its denouement, the film was far ahead of its time. In times of #MeToo, it is worth a second look.

Trishagni (1988): Noted screenplay writer Nabendu Ghosh's debut film as a director was based on Saradindu Bandopadhyay's story, *Maru o Sangha* (Desert and the Monastery). The film dissected desire in the context of Buddhism. Ghosh got the national award for best debut film by a director.

Ek Din Achanak (1989): Mrinal Sen's film was based on eminent Bengali writer Ramapada Chowdhury's work, *Beej*.

Some other films inspired by Bengali literature in the 1980s were Buddhadev Dasgupta's *Andhi Gali* (1984), which was based on Dibyendu Palit's *Ghar Baari*. Kalpana Lajmi's feminist *Ek Pal* (1986) emerged from Maitreyi Devi's work. Dasgupta passed away on 10 June 2021.

Goutam Ghose's bilingual *Mahayatra/Antarjali Jatra* (1987) was based on Kamal Kishore Majumdar's most well-known work, which was set in nineteeth-century Bengal. Gulzar's *Ijaazat* (1988) was made from Subodh Ghosh's short story, *Jatugrih*.

Urdu

The first Urdu novel, *Umrao Jaan Ada* (1905), took a nostalgic look at Lucknow's elite-sponsored courtesan culture of the nineteenth century. Filmmaker Muzaffar Ali recreated on celluloid Mirza Hadi Ruswa's work. His *Gaman* (1978) had captured the plight of the rural migrant—nowhere men trapped physically and emotionally in a nowhere place. Ali said, '*Umrao*

Jaan [1981] was also about a migration which had taken place a hundred years ago. It was the story of human helplessness that drew me towards it.'[11]

A painter, Ali saw the novel equally as a canvas. The movie lacked the acuity of the novel. The general view was that the director had focused more on producing a painstakingly detailed visual portrait than delivering a sharp testament of the times.

B.R. Chopra's *Tawaif* (1985) was based on Aleem Masroor's novel, *Bahut Der Kar Di,* and owed its core to Chopra's own

Director-producer Muzaffar Ali was also one of the three art directors of *Umrao Jaan*

Sadhna (1958). The love triangle overturned the formula of the golden-hearted dancing girl who must die or sacrifice her love.

Of all the writers whose works were filmed in Bombay, Rajinder Singh Bedi had one of the deepest engagements with the industry. He wrote dialogues for a cache of memorable movies (*Devdas, Madhumati* and *Anupama*) and formed a production house, Cine Cooperative, with director Amar Kumar and actors Balraj Sahni and Geeta Bali. But after the group's first venture, *Garam Coat* (1955), based on Bedi's own poignant tale, fizzled out, they shut shop. At fifty-five, Bedi made his directorial debut with the award-winning *Dastak* (1970), based on his radio play, *Naql-e-Makani.*

Bedi's most feted novel, *Ek Chadar Maili Si,* had earned him the Sahitya Akademi award in 1965. He 'had wanted to make this film himself, way back in the Sixties with Geeta Bali and Dharmendra in the lead. But the project was shelved with Geeta's sudden death.'[12] The film was finally made in 1986, two years after his death, by director Sukhwant Dhadda, with veteran director Phani Majumdar writing the screenplay.

Actors Hema Malini and Rishi Kapoor played the lead in *Ek Chadar Maili Si*, which was about an old Punjabi custom where a young *devar* marries his elder brother's widow. The film failed to capture the human tragedy created by such a situation. Barring Punjab, where it did brisk business, the film vanished like late-spring mist.

Another pillar of Urdu literature and Bedi's friend, Krishan Chander, had profusely praised *Ek Chadar Maili Si*, the novel. Prolific in Bombay like Bedi, Chander had written the sharp and thoughtful dialogues of *Andolan* (1951) and *Faraar* (1955) and many more films. His own novel, *Yahan Se Sheher Ko Dekho* (1983), was turned into a little-known film by R.K. Munir.

Tamil

Pehla Adhyay (1981): Vishnu Mathur, better known for his documentaries, turned Tamil feminist writer C.S. Lakshmi's short story, *Milechan,* into an avant-garde film about the loneliness of a college student in Bombay.

—————————— SHORT TAKE ——————————

Kafan in Telugu

Mrinal Sen's Telugu film, *Oka Oorie Katha* (1977) was dubbed and released in Hindi as *Kafan* (1981). The film was based on Premchand's novel of the same name.

Kannada

Sookha (1983): U.R. Ananthamurthy's story was filmed by M.S. Sathyu, earlier made as *Bara* in Kannada. 'The story is about the nexus between police and a ruling politician, where an idealistic administrator gets caught in the power game. Famine is a backdrop,' said Sathyu.[13]

Malayalam

Chirutha (1981): The NFDC film, directed by Tanvir Ahmed, was based on renowned Malayalam writer Thakazhi S. Pillai's *Two Measures of Rice*. Shot in the backwaters of the Alleppey district, the film humanised the plight of paddy cultivators in 1948 rural Kerala. Few saw the movie.

Gujarati

Mirch Masala (1986): Gujarati writer Chunilal Madia's fiery tale of female rebellion against sexual exploitation in rural Saurashtra was turned into a film by Ketan Mehta.

Rajasthani

Parinati (1989): Prakash Jha's creative interpretation of Vijaydan Detha's soul-crushing Rajasthani folktale.

Sanskrit

Utsav (1984): Producer Shashi Kapoor and director Girish Karnad, the film lavishly and lovingly blended and recreated two ancient Indian plays—*Charudutta* by Bhasa and Sudraka's *Mrichchhakatika* (The Clay Cart).

Punjabi

Waaris (1988): Based on *Kaare-Haathi,* written by Lahore-born Punjabi novelist and journalist Sohan Singh Hans. Before its release, Hans had filed an application in a Patiala court claiming that the film was based on his novel and obtained a stay on the release. He eventually got what he wanted. The opening credit clearly mentions, 'Based on a Punjabi novel, "Kaare-Haathi" written by Sohan Singh Hans.'

English

Man Pasand (1980): The film was dedicated to the genius of Irish playwright G.B. Shaw and based on his work, *Pygmalion*, but it was Basu Chatterjee's least satisfying liaison with literature.

Kanhaiyaa (1981): Master Rajoo played the lead in this desi version of Oliver Twist. Naseeruddin Shah also acted in the film.

Angoor (1982): Inspired from Shakespeare's *Comedy of Errors* and adroitly localised by Gulzar. Of all the filmed literary works, this was the biggest box-office success.

Masoom (1983): Shekhar Kapur's desi tadka of Eric Segal's *Man, Woman and Child*.

Khudgarz (1987): Rakesh Roshan's mast masala adaptation of Jeffrey Archer's *Kane and Abel*.

Gawaahi (1989): Producer Viveck Vaswani and director Anant Balani's dissatisfying venture based on Ayn Rand's courtroom thriller, *Night of January 16th*. It starred Zeenat Aman and Shekhar Kapur in key roles.

Massey Sahib (1985): Director Pradeep Kishen's film was inspired by *Mister Johnson,* written by the adventurous Irish novelist, Joyce Carey. Harish Trivedi, professor of English at Delhi University said, '*Massey Sahib* was an arthouse film made with integrity. Raghubir Yadav was outstanding in the title role. But several key aspects of the novel were left out from the celluloid adaptation. This was unlikely due to ignorance, more probably an artistic decision. For instance, the novel hinges on the fact that Mister Johnson is a black character serving a white master; this racial equation can hardly be replicated in the Indian colonial situation...All intercultural adaptations have their own problems, but here they were especially acute.'[14]

Russian

Sahib Bahadur (1980): Chetan Anand's remake of his film, *Afsar.* Both were inspired by Nikolai Gogol's *The Office Inspector.*

French

Eent Ka Jawab Patthar (1982): Inspired by Alexander Dumas's *The Count of Monte Cristo*, director Pachhi's film had actor Surendra Pal in the once-in-a-lifetime lead role.

Brides Are Not for Burning

Dowry-related violence, especially burning of brides, spiked in the 1970s and 1980s. Perpetrators often tried to pass off these cases as suicide. Many gruesome incidents were front-paged in newspapers. Women's movements against dowry also gathered steam during this time. Consequently, an amendment was brought in 1986 to strengthen the vague and toothless Dowry Prohibition Act of 1961. The 1980s saw many films focused around the regressive social practice:

Sau Din Saas Ke (1980): The spunky bride (Reena Roy) gets the better of her mother-in-law (Lalita Pawar), who first tries to harass her, and then tries to get her killed. Director Vijay Sadanah's film entertained, even if it didn't educate.

Dahej (1981): Not much is known about producer-director-writer-lyricist Indrajit Hassanpuri's film except that it carried a song fawning over Sanjay Gandhi.

Jawalaa Dahej Ki (1982): The devastating 'economy' of dowry was tellingly bared in this Arun Govil and Shoma Anand film.

Dulha Bikta Hai (1982): The hero takes revenge on those who refuse to marry his sisters by wooing theirs. One of Raj Babbar's solo winners.

Ek Din Bahu Ka (1983): Karate-kicking bahu (Swapna) avenges the wrongs caused by greedy sasur-*ji* (Om Prakash).

Shubh Kaamna (1983): Dowry is central to this romantic drama directed by K. Vishwanath. The scene where hero Rakesh Roshan exposes the hypocrisy of Utpal Dutt is innovative.

Agnidaah (1985): The movie with the catchline, 'Brides are not for burning', seems to have disappeared from everywhere, including the net. A Zarina Wahab-Karan Razdan starrer.

Bahu Ki Awaaz (1986): Director Shashilal Nair's anti-dowry vigilante film in which Supriya Pathak goes on a killing spree in the climax.

New Delhi Times (1986): An old man narrates his tale of woe—how his daughter was beaten up, declared insane and then just disappeared—to a woman lawyer (Sharmila Tagore). The scene leaves an impression, like the movie on political corruption.

Sasti Dulhan Mehenga Dulha (1986): Director Bhappi Sonie's maudlin drama flopped at the cash counters.

Bandook Dahej Ke Seeney Par (1989): Anita Kanwar, Sonika Gill and Prema Narayan mount a tirade against dowry. Guns and horses play support roles.

Billoo Baadshah (1989): Top Odisha director Sisir Misra's family drama. In one of the scenes, a character says chillingly, 'Our neighbours are very bad. If she [the bride] gets anything less in dowry, then they will taunt her so ruthlessly that she would pour kerosene and set herself aflame. And people would say that the mother-in-law has killed her for dowry.'

Hard News

The jholawala journalist often played cameos as well as central parts in a bunch of movies of varying quality during the decade. Some hacks were ramrod straight, others crooked like a fish hook.

Aakrosh (1980): In a small town lorded over by a select elite, a small, independent publisher-journalist running a newspaper, 'Rashtrahit', wants to publish an ugly truth. He is thrashed. We don't hear of him again.

Jaane Bhi Do Yaaro (1983): Calculating and corrupt, the woman editor of 'Khabardar' stands out as a counterpoint to the filmy breed of scribes, generally projected as honest.

Be-Aabroo (1983): The local version of the Hollywood rape and revenge flick, *I Spit on Your Grave* (1978), was a surprise box-office biggie. The woman journalist protagonist (Anu Dhawan) hardly went to office.

Kamla (1984): Based on a real-life expose of women bought and sold in Rajasthan. Marc Zuber played a better-looking version of the *Indian Express* investigative reporter, Ashwini Sarin. The film didn't create half as much sensation as the news story.

Mashaal (1984): The story of an editor who turns into a mafia don and a wayward street kid who becomes a reporter. Directed by Yash Chopra and written by Javed Akhtar, the film got its name from the newspaper.

Meri Izzat Bachao (1984): A woman journalist (Anu Dhawan) is after a gang that forces gullible girls into making blue films. It was an exploitative C-grade yarn, which became a surprise hit.

Surkhiyan, The Headlines (1985): Although patchy and preachy at times, director-writer Ashok Tyagi's movie strove hard to explain how sensationalism replaced seriousness in the newspaper industry. Kulbhushan Kharbanda was good as the unscrupulous owner-publisher who runs 'Morning News' and 'Daily Sunset'.

New Delhi Times (1986): A taut and immensely watchable political drama, written by Gulzar and directed by Kalimpong-born Ramesh Sharma. Shashi Kapoor played the intrepid editor (modelled on Arun Shourie of *Indian Express*) and controversially received the national award for best actor for a modest performance. DD once refused to telecast it.

Aaj (1987): Raj Babbar, editor of 'News of India', drinks alcohol in office and talks about the role of truth in journalism. Debutant heroine Anamika Pal, also the city's richest man's daughter, works as a reporter and works on a story on missing persons. Shoddy script, shoddily executed.

Mr. India (1987): The film had an editor and a reporter, but it wasn't exactly about journalism as we know it.

Main Azaad Hoon (1989): Writer Javed Akhtar's desi take on *Meet John Doe* (1941) was among the first films to deal with fake news. The new owner of 'National Voice' is immoral and arrogant and wants to sell news at any cost, and the title character is a figment of a columnist's (Shabana Azmi) imagination. Sporadically lapses into melodrama but also hard-hitting in parts.

Sachche Ka Bolbala (1989): Dev Anand had a penchant for turning headlines into films. The movie was built around a 'daring and forthright editor', his son Suneil Anand said. The flop had only one positive fallout: the filmmaker-actor was made an honorary member of Delhi's Press Club of India.

Caste Inequity

The term Dalit grabbed political prominence in 1972 after the formation of the radical Dalit Panthers. However, in 1980s Hindi cinema, the word was seldom used to describe any member of the Scheduled Caste. Most films continued to use the term Harijan, first used by Mahatma Gandhi in the 1930s. Here are some arthouse and mainstream films that engaged with caste, directly or indirectly:

Pehla Kadam (1981): Seasoned director Kidar Sharma's well-intended but ultimately dissatisfying reformist film—framed in village-theatre style—encapsulated an illiterate Harijan school sweeper's resolve to read and write with the help of his spunky wife.

Sadgati (1981): Satyajit Ray's fifty-two-minute telefilm captured the essence of Premchand's heart-wrenching yarn that's as much an indictment of poverty as the caste system.

Souten (1983): A mainstream film that took an offbeat path and reaped cash rewards. Dr Sriram Lagoo and Padmini Kolhapure play Harijans in Sawan Kumar Tak's tale of an imagined love triangle. The film isn't serious about discussing caste, just uses it to appear superficially different.

Sant Ravidas Ki Amar Kahani (1984): An important addition to the pantheon of devotionals. Based on the life of the fifteenth-century saint venerated by Dalits, veteran director Babubhai Mistry's film speaks out against untouchability and other forms of discrimination.

Jaag Utha Insan (1984): Director K. Vishwanath engages seriously with every form of caste prejudice in this tragic love story of a Harijan flautist (Mithun) and a Brahmin dancer (Sridevi). If only producer-actor Rakesh Roshan had shown more guts and gone for a happy ending!

Paar (1984): Their caste is not specified in Goutam Ghose's realist venture. But it's obvious that the couple played by Naseeruddin Shah and Shabana Azmi, who goad a group of pigs across a swollen river for money, are extremely poor Dalits.

Ghulami (1985): Director J.P. Dutta's film set in feudal Rajasthan led to riots in the western state. In Jammu, it also led to a violent agitation and arrests. The film takes a penetrating look at caste discrimination with dialogues such as '*Ghodi pe chhadna oonchi jaatwalon ka kaam hai, aapni jaat bhool gaye kya* (Only the upper caste rides on horses. Have you forgotten your caste)?' Those lines, sadly, remain relevant even today.

Damul (1985): A crafty Rajput leader seeks to depose the long-standing Brahmin sarpanch. He sets up a Harijan as a dummy candidate. Village politics gets dangerous and dirty in this Prakash Jha film where caste is the basis of loyalty and votes.

Saveray Wali Gaadi (1986): Director Bharathiraja's flop where young poet Ravidas (Sunny Deol) is a *nai* (barber) by caste. The dialogues are pithy and pungent but the love story fails to connect with the audience.

Chameli Ki Shaadi (1986): Basu Chatterjee's inter-caste love story flopped despite being enjoyable and meaningful. The climax feels like a sermon though.

Mahayatra (1987): The protagonist of Goutam Ghose's bilingual is a *chandal* (Shatrughan Sinha), an 'untouchable', who lives in the cremation grounds. A powerful film set in nineteenth century India, it interrogates the manipulative rituals that protect and propel caste privileges and patriarchy.

Bhed Bhav (1988): Director Navin Kumar's film ham-handedly poked at entrenched casteism as well as communalism. Neeta Mehta, now a preacher, figures in a strong role.

Batwara (**1989**): Another exposition of caste and feudalism in hinterland Rajasthan. Dharmendra is a retired *fauji*, and Amrita Singh is of *chhoti jati* (lower caste). The sadistic casteist cop (Amrish Puri) tortures a *chhoti jaati ka* dacoit. Later, after killing him, Puri says, '*Keede makaude to marte hi rehte hain* (Insects keep dying).'

Bhim Garjana (**1989**): The biographical film on Baba Saheb Ambedkar fails to capture the depth and range that its protagonist deserved.

NOTES

REEL 1: Explaining the Eighties

1. *Romancing with Life*, Penguin/Viking, 2007, pp. 255
2. *India Today*, 28 February 1978
3. *Film Information*, 5 January 1980
4. Author's phone interview with Rakesh Bedi, 6 April 2020
5. *Bollywood Showplaces: Cinema Theatres in India*, E & E Plumridge, 2002, pp. 53
6. *Screen*, 25 December 1987
7. *70 Years Of Indian Cinema (1913-83)*, CINEMA India-International, 1985
8. Ashok Joshi and Alok Rastogi, 'Hukkam ya hukam ke ghulam? Darshakon aur malikon ke beech base yeh cinema manager', *Madhuri*, 30 April 1982
9. Ibid
10. Ibid
11. Ibid
12. Alok Rastogi, 'Yeh dwarpal kitne khushhal', *Madhuri*, 30 April 1982
13. Author's Interview with Shahzad Ahmad, projectionist, Kalpana cinema, Saharanpur, 28 May 2017
14. Udaya Tara Nayar, 'Black marketing in cinema tickets, authorities and cinema goers to blame?' *Screen*, 14 November 1980
15. *Film Information*, 25 July 1987
16. *Film Information*, 10 October 1987
17. *Film Information*, 16 March 1985
18. Madhu Jain, 'New crop of young stars invade Bombay film industry, spark off major new trend', *India Today*, 30 June 1986

19. *Film Information*, 24 January 1987
20. Ibid
21. Avijit Ghosh, 'You can't go to the movies in this Punjab town', *The Times of India*, 18 February 2018
22. Ibid
23. *Trade Guide*, 3 January 1987
24. *Film Information*, 13 May 1989
25. Avijit Ghosh, 'Bollywood Returns To Kashmir, Movies Don't', *The Times of India*, 27 September 2013
26. *Film Information*, 11 January 1986
27. *Film Information*, 16 May 1987
28. *Film Information*, 10 January 1987
29. *Film Information*, 30 May 1987
30. Qtd. in M. Rahman, 'Hindi film industry presents a contradictory picture; chaos and flops rule', *India Today*, 31 May 1988
31. Ibid
32. *The Indian Media Business*, Sage Publications India, 2003, pp. 123
33. Ibid
34. 'Buddies, Badmen, Peers and Contemporaries', *Khullam Khulla: Rishi Kapoor Uncensored*, HarperCollins Publishers India, 2017
35. 'Appendix B: Terrorism Piracy Cases', *Film Piracy, Organized Crime, and Terrorism*, RAND, Safety and Justice Program and the Global Risk and Security Center, 2009, pp. 129
36. *Aspects of the Black Economy in India*, National Institute of Public Finance and Policy, 1986, pp. 329
37. *Film Information*, 8 August 1987
38. *Film Information*, 24 January 1987
39. Ibid
40. Author's phone interview with Deepak Bahry, 22 August 2017
41. Op cit, *Madhuri*, 30 April 1982
42. Ibid
43. *Film Information*, 8 August 1987
44. Author's interview with Sudhir Mishra, 8 February 2019
45. *Film Information*, January 1985

REEL 2: The Great Piracy Bazaar

1. V.P. Sathe, 'Looking Back, Looking Ahead', *Film Information*, 18 December 1982

2. Ibid

3. *Film Information*, 14 January 1984

4. Ibid

5. Author's interview with film distributor Sanjay Mehta, 9 March 2018

6. Author's interview with producer-director K. Ravi Shankar, 8 February 2019

7. Author's interview with producer-director B. Subhash, 8 February 2019

8. Umesh Mathur, 'Collapse of the UK market', *Screen*, 22 February 1980. However, a 1984 article in *India Today* put the number of theatres as 159.

9. Ibid

10. 'Piracy, Piracy', *The Times of India*, 17 August 1980

11. 'Flashback 1980', *Trade Guide*, 3 January 1981

12. Sumit Mitra, 'Manmohan Desai and Prakash Mehra stand out as remarkable survivors with big budget films' *India Today*, 31 May 1984

13. Ibid

14. Written reply in Lok Sabha by Union I&B minister Ajit Kumar Panja, 20 April 1987

15. Written reply in Lok Sabha by Union I&B minister Ajit Kumar Panja, 30 November 1987

16. 'Appendix B: Terrorism Piracy Cases', *Film Piracy, Organized Crime, and Terrorism*, RAND, Safety and Justice Program and the Global Risk and Security Center, 2009

17. Op cit, *India Today*, 31 May 1984

18. 'As the Video Virus Spreads', *The Times of India*, 22 January 1984

19. *Film Information*, 14 January 1984

20. 'Hindi film industry presents a contradictory picture; chaos and flops rule', *India Today*, 31 May 1988

21. *Film Information*, 14 January 1984

22. Op cit, *The Times of India*, 22 January 1984

23. Op cit, *The Times of India*, 22 January 1984

24. *Film Information*, 31 December 1983

25. Op cit, *The Times of India*, 22 January 1984

26. *Film Information*, 31 December 1983

27. *Film Information*, 7 January 1984

28. *Media Consumption and Everyday Life in Asia*, Routledge, 2008
29. *Film Information*, 31 December 1983
30. *Trade Guide*, 3 January 1987
31. Op cit, *Film Information*, 24 January 1987
32. Ibid
33. Yusuf Khan, 'Video piracy forces cinema halls' sale', *The Times of India*, 28 September 1984
34. Ibid
35. 'Two Ahmedabad Cinemas bow to Video-TV', *Trade Guide*, 4 January 1986
36. *Film Information*, 17 June 1989
37. Qtd. from UK's *VideoWeek* magazine in *Film Information*, 29 December 1984
38. Ibid
39. *Film Information*, 31 December 1983
40. 'Calcutta video libraries open', *Film Information*, 2 January 1988
41. *Trade Guide*, 3 January 1987
42. Ibid
43. Author's interview with Amit Khanna, 5 February 2019
44. Author's phone interview with director Anil Sharma, 5 February 2019
45. Author's phone interview cameraman S.M. Anwar, 2 March 2018
46. Op cit, *India Today*, 30 June 1983
47. *Film Information*, 4 January 1983
48. 'Steps to check video piracy', *The Times of India*, 26 May 1990
49. *Film Information*, 2 January 1988
50. *Film Information*, 5 January 1985
51. Author's phone interview with Pavan Kaul, 18 July 2020
52. Ibid
53. Anupama Chopra, 'Music Mania' *India Today*, 15 November 1994
54. 'India', *Media Piracy in Emerging Economies*, Social Science Research Council, 2011, pp. 353
55. Author's interview with Vinod Pande, 2018
56. Op cit, Hasan Kamal
57. Ibid
58. *Film Information*, 3 December 1988
59. Op cit, 'India', *Media Piracy in Emerging Economies*, Social Science Research Council, 2011, pp. 353-354

60. *Screen*, 29 December 1989

61. Mohd Irfan, 'Raj Kumar Barjatya: Keeping the tradition alive', *Screen*, 29 December 1989

62. Shama Bhagat, 'Raam Laxman: The music will be remembered forever', *Screen*, 29 December 1989

REEL 3: Cut, Cut, Cut! The Art of Getting Around Scissorhands

1. 'Film censorship deteriorates into a license to dictate national standards of morality', *India Today*, 15 October 1980

2. 'I don't eat men for breakfast: Zeenat Aman', *The Times of India*, 2 May 1982

3. 'Eyecatchers', India Today, 31 October 1980.

4. Ibid

5. *Encyclopaedia of Indian Cinema*, British Film Institute and Oxford Univeristy Press, 1994, pp. 448

6. Author's phone interview with Vinod Talwar, 26 November 2019

7. '11 censor decisions since 1979 challenged', *Screen*, 8 July 1993. The answer was provided by the Ministry of Information and Broadcasting in a written reply to a question by Dr Rudra Pratap Singh at the meeting of the Consultative Committee of Members of Parliament on 24 June 1983.

8. 'Threatening call to Film censor panel member', *The Times of India*, 10 May 1982

9. 'Censors against use of derogatory words', *Film Information*, 7 January 1984

10. Trade Guide, 4 January 1986

11. V. Verma, 'Rajkumar Kohli's saga of triumph', *Screen*, 2 January 1987

12. Ibid

13. *Film Information*, 10 October 1987

14. *Freedom: My Story*, HarperCollins Publishers India, 2017, pp. 15

15. Author's interview with Manmohan Shetty, 9 February 2016

16. Amit Agarwal, 'No cabarets please, we're Doordarshan', *The Times of India*, 16 April 1990

17. 'New Delhi Times', *The Times of India*, 4 March 1986

18. Op cit, Agarwal

19. *Film Information*, 28 February 1987

20. Author's interview with Vimal Kumar, 9 February 2019

21. Ibid

22. Author's interview with K. Ravi Shankar, 8 February 2019

23. 'Sex?...We have titillation, not sex: Bikram Singh, chairman, CBFC', *Film Information*, 24 October 1987

24. Sunil Sethi and Chander Uday Singh, 'Demand for Meri Aawaz Suno soars as govt bans film for "violence, vulgarity"', *India Today*, 31 January 1982

25. Ibid

REEL 4: The Great Strike of 1986

1. 'Bollywood goes on strike'. The article was originally published in *Link* magazine, 4 January 1987. Republished in *Hindi Cinema: An Insider's View*, Oxford University Press, 2009, pp. 149

2. Op cit, *Hindi Cinema: An Insider's View*, pp. 150

3. *Unfinished Innings: Recollections and Reflections of a Civil Servant*, Orient Longman, 1996, pp. 174

4. Mithilesh Sinha, 'Cinema Band' *Madhuri*, 21 November 1986

5. Ibid

6. Ibid

7. 'CM to consult Delhi on film bandh', *The Times of India*, 5 November 1986

8. 'Strike while it's hot', *The Times of India*, 2 November 1986

9. Ibid

10. Op cit, 'Strike while it's hot'

11. K. Brahmanandam, 'World's largest film industry ends strike', UPI, 10 November 1986. Some industry hands said the number of workers affected was 400,000.

12. Op cit, 'CM to consult Delhi on film bandh'

13. Op cit, 'Bombay Strike'

14. Author's interview with Amit Khanna, 5 February 2019

15. Op cit, 'Bollywood goes on strike', pp. 147

16. The UNI report was published with the headline, 'Amitabh meets PM on stir', *The Times of India*, 7 November 1986

17. Op cit, *The Times of India*, 2 November 1986

18. Amjad Khan, 'Look Ahead in Anger', *The Times of India*, 9 November 1986

19. Op cit, *The Times of India*, 5 November 1986
20. Op cit, 'Amitabh meets PM on stir'
21. 'Film stir called off', *The Times of India*, 9 November 1986
22. M. Rahman, 'Bombay film industry strike ends, But Amitabh Bachchan, Sunil Dutt cast as villains', *India Today*, 30 November 1986
23. 'Bitter-sweet Eid', Editorial, *Indian Express*, 12 November 1986
24. Op cit, *Unfinished Innings*, pp. 174
25. Op cit, *Unfinished Innings*, pp. 178
26. 'Hope '86 mesmerises crowds', *The Times of India*, 14 December 1986
27. Ibid
28. 'The Revolt of 1986, About our stars and studios', *Screen*, 26 December 1986
29. *Film Information*, 7 November 1987

REEL 5: New Wave 2.0: Progress and Stagnation

1. For more details, refer to *India's Film Society Movement: The Journey and Its Impact*, Sage Publications India, 2017
2. Ibid, pp. 127
3. Govind Nihalani, 'Gandagi ko dhak dene se badboo kam nahi ho jaati', *Dharamyug*, 24-30 November 1985
4. Prakash Jha, 'Manoranjan ke naam par purey ke purey mahaul ko napunsak nahi banaya ja sakta hai', *Dharamyug*, 24-30 November 1985
5. Author's interview with Manmohan Shetty, 9 February 2019
6. Op cit, 'Gandagi ko dhak dene se badboo kam nahi ho jaati'
7. 'Young Filmmakers strike gold', *Sunday*, 29 March 1981, republished in *Hindi Cinema: An Insider's View*, Oxford University Press, 2009, pp. 155
8. V.P. Sathe, 'NFDC and video business grows abroad', column, 'Looking Back, Looking Ahead', *Film Information*, 1 January 1983
9. Author's interview with Sudhir Mishra, 10 February 2019
10. Author's phone interview with M.K. Raina, 3 April2020
11. Ibid
12. Written reply in Parliament by Union I&B minister Ajit Kumar Panja to a question by Prof. Chand Parashar, 2 March 1987

13. Lata Lal, 'Rashtriya Film Vikas Nigam: Aath varshon ki Sarthak Upladhiyan', *Madhuri*, 12 August 1988. The article doesn't specify where the data came from but the source, it seems, is NFDC.

14. Ibid

15. Op cit, Shetty

16. Author's interview with Shyam Benegal, 8 February 2019

17. Op cit, *Madhuri*

18. Op cit, Shetty

19. *Jaane Bhi Do Yaaro*, HarperCollins, 2010, pp. 46

20. Author's telephone interview with Subhankar Ghosh, 6 May 2012

21. 'Lens Eye: Interview with Govind Nihalani', *The Times of India*, 16 November 1986

22. Op cit, *Hindi Cinema: An Insider's View*, pp. 160

23. Op cit, *Film Information*, 1 January 1983

24. Answer of Union I&B minister V.N. Gadgil to a question in Parliament by Eduardo Faleiro, 25 March 1985

25. 'Hukkam ya hukam ke ghulam', *Madhuri*, 30 April 1982

26. Ibid

27. NFDC Annual Report (2005-2006)

28. Ibid

29. Author's interview with Muzaffar Ali, 17 February 2019

30. Ibid

31. Op cit, Raina

32. Op cit, Shetty

33. Op cit, Benegal

34. Ibid

35. Author's email interview with Saeed Mirza, 17 March 2020

36. Op cit, Mishra

37. Ibid

38. Ibid

REEL 6: New Wave 2.0: Movers and Shakers

1. Author's interview with Manmohan Shetty, 9 February 2019

2. *Filmfare*, 16 February 1985

3. Op cit, Shetty

4. Author's interview with M.K. Raina, 29 November 2011

5. *Unlikely Hero: Om Puri*, Roli Books, 2009, pp. 113

6. Ibid

7. *Encyclopaedia of Indian Cinema*, British Film Institute and Oxford Univeristy Press, 1994, pp. 444

8. From the article, 'Young Filmmakers strike gold', *Sunday*, 29 March 1981, republished in *Hindi Cinema: An Insider's View*, Oxford University Press, 2009, pp. 155-156

9. Author's interview with Shyam Benegal, 8 February 2019

10. Author's email interview with Victor Banerjee, 29 April 2020

11. Op cit, Benegal

12. Author's email interview with Shama Zaidi, 19 February 2019

13. Author's phone interview with Madan Jain, 7 April 2020

14. Op cit, Banerjee

15. Author's phone interview with Rakesh Bedi, 6 April 2020

16. Interview, wildlifefilmsindia.com, YouTube, 2 September 2018

17. Author's email interview with Nandita Puri, 1 March 2020

18. Ibid

19. Avijit Ghosh, '20 years on, Smita's eyes still light up memories', *The Times of India*, 6 December 2011

20. *Mother Maiden Mistress: Women in Hindi Cinema (1950-2010)*, HarperCollins Publishers India, 2012, pp. 138

REEL 7: How the South Shook Up the North

1. Author's interview with K. Ravi Shankar, 8 February 2019

2. Author's phone interview with producer G.A. Seshagiri Rao, 14 February 2019

3. Ibid

4. Author's phone interview with Raj Babbar, 8 July 2020

5. Author's phone interview with Rakesh Bedi, 6 April 2020

6. Author's email interview with writer Kamlesh Pandey, 4 February 2019

7. Author's phone interview with director T. Rama Rao, 14 February 2019

8. From Ali's column, 'All about stars and studio', *Screen*, 28 December 1984

9. Sumit Mitra, 'Manmohan Desai & Prakash Mehra...', *India Today*, 31 May 1984

10. Ibid

11. Harmeet Kathuria, 'Dilip Kumar's role was written keeping NTR

in mind: K. Raaghavendra Rao', *Film Information*, 29 December 1984

12. Op cit, T. Rama Rao

13. Op cit, G.A. Seshagiri Rao

14. 'Lens Eye: The wave that came in from the south', *The Times of India*, 22 July 1984. The article also provides the backdrop to the phenomenon.

15. Op cit, Pandey

16. Ibid

17. Ibid

18. 'Film review: Sasural, A highly entertaining film', *The Times of India*, 7 May 1961.

19. Op cit, Babbar

20. Op cit, T. Rama Rao

21. Ibid

22. Author's interview with Vimal Kumar, 9 February 2019

23. Op cit, K. Ravi Shankar

24. Ibid

25. Ibid

26. Op cit, G.A. Seshagiri Rao

27. T. Shankar, 'From Rama Naidu: Larger than life', *Screen*, 2 January 1987

28. Khalid Mohamad, 'Film Review, Ek Duuje…Overdone love story', *The Times of India*, 7 June 1981

29. K. Balachander on Kamal Haasan, *Screen*, 22 February 1980

30. 'Lens Eye: Kamal Haasan interview: "I can cry or kung fu"', *The Times of India*, 14 August 1983

31. 'Lens Eye: Rajinikanth: "Call me Panther"', *The Times of India*, 21 January 1984

32. Rajinikanth interview: 'I am growing up…', *Film Information*, 28 January 1984

33. Author's interview with film distributor Sanjay Mehta, 9 March 2018

REEL 8: Six Stars—and Three Others—Who Defined the Decade

1. *Flashback: 175 Years of Entertainment Entertainment Entertainment*, Bennet Coleman and Company, 2013, pp. 127

2. *Khullam Khulla: Rishi Kapoor Uncensored*, HarperCollins Publishers India, 2017, pp. 184

3. Author's interview with Rameshwari, 26 February 2018

4. *Talking Films: Conversations on Hindi Cinema with Javed Akhtar*, Oxford University Press, 1999, pp. 85

5. Khalid Mohamed, 'I hate the label "superstar": Amitabh Bachchan', *The Times of India*, 1 August 1982

6. 'Shahenshah comes to town', *Movie*, March 1988

7. *Film Information*, 27 February 1988

8. Op cit, *Movie*

9. Author's phone interview with Ravi Tandon, 19 and 24 September 2017

10. Author's phone interview with G.A. Seshagiri Rao, 14 February 2019

11. Sridevi interviewed by Khalid Mohamed, *Filmfare*, December 1992 (access at: sridevi.org)

12. Deepa Gahlot, 'Some made good, some faded away', *Filmfare*, 1 January 1984

13. Op cit, G.A. Seshagiri Rao

14. Ali, 'Farewell, Orwell's 1984', Column: 'About our stars and studios' *Screen*, 28 December 1984

15. Op cit, Rameshwari

16. Sridevi interview to Komal Nahta, *Film Information*, 24 January 1987

17. Author's interview with K. Ravi Shankar, 8 February 2019

18. Author's interview with T. Rama Rao, 14 February 2019

19. Op cit, G.A. Seshagiri Rao

20. Ibid

21. Ibid

22. Op cit, Rameshwari

23. Author's interview with Shatrughan Sinha, 31 January 2018

24. Op cit, Rameshwari

25. Satish Jain, 'Jitendra: Dakshini samrajya dhah raha hai (Jeetendra's southern empire is collapsing)', *Madhuri*, 20 June 1986

26. Ibid

27. Op cit, Ravi Shankar

28. 'From Koi Shaque! Mithun's political life comes full circle'. *The Times of India*, 8 March 2021

29. Author's phone interview with Deepak Bahry, 22 August 2017.

30. Author's interview with B. Subhash, 8 February 2019

31. Ibid

32. *Film Information*, 1 January 1983

33. Avijit Ghosh, '"Sexy at 60": Mithun Chakraborty interviewed', July 2010

34. 'I'll never go hungry now: Mithun Chakraborty', *The Times of India*, 2 April 1983

35. Author's email interview with Umesh Mehra, 8 February 2019

36. Ibid

37. *Disco Dancer: A Comedy In Five Acts*, HarperCollins Publishers India, 2011, pp. xv

38. Op cit, Sanjay Mehta

39. Harmeet Kathuria, 'Even Kamal Babu had said that Mithun was miscast in Pyar Jhukta Nahin: Sadana', *Film Information*, 26 January 1985

40. Op cit, *Madhuri*, 1986

41. Author's email interview with Simi Garewal, 6 April 2018

42. *Screen*, 2 September 1983

43. Op cit, 'Sexy at 60'

44. Op cit, Ravi Shankar

45. Author's interview with Vimal Kumar, 9 February 2019

46. Op cit, Sanjay Mehta

47. 'We're friends, not lovers: Mithun Chakraborty', *The Times of India*, 21 June1987

48. *Film Information*, 13 June 1987

49. Madhu Jain, 'Govinda: The Virar boy who turned tinsel town phenomenon', *India Today*, 30 June 1986

50. Govinda interview on video magazine *Lehren Retro*, (youtube.com/ watch?v=RVf9uAUgtAM)

51. Ibid

52. Author's interview with Shibu Mitra, 15 March 2019

53. Op cit, Vimal Kumar

54. Ibid

55. Ibid

56. Ibid

57. Priya Gupta, 'One day Mummy predicted her own death to me: Govinda', *Mumbai Times*, 22 November 2014

58. Ibid

59. Khalid Mohamed, 'I know I am the best: Rekha', *The Times of India*, 29 July 1984

60. Op cit, Vinod Pande

61. Ibid

62. Author's interview with Muzaffar Ali, 17 February 2019

63. The Kader Khan profile is sourced from the obituary written by Avijit Ghosh in *The Times of India*, 2 January 2019

64. 'Bhanu Athaiya returns Oscar fearing theft', *The Times of India*, 15 December 2012

65. The Saroj Khan profile is sourced from the obituary written by Avijit Ghosh in *The Times of India*, 6 July 2020

REEL 9: Rising Sons and Promising Outsiders

1. Author's interview with Mahesh Bhatt, 7 February 2019

2. Ibid

3. *Sanjay Dutt: The Crazy Untold Story of Bollywood's Bad Boy*, Juggernaut Books, 2018, pp. 40-42

4. 'I am fed up of blowing bubble gum': Kumar Gaurav in an interview to *The Times of India*, 28 April 1985

5. Author's telephone interview with Mahesh Bhatt, 8 and 9 January 2012

6. Ibid

7. Author's email interview with Akash Khurana, 10 February 2020

8. 'Dad used to slap me, so what', *The Times of India*, 17 June 1984

9. Author's interview with Shatrughan Sinha, 31 January 2018

10. Author's email interview with Suneil Anand, 27 April 2020

11. *Romancing with Life*, Penguin/Viking, 2007, pp. 276

12. Op cit, Suneil Anand

13. Ibid

14. Qtd. in *The Kapoors: The First Family of Indian Cinema*, Penguin/ Viking, 2005,pp. 315 (which quotes from Bunny Reuben's book, *Raj Kapoor, The Fabulous Showman: An Intimate Biography*, National Film Development Corporation, 1988)

15. *Film Information*, December 14, 1985

16. Op cit, *The Kapoors*, pp. 317

17. Ronjita Kulkarni, 'I was too foreign looking in Bollywood: Karan Kapoor', rediff.com, 2016

18. Ibid
19. Author's email interview with M.S. Sathyu, 18 April 2020
20. 'I'll only do films I believe in: Anil Kapoor', *The Times of India*, 22 January 1989
21. Author's interview with Anupam Kher, 19 August 2017
22. Author's phone interview with Raj Babbar, 8 July 2020
23. Ibid
24. Ibid
25. Ibid
26. Ibid
27. Ibid
28. Ibid
29. Producer Tahir Hussain quoted in *Film Information*, 14 September 1985
30. Op cit, Raj Babbar

REEL 10: Movers and Moguls: Top and Flop Filmmakers of the 1980s

1. *Film Information*, 4 January 1986
2. *Film Information*, 7 January 1984
3. 'An evening with MD', *Film Information*, 14 January 1984
4. Sumit Mitra, 'Manmohan Desai and Prakash Mehra stand out as remarkable survivors with big budget films', *India Today*, 31 May 1984
5. Udaya Tara Nayar, 'Ramesh Sippy: Trend setter in Hindi cinema', *Screen*, 12 December 1980
6. Author's phone interview with S.M. Anwer, 2 March 2018
7. 'Mediocrity works in Indian cinema: Basu Chatterjee talks to Sriprakash Menon', *The Times of India*, 21 July 1996
8. *Echoes and Eloquences: The Life and Cinema of Gulzar*, Rupa Publications India, 2007, pp. 225
9. Author's phone interview with Raj Babbar, 8 July 2020
10. 'Disco Dancer: Sure to turn you off', *The Times of India*, 19 December 1982
11. 'From Indian films in the USSR and Russia: Past, Present and Future', article by Elena Igorevna Doroshenko, in *Media Consumption and Everyday Life in Asia*, Routledge, 2008
12. Ibid

13. Author's interview with B. Subhash, 8 February 2019
14. Ibid
15. Avijit Ghosh, '"Sexy at 60": Mithun Chakraborty interviewed', July 2010.
16. Op cit, B. Subhash
17. Ibid
18. Madhu Jain, 'Hit director brings realism to films', *India Today*, 28 February1989
19. *Film Information*, 5 September 1987
20. Ibid
21. Author's phone interview with Madan Jain, 26 March 2020
22. Author's phone interview with Sujata Mehta, 19 April 2020
23. Author's phone interview with Anil Sharma, 5 February 2019
24. Ibid
25. Ibid
26. Author's interview with Manmohan Kapur, 9 February 2019
27. Author's phone interview with Saleem (of Faiz-Saleem), 15 February 2019
28. *Mother Maiden Mistress: Women in Hindi Cinema (1950-2010)*, HarperCollins Publishers India, 2012, pp.134
29. Author's telephone interview with Mahesh Bhatt, 8 January 2012
30. Author's interview with Mahesh Bhatt, 7 February 2019
31. Ibid
32. Ibid
33. Ibid
34. Ibid
35. Author's email interview with Akash Khurana, 10 February 2020
36. 'I wish I could make a film like Manmohan Desai. But I can't: Mahesh Bhatt'. *Film Information*, 28 January 1984
37. Ibid
38. Simran Bhargava, 'Bollywood dreamboat: Qayamat Se Qayamat Tak makes Aamir Khan a teenage sensation', *India Today*, 15 December 1988
39. *I'll Do It My Way: The Incredible Journey of Aamir Khan*, Om Books International, 2012, pp. 25
40. *Sex in Cinema: A History of Female Sexuality in Indian Films*, Rupa Publications India, 2010, pp. 234
41. Author's phone interview with Dr Achala Nagar, 31 January 2020

42. Ibid
43. Ibid
44. *Islamicate Cultures of Bombay Cinema*, Tulika Books, 2009, pp. 207
45. Author's email interview with Jijo Punnoose, 28 April 2020
46. Punnoose and Navodaya website
47. Author's phone interview with Manju Malhotra, 7 December 2019
48. Udaya Tara Nayar, 'The excitement never dies: Harmesh Malhotra', *Screen*, 19 June 1998
49. *Film Information*, 24 January 1987
50. Ibid
51. 'Dream Run, Defeat and Depression', *Khullam Khulla: Rishi Kapoor Uncensored*, HarperCollins Publishers India, 2017
52. *Movie*, February 1987
53. Author's email interview with Umesh Mehra, 8 February 2019
54. Ibid
55. Ibid
56. Ibid
57. Dhiraj Shetty, 'The story is the hero, boss: Pankaj Parashar interviewed', rediff.com, 10 January 2003
58. Op cit, Mehta
59. Author's interview with Rameshwari, 28 February 2018
60. 'Esmayeel Shroff passes away', *The Times of India*, 27 October 2020
61. Author's email interview with Suneil Anand, 27 April 2020
62. Author's phone interview with Vinod Pande, 30 April 2018

REEL 11: Also Starring: Dacoits and Devotionals; Suspense and Sex Movies

1. *Encyclopaedia of Indian Cinema*, British Film Institute and Oxford Univeristy Press, 1994, pp. 470
2. Author's phone interview with Sujata Mehta, 19 and 24 April 2020
3. Author's interview with Saleem (of Faiz-Saleem), 15 February 2019
4. Author's interview with Javed Khan, 24 November 2019
5. Ibid
6. Ibid
7. Ibid

8. 'Phoolan warns film director', *The Times of India*, 31 August 1982
9. *A Pictorial History of Indian Cinema*, Hamlyn, 1979, pp. 17
10. Avijit Ghosh, 'Sant Ravidas unleashed frontal attack on untouchability, Ronki Ram', *The Times of India*, 28 August 2019
11. *In a Cult Of Their Own: Bollywood Beyond Box Office*, Rupa Publications India, 2018, pp. 243. Rishi Majumder also mentions the same facts in the article, 'Ramsay International', for *The Times of India's* Crest Edition, 7 July 2012. Shamya Dasgupta has also written a book on the Ramsay brothers: *Don't Disturb the Dead: The Story of the Ramsay Brothers*, HarperCollins Publishers India, 2017.
12. Qtd. in 'Horror filmmaker Shyam Ramsay dead', Avijit Ghosh, *The Times of India*, 19 September 2019
13. Op cit, *In a Cult Of Their Own*, pp. 244
14. Qtd. in op cit, 'Horror filmmaker…'
15. Author's interview with K.M. Bhakri, 22 November 2019
16. Op cit, Javed Khan
17. Op cit, K.M. Bhakri
18. Op cit, Javed Khan
19. Ibid
20. Author's interview with Vinod Talwar, 26 November 2019
21. Ibid
22. *Freedom: My Story*, HarperCollins Publishers India, 2017, pp. 91
23. Ibid, pp. 97
24. *Film Information*, 12 April 1988

REEL 12: Disco Outbreak and Unsung Classics

1. *Made in India: Adventures of a Lifetime*, HarperCollins Publishers India, 2015, pp. 211
2. *Screen*, 25 December 1981
3. Author's phone interview with lyricist Hasan Kamal, 5 March 2018
4. Author's interview with K. Ravi Shankar, 8 February 2019
5. Op cit, Hasan Kamal
6. Ibid
7. Author's interview with producer-director B. Subhash, 8 February 2019

8. Vinod Tiwary, 'Jawan dilwalon ke liye hai mera sangeet: Bappi Lahiri', *Madhuri*, 11 April 1986
9. *Film Information*, 24 January 1987
10. Op cit, Ravi Shankar
11. Avijit Ghosh, 'Kabhi Alvida Na Kehna', *The Times of India*, 17 February 2022
12. Op cit, Hasan Kamal
13. Op cit, Subhash
14. Op cit, 'Jawan dilwalon ke liye hai mera sangeet: Bappi Lahiri'
15. Information obtained from the website, websiteitwofs.com
16. Avijit Ghosh, 'Ajit Varman's music was sensitive, nuanced', *The Times of India*, 17 December 2016
17. Ibid
18. Ibid
19. Ibid
20. Author's interview with Shyam Benegal, 8 February 2019
21. Ibid
22. Ibid

REEL 13: When Lamba Rhymed with Khambha

1. *Talking Songs: Javed Akhtar in Conversation with Nasreen Munni Kabir and Sixty Selected Songs by Javed Akhtar*, Oxford University Press, 2005, pp. 33
2. Author's interview with Hasan Kamal, 5 March 2018
3. Author's interview with Maya Govind, 5 March 2018
4. Vinod Tiwary, 'Jawaan dilwalon ke liye hai mera sangeet: Bappi Lahiri' *Madhuri*, 11 April 1986
5. Op cit, *Talking Songs*
6. Author's interview with Muzaffar Ali, 17 February 2019
7. Avijit Ghosh, 'Meet the man whose song made Ranu Mandal famous: Santosh Anand', *The Times of India*, 6 September 2019
8. Author's phone interview with Yogesh, 26 February 2018
9. Qtd. in Avijit Ghosh, 'Lyricist Yogesh, who wrote Kahin Door Jab Din Dhal Jaaye, no more', *The Times of India*, 30 May 2020. The Yogesh section borrows from this article.
10. Shantiswarup Tripathi, 'Rafi Saab meri taleem thhey', Shabbir Kumar: interviewed, *Dharamyug*, 30 July 1989

11. 'Mohd Aziz to Bollywood Dynasty', 13 April 2015
12. Shantiswarup Tripathi, 'Main apni aawaz mein gata hoon: Suresh Wadkar interviewed', *Dharamyug*, 30 July 1989
13. Ibid
14. The Bhupinder section partly borrows from the obituary published in *The Times of India*, 19 July 2022. It was written by Avijit Ghosh and Bela Jaisinghani.

REEL 14: Literature, Dowry, Journalism and Caste Inequity

1. Author's phone interview M.K. Raina, 3 April 2020
2. Author's email interview with Mridula Garg, 5 August 2020
3. Author's phone interview with Rachana Yadav, 7 August 2020
4. Ibid
5. Op cit, Garg
6. Op cit, Yadav
7. Author's text exchange with Shaival, 7 August 2020
8. Ibid
9. Author's email interview with Mahesh Eklunchwar, 7 August 2020
10. Ibid
11. Author's interview with Muzaffar Ali, 17 February 2019
12. Nirupama Dutt, 'Punjabi film fare', *The Tribune*, 5 December 2004
13. Author's interview with M.S. Sathyu, 18 April 2020
14. Author's interview with Harish Trivedi, 20 March 2020

BIBLIOGRAPHY

Acharya, Shankar N. and Associates. *Aspects of the Black Economy in India*, National Institute of Public Finance and Policy, 1986.

Anand, Dev. *Romancing with Life*, Penguin/Viking, 2007

Bhargava, Anil. *Binaca Geetmala Ka Sureela Safar*, Cine Sahitya Prakashan, 2007

Bhaskar, Ira and Richard Allen. *Islamicate Cultures of Bombay Cinema*, Tulika Books, 2009

Biddu. *Made in India: Adventures of a Lifetime*, HarperCollins Publishers India, 2015

Bhattacharya, Aniruddha and Balaji Vittal. *R.D. Burman: The Man, The Music*, HarperCollins Publishers India, 2011

Chatterjee, Bishwanath. *Hindi Film Geet Kosh (1971-1980)*, vol 5, Delight Press, 1991

Chatterjee, Saibal. *Echoes and Eloquences: The Life and Cinema of Gulzar*, Rupa Publications India, 2007

Chaudhuri, Diptikirti. *Written by Salim-Javed: The Story of Hindi Cinema's Greatest Screenwriters*, Penguin Books, 2015

Daniels, Christina. *I'll Do It My Way: The Incredible Journey of Aamir Khan*, Om Books International, 2012

Cherian, V.K. *India's Film Society Movement: The Journey and Its Impact*, Sage Publications India, 2017

Chintamani, Gautam. *Qayamat Se Qayamat Tak: The Film That Revived Hindi Cinema*, HarperCollins Publishers India, 2016

Ghosh, Avijit, *40 Retakes: Bollywood Classics You May Have Missed*, Tranquebar Press, Westland Books, 2013

Godbole Madhav. *Unfinished Innings: Recollections and Reflections of a Civil Servant*, Orient Longman, 1996

Gooptu, Sharmistha, Avijit Ghosh and Srijana Mitra Das. *Flashback: 175 Years of Entertainment Entertainment Entertainment*, Bennet Coleman and Company, 2013

Gulati, Leela and Jasodhara Bagchi(ed).'Abode Of Colour: Vijaya Mehta', *A Space of Her Own: Personal Narratives Of Twelve Women*, Sage Publications India, 2005

Hood, John W. *The Essential Mystery: Major Filmmakers of Indian Art Cinema*, Orient BlackSwan, 2009

Hamraaz, Har Mandir Singh. *Hindi Film Geet Kosh (1981-1985)*, vol 6, Digital Mudrak, 2018

Jalil, Rakhshanda. *Shahryar: A Life in Poetry*, HarperCollins Publishers, 2018

Jain, Madhu. *The Kapoors: The First Family of Indian Cinema*, Penguin/Viking, 2005

Kabir, Nasreen Munni and Javed Akhtar. *Talking Films: Conversations on Hindi Cinema with Javed Akhtar*, Oxford University Press, 1999

____.*Talking Songs: Javed Akhtar in Conversation with Nasreen Munni Kabir and Sixty Selected Songs by Javed Akhtar*, Oxford University Press, 2005

Kapoor, Rishi with Meena Iyer. *Khullam Khulla: Rishi Kapoor Uncensored*, HarperCollins Publishers India, 2017

Kazmi, Fareed. *Sex in Cinema: A History of Female Sexuality in Indian Films*, Rupa Publications India, 2010

Kidwai, Rasheed. *Neta Abhineta: Bollywood Star Power in Indian Politics*, Hachettte Book Publishing India, 2018

Kim Youna (ed). *Media Consumption and Everyday Life in Asia*, Routledge, 2008

Kohli Vanita. *The Indian Media Business*, Sage Publications India, 2003

Liang, Lawrence and Ravi Sundaram. 'India', *Media Piracy in Emerging Economies*, ed. Joe Karaganis, Social Science Research Council, 2011, pp. 339-398

Manuel Peter. *Cassette Culture: Popular Music and Technology in North India*, University of Chicago Press, 1993

Mehta Monika. *Censor and Sexuality in Bombay Cinema*, Permanent Black, 2011

Pal, Anuvab. *Disco Dancer: A Comedy In Five Acts*, HarperCollins Publishers India, 2011

Paranjpye, Sai. *A Patchwork Quit: A Collage of My Creative Life*, HarperCollins Publishers India, 2020

Patil, Arunaraje. *Freedom: My Story*, HarperCollins Publishers India, 2017

Puri, Nandita C. *Unlikely Hero: Om Puri*, Roli Books, 2009

Raag, Pankaj. *Dhuno Ki Yatra (Hindi Filmon Ke Sangeetkar: 1931-2005)*, Rajkamal Prakashan, 2006

Rajadhyaksha Ashish and Paul Willemen. *Encyclopaedia of Indian Cinema*, British Film Institute and Oxford Univeristy Press, 1994

Ramachandran T.M. (ed). *70 Years Of Indian Cinema (1913-83)*, CINEMA India-International, 1985

Rangoonwalla, Firoze. *A Pictorial History of Indian Cinema*, Hamlyn, 1979

Ray Bibekananda. *Conscience of the Race: India's Offbeat Cinema*, Publication Division, Ministry of Information and Broadcasting, Government of India, 2005.

Roychoudhury, Amborish. *In a Cult Of Their Own: Bollywood Beyond Box Office*, Rupa Publications India, 2018

Saari Anil. *Hindi Cinema: An Insider's View*, Oxford University Press, 2009

Somaaya Bhawana, Jigna Kothari and Supriya Madangarli. *Mother Maiden Mistress: Women in Hindi Cinema (1950-2010)*, HarperCollins Publishers India, 2012

Shah, Naseeruddin. *And Then One Day: A Memoir*, Penguin/Hamish Hamilton, 2014

Singh, Jai Arjun. *Jaane Bhi Do Yaaro*, HarperCollins, 2010

Thoraval Yves. *The Cinemas of India*, Macmillan India, 2000

Treverton, Gregory F., Carl Matthies, Karla J. Cunningham, Jeremiah Goulka, Greg Ridgeway and Amy Wong. 'Apendix B: Terrorism Piracy Cases', *Film Piracy, Organized Crime, and Terrorism*, RAND, Safety and Justice Program and the Global Risk and Security Center, 2009, pp. 117-139 (jstor.org/stable/10.7249/mg742mpa.16, last accessed 25 January, 2023)

Usman, Yasser. *Rekha: The Untold Story*, Juggernaut Books, 2016

_____.*Sanjay Dutt: The Crazy Untold Story of Bollywood's Bad Boy*, Juggernaut Books, 2018

Vasudev, Aruna. *Liberty and Licence in the Indian Cinema*, Vikas Publishing House, 1978

Vinnels, David and Brent Skelly. *Bollywood Showplaces: Cinema Theatres in India*, E&E Plumridge, 2002.

Newspapers and Magazines

Dharamyug; *Film Information*; *Filmfare*; *Hindustan Times*; *India Today*; *Indian Express*; *Madhuri*; *Movie*; *Sarika*; *Screen*; *Star & Style*; *The Statesman*; *The Times of India*; *Trade Guide*

Archives

Nehru Memorial Museum and Library, New Delhi
Parliament Library, New Delhi
The National Film Archive of India (NFAI), Pune

Websites

swarganga.org
hindigeetmala.net

Interviews

The following personalities were interviewed either in person, on phone or via email beween 2018 and 2021:

Achala Nagar; Amit Khanna; Anil Sharma; Ashim Samanta; B. Subhash; Deepak Bahry; G.A. Seshagiri Rao; Hasan Kamal; Harish Trivedi; Javed Khan; Jijo Punnoose; Kamlesh Pandey; K. Ravi Shankar; K.M. Bhakri; Madan Jain; Mahesh Bhatt; Mahesh Eklunchwar; Manmohan Kapur; Manmohan Shetty; Maya Govind; M.K. Raina; Mridula Garg; M.S. Sathyu; Muzaffar Ali; Nandita Puri; Pavan Kaul; Rachana Yadav; Raj Babbar; Rakesh Bedi; Rameshwari; Ravi Tandon; Saleem (Faiz); Sanjay Mehta; Shaival; Shama Zaidi; Shatrughan Sinha; Shibu Mitra; Shyam Benegal; Shyam Shroff; Simi Garewal; S.M. Anwer; Sudhir Mishra; Sujata Mehta; T. Rama Rao; Umesh Mehra; Victor Banerjee; Vimal Kumar.

INDEX

Song Index

Books, Films and Names Index

Shakti Kapoor was busy playing the bad guy in the 1980s. He often indulged in comic villainy. (Photo Credit: Manmohan Kapoor)

Debutant director Vinod Pande's *Ek Baar Phir*, the sleeper hit of 1980, was shot entirely in London. (Photo Credit: Vinod Pande)

Naseeruddin Shah and Rekha in *Umrao Jaan* (1980).
(Photo Credit: Muzaffar Ali)

Politician Vasant Sathe with *Ek Baar Phir* director Vinod Pande and
Deepti Naval at Tashkent Film festival. (Photo Credit: Vinod Pande)

Farooq Sheikh, Ravi Baswani and Rakesh Bedi in the comedy film *Chashme Buddoor* (1981). Sheikh and Baswani are no more. (Photo Credit: Rakesh Bedi)

Dancer Helen continued to delight in the 1980s. Here she is in *Heeron Ka Chor* (1982). (Photo Credit: Manmohan Kapoor)

Shabana Azmi and Naseeruddin Shah in Shyam Benegal's *Mandi* (1983). (Photo Credit: Shyam Banegal)

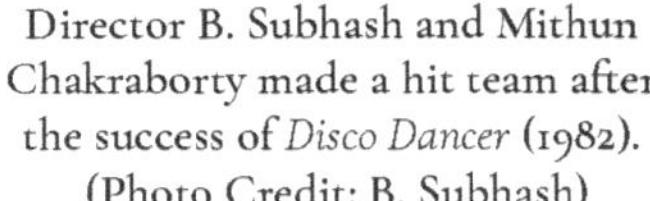

Director B. Subhash and Mithun Chakraborty made a hit team after the success of *Disco Dancer* (1982). (Photo Credit: B. Subhash)

Smita Patil and Shabana Azmi in *Mandi*. (Photo Credit: Shyam Benegal)

The blockbuster *Chhota Chetan* (1984) kick-started the short-lived trend of 3D films in the '80s. (Photo Credit: Jijo Punnoose)

Rajesh Khanna and Tina Munim made a hit pair in *Souten* (1983). Here the two can be seen in *Insaaf Main Karoonga* (1985). (Photo Credit: Manmohan Kapoor)

Hema Malini played a dacoit in *Sitapur ki Geeta* (1987). Sridevi and Zeenat Aman also starred in similar films where the male actors played second fiddle. (Photo Credit: Manmohan Kapoor)

Pran, a popular character actor was the villain in *Sitapur Ki Geeta.*

Dharmendra and Rati Agnihotri in *Hukumat* (1987). (Photo Credit: Anil Sharma)

Director Harmesh Malhotra and lead actor Sridevi's superhit *Nagina* (1986) spurred the snake-woman subgenre and birthed the snake dance at parties. (Photo Credit: Manju Malhotra)

Aamir Khan and Juhi Chawla in B. Subhash's flop, *Love Love Love* (1989). (Photo Credit: B. Subhash)

Bindiya Goswami's acting career didn't proceed to the desired level in the 1980s. She later married director J.P. Dutta and quit films. (Photo Credit: Manmohan Kapoor)

Models made major inroads into Hindi cinema in the 1980s. Here is Javed Khan, a popular hero of 1980s horror films, and Kimi Katkar in an advertisement. Both began their career as models.

Mithun Chakraborty became a hugely popular action-dance star in the 1980s.

The mujra song was an essential part of the dacoit film menu. Actor and dancer Jayshree T was adept at the task.

INSPIRED BY THE PRIME MINISTER
RAJIV GANDHI'S
CRUSADE AGAINST RED TAPISM,
FAVOURITISM AND CORRUPTION
THE GREATEST ENEMY OF COUNTRY'S PROGRESS
AND
DEDICATED TO HONEST POLICEMEN
WHO LAID THEIR LIVES FOR THIS CRUSADE.

Filmmakers weren't shy of praising the people in power in the 1980s. Here's how Pramod Chakraborty's *Shatru* (1986) opens.

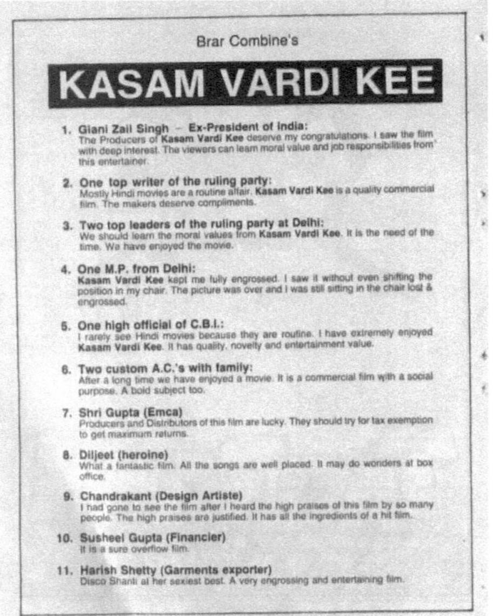

Brar Combine's

KASAM VARDI KEE

1. **Giani Zail Singh — Ex-President of India:**
   The Producers of **Kasam Vardi Kee** deserve my congratulations. I saw the film with deep interest. The viewers can learn moral value and job responsibilities from this entertainer.

2. **One top writer of the ruling party:**
   Mostly Hindi movies are a routine affair. **Kasam Vardi Kee** is a quality commercial film. The makers deserve compliments.

3. **Two top leaders of the ruling party at Delhi:**
   We should learn the moral values from **Kasam Vardi Kee**. It is the need of the time. We have enjoyed the movie.

4. **One M.P. from Delhi:**
   Kasam Vardi Kee kept me fully engrossed. I saw it without even shifting the position in my chair. The picture was over and I was still sitting in the chair lost & engrossed.

5. **One high official of C.B.I.:**
   I rarely see Hindi movies because they are routine. I have extremely enjoyed **Kasam Vardi Kee**. It has quality, novelty and entertainment value.

6. **Two custom A.C.'s with family:**
   After a long time we have enjoyed a movie. It is a commercial film with a social purpose. A bold subject too.

7. **Shri Gupta (Emca)**
   Producers and Distributors of this film are lucky. They should try for tax exemption to get maximum returns.

8. **Diljeet (heroine)**
   What a fantastic film. All the songs are well placed. It may do wonders at box office.

9. **Chandrakant (Design Artiste)**
   I had gone to see the film after I heard the high praises of this film by so many people. The high praises are justified. It has all the ingredients of a hit film.

10. **Susheel Gupta (Financier)**
    It is a sure overflow film.

11. **Harish Shetty (Garments exporter)**
    Disco Shanti at her sexiest best. A very engrossing and entertaining film.

Trade magazines would usually dedicate a page for endorsement of films in the 1980s. See for example, the endorsement of Shibu Mitra's *Kasam Vardi Kee* (1989). (Photo Credit: *Film Information*, 1989)

Vinod Khanna endorsed this popular
soap advertisement in the 1980s.

Dev Anand and Tina Munim on the poster
of *Man Pasand* (1980). The film was inspired
by George Bernard Shaw's play *Pygmalion*.

Raw and urgent, Govind Nihalani's *Aakrosh* (1980) was a hard-hitting take on the exploitation of tribals.

Amjad Khan with Ashok Kumar and Pran in Shibu Mitra's *Maan Gaye Ustad* (1981). (Photo Credit: Manmohan Kapoor)

Real-life dacoits, Madho Singh and Mohar Singh acted in *Chambal Ke Daku* (1982). Their muscular presence contributed to the film's modest success.

Sumbandh (1982) was a rare film that dealt with male impotence.

Ardh Satya (1983) poster

Director Shekhar Kapur's *Masoom* (1983)
was a critical and commercial success.

Lyricist Amit Khanna also directed *Sheeshay Ka Ghar* (1984). Raj Babbar and Padmini Kolhapure played lead roles.

Sujata Mehta played the protagonist in *Pratighaat*. It was the biggest hit of 1987.

Dipika Chikhalia acted in the horror film, *Raat Ke Andhere Mein* (1987). She later became famous playing Sita in *Ramayan* on TV. She was also a Lok Sabha MP for BJP from Baroda.

Amitabh Bachchan-starrer *Main Azaad Hoon* (1989) foresaw fake news.

www.ingramcontent.com/pod-product-compliance
Lightning Source LLC
LaVergne TN
LVHW041449170726
843492LV00005B/1155